A THOUSAND TEACHINGS

A THOUSAND TEACHINGS

The *Upadeśasāhasrī* of Śaṅkara

Translated and Edited by
SENGAKU MAYEDA

Foreword by
JOHN M. KOLLER

STATE UNIVERSITY OF NEW YORK PRESS

First published in U.S.A. by
State University of New York Press, Albany

Printed in the United States of America

Published in Japan by University of Tokyo Press, 1979

For information, address State University of New York Press, State University Plaza, Albany, N.Y. 12246

Production by Dana Foote
Marketing by Bernadette LaManna

Library of Congress Cataloging in Publication Data

Śaṅkarācārya.
[Upadeśasāhaśrī. English]
A thousand teachings : the Upadeśasāhasrī of Śaṅkara / translated and edited by Sengaku Mayeda ; foreword by John M. Koller.
p. cm.
Translation of: Upadeśasāhaśrī.
Reprint, with new foreword. Originally published: Tokyo : University of Tokyo Press, 1979.
Includes bibliographical references and index.
ISBN 0–7914–0943–0 (hard : alk. paper). —ISBN 0–7914–0944–9 (pbk. : alk. paper)
1. Advaita. I. Title.
B133.S49U6213 1992
181′.482—dc20 91-9641
CIP

10 9 8 7 6 5 4 3 2 1

To Norman

CONTENTS

A THOUSAND TEACHINGS (TRANSLATION AND NOTES)

II. Prose Part (*Gadyabandha*)

FOREWORD

We are fortunate to have Śaṅkara's *A Thousand Teachings* available in this excellent translation at an affordable price. No other Vedānta text is so accessible and so effective in introducing students to the central issues of Advaita Vedānta. Śaṅkara (700 – 750) is generally regarded as one of India's greatest philosophical and religious thinkers, and *A Thousand Teachings* is the best introduction to his thought. Because of his critique of Mīmāṃsā, Sāṃkhya, Buddhism, and the other traditions, it is also an excellent introduction to the whole field of Indian philosophy. In my experience this text is without equal in successfully engaging students in thinking about the central issues that have shaped the on-going Advaita tradition and that have dominated the history of Indian philosophy.

In *A Thousand Teachings,* the only clearly authentic work of Śaṅkara that is not in the form of a commentary, we find the central teachings of non-dualistic Vedānta set out in clear and direct language. Philosophers will be impressed by the careful conceptual analysis and vigorous argumentation Śaṅkara employs to support his own views and to refute the competing views of others. In the second chapter of the prose part, the philosophical centerpiece of the text, the teacher keeps questioning the student, pushing him to analyze his claims and to examine the arguments supporting them. In doing so, the student repeatedly challenges the teacher's claims and arguments, creating a profound and subtly argued philosophical dialogue in the process.

Students of religious thought, on the other hand, will find this text an interesting example of how reason is used to support revelation, for Śaṅkara acknowledges that despite the power of reason, ultimately it is *Śruti* (revelation) that is the source of truth. Furthermore, though reason can clarify truth and remove objections to it, its confirmation is not found in logic, but in experience, in the experience of meditative insight. This understanding of the relationship between revelation, reasoning, and meditation — typical of much Indian thought — underlies the organization of the text. Of the three chapters of the prose part, the first recalls the *Śruti* teachings concerning liberating knowledge, the second provides rational clarification and removes conceptual difficulties, and the third directs the seeker of knowledge to meditation.

In Part I, in the nineteen chapters addressed to students as a kind of textbook of Vedānta, Śaṅkara combines the authority of revelation (*śruti*) with philosophical reasoning to answer the main questions raised by a non-dualistic interpretation of reality. Each short chapter addresses a specific question, as illustrated here by a brief analysis of the first four chapters.

Chapter 1, "Pure Consciousness," takes up the question, Why is knowledge alone capable of realizing final beatitude? Why not action? Śaṅkara explains that since the Self is of the nature of pure consciousness, knowledge, because it is also of the nature of pure consciousness can be effective in removing the ignorance that stands in the way of blissful self-realization. Action, on the other hand, because it belongs to the body, and therefore is not of the nature of pure consciousness, cannot be effective in removing this ignorance.

Chapter 2, "Negation," addresses the question, Why is the way of negation effective in realizing the Self? Here Śaṅkara explains that what is of the nature of object can be negated, but what is of the nature of pure subject can never be negated. Therefore negation can serve as an effective way of discriminating the pure Self from the self identified as an object.

Chapter 3, "The Lord," continues the discussion of negation, addressing the question, If the way of negation is followed to its limit, wouldn't we arrive at mere nothingness, the nihilistic emptiness (*śūnyatā*) of the Buddhists? Śaṅkara answers that negation removes only the qualities falsely imposed on the pure Self. What is negated is not *Ātman,* but the characteristics of objects that are non-*Ātman,* superimposed on *Ātman* through ignorance. This is why negation arrives not at nihilistic emptiness but at *Ātman,* the ultimately real.

Chapter 4, "I-Notion," asks, How can action, which is rooted in identification of Self with the agent, produce its result when this identification has been removed by the knowledge that the true Self is not an agent? Śaṅkara answers that actions undertaken as a result of ignorant identification with agency continue to produce their results, but when it is realized that Self is not agent then no new actions and results are produced. Agency and action result from mistaking the body for the Self. "A man who has knowledge of *Ātman,* which negates the notion that body is *Ātman* . . . is released even without wishing," says Śaṅkara [I.4.5].

In Part Two, addressed to teachers, Śaṅkara explains how the teacher should guide a student who is seeking liberation from the suffering of *saṃsāra.* Chapter 2, the heart of this part of the text, is in the form of a dialogue which may well represent actual exchanges between Śaṅkara and his students. The student displays a highly critical intelligence, refusing to accept the teacher's word when it runs counter to his own understanding. Time and again, the student objects to questionable distinctions, questions the appropriateness of examples, and challenges the teacher's analyses and arguments. But these philosophical exchanges are not motivated by mere curiosity; they are important means of arriving at the truth that will deliver one from the bondage of suffering.

The dialogue begins with the student asking, "How can I be released from transmigratory existence?" Noting that he experiences suffering in both the waking and dreaming state, he asks about the cause of this suffering: "Is it indeed my own nature or [is it] due to some cause, my own nature being different?" The student is keenly aware that if suffering is an inherent feature of human existence no release is possible. He goes on to say, "If [this is] my own nature, there is no hope for me to attain final release, since one cannot avoid one's own nature. If [it is] due to some cause, final release is possible after the cause has been removed."

When the teacher replies, "This is not your own nature but is due to a cause," the student asks, "What is the cause? And what will remove it? And what is my own nature?" Upon being told that the cause is ignorance, which can be removed by knowledge, the student asks, "What is that nescience? And what is its object?

And what is knowledge . . . ?" [II.2.46~49]

In the continuing dialogue the teacher explains the fundamental Vedic teaching presented in the Upaniṣads: One's innermost being, the *Ātman,* is the ultimate reality, *Brahman.* The knowledge wherein this identity is realized removes the ignorance constituted by wrong identification with the body-mind and recovers the original perfection of the Self, releasing one from the sufferings of this *saṃsāric* existence.

Thus, in response to the student's questions the main concerns of Advaita Vedānta are addressed, namely: (1) How is release from suffering possible? (2) Is suffering inherent in human existence? (3) Or is it caused by something outside of one's own nature? (4) What is the nature of the Self? (5) What is the cause of suffering? (6) If the cause is ignorance, how can it be removed? (7) What is ignorance? (8) How is ignorance related to knowledge? (9) How is it possible for the self, said to be of the nature of knowledge, to be ignorant? (10) If the ignorance which causes suffering does not belong to the Self, then how can it cause the self to suffer?

To answer these questions the teacher must explain the difference between what is truly real (*sat*) and what only appears to be real (*māyā*), and explain how what is merely appearance can be superimposed on what is ultimately real. In these explanations the unique response of Advaita Vedānta to the generic problem of how to attain release from suffering is fully laid out in this rich dialogue.

Let me turn now to Professor Sengaku Mayeda's translation of the text and his critical study of Śaṅkara's life and thought. The translation is a model of accuracy that allows the force of the original to shine through. The notes following each chapter are helpful and to the point.

The introduction to the life and thought of Śaṅkara by Professor Mayeda is a masterpiece that will be appreciated by students and teachers alike. Through a careful examination of *A Thousand Teachings* in the larger context of Śaṅkara's other works and in relation to its place in the whole field of Indian philosophy, Professor Mayeda has given us an excellent introduction to Śaṅkara, opening the door to a deep appreciation of his thought and to further study.

JOHN M. KOLLER
Troy, New York

PREFACE

Śaṅkara (700–750) has usually been regarded as the greatest philosopher of India since P. Deussen praised his philosophy and compared it with those of Parmenides and Kant.[1] It has also been pointed out that, like Meister Eckhart, he was not so much a philosopher as a theologian.[2] Śaṅkara was indeed a metaphysician or theologian, but, like Gotama Buddha and other great religious teachers, he was primarily concerned with the salvation of people suffering in transmigratory existence here in this present world and not with the establishment of a complete system of philosophy or theology.[3]

This book contains an annotated English translation[4] of Śaṅkara's *Upadeśasāhasrī* or "A Thousand [Verses of] Teachings,"[5] accompanied by an Introductory Essay. The translation is based upon my edition of the text which has been published in a romanized version of the Sanskrit (*Śaṅkara's Upadeśasāhasrī, Critically Edited with Introduction and Indices*. Tokyo: The Hokuseido Press, 1973).

As already stated in the Preface there, it is not my purpose to point out yet again the importance of the *Upadeśasāhasrī* in the history of the Advaita Vedānta, which has been the main current of thought in India for many centuries. But it is perhaps necessary to describe briefly the character of the *Upadeśasāhasrī*.

The *Upadeśasāhasrī* consists of two parts, one in verse and the other in prose. The verse or Metrical Part (*Padyabandha*) comprises nineteen chapters (*prakaraṇa*). Manuscripts indicate that the two parts were regarded as independent works, as it were, and studied or commented upon separately. They also suggest the possibility that any single chapter could be selected, copied, and studied apart from the rest.[6] This means that reading of the text may begin anywhere.

In the Metrical Part, perforce translated here into prose, three kinds of meter are used, but the prevailing one is *anuṣṭubh,* which consists of 8 syllables to a quarter. Chapters 8, 10, and 19 are entirely composed in the *vaṃśastha* meter with 12 syllables to a quarter. This meter is also used in verses 41–50 of Chapter 14, verse 54 of Chapter 15, and verses 68–74 of Chapter 16. The only use of the *sragdharā* meter, which has 21 syllables to a quarter, is found in verse 81 of Chapter 17.

In the Metrical Part, the author discusses and repeatedly explains many basic problems of Advaita or "non-dualism" from different points of view, sometimes in the form of a dialogue. He first denies the validity of all kinds of action caused by ignorance (*ajñāna*). At the same time he asserts that knowledge (*vidyā*) is the remover of ignorance which is the cause of transmigratory existence (*saṃsāra*). He states that *Ātman* (Self) cannot be negated and explains the identity of *Ātman* with the Lord (*īśvara*). Again making clear the nature of actions, he points out the cause of delusion, sharply distinguishes *Ātman* from the intellect (*buddhi*) and declares that, from the standpoint of the highest truth (*paramārtha*), I (= *Ātman*) am the supreme *Brahman,* or absolute. The main topic is the great sentence (*mahāvākya*) "*tat tvam asi*" (Thou art That), to which the longest chapter, the eighteenth, consisting of 230 verses, is devoted. All these subjects are not systematically expounded. The entire exposition is pervaded by the author's firm faith in *Ātman.* He passionately refutes the teachings of other philosophical schools—Lokāyata, Buddhist, Jain, Sāṃkhya, Vaiśeṣika, and so forth. This vigor of his polemic is easily seen in verse I, 16, 65: "As [their assumptions] contradict the scriptures and reasoning, they should never be respected. Their faults can be pointed out hundreds and thousands of times."

The Prose Part opens, in a simple style, with the declaration that the author will explain how to teach the means of final release (*mokṣa*) for the benefit of the seekers after final release; the means is knowledge of the identity of *Ātman* with *Brahman.* He describes the qualifications of a pupil who is to receive an invitation to knowledge, and also the qualifications of a teacher: a pupil should be a seeker after final release (*mumukṣu*) while a teacher should already be released (*mukta*).

In the Vedānta school there are three stages in the attainment of final release: (a) hearing (*śravaṇa*), (b) thinking (*manana*), and (c) meditation (*nididhyāsana*).[7] They appear to correspond to the first, second, and third chapters, respectively, of the Prose Part.[8] In the first chapter the teacher expounds to a pupil the purport of the scriptures using numerous citations from both the revealed texts (*śruti*) and the traditional texts (*smṛti*). In the second chapter the pupil reflects on the purport of the scriptures over and over again by means of his own reasoning and by discussing with the teacher such fundamental themes as nescience (*avidyā*) and superimposition (*adhyāropaṇā*). The third chapter describes the *parisaṃkhyāna* meditation.

The Prose Part must have been written on the basis of Śaṅkara's practical and pedagogical experiences. The question and answer exchanges between a teacher and his pupil in the Prose Part probably were based upon such interchanges between the author and his disciples. The Prose Part is a handy guide for teachers, while the Metrical Part is, as it were, a textbook for the pupils.

Four years have already passed since the publication of my edition of the text, though I had intended to publish the translation without delay. One of the reasons for this delay was the fact that there was nobody who could look over my English, which is not my mother tongue. Fortunately Mr. Trevor Leggett, who is not only a specialist in Japanese Buddhism and culture but also versed in Śaṅkara's philosophy, kindly read the manuscript of this translation and suggested changes in English expression. Without his warmhearted cooperation this translation could not have been completed. I would like to express my deepest gratitude to him.

Thanks are also due to Dr. Marie G. Wanek, my former student in Indian philosophy at the University of Pennsylvania, who also helped me improve my English translation.

Publication of this book was aided by a grant from the Ministry of Education, Science and Culture, Japan, and by the annual publication subsidy of the University of Tokyo Press. I am grateful for the support of these organizations.

March 26, 1977

SENGAKU MAYEDA

Notes to the Preface

[1]P. Deussen, *The System of the Vedânta* (Reprint edition. New York: Dover Publications, Inc., 1973), p. 48.

[2]R. Otto, *Mysticism East and West* (New York: Collier Books, 1962), p. 33.

[3]Cf. K. H. Potter, *Presuppositions of India's Philosophies* (Englewood Cliffs, N. J.: Prentice-Hall, 1963), p. 165. According to Potter's classification, Śaṅkara and Rāmānuja, as well as Gotama Buddha, are both path philosophers and speculative philosophers (*ibid.*, pp. 36–37). Potter also says: "Śaṃkarācārya . . . seems to teeter between leap and progress philosophy . . ." (*ibid.*, p.100).

[4]The Upad has been translated into modern Indian languages such as Marathi, Bengali, Kanarese, and Hindi:

(a) *Śaṃkarācārya-kṛta-Upadeśasāhasrī, Marāṭhībhāṣāṃtara,* ed. by Sitārāma Mahādeva Phaḍake. Poona: Bhāratabhūṣaṇa Press, 1911.

(b) *Śrīmac-Chaṅkara-viracitā Upadeśasāhasrī, Mūla, Anvaya, Vāṅgālā Pratiśabda, Rāmatīrtha-ṭīkā, Vaṅgālānuvāda Evaṃ Tātparyāsaha,* by Śrīyukta Akṣayakumāra Śāstrī. Calcutta: Metcalfe Press, 1915.

(c) *Prakaraṇagaḷu, Sampuṭi I.* (*Upadeśasāhasrī, Gadya, Padya*; *Aparokṣānubhūti*; *Advaitānubhūti*), by Śrī Saccidānandasarasvatī. Holenarasipuram: Adhyātma Prakāśa Kāryālaya, 1949.

(d) *Śrīmad-ādya-Śaṅkarācāryakṛta-Upadeśasāhasrī, Hindī Anuvāda Sahit,* tr. by Munilāl. Benares: Bhārgava Pustakālaya, 1954.

There is an English translation of the whole text of the Upad:

(e) *A Thousand Teachings in Two Parts—Prose and Poetry—of Srî Sankarâchârya, tr. into English with Explanatory Notes* by Swâmi Jagadânanda. Madras: Sri Ramakrishna Math, 1949.

However, this translation seems to be more faithful to Rāmatīrtha's commentary, *Padayojanikā*, than to the original, as I have pointed out elsewhere (*Philosophy East and West*, vol. 12, no. 3, 1962, pp. 261–263).

There is a German translation of the Prose Part of the text:

(f) *Upadeshasāhasrī von Meister Shankara, aus dem Sanskrit übersetzt und erläutert* von Paul Hacker. Bonn: Röhrscheid Verlag, 1949.

This is based upon the text contained in the *Minor Works of Śri Śaṅkarācārya* (Poona: Oriental Book Agency, 1952). It is a very reliable translation and its footnotes are useful.

The eighteenth chapter of the Metrical Part has been translated into English and French:

(g) *"That Thou Art" by Śrī Śaṃkara (Chapter Eighteen of the Upadeśa Sāhasrī)*, tr. by A. J. Alston. London: Shanti Sadan, 1967.

This is based on D. V. Gokhale's edition: *Shrî Shankarâchârya's Upadeshasâhasrî with the Gloss Padayojanikā by Shrî Râmatîrtha* (Bombay: The Gujarati Printing Press, 1917).

(h) Guy Maximilien, *Tattvamasi de Śaṅkara*: *Texte avec introduction, traduction et notes* (Thèse de troisième cycle en Sorbonne, 1974, unpublished).

The present writer contributed his English translation of the Prose Part based on Mayeda Upad to: *A Source Book of Advaita Vedānta*, ed. by Eliot Deutsch and J. A. B. van Buitenen (Honolulu: The University Press of Hawaii, 1971, pp. 122–151) and a Japanese translation of the Prose Part to: *Annual of Oriental and Religious Studies*, no. 10 (1973), pp. 44–58, no. 8 (1971), pp. 57–69, and no. 15 (1978), pp. 38–40.

In preparing my English translation I have taken the above listed translations in European languages into consideration. In addition, I consulted the following three commentaries on the text:

(i) Ānandajñāna's *Upadeśasāhasrīṭīkā* (alias *Upadeśasāhasrīvivṛti*)—this is unpublished. The manuscript 2552 (Eggeling 2279) in the India Office Library (London) has been utilized.

(ii) Bodhanidhi's *Upadeśa[sahasra]granthavivaraṇa*—this is unpublished and comments on the Metrical Part alone. The manuscript 776 (TR 164) in the Adyar Library (Madras) has been utilized.

(iii) Rāmatīrtha's *Padayojanikā*—this has been published several times in India (see Mayeda Upad, pp. 19–21).

For descriptions of the printed editions of the text, see Mayeda Upad, pp. 19–21.

5 The full title of the text is *Sakalavedopaniṣatsāropadeśasāhasrī* or "A Thousand [Verses of] Teachings, which is the Essence of all the Upaniṣads of the Veda"; this title appears in colophons of manuscripts and printed editions of the text. Cf. Mayeda Upad, p. 68, note 11.

6 The formation of the text is described in Mayeda Upad, pp. 65–68.

7 This is based upon Bṛh.Up. II,4,5 (= IV,5,6): *ātmā vā are draṣṭavyaḥ śrotavyo mantavyo nididhyāsitavyaḥ* (*Ātman* should be seen, heard of, reflected on, and meditated upon). In his *Vedāntasāra* [XXX] 196 Sadānanda adds one more stage called "concentration" (*samādhi*).

8 Cf. P. Hacker, *Upadeshasāhasrī von Meister Shankara*, p.9.

ABBREVIATIONS

Ait. Up. = *Aitareya Upaniṣad.*
BhG = *Bhagavadgītā.*
Bṛh. Up. = *Bṛhadāraṇyaka Upaniṣad.*
BS = *Brahmasūtra.*
BSBh = Śaṅkara, *Brahmasūtrabhāṣya* (Bombay: Nirṇaya-Sâgar Press, 1934).
BUBh = Śaṅkara, *Bṛhadāraṇyakopaniṣadbhāṣya* (Ānandāśrama Sanskrit Series, vol. 15, 1939).
Chānd. Up. = *Chāndogya Upaniṣad.*
Eigen = P. Hacker, "Eigentümlichkeiten der Lehre und Terminologie Śaṅkaras: Avidyā, Nāmarūpa, Māyā, Īśvara", *Zeitschrift der Deutschen Morgenländischen Gesellschaft*, vol. 100 (1950), pp. 246–286.
GBh = Śaṅkara, *Bhagavadgītābhāṣya* (Bombay: Nirṇaya-Sâgar Press, 1936).
GK = Gauḍapāda, *Gauḍapādīyakārikā* (see GKBh).
GKBh = Śaṅkara, *Gauḍapādīyabhāṣya* (Ānandāśrama Sanskrit Series, vol. 10, 1900).
Kaṭh. Up. = *Kaṭha Upaniṣad.*
Kauṣ. Up. = *Kauṣītaki Upaniṣad.*
Māṇḍ. Up. = *Māṇḍūkya Upaniṣad.*
Manu = *Manusmṛti.*
Mayeda Upad = S. Mayeda, *Śaṅkara's Upadeśasāhasrī, Critically Edited with Introduction and Indices* (Tokyo: The Hokuseido Press, 1973).

M.N. Up. = *Mahānārāyaṇa Upaniṣad.*

Naiṣ = Sureśvara, *Naiṣkarmyasiddhi* (*The Naiṣkarmya-Sidddi of Sureśvarācārya with the Candrikā of Jñānottama*, edited with notes and index by the late Colonel G.A. Jacob and revised with introduction and explanatory notes by M. Hiriyanna. Bombay Sanskrit and Prakrit Series No. XXXVIII, 1925).

Nakamura I = H. Nakamura, *Shoki no Vedānta Tetsugaku* (= Early Vedānta Philosophy. Shoki Vedānta Tetsugakushi, vol. I. Tokyo: Iwanami Shoten, 1950).

Nakamura II = H. Nakamura, *Brahmasūtra no Tetsugaku* (= The Philosophy of Brahmasūtra. Shoki Vedānta Tetsugakushi, vol. II. Tokyo: Iwanami Shoten, 1951).

Nakamura III = H. Nakamura, *Vedānta Tetsugaku no Hatten* (= The Development of Vedānta Philosophy. Shoki Vedānta Tetsugakushi, vol. III. Tokyo: Iwanami Shoten, 1955).

Nakamura IV = H. Nakamura, *Kotoba no Keijijōgaku* (= The Metaphysics of Language. Shoki Vedānta Tetsugakushi, vol. IV. Tokyo: Iwanami Shoten, 1956).

PBh = Śaṅkara, *Padabhāṣya* (*The Kena Upanishad with Sri Shankara's Commentaries*, ed. by Sri Swami Saccidanandendra Sarasvati. Holenarasipur: Adhyatma Prakasha Karyalaya, 1959).

Praś. Up. = *Praśna Upaniṣad.*

Sś = Sarvajñātman, *Saṃkṣepaśārīraka* (*The Saṁkṣepaśārīraka of Sarvajñātman, Critically edited with Introduction, English Translation, Notes and Indexes* by N. Veezhinathan. Madras: University of Madras, 1972).

Śvet. Up. = *Śvetāśvatara Upaniṣad.*

Taitt. A. = *Taittirīya Āraṇyaka.*

Taitt. Up. = *Taittirīya Upaniṣad.*

Unters = P. Hacker, *Untersuchungen über Texte des frühen Advaitavāda, 1. Die Schüler Śaṅkaras.* Mainz: Verlag der Akademie der Wissenschaften und der Literatur, 1950).

Up. = *Upaniṣad.*

Upad = Śaṅkara, *Upadeśasāhasrī* (see Mayeda Upad).

VP = Dharmarāja Adhvarin, *Vedāntaparibhāṣā* (*Vedāntaparibhāṣā by Dharmarāja Adhvarin, ed. with an English Translation* by S.S. Suryanarayana Sastri. The Adyar Library Series, No. 34, 1942).

WZKSO = *Wiener Zeitschrift für die Kunde Süd- und Ostasiens.*

AN INTRODUCTION TO THE LIFE AND THOUGHT OF ŚAṄKARA

I. THE LIFE AND WORKS OF ŚAṄKARA

There are many works which profess to be biographies of Śaṅkara.[1] The most famous of all is the *Śaṅkaradigvijaya*, written by Vidyāraṇya in the fourteenth century.[2] All these biographies were composed hundreds of years after Śaṅkara's death and are filled with legendary stories and incredible anecdotes, some of which are mutually contradictory. Today there are no extant materials from which to reconstruct his life with certainty.

Setting the date of Śaṅkara's birth is probably one of the most controversial problems in the history of Indian philosophy, not only because he is one of the greatest Indian philosophers but also because a solution is inseparable from the correct understanding of one of the most important and critical periods of the history of Indian thought. It has been customary to adopt the birth and death dates asserted by K. B. Pathak in 1882,[3] 788 and 820, but these dates have no firm basis. After reviewing and criticizing all the conflicting opinions, Hajime Nakamura proposed in 1950 that the dates should be shifted to 700–750.[4] This view has been accepted by such scholars as L. Renou[5] and D. H. H. Ingalls.[6]

During the fifth and sixth centuries the Huns invaded India from the central Asian steppes, and the political system of the Gupta empire, under which India had enjoyed her golden age of classical culture, was completely broken up in the sixth century. In the seventh century King Harṣa restored peace in North India, but after his death India fell into chaos again. Thus Śaṅkara was active in composing his works and propagating his teachings during an era of political division and social unrest in India; Buddhism was on the wane and Hinduism on the rise.

Tradition says that Śaṅkara was born into a pious Nambūdiri Brahmin family[7] in a quiet village called Kālaḍi on the banks of the Cūrṇā (or Pūrṇā, Periyāṛu) River in Kerala, South India.[8] He is said to have lost his father, Śivaguru, early in his life. Śaṅkara renounced the world and became a *saṃnyāsin* (ascetic) against his mother's will, and went to Govinda (670–720)[9] to receive instruction. No reliable information about Govinda is available,[10] but he is traditionally said to have been a pupil of Gauḍapāda (640–690).[11] Gauḍapāda is notable as the author of an important Vedānta work, *Gauḍapādīyakārikā*, in which the influence of Mahāyāna Buddhism is evident and, especially in its last chapter, even dominant.[12]

It is said that Śiva, one of the principal gods in Hindusim, was Śaṅkara's family deity and also that he was, by birth, a Śākta, or worshipper of Śakti, the consort of Śiva and female personification of divine energy. Later he came to be regarded as a worshipper of Śiva and even as an incarnation of Śiva himself. But his doctrine is very far removed from Śaivism and Śāktism. It can be ascertained from his works that he had some faith in, or was favorable to, Vaiṣṇavism.[13] It is likely that he was familiar with Yoga, since he is the author of the *Yogasūtrabhāṣyavivaraṇa*, the exposition of Vyāsa's commentary on the *Yogasūtra*, a basic text of the Yoga school.[14] A recent study, though not fully acceptable, has suggested that he was first an adherent of Yoga and later became an Advaitin.[15]

Biographers narrate that Śaṅkara first went to Kāśī (Vārāṇasī), a city celebrated for learning and spirituality, and then travelled all over India, holding discussions with philosophers of different creeds. His heated debate with Maṇḍanamiśra, a philosopher of the Mīmāṃsā school, whose wife served as an arbiter, is perhaps the most interesting of the episodes reported in his biography[16] and may reflect a historical fact: keen conflict between Śaṅkara, who regarded the knowledge of *Brahman* as the only means to final release, and the Mīmāṃsā school, which emphasized the performance of ordained duty and the Vedic rituals, and to which belonged eminent philosophers such as Kumārila Bhaṭṭa, Prabhākara, and Maṇḍanamiśra. It is traditionally believed that Kumārila was Śaṅkara's senior contemporary and that Prabhākara was

Kumārila's pupil, though he later established the Prabhākara school in opposition to his teacher.[17] Maṇḍanamiśra was another contemporary who held Advaitic views different from Śaṅkara's. It has been remarked that "during the age of Śaṃkara and for some centuries following it, Maṇḍana's authority on questions relating to Advaita was recognized to be at least as high and important as that of Śaṃkara himself."[18]

Śaṅkara would not teach his doctrine to city dwellers. In cities the power of Buddhism was still strong, though already declining, and Jainism prevailed among the merchants and manufacturers. Popular Hinduism occupied the minds of ordinary people while city dwellers pursued ease and pleasure. There were also hedonists in cities,[19] and it was difficult for Śaṅkara to communicate Vedānta philosophy to these people. Consequently he propagated his teachings chiefly among *saṃnyāsins*, who had renounced the world, and intellectuals in the villages, and he gradually won the respect of Brahmins and feudal lords.[20] He made enthusiastic efforts to restore the orthodox Brahmanical tradition, without paying attention to the *bhakti* (devotional) movement, which had made a deep impression on ordinary Hindus in his age.

It is very likely that Śaṅkara had many pupils, but we know only four from their writings: Padmapāda, Sureśvara, Toṭaka (or Troṭaka), and Hastāmalaka.[21] Padmapāda wrote a commentary on Śaṅkara's commentary on the first four *sūtras* (aphorisms) of the *Brahmasūtra*, called *Pañcapādikā*, on which in the middle of the tenth century A.D.[22] Prakāśātman composed a commentary entitled *Pañcapādikāvivaraṇa*. The Vivaraṇa school which Padmapāda started was the most influential among the later Advaitins until it was overshadowed by the Bhāmatī school. Sureśvara is known as the commentator on Śaṅkara's commentaries on the *Bṛhadāraṇyaka Upaniṣad* and the *Taittirīya Upaniṣad*. His independent work *Naiṣkarmyasiddhi* is "intended to reiterate the views embodied in the *Upadeśasāhasrī*" of Śaṅkara.[23] Toṭaka and Hastāmalaka are the authors of the *Śrutisārasamuddharaṇa* and the *Hastāmalakaślokāḥ*, respectively, but their influence upon the development of the Advaita Vedānta seems to be negligible.

It is also traditionally believed that Śaṅkara founded four monasteries (*maṭha*), at Śṛṅgeri (Śṛṅgerimaṭha, South), Purī

(Govardhanamaṭha, East), Dvārakā (Śāradāmaṭha, West), and Badarīnātha (Jyotirmaṭha, North). The most important of the four is the one at Śṛṅgeri in Mysore Province. In founding monasteries he was probably inspired by the Buddhist *vihāra* (monastery) system.[24] In any case, the monasteries must have played a significant role in the development of his teachings into the leading philosophy of India.

More than three hundred works—commentaries, expositions, and poetry—are attributed to him.[25] Most of them are not accepted as authentic.[26] His masterpiece is the *Brahmasūtrabhāṣya*, the commentary on the *Brahmasūtra*, which is the fundamental text of the Vedānta school. In fact, we should define Śaṅkara as the author of the *Brahmasūtrabhāṣya*, and use it as the yardstick against which to measure the authenticity of other works ascribed to him.[27] Śaṅkara also wrote commentaries on the *Bṛhadāraṇyaka*, *Chāndogya*, *Aitareya*, *Taittirīya*, *Kena*,[28] *Īśā*, *Kaṭha*, *Muṇḍaka*, *Praśna*, and *Māṇḍūkya Upaniṣad*.[29] Those commentaries are probably all genuine, but the commentary on the *Śvetāśvatara Upaniṣad*, which is traditionally ascribed to him, may be spurious.[30] The commentaries on the *Gauḍapādīyakārikā* and the *Adhyātmapaṭala* of *Āpastamba-Dharmasūtra* seem to have been written by Śaṅkara himself.[31] As I have already mentioned, he is probably the author of the *Yogasūtrabhāṣyavivaraṇa*.[32] These works are all commentaries on one or another text. The *Upadeśasāhasrī*, which is translated here, is the only non-commentarial work whose authenticity has been conclusively demonstrated.[33]

Penetrating insight, analytical skill, and lucid style characterize Śaṅkara's works. He cannot be called a particularly original philosopher,[34] but it has to be remembered that in India it is not originality but fidelity to tradition which is the great virtue. He was an excellent exegete, with an approach to truth which was psychological and religious rather than philosophical.[35] He was really not so much a philosopher as a pre-eminent religious leader and a most successful religious teacher. His works show him to have been not only versed in the orthodox Brahmanical traditions but also well acquainted with Mahāyāna Buddhism, so much so that he was often criticized as a "crypto-Buddhist" (*pracchannabauddha*) by his opponents because of the similarity between his doctrine and Buddhism. Against this criticism, it should be noted that he made full use of his knowledge of Buddhism to attack Buddhist doctrines vigorously, or to assimilate them into his own Vedāntic nondualism, and he made great exertions to "revedanticize" the Vedānta philosophy, which had been made extremely Buddhistic by his predecessors. The basic structure of his philosophy is nearer to Sāṃkhya, a philosophic system of nontheistic dualism, and to the Yoga school, than to Buddhism.

It is said that Śaṅkara died at Kedārnātha in the Himalayas. The Advaita Vedānta school he founded has always been preeminent in the learned circles of India. His doctrine has been the source from which the main currents of modern Indian thought are derived.

Notes to Introduction, I

1 For example, (1) Anantānandagiri, *Guruvijaya*; (2) Ānandagiri, *Śaṅkaravijaya* [ed. by Jayanārāyaṇa Tarkapañcānana. Calcutta: Asiatic Society of Bengal, 1868; ed. by Pandit Jibananda Vidyasagara. Calcutta: Sarasudhanidhi Press, 1881]; (3) Govindanātha, *Śaṅkarācāryacarita* [Trichur: The Kerala Publishing House, 1926]; (4) Citsukhācārya, *Bṛhatśaṅkaravijaya*; (5) Cidvilāsa, *Śaṅkaravijayavilāsa*; (6) Parameśvara, *Ācāryavijayacampū*; (7) Rājacūḍāmaṇidīkṣita, *Śaṅkarābhyudaya*; (8) Vallīsahāya, *Śaṅkaravijaya*; (9) Vidyāśaṅkara, *Śaṅkaravijaya*; (10) Vidvadbālakakāśīlakṣmaṇa Śāstri, *Guruvaṃśakāvya* [Śrīraṅgam: Śri Vāṇi Vilās Press, n.d.]; (11) Vyāsācala, *Śaṅkaravijaya*; (12) Sadānanda, *Śaṅkaravijayasāra*; (13) Sadāśivabrahmendra, *Gururatnamālā*; and (14) Sarvajña Sadāśivabodha, *Puṇyaślokamañjarī*, and its *Pariśiṣṭa* by Ātmabodha.

2 Editions: (1) Bombay: Gaṇpat Kṛṣṇājī's Press, 1864; (2)Ānadāśrama Sanskrit Series, vol. 22 (Poona), 1891; (3) Hardvār: Śrī Śravaṇanātha Jñānamandir, 1943 — this edition contains a Hindi translation by P. Baladeva Upādhyāya; and (4) Sringeri: The Sringeri Matha, 1956. The first chapter of the *Śaṅkaradigvijaya* was translated into German by P. Deussen in his *Allgemeine Geschichte der Philosophie*, I, 3 (Leipzig: F. A. Brockhaus, 1908), pp. 181 – 189.

3 *Indian Antiquary*, XI (1882), pp. 174–175.

4 Nakamura I, pp. 63–121. In opposition to this view K. K. Raja published an article, "On the Date of Śaṃkarācārya and Allied Problems," in the *Adyar Library Bulletin* (vol. XXIV, pts. 3–4, 1960, pp. 125–148) suggesting that the works of Śaṅkara were composed toward the close of the eighth century. P. Hacher places him before or around 700 A.D. (*Orientalistische Literaturzeitung* 59, 1964, p. 235–236). Cf. Giuseppe Morichini's review of Nakamura's book, *East and West*, 1960, pp. 33–39.

5 *Journal Asiatique*, Vol. CCXLIII (1955), no. 2, pp. 249–251.

6 *Philosophy East and West*, Vol. 3 (1954), p. 292, n. 2.

7 The Nambūdiris are the only original Brahmins of Kerala, whose origins cannot be traced back outside Kerala. Even today they form a unique community among the many kinds of Brahmins in India, preserving some of the ancient Vedic and early

post-Vedic traditions and rites which are extinct elsewhere. It is of interest to note that insofar as they adhered to any philosophical system at all, it was to the Bhāṭṭa school of Pūrva Mīmāṃsā, which Śaṅkara severely attacked in his works. It is said that Advaita was adopted by many Nambūdiris only after having become quite popular in other parts of India. See J. F. Staal, "Notes on Some Brahmin Communities of South India," *Art and Letters, India, Pakistan, Ceylon*, vol. XXXII (1958), no. 1, pp. 1–7.

8 At present there is a walled enclosure overlooking the ghat in Kālaḍi which contains sites known traditionally as Śaṅkara's birthplace, the place where his house stood, and the place on which the remains of his mother were cremated. This compound also contains two shrines, the Śāradā and the Śaṅkara, and a *pāṭhaśālā* which offers instruction in *Veda* and *Vedānta* in a traditional way.

9 Nakamura III, p. 244.

10 Tradition has it that Govinda was the author of the commentaries on the Chānd. Up., *Devatākāṇḍa*, and BS, though they are not extant. He is also reported to have written the *Yogatārāvali*, which is unpublished. See M. Raṅgācārya, *The Sarva-Siddhānta-Saṅgraha of Śaṅkarācārya* (Madras: Government Press, 1909), p. viii; Nakamura III, pp. 244–247.

11 In his paper (*Adyar Library Bulletin*, vol. XXIV, pts. 3–4, pp. 125–148) K. K. Raja assigns Gauḍapāda to the fifth century A.D. and denies the tradition that makes him a *paramaguru* of Śaṅkara, interpreting the Sanskrit term as "supreme preceptor" instead of the more usual "teacher's teacher." See T.M.P. Mahadevan, *Gauḍapāda: A Study in Early Advaita* (Madras: University of Madras, 1960), pp. 15–16. Nakamura, on the other hand, regards him as an editor of the *Kārikā* rather than its author and accepts the tradition that he was Śaṅkara's teacher's teacher. See Nakamura III, pp. 589–602.

12 See Introduction, II, p. 13. The *Gauḍapādīyakārikā* is also called *Māṇḍūkyakārikā*, *Māṇḍūkyopaniṣatkārikā*, and *Āgamaśāstra* (cf. Nakamura III, pp. 520–523).

13 See Nakamura III, p. 531; P. Hacker, "Relations of Early Advaitins to Vaiṣṇavism", WZKSO, vol. IX (1965), pp. 147–154. This may be related to the fact that Śaṅkara pays the highest regard to the BhG among the non-Vedic texts (see S. Mayeda, "The Authenticity of the Upadeśasāhasrī Ascribed to Śaṅkara," *JAOS*, vol. 85, No. 2, 1965, pp. 187–188; Mayeda Upad, p. 44). It should be noted here that a large percentage of the present Nambūdiris (see note 7) have Nārāyaṇan for their individual name, that the name Nārāyaṇa is very sacred to them, and that the most famous temple of Kerala is the Guruvāyur temple where Kṛṣṇa is worshipped and whose priests are drawn only from particular Nambūdiri families. Cf. J. F. Staal, *Art and Letters, India, Pakistan*, vol. XXXII (1958), no. 1, p. 5.

14 See note 32, below, and Introduction, III, B, note 63, pp. 64–65.

15 See P. Hacker, "Śaṅkara der Yogin und Śaṅkara der Advaitin," WZKSO, vol. XII-XIII (1968/1969), p. 119–148. It may, however, be necessary to reexamine his opinion. Cf. H. Nakamura, "Notes to Śaṅkara's *Yogasūtrabhāṣyavivaraṇa* [I]" (*Journal of Indian and Buddhist Studies*, Vol. XXV, no. 1, 1976, p. 77).

16 Mādhava, *Śaṅkaradigvijaya* VIII. Cf. T.M.P. Mahadevan, *Homage to Śaṅkara* (Jayanti Series no. 4. Madras: Ganesh and Co., 1959), pp. 18–23. Tradition says that Maṇḍanamiśra, converted to the Vedānta, was named Sureśvara by Śaṅkara. This tradition seems to be baseless, though the question may have not yet been settled. See M. Hiriyanna, *Journal of the Royal Asiatic Society of Great Britain and Ireland* (1923), pp. 259–263; (1924), pp. 96–97; M. Hiriyanna, *The Naiṣkarmya-Siddhi of Sureśvarācārya with the Candrikā of Jñānottama* (Bombay Sanskrit and Prakrit Series no. XXXVIII. Bom-

bay, 1925), p. xxxii; S. Kuppuswami Sastri, *The Brahmasiddhi by Ācārya Maṇḍanamiśra with Commentary by Śaṅkhapāṇi, Edited with Introduction, Appendices and Indexes* (Madras Government Oriental Manuscripts Series no. 4. Madras, 1937), pp. xxiv f.; Dinesh Chandra Bhattacharya, *Indian Historical Quarterly*, vol. VII (1931), pp. 301–308; Amarnath Roy, *ibid.*, vol. VII (1931), p. 632; J. M. Van Boetzelear, *Sureśvara's Taittirīyopaniṣadbhāṣyavārtikam* (Leiden: E. J. Brill, 1971), p. 1.

17 Cf. S. Dasgupta, *A History of Indian Philosophy*, vol. I (Cambridge, 1951), pp. 370–372.

18 K. K. Raja, "On the Date of Śaṃkarācārya and Allied Problems," pp. 142–143. Cf. S. Kuppuswami Sastri, *The Brahmasiddhi*, p. lix; L. Schmithausen, *Maṇḍanamiśra's Vibhramavivekaḥ mit einer Studie zur Entwicklung der indischen Irrtumslehre* (Wien: Kommissionsverlag der Österreichischen Akademie der Wissenschaften, 1965); Tilmann Vetter, *Maṇḍanamiśra's Brahmasiddhiḥ, Brahmakāṇḍaḥ, Übersetzung, Einleitung und Anmerkungen* (Wien: Kommissionsverlag der Österreichischen Akademie der Wissenschaften, 1969); M. Biardeau, *La philosophie de Maṇḍana Miśra vue à partir de la Brahmasiddhi* (Publications de l'École française d'extrême-Orient vol. LXXVI. Paris, 1969).

19 H. Nakamura, "Śaṅkara Tetsugaku no Rekishiteki Shakaiteki Tachiba," *Dr. Hakuju Ui's Felicitation Volume* (Tokyo: Iwanami Shoten, 1951), p. 361.

20 See Upad II,1,2 and its notes 3 and 6.

21 P. Hacker, Unters.

22 See K. Cammann, *Das System des Advaita nach der Lehre Prakāśātmans* (Münchener Indologische Studies Bd 4. Wiesbaden: Otto Harrassowitz, 1965), pp. 4–8.

23 M. Hiriyanna, *The Naiṣkarmya-Siddhi of Sureśvarācārya*, p. viii.

24 P. V. Kane, *History of Dharmaśāstra*, Vol. II, Pt. II (Government Oriental Series Class-B, No. 6. Poona: Bhandarkar Oriental Research Institute, 1941), p. 907; K. A. Nilakanta Sastri, *A History of South India* (Oxford: Oxford University Press, 1958), p. 417.

25 Cf. Th. Aufrecht, *Catalogus Catalogorum,* 3 vols. Leipzig, 1891 – 1903.

26 In India it has been a common practice to lend a book authenticity by attributing it to a famous author. Besides, all the heads (*Jagadguru*) of the Śṛṅgerimaṭha have had the title Śaṅkarācārya, and any literary or philosophical work written by any of these heads could be legitimately called a work of Śaṅkarācārya. Cf. K. K. Raja, *Adyar Library Bulletin* (vol. XXIV, pts. 3–4), pp. 127–128. It is thus not easy to decide which works were really written by our Śaṅkara. P. Hacker pointed out that Śaṅkara's contemporaries had styled him Bhagavat, Bhagavatpāda, and Bhagavatpūjyapāda and that the BSBh is invariably ascribed to Śaṅkara-Bhagavat, -Bhagavatpāda, or -Bhagavatpūjyapāda in the colophons. From this fact he concluded that "we are entitled to regard provisionally as genuine those works that are described in their colophons as productions of the Bhagavat, whereas all the works that are usually attributed to Śaṅkara-Ācārya in the colophons are suspicious of being spurious" (P. Hacker, "Śaṅkarācārya and Śaṅkarabhagavatpāda," *New Indian Antiquary*, vol. IX, 1947, pp. 182–183). He applied this method and concluded that all the commentaries on the *Prasthānatrayī* are genuine. But he denied the authenticity of the *Śvetāśvataropaniṣadbhāṣya* in its present form. Cf. P. Hacker, WZKSO, vol. XII-XIII (1968/1969), p. 147.

27 Cf. Mayeda Upad, p. 22.

28 There are two commentaries on the *Kenopaniṣad* which are ascribed to one and the same author, Śaṅkara; one is entitled *Padabhāṣya* and the other *Vākyabhāṣya*. Both of them seem to be genuine. See S. Mayeda, "On Śaṅkara's Authorship of the Kenopaniṣadbhāṣya," *Indo-Iranian Journal*, vol. X (1967), no. 1, pp. 33–55.

[29] Cf. S. Mayeda, "On the Author of the Māṇḍūkyopaniṣad- and the Gauḍapādīya- Bhāṣya," *Professor V. Raghavan's Felicitation Volume, Adyar Library Bulletin*, vols. 31–32 (1967–68), pp. 73–94.

[30] See note 26, p. 9; Ānandāśrama Sanskrit Series No. 9 (1918), pp. [1]–[2]; S. Mayeda, "Nārāyaṇa's Kenopaniṣaddīpikā," *Journal of Indian and Buddhist Studies*, vol. XX (1972), no. 2, p. 97.

[31] See note 29 and P. Hacker, WZKSO, Vol. XII-XIII (1968/1969), S. 147.

[32] T. Chandrasekharan (ed.), *Pātañjalayogasūtrabhāṣyavivaraṇam* (Madras Government Oriental Series no. XCIV. Madras, 1952). On Śaṅkara's authorship of this *Vivaraṇa*, see Introduction, III, B, note 63, pp. 64–65.

[33] Mayeda Upad, pp. 22–64. There are many other non-commentarial works ascribed to Śaṅkara but their authenticity is very doubtful. For example, the following works do not seem to be authentic, though they are widely accepted as Śaṅkara's works: (1) The *Vivekacūḍāmaṇi*—see D. H. H. Ingalls, "The Study of Śaṅkarācārya," *Annals of the Bhandarkar Oriental Research Institute*, vol. XXXIII (1952), p. 7; S. Mayeda, "Śaṅkara's Upadeśasāhasrī: Its Present Form," *Journal of the Oriental Institute*, vol. XV (1966), nos. 3–4, p. 252, footnote 3; (2) The *Saundaryalaharī*—see W. Norman Brown, *The Saundaryalaharī, or Flood of Beauty traditionally ascribed to Śaṅkarācārya* (Harvard Oriental Series 43. Cambridge: Harvard University Press, 1958), pp. 25–30; (3) The *Sarvasiddhāntasaṅgraha*—see P. Hacker, *New Indian Antiquary*, vol. IX (1947), pp. 184–185; (4) *Vākyavṛtti* and *Laghuvākyavṛtti*—see S. Mayeda, "On the Vākyavṛtti," *Professor H. Nakamura's Felicitation Volume* (Tokyo: Shunjūsha, 1973), pp. 57–69.

[34] Nakamura IV, pp. 420–437. Taking up ideas which have generally been regarded as characteristic of Śaṅkara's teachings, Nakamura has shown that each of those had already been expressed by some of his predecessors and that Śaṅkara himself was not the originator.

[35] Cf. Eigen, p. 256; D. H. H. Ingalls, "Śaṁkara on the Question: Whose Is Avidyā?" *Philosophy East and West*, vol. 3 (1953), no. 4, p. 72.

II. ŚAṄKARA'S CENTRAL DOCTRINE AND HIS POSITION IN THE HISTORY OF THE VEDĀNTA

All the systems of Indian philosophy, including materialism (Lokāyata), Jainism, and Buddhism, have as their ultimate objective the attainment of final release (*mokṣa*) from transmigratory existence (*saṃsāra*), a fact which Western philosophers have not always appreciated. In India philosophic speculation is simply a practical means to the goal. It is pursued out of a deep craving for the realization of the religious purpose of life, though, of course, there are considerable differences of degree in earnestness and enthusiasm among Indian philosophers and thinkers.

It was the knowledge of *Brahman*, the absolute, that Śaṅkara taught to his followers over and over again. The teaching that *Ātman*, one's inner Self (*pratyagātman*), is wholly identical with *Brahman*[1] is not only the starting point of his philosophy but also its goal. Śaṅkara's central doctrine is *Ātman*'s identity with *Brahman*; this truth arrived at by Upaniṣadic thinkers was the culmination of the serious quest for universal truth which Ṛgvedic poet-thinkers had first begun probably before 1000 B.C. In Śaṅkara's view the knowledge of this truth is the means (*sādhana*) to final release. He says:

> When the knowledge (*vidyā*) [of *Brahman*] is firmly grasped, it is conducive to one's own beatitude and to the continuity [of the knowledge of *Brahman*]. And the continuity of knowledge [of *Brahman*] is helpful to people as a boat is helpful to one wishing to get across a river. (*dṛḍhagṛhītā hi vidyātmanaḥ śreyase santatyai ca bhavati / vidyāsantatiś ca prāṇyanugrahāya bhavati naur iva nadīṃ titīrṣoḥ*—Upad II,1,3)

Philosophy is not his aim but is rather a vital weapon with which to fulfil his aim, which is to rescue people out of transmigratory existence. Logic and theory are subordinate to this end.

Śaṅkara is an epoch-making reformer of the Vedānta school of philosophy, the founder of which is traditionally said to be Bādarāyaṇa (100–1 B.C.).[2] Bādarāyaṇa is regarded as the author of the *Brahmasūtra*[3] which, together with the Upaniṣads and the *Bhagavadgītā*,[4] constitute the threefold canon (*prasthānatraya*) of the Vedānta school.

Though the *Brahmasūtra* is attributed to Bādarāyaṇa, it cannot be considered a work composed by a single author; it was based upon about 700 years' activities by many scholars, and was given its present form probably around 400–450 A. D.[5] Before the composition of the *Brahmasūtra* there must have been different interpretations of the Upaniṣads and various theories on metaphysical problems related to the Upaniṣads, which latter contain diverse, even mutually contradictory, and unsystematized teachings. The *Brahmasūtra* summarized, arranged, criticized, unified, and systematized those different or conflicting interpretations and theories.

In consolidating the Vedāntic position, the *Brahmasūtra* made a special point of refuting the dualism of the then prevailing Sāṃkhya school which posited *Puruṣa* (Spirit) and *Prakṛti* (Matter) as the independent ultimate causes of the Universe. The *Brahmasūtra* maintained instead that *Brahman* alone is the absolute ultimate cause of the Universe. Thus the *Brahmasūtra* characterized Vedānta as a monistic system devoted to inquiry into *Brahman* (*brahmajijñāsā*, BS I,1,1). This characterization distinguished the Vedānta not only from the Sāṃkhya, which is of all the Indian philosophic systems doctrinally most akin to it, but also from the sister system, Mīmāṃsā, which has *dharma*[6] as the object of its inquiry.

The most crucial problem among the Vedāntins is the relationship between *Brahman*, or absolute, and the individual Self, *Ātman*. Controversy concerning this problem led to the splitting up of the Vedānta school into many minor schools. The *Brahmasūtra* indicates that at the time of its composition this was already a significant problem.[7] Today it is generally accepted that the central doctrine of the Upaniṣads is the identity of *Brahman* and *Ātman*. The *Brahmasūtra*, however, declares that the individual *Ātman* is a portion (*aṃśa*) of *Brahman* (BS II,3,43). According to

Śaṅkara, Bhāskara, and Rāmānuja, the three commentators on the text, this theory is based upon *Bhagavadgītā* XV,7. The individual *Ātman* is different from *Brahman* (*nānā*, BS II,3,43; *vaiśeṣya*, BS I,2,8; *bheda*, BS II,1,22) but it is also described as non-different (*avaiśeṣya*, BS III,2,25).[8] This fact indicates that the *Brahmasūtra* stands in the line of difference-and-non-difference (*bhedābheda*), although this technical expression is not used in the text.[9] As the *Brahmasūtra* itself suggests (BS III,2,27), it is probable that the above view reflects an intention to synthesize two contradictory teachings in the Upaniṣads, one being the teaching that the individual *Ātman* is different from *Brahman*[10] and the other that of their non-difference.[11]

During the period between the *Brahmasūtra* and Śaṅkara the Vedānta experienced a significant transformation. There was a buddhification of the Vedānta tradition. In this period the *Gauḍapādīyakārikā*, which is traditionally ascribed to Gauḍapāda, was composed, comprising four chapters (*prakaraṇa*), ostensibly to explain the *Māṇḍūkyopaniṣad*.[12] Modern scholarship has revealed that the *Māṇḍūkyopaniṣad* already shows Buddhist influence[13] and that the *Gauḍapādīyakārikā* is a work greatly influenced by Buddhism; each succeeding chapter of the *Gauḍapādīyakārikā* is more Buddhistic than that preceding it.[14] It seems to me that the *Māṇḍūkyopaniṣad* and the four chapters of the *Gauḍapādīyakārikā* represent five stages of increasing Buddhist influence upon the Vedānta tradition. The fourth chapter, which constitutes nearly half of the whole text, has hardly anything to do either with the Upaniṣads or with the *Brahmasūtra* and may well be regarded as a Buddhist text.[15]

Śaṅkara's composition of the commentary on the *Gauḍapādīyakārikā* is an epochal event in the history of the Vedānta, since it may be said that this commentary represents a turning point in the Vedānta tradition, which until then had been becoming more and more Buddhistic. It was in consonance with the general tendency of Śaṅkara's time, for the age of the happy coexistence of Buddhism and Hinduism had already passed when he was born, and his age was marked by a Hindu revival.[16] Although he tried to Vedānticize the *Gauḍapādīyakārikā*, an extremely Buddhistic text, he did not ignore the Buddhistic elements in the work; as I have shown elsewhere,[17] he skillfully gave them a Vedāntic character and adopted them into his own system.[18] Thus the Vedānta in the *Brahmasūtra*, which may be characterized as realistic monism, was transformed into illusionistic monism, which regards everything but *Brahman* as unreal. At the same time the difference between the individual *Ātman* and *Brahman* is looked upon as due to nescience (*avidyā*) and therefore unreal. Śaṅkara asserted that, although the individual *Ātman* appears to be different from *Brahman* in the sphere of nescience, they are wholly identical from the standpoint of the highest truth (*paramārtha*). This view of the relationship between *Ātman* and *Brahman* is called "non-dualism" (*advaitavāda*), in contrast with the theory of difference-and-non-difference (*bhedābhedavāda*) which was overshadowed by it, in spite of the vain efforts by Bhāskara, probably soon after the death of Śaṅkara, to revive it by writing another commentary on the *Brahmasūtra* from the standpoint of that older tradition.[19]

The Advaitic tradition started long before Śaṅkara; it has its origin in the Upaniṣads. The *Gauḍapādīyakārikā* is the earliest extant text that advocated illusionistic *Advaita*.[20] It was, however, Śaṅkara who established the illusionistic *Advaita* tradition based on the concept of nescience[21] and the Sāṃkhyan dualism, and made it the main current of the Vedānta.

Śaṅkara's *Upadeśasāhasrī* is dedicated to explaining the identity of *Ātman* and *Brahman* and repeatedly teaches that the knowledge of that identity is the means to final release. In the following pages we shall see his demonstration of the *Brahman-Ātman* identity, and his view of final release.

Notes to Introduction, II

1 In his *Mysticism East and West* (pp. 28–29), R. Otto points out the similarity between Śaṅkara and Meister Eckhart on this point.

2 Nakamura II, p. 55.

3 In his BSBh Śaṅkara does not clearly say that the author of the BS is Bādarāyaṇa. When he comments, however, on the last *sūtra* he says, "*ata uttaraṃ bhagavān bādarāyaṇa ācāryaḥ paṭhati*" (p. 905), so it is likely that he regards Bādarāyaṇa as the author of the whole text. It seems that the identification of Veda-Vyāsa with Bādarāyaṇa begins with Vācaspatimiśra (Maṅgalācaraṇa of his *Bhāmatī*). Later it became usual to identify Bādarāyaṇa with Veda-Vyāsa and with Vyāsa, who is regarded as the author of the *Mahābhārata* and other *Smṛtis*. Cf. Nakamura II, pp. 52–58; P. V. Kane, *History of Dharmaśāstra*, vol. V, pt. II (Poona: Bhandarkar Oriental Research Institute,

1962), pp. 1160–1173. It should be noted here that Sureśvara, one of Śaṅkara's pupils, may be attributing the BS to Jaimini when he says: *yadi hy ayam abhiprāyo 'bhaviṣyat "athāto brahmajijñāsā / janmādy asya yataḥ" ity evamādibrahmavastusvarūpamātrayāthātmyaprakāśanaparaṃ gambhīranyāyasaṃdṛbdhaṃ sarvavedāntārthaṃīmāṃsanaṃ śrīmacchārīrakaṃ nāsūtrayiṣyat* (Naiṣ I, 91). But M. Hiriyanna in his edition of the Naiṣ rejects this interpretation, asserting that it is better to suppose "that when he wrote the passage, our author was thinking more of the harmony between these two pre-eminently orthodox systems than the difference in their authorship." (*The Naiṣkarmya-Siddhi of Sureśvarācārya with the Candrikā of Jñānottama*, p. 230). On the other hand, H. Nakamura has proposed a new theory that, just as there were some people who attributed the present BS to Bādarāyaṇa, there were probably others who ascribed it to Jaimini, and he rejects S. K. Belvalkar's opinion that Jaimini also wrote a *Śārīraka-Sūtra* (Nakamura II, pp. 42–44).

4 Cf. J. N. Farquhar, *An Outline of the Religious Literature of India* (Reprint edition, Delhi: Motilal Banarsidass, 1967), p. 128 and p. 173.

5 See Nakamura II, pp. 94–96.

6 The term *dharma* in the Mīmāṃsā has a particular meaning. The *Mīmāṃsāsūtra* I,1,2 defines it as "that which is indicated by the Vedic injunction as conducive to welfare." Cf. Ganganatha Jha, *Pūrva-Mīmāṃsā in Its Sources* (Benares: Benares Hindu University, 1942), pp. 172–174.

7 Cf. BS I,4,19–22. It has been pointed out that Kāśakṛtsna stood in the line of *bhedābheda*, regarding the individual *Ātman* as a portion (*aṃśa*) of *Brahman* (Nakamura II, pp. 7–12. Cf. *BS* II,3,43). Auḍulomi held the opinion that they are different in the state of transmigration which is real and non-different in the state of final release (Nakamura II, pp. 22–23. Cf. Ānandajñāna on BS I,4,21). Āśmarathya was of the opinion that they are in the relationship of the material cause and its modification (*prakṛtivikārabhāva*, Bhāskara on BS I,4,21. Cf. Nakamura II, pp. 25–26).

8 See Nakamura II, p. 273 and p. 448.

9 See *ibid.*, pp. 446–451.

10 In his BSBh (III,2,27, p. 658), Śaṅkara quotes Māṇḍ. Up. III,1,8; 2, 8 and Bṛh. Up. III,7,15 as examples of texts on the difference between *Ātman* and *Brahman*.

11 In his BSBh (III,2,27, p. 658), Śaṅkara quotes Chānd. Up. VI,8,7; Bṛh. Up. I,4, 10; III,4,1; 7,3 as examples of texts on the non-difference. In his Upad II,1,6 he says that first of all a teacher should teach his pupil the *Śrutis* which are concerned primarily with the oneness of *Ātman* with *Brahman*, and he quotes as examples Chānd. Up. III, 14,1; VI,2,1; VII,24,1; VII,25,2; Ait. Up. I,1,1.

12 V. Bhattacharya rejected the tradition that the GK interprets the Māṇḍ. Up. and asserted that the Māṇḍ. Up., being based upon the GK, came into existence after the GK. See V. Bhattacharya, "Māṇḍūkya Upaniṣad and the Gauḍapāda Kārikā," *Indian Historical Quarterly* I (1925), pp. 119 – 125; V. Bhattacharya, *The Āgamaśāstra of Gauḍapāda* (University of Calcutta, 1952), pp. 46 – 52; R. D. Karmarkar, *Gauḍapāda-Kārikā* (Government Oriental Series, Class B, no. 9, 1953), pp. xxxi – xxxiii; Nakamura III, pp. 557 – 565.

13 Especially Māṇḍ. Up. VII and XII. See Nakamura III, pp. 289–303 and 559–561.

14 Nakamura III, pp. 562–589.

15 *Ibid.*, p. 587.

16 Cf. Nilakanta Sastri, *A History of South India* (Madras: Oxford University Press, 1958), pp. 411–417.

17 S. Mayeda, "On the Author of the Māṇḍūkyopaniṣad- and the Gauḍapādīya-

Bhāṣya," *Professor V. Raghavan's Felicitation Volume, Adyar Library Bulletin*, vols. 31–32 (1967–68), pp. 73–94. For example, the term *dharma* in GK IV is no doubt used in a Buddhist sense, *i.e.*, "a thing" or "an object of knowledge" (cf. V. Bhattacharya, "The Gauḍapāda-Kārikā on the Māṇḍūkya Upaniṣad," *Proceedings of the Second All-India Oriental Conference*, 1920, p. 442, and Nakamura III, pp. 507–508); but Śaṅkara explains it as *Ātman* in GKBh IV, 1, p. 156; 10, p. 162; 46, p. 189; 53, p. 193; 81, p. 207; 91, p. 215; 92, p. 215; 96, p. 218; 99, p. 220. He sometimes does not interpret it (GKBh IV, 6; 8; 21; 33; 98). This fact probably does not indicate ignorance of the Buddhist usage of the term, but rather an intentional misinterpretation by Śaṅkara so as to give the text an Advaitic character.

[18] This is the reason why Śaṅkara has been censured as "crypto-Buddhist" (*pracchannabauddha*) by some of his opponents. But in fact he was a genuine Vedāntin who was faithful to the orthodox Brahmanical tradition and antagonistic to Buddhism, although the traditional claims that he persecuted the Buddhists and the Jains and destroyed their books (see J. N. Farquhar, *An Outline of the Religious Literature of India*, p. 175) are difficult to credit. His successful absorption of Buddhism into Vedānta represents a victory over Buddhism and not a surrender to it. Hinduism is all-inclusive. Among the six systems of Indian philosophy Vedānta has been most flexible and has always had extraordinary absorptive capacity. Without losing its own basis Vedānta has continued to be revitalized by incorporating foreign elements into its own system, whereas all other systems have either died out or barely survived.

[19] On Bhāskara's *bhedābhedavāda* and other related theories, see P. N. Srinivasachari, *The Philosophy of Bhedābheda* (Adyar: The Adyar Library, 1950); S. Dasgupta, vol. III (1961), pp. 1–11. According to Aufrecht's *Catalogus Catalogorum* (I, pp. 383–386), there are 49 different commentaries on the BS which were composed from various philosophic standpoints. After Bhāskara, Rāmānuja, identifying *Brahman* with Nārāyaṇa, attacked Śaṅkara's system and wrote a sectarian commentary from the philosophic standpoint styled *viśiṣṭādvaita* (Non-dualism of the qualified One). On the meaning of this compound, see J. A. B. van Buitenen, *Rāmānuja on the Bhagavadgītā* (Gravenhage: H. L. Smits, 1953, p. 1, n. 1). There are supposed to be five (or ten) famous schools of Vedānta (*pañcavedāntasaṃpradāya*) which hold characteristic and differing philosophic views concerning the relationship between *Brahman* and *Ātman*. They are: (1) Advaitavāda of Śaṅkara [non-sectarian]; (2) Viśiṣṭādvaitavāda of Rāmānuja (1017–1137) [Śrīvaiṣṇava Sect]; (3) Dvaitādvaitavāda of Nimbārka (1062–1162) [Nimbārka Sect]; (4) Dvaitavāda of Madhva (1230) [Mādhava Sect]; and (5) Śuddhādvaitavāda of Vallabha (sixteenth century) [Vallabhācārya Sect]. Cf. J. N. Farquhar, *An Outline of the Religious Literature of India*, p. 287; Nakamura II, p. 99; Roma Chaudhuri, *Doctrine of Srikantha* (Pracyavani Research Series no. XI, Calcutta, 1962), vol. I, p. 2.

[20] No use of the term *avidyā* occurs in the GK although Śaṅkara uses it in his commentary on the GK (see S. Mayeda, "On the Author of the Māṇḍūkyopaniṣad- and the Gauḍapādīya-Bhāṣya," pp. 73–94). Gauḍapāda's illusionism is based upon the concept of *māyā*, influenced by Mahāyāna Buddhism. It is not always easy to determine the meanings in which the term *māyā* is used in the GK. But it is certain that the term *māyā* there is far removed from that in works of later Advaitins, where it means the material cause of the universe indescribable as being or non-being (*sadasadbhyām anirvacanīya-*). As far as I can see, the meanings of *māyā* in the GK are: (1) the miraculous power of god or synonyms for him such as *ātman* (GK II,12; 19; III,10, 24 [twice]—one of which is Indra's *māyā* in the quotation from *Ṛgveda* VI,47,18 = Bṛh

Up. II,5,19—; 27; 28 [twice]), *citta* (GK IV,61 [twice]), and *manas* (GK III, 29 [twice]), and (2) (magical) illusion (GK 1,7; II,31; IV,58. *māyāmaya,* GK IV,59; 69; *māyāmātra,* GK I,17; *māyopama,* GK IV, 58; *māyāhastin,* GK IV, 44).

[21]In his *Brahmasiddhi,* Maṇḍanamiśra, Śaṅkara's senior contemporary, also advocated a non-dualism very similar to Śaṅkara's but with a slight difference. But Maṇḍanamiśra did not attain the prestige of Śaṅkara, and some of the Advaitins such as Sureśvara, Vimuktātman, Sarvajñātman, Prakāśātman, and Ānandānubhava took up an attitude of overt opposition to him. See S. Kuppuswami Sastri, *The Brahmasiddhi by Ācārya Maṇḍanamiśra with Commentary by Śaṅkhapāṇi, Edited with Introduction, Appendices and Indexes* (Madras Government Oriental Manuscripts Series no. 4. Madras, 1937), p. lix.

III. *ĀTMAN*'S IDENTITY WITH *BRAHMAN*

Śaṅkara holds that *Brahman* is *Ātman* and *Ātman* is *Brahman*, but this truth may be approached along different lines. When Śaṅkara undertakes his search for the truth—or, rather, when he explains to his pupils or readers the truth that he has already attained—he does it from two different starting points. Accordingly, in the *Upadeśasāhasrī*, two different approaches are recognizable. When in his search for the truth he sets out from *Brahman* as the ultimate cause of the universe, he comes, through a theological or cosmological approach, to the knowledge that *Brahman* is *Ātman*. When his investigation sets out from the inner *Ātman*, he arrives, through a psychological or epistemological approach, at the knowledge that *Ātman* is *Brahman*. The second line of approach is adopted much more frequently than the first in Śaṅkara's works, including the *Upadeśasāhasrī*. However, neither of them can be complete by itself, and there is a third aspect which is that the knowledge of *Brahman* and *Ātman* is attainable only through the *Śrutis*, and so the conclusion arrived at by the two approaches is to be confirmed and authenticated by the *Śrutis*. Through an exegesis of the *Śrutis*, Śaṅkara determines that the *Śrutis* state the truth of the identity of *Brahman* and *Ātman*. In the following pages I would like to examine his doctrine in greater detail through his discussions and speculations along the three different lines of approach.

A. Theological and Cosmological Approach

1. A Cosmological Proof of the Identity

The *Brahmasūtra* (I,1,2) defines *Brahman* as "that from which the origination, subsistence, and dissolution of this universe proceed." *Brahman* as the ultimate cause of the universe is regarded as different in essence from this material universe (BS II,1,4). It is Being (*sat*, BS II,3,9). Although the *Brahmasūtra* does not explicitly characterize *Brahman* as Knowledge (*jñāna*) or Pure Consciousness (*caitanya*, *cit*), the *Brahmasūtra* seems to assume it[1*] in its presentation (BS I,1,5; 1,9; 1,10; II,2,3; 2,9; III,2,16). Later Vedānta writers[2] describe the positive nature of *Brahman* as Being-Consciousness-Bliss (*sac-cid-ānanda*). Though this well-known expression is not found in the *Brahmasūtra*, the description of *Brahman* there may well point to it.[3] *Brahman* in the *Brahmasūtra* seems to be conceived as the personal Being rather than impersonal principle.[4] This is clear from the fact that the word "*paraḥ*" (the Highest One in the masculine form) is used for *Brahman* (neuter form).[5] The same thing is true of Śaṅkara's work, in which (*paraṃ*) *brahma* (*n*), and *paramātman* are interchangeable with *īśvara* (the Lord).[6]

According to the dualistic Sāṃkhya, *Puruṣa* (Spirit) and *Prakṛti* (Matter) are respectively the efficient cause and the material cause of the universe. Against this theory the *Brahmasūtra* maintains that *Brahman* is both the efficient and the material cause (BS I,4,23–27).[7] There is no other ultimate cause of the universe than *Brahman*. Thus the creation of the universe is nothing but self-creation (*ātmakṛti*, BS I,4,26). *Brahman* is the creator of all things and *Brahman* transforms itself into all things.[8] The *Brahmasūtra* calls this type of creation "transformation" (*pariṇāma*, BS I,4,26). Thus it is certain that the *Brahmasūtra* holds *satkāryavāda* as its theory of causation (BS II,1,7; II,1,16–20).

There are three representative types of cosmological theory in India. The first is the *pariṇāmavāda*, the theory of transformation; this is based upon the theory (*satkāryavāda*) that the effect, though different in appearance or phenomenally, is substantially identical with the cause, and pre-exists latently in it. The second is the *ārambhavāda*, the theory of atomic agglomeration, which is based on the theory (*asatkāryavāda*) that the effect, being something newly produced, does not pre-exist in the cause. The third is the *vivartavāda*, the theory of false appearance, which is closely connected with the first and peculiar to the Advaita Vedānta school. Although the *Brahmasūtra* sharply attacks the Sāṃkhya system, the

* Footnotes to section III, A begin on p. 58.

Vedānta of the *Brahmasūtra* is very similar in its fundamental cosmological theory to the Sāṃkhya, which also maintains *pariṇāmavāda* and *satkāryavāda*, and it is essentially different from the Nyāya-Vaiśeṣika which adopts *ārambhavāda* and *asatkāryavāda*.

By postulating *Brahman* as the only ultimate cause of the universe, the monism of Vedānta encountered theoretical difficulties which the Samkhyan dualism avoided by proposing two ultimate causes, Puruṣa and Prakṛti, and which are more or less inherent in any types of monism or monotheism:

1. If *Brahman* is one Being (*sat*) alone without any distinction, how is the manifoldness of the universe possible?[9]

2. If *Brahman* is Pure Consciousness (*cit*) and if *satkāryavāda* is to be assumed, how can it create this material world?[10]

3. If *Brahman* is Bliss (*ānanda*), why did it create this world full of sufferings? Is it not possessed of the faults of unfairness (*vaiṣamya*) and lack of compassion (*nairghṛṇya*)?[11]

The *Brahmasūtra* tried to solve these problems but could not do so satisfactorily[12]; its replies were too crude and naïve to silence the opponents. These problems remained to be solved by Śaṅkara and other later Vedānta philosophers.

In order to solve them, especially the first and second ones, Śaṅkara introduces into the Vedānta system a new principle called "Unevolved Name-and-Form" (*avyākṛte nāmarūpe*), for which he depends upon the *Chāndogya Upaniṣad*[13] and which is peculiar to Śaṅkara's cosmology. As P. Hacker first pointed out,[14] in the *Brahmasūtrabhāṣya* the term means a kind of primary material or state out of which the world evolves. In the *Upadeśasāhasrī* (II,1,18) also, when he says that the highest *Ātman* is "the evolver of that Unevolved Name-and-Form" which is the seed of the world (*jagadbījabhūta*), and which is different in essence from the highest *Ātman*, he certainly means by the term a kind of primary material of the world, which corresponds to *Prakṛti* in the Sāṃkhya doctrine. In the Sāṃkhya everything material, including the intellect (*buddhi*), I-consciousness (*ahaṃkāra*), mind (*manas*), and the senses, evolves from the *Prakṛti*. Similarly, for Śaṅkara everything material evolves from Unevolved Name-and-form, which according to the *Upadeśasāhasrī* (II,1,18–22) itself first evolved from *Brahman*. On the authority of the *Taittirīya Upaniṣad* (II,1,1), the *Brahmasūtra* (II,3,1–7) simply maintains that ether, the first of the five material elements, arose from *Brahman*. But Śaṅkara says:

> [Originally] unevolved, this Name-and-Form took the name-and-form of "ether" in the course of its evolution from this very *Ātman* (= *Brahman*). And in this manner this element named "ether" arose from the highest *Ātman* . . . (Upad II,1,19).

In the *Brahmasūtra* ether arises directly from *Brahman*. According to Śaṅkara, however, the Unevolved Name-and-Form first of all evolves from *Brahman* and then becomes something describable as "ether." Therefore, ether arises from *Brahman* only indirectly. From this name-and-form called ether there arose air; from air, fire; from fire, water; from water, earth, in that order. Further, ether entered into air, air into fire, fire into water, water into earth; so arose the five gross elements. From earth rice, barley, and other plants consisting of the five elements are produced. From them, when they have been eaten, blood and sperm are produced in the bodies of women and men respectively. Blood and sperm, produced by churning with the stick of sexual passion, driven by nescience and sanctified with sacred formulas, are poured into the womb at the proper time. By saturation with fluid from the womb, they become an embryo, which is delivered in the ninth or tenth month (Upad II,1,20). In this manner the body consists of nothing but name-and-form. The mind and sense organs also consist only of name-and-form (Upad II,1,22).

In this context Śaṅkara then asserts on the authority of the *Śrutis*[15] and the *Smṛtis*[16] that *Brahman*, after creating the body, entered the name-and-form of the body as *Ātman*. Therefore, *Brahman* is *Ātman*, which is different from the mind, the senses, the body, and the like, since they consist of name-and-form, although through nescience ordinary people identify *Ātman* with the body, the mind, or a combination of the two.

The above is an outline of Śaṅkara's cosmological view and his cosmological demonstration of *Brahman*'s identity with *Ātman*. The originality of his cosmology lies in introducing into his basically traditional view a new concept, Unevolved Name-and-Form. But to evaluate properly his position in the history of the Vedānta we must make a more detailed examination.

2. Characteristics of Śaṅkara's Cosmological View

In the *Brahmasūtra* (II,3,1–7) the material element ether is treated as a direct transformation of its sole cause *Brahman*, on the authority of the *Taittirīya Up.* (II,1,1). This theory, however, contradicts the Vedānta system itself, since the latter holds to *satkāryavāda*, which cannot admit that a material element, ether, can evolve directly from *Brahman*, which is Pure Consciousness.

According to Śaṅkara, originally Unevolved Name-and-Form evolves from *Brahman*, and in the course of its evolution becomes ether. Therefore, ether evolves indirectly from *Brahman*. Consequently his introduction of "Unevolved Name-and-Form" into the Vedānta system may be effective in explaining the manifoldness of the universe, the creation of this material world, and other theoretical difficulties which the monism of the *Brahmasūtra* had to face. However, in doing so, Śaṅkara comes near to a dualism like that of Sāṃkhya. The acceptance of a cause other than *Brahman* leads to the abandonment of monism, the basic standpoint of the Vedānta.

It is certain that Śaṅkara was well aware of this theoretical difficulty. In his conception, Unevolved Name-and-Form is the supersensible seed of the world (*jagadbījabhūta*), which is not describable as "this" or anything else (*tattvānyatvābhyām anirvacanīya-*)[17] and is known only to *Brahman* itself (*svayaṃvedya*, Upad II,1,18). But he is always careful never to define it as an independent material cause of the world. On the one hand he stresses its essential difference from *Brahman* (*svātmavilakṣaṇa*, Upad II,1,18). On the other hand he asserts that it evolves from *Brahman* (*te nāmarūpe . . . vyākriyamāṇe . . . ātmanaḥ*, Upad II,1,19). Thus he shows its difference from *Prakṛti* of Sāṃkhya. He also denies its independence of *Brahman*, by characterizing it as abiding in *Brahman* (*svātmastha*, Upad I,1,18).

In the *Upadeśasāhasrī* (II,1,19) he tries to explain the relationship between *Brahman* and Unevolved Name-and-Form. He compares their relationship with that between "clear water" and "dirty foam" which arises from clear water:

> [Originally] unevolved, this name-and-form took the name-and-form of ether in the course of its evolution from this very *Ātman*. And in this manner this element named "ether" arose

from the highest *Ātman*, as dirty foam from clear water. Neither is foam [identical with] water, nor absolutely different from water, since it is not seen without water. But water is clear and different from foam, which is of the nature of dirt. Likewise, the highest *Ātman* is different from name-and-form which corresponds to foam; *Ātman* is pure, clear, and different in essence from it. . . . (*te nāmarūpe 'vyākṛte satī vyākriyamāṇe tasmād etasmād ātmana ākāśanāmākṛtī saṃvṛtte / tac cākāśākhyaṃ bhūtam anena prakāreṇa paramātmanaḥ saṃbhūtaṃ, prasannāt salilān malam iva phenam / na salilaṃ na ca salilād atyantabhinnaṃ phenam / salilavyatirekeṇādarśanāt / salilaṃ tu svaccham anyat phenān malarūpāt / evaṃ paramātmā nāmarūpābhyām anyaḥ phenasthānīyābhyāṃ śuddhaḥ prasannas tadvilakṣaṇaḥ / . . .* Upad II,1,19).

This simile is a variation of the simile of the sea and its waves, foam, or other modifications. It is logically appropriate for the *bhedābhedavāda*, which asserts that the relationship between *Brahman* and *Ātman*, or *Brahman* and the phenomenal world, is both different and non-different, as the sea is different and non-different from the waves.

However, the parallel simile plays a different role in the passage quoted above. There it is stressed that foam, which is of the nature of dirt, is essentially different from clear water. Although foam is different in its nature, it is not regarded as absolutely different from water for the very weak reason that it is not seen without water; this aspect of their non-difference is only touched on. Such relationship of clear water and foam is not that of *bhedābheda*, since the *bhedābheda* relation presupposes an essential non-difference between two things.

It is more significant that Śaṅkara describes water as "clear" (*prasanna, svaccha*) and "pure" (*śuddha*), while he characterizes foam as "being of the nature of dirt" (*malarūpa*, Upad II,1,19). Hacker has commented: ". . . but here he is satisfied with a simile which indeed attributes lower value but not lower reality to the world than to *Brahman*."[18] If we set the above quotation (Upad II,1,19) apart from the whole context of the *Upadeśasāhasrī*, this comment is correct, but, looking at the whole work, I would think that the above simile also ascribes a lower reality to foam, because the term "dirt" used in contrast with "clear" and "pure" hints not only at a judgment of value but also at the important concept of *avidyā*. In the first chapter of the *Upadeśasāhasrī*, where our present cosmological discussion appears, Śaṅkara does not use similes suitable to his illusionism, such as a snake and a rope, or silver and mother-of-pearl. This is probably because the first chapter is meant for a novice at the first stage of the Vedāntic education who has just been initiated into Śaṅkara's Vedānta and is unfamiliar with the illusionistic way of thinking. In such a context it is possible to interpret "dirt" as standing for the term *avidyā*, which is first taken up for discussion in the second chapter of the *Upadeśasāhasrī*, intended for a pupil at the second stage of the Vedāntic education.

In the *Upadeśasāhasrī* the adjectives *nirmala* (clear) and *śuddha* (pure) are used only for the real *Ātman*. The word "dirt" is compared to something unreal, in contrast with something real. For example:

> As superimposition is [made] upon *Ātman*, so [its] negation is [made from *Ātman*], just as the superimposition of dirt upon the sky and negation of it therefrom are made by the foolish
> (*ātmanīha yathādhyāsaḥ pratiṣedhas tathaiva ca* /
> *malādhyāsaniṣedhau khe kriyete ca yathābuddhaiḥ* // Upad II,18,22).
> . . . A general rule cannot be made that superimposition is made only on that which is adventitiously established and not on that which is permanently established, for dirt and other things on the surface of the earth are seen to be superimposed upon the sky [which is permanently established]
> (. . . *na hi kādācitkasiddhāv evādhyāropaṇā na nityasiddhāv iti niyantuṃ śakyaṃ, ākāśe talamalādyadhyāropaṇadarśanāt*—Upad II,2, 61).

The analogy of dirty foam seems to be capable of expressing the same illusoriness as that of the unreal snake superimposed upon a rope (Upad II,2,109, etc.). Moreover, in the *Upadeśasāhasrī* this world, which originally evolved from the name-and-form and corresponds in the analogy to foam, is described as the "outcome of *avidyā*" (*avidyāprabhava*, Upad I,17,20) and "superimposition due to *avidyā*" (*avidyādhyāsa,* Upad I,6,3). This is also ascertained from the *Brahmasūtrabhāṣya*, where the name-and-form is described as "made of *avidyā*" (*avidyākṛta*), "falsely constructed by *avidyā*" (*avidyopasthāpita*), "falsely imagined through *avidyā*" (*avidyākalpita*), "superimposed through *avidyā*" (*avidyādhyasta, avidyādhyāropita*), and "consisting of *avidyā*" (*avidyātmaka*).[19]

In the Sāṃkhya system Prakṛti is a real, independent, and eternal cause of the universe together with Puruṣa. Śaṅkara has tried to save monism by characterizing name-and-form as unreal and as falsely constructed upon *Brahman* through *avidyā*. But, while doing so, he introduced another difficult problem, *avidyā*, for his followers. What is *avidyā*? This problem gave birth to very great controversy among the followers of Śaṅkara himself, just as later the problem of the relationship between *Brahman* and *Ātman* was to play a central role in the division of the whole Vedānta school.

It has been generally believed that Śaṅkara advocated *vivartavāda*, which is based upon *satkāraṇavāda*.[20] However, Nakamura[21] and Hacker[22] have pointed out that Śaṅkara either was not aware of an illusionistic usage of the word *vivarta* or else deliberately disregarded it, and that he did not advocate the so-called *vivartavāda*. In fact, his cosmological view as described here cannot be labelled *vivartavāda*. What is it then?

Śaṅkara's special expression, "Unevolved Name-and-Form," was not adopted even by the pupils he taught personally. One of the reasons for this may be that historically the phrase is remote from any connotation of illusion. Consequently some qualification like *avidyā* (or dirt) is needed in addition in order to associate the concept of illusion with this realistic phrase, and as a result the use of the phrase "name-and-form" must have introduced a double theoretical difficulty into Vedāntic monism. Padmapāda, one of Śaṅkara's personal pupils, used the term *avidyā* (or *māyā*) for the material cause of the world, probably because of his awareness of the difficulty. Padmapāda distinguished the usage of *vivarta* from that of *pariṇāma*, and his commentator Prakāśātman in the tenth century gave a definition to *vivarta*. Since then the cosmology of the Advaita Vedānta has moved from *pariṇāmavāda* to *vivartavāda*; according to this theory, the world is the *pariṇāma* of *avidyā* and the *vivarta* of Brahman.[23]

Hacker defines Śaṅkara's cosmological view as "a kind of illusionistic *pariṇāmavāda*."[24] It seems to me that it is in its essence different from the realistic *pariṇāmavāda* of the early Vedānta, because besides *Brahman* Śaṅkara postulates an illusory Unevolved Name-and-Form which corresponds to *avidyā* (or *māyā*). According to the early Vedāntic theory, the world is the *pariṇāma* of *Brahman*. According to Śaṅkara, the world is the evolution of Unevolved Name-and-Form. The relationship between *Brahman* and the world is comparable to that between pure water and foam whose nature is dirt. They are essentially different from each other; *Brahman*, the cause of the universe, is real, while the world, the effect, is unreal. Śaṅkara does not use a technical term with which to express his new cosmological view, but its contents are much closer to *vivartavāda* than to *pariṇāmavāda*. It might be styled as "early *vivartavāda*."

3. Śaṅkara's View of Gross Elements

When Advaita writers explain how the subtle elements are combined to produce gross elements, they resort to the theory of *trivṛtkaraṇa* "compounding each gross element from all three subtle elements"[25] or to that of *pañcīkaraṇa* "compounding each gross element from all five subtle elements."[26] Does Śaṅkara hold the former theory or the latter? This is another point to be examined in his cosmological view.

On the basis of *Chāndogya Up.* (VI,3,2; 3) the *Brahmasūtra* cites the theory of *trivṛtkaraṇa*, which assumes the existence of three elements, fire, water, and food, although the *Brahmasūtra* itself accepts five elements, namely earth, water, fire, air, and ether, in accordance with *Taittirīya Up.* (II,1). In this respect the *Brahmasūtra* is eclectic and theoretically inconsistent. Vācaspatimiśra (ninth century) and Amalānanda (thirteenth century) preferred *trivṛtkaraṇa* to *pañcīkaraṇa* since they did not accept that air and ether also have parts of other elements incorporated in them, and because there is no authority for *pañcīkaraṇa* in the Veda.[27] Later, Sadānanda[28] and Dharmarāja[29] established the theory of *pañcīkaraṇa* while disregarding that of *trivṛtkaraṇa*, although they were still relying upon the *Chāndogya Up.* (VI) for scriptural support.

In his *Brahmasūtrabhāṣya* Śaṅkara refers to the five gross elements and comments on *trivṛtkaraṇa*, which the *Brahmasūtra* mentions, but he does not refer to *pañcīkaraṇa*. In the *Upadeśasāhasrī* this term is not used, but the author seems to suggest *pañcīkaraṇa* when he says:

This name-and-form . . ., [originally unevolved], took the

name-and-form of "ether" in the course of its evolution. Becoming grosser in the course of evolution, the name-and-form from ether becomes air; from air, fire; from fire, water; from water, earth. In this order each preceding [element] has entered each succeeding one and the five gross elements, [ether, air, fire, water, and] earth, have come into existence. Consequently earth is characterized by the qualities of the five gross elements . . . (*te nāmarūpe 'vyākṛte satī vyākriyamāṇe phenasthānīye ākāśanāmākṛtī saṃvṛtte // 19 // tato 'pi sthūlabhāvam āpadyamāne nāmarūpe vyākriyamāṇe vāyubhāvam āpadyete, tato 'py agnibhāvam, agner abbhāvam, tataḥ pṛthvībhāvam ity evaṃkrameṇa pūrvapūrvo[ttaro] ttarānupraveśena pañcamahābhūtāni pṛthivyantāny utpannāni / tataḥ pañcamahābhūtaguṇaviśiṣṭā pṛth[i]vī*—Upad II,1,19–20).

This passage may not be strong enough evidence to lead us to the conclusion that Śaṅkara supported the so-called *pañcīkaraṇa*, but at least it enables us to suppose that he held a very similar idea. Moreover, of his works which can be regarded as authentic only the *Brahmasūtrabhāṣya* (II,4,20–2) and the *Chāndogyopaniṣadbhāṣya* (VI, 3,2–4) that refer to *trivṛtkaraṇa*. This reminds us that the term *ānanda* is referred to only when the text to be interpreted forces him to mention it.[30] We may infer, after our examination above, that he held a kind of *pañcīkaraṇa*, accepting the five gross elements, and therefore disregarded *trivṛtkaraṇa*. In this sense it may be said that Śaṅkara paved the way for the later establishment of the theory of *pañcīkaraṇa*.[31]

In any case, it should be emphasized that Śaṅkara did not intend to establish any system of cosmology of his own, but only to make use of cosmological discussion for the purpose of leading his pupils to final release. What he really wants to say is simply that from a cosmological point of view *Brahman* is identical with *Ātman*.

B. Psychological and Epistemological Approach

If *Ātman* is identical with *Brahman, Ātman* must be Pure Consciousness (*caitanya*)—eternal, changeless, ever-free, and fearless exactly in the same manner as *Brahman* is. However, what ordinary people conceive to be *Ātman* is far removed from *Brahman*, the Absolute. How and why can *Ātman* be *Brahman*? In order to answer this question it is necessary to investigate the nature of *Ātman* which is called "inner Self" (*pratyagātman*) and to approach it through an analysis of psychological and epistemological facts which are generally regarded as associated with, or based upon, *Ātman* or as its attributes.

1. Structure of the Individual

The Vedāntic view of the structure of the individual, which is akin to the Sāṃkhya-Yoga view, has its origin in the Upaniṣads and has already been established in the *Brahmasūtra*. In the *Upadeśasāhasrī* and his other works Śaṅkara tries neither to improve upon it nor to create a new theory; he seems to adopt the then generally accepted opinion.

According to Buddhism, which maintains non-existence of any permanent *Ātman*, the individual consists of five aggregates (*skandha*): matter (*rūpa*), perception (*vedanā*), mental conceptions and ideas (*saṃjñā*), volition (*saṃskāra*), and consciousness (*vijñāna*); the first one is the body of the individual and the other four constitute the mind. There is therefore no room for *Ātman* in the Buddhist system. In the Vedānta and in the other philosophical systems of India, on the other hand, it is the essence of the individual. In addition to *Ātman*, Śaṅkara recognizes five more components of the individual, which constitute the limiting adjunct (*upādhi*) of *Ātman*[1]*: the body, gross (*sthūla*) and subtle (*sūkṣma*); the principal vital air (*mukhyaprāṇa*); the five organs of action (*karmendriya*); the five senses (*buddhīndriya*); and the internal organ (*antaḥkaraṇa*).

The gross body is the perceptible body which perishes at the time of death and consists of the five elements (Upad I,16,1–2). Śaṅkara refers to the subtle body (*liṅga*, Upad I,11,14; 15,10) without any explanation, but the *Brahmasūtra* discusses it in detail.[2] In the *Brahmasūtrabhāṣya* Śaṅkara describes it as "the subtle parts of the elements, which subtle parts constitute the seed of the [gross] body."[3] The gross body is dissolved at death, but this sublte body is assumed to accompany *Ātman* when it transmigrates. According to the *Brahmasūtra* (IV,2,11; BSBh IV,2,11), bodily warmth belongs to the subtle body since it is not felt in the body after death,

*Footnotes to section III, B begin on p. 60.

whereas form and other bodily qualities continue to be perceived. The subtle body persists as long as one does not attain final release; it does not originally belong to *Ātman* (Upad I,15,10).

Nothing about the principal vital air is known from the *Upadeśasāhasrī*, though the *Brahmasūtra* refers to it.[4] According to the *Brahmasūtra* (II,4,12) and Śaṅkara's commentary on it, it has five functions (*pañcavṛtti*): expiration (*prāṇa*); inspiration (*apāna*); *vyāna* (a sort of combination of both; that which supports life when the breath is held with a great effort); *udāna* (the faculty which at death brings about the passing of the *Ātman* from the body); and *samāna* (the principle of digestion).[5]

The rest of the components are jointly termed in the *Brahmasūtra* (II,4,1) *prāṇa* (life organ), which is synonymous with *indriya* (BS II,4,17). The principal vital air, which is concerned with unconscious life, is by nature different (*vailakṣaṇya*, BS II,4,19) from *prāṇa*, the organs (BS II,4,11; 17) which are related to conscious life.[6] Among these life organs, the five organs of action which are concerned with activity (*karman*) are speech, hand, feet, generation, and evacuation (Upad I, 16,3).

The senses have perception (*buddhi*) of their objects as their purpose (Upad I,16,3).[7] They are the cause of perception of their objects (BSBh II,4,19, p. 587).[8] There are five senses: auditory (*śrotra*), cutaneous (*tvac*), visual (*cakṣus*), gustatory (*rasana*), and olfactory (*ghrāṇa*), since there are five different perceptions (*buddhibheda*), having as their respective objects sound (*śabda*), touch (*sparśa*), form-color (*rūpa*), taste (*rasa*), and smell (*gandha*) (BSBh II,4,6, p. 572. Cf. Upad I,3,113–116).[9] According to Śaṅkara's cosmology, the auditory and other senses as well as the body and things external are evolutes of the five elements (ether, air, fire, water, and earth). The five elements are in turn evolutes of the Unevolved Name-and-Form. Sound and other objects of the senses are qualities (*guṇa*) of ether and other elements respectively. As in the Nyāya system,[10] each sense is thought to have as its object something of its own kind (Upad II,16,2); for example, the auditory sense has sound, a quality of ether, as its object. Like external objects, however, the senses are material and have no consciousness at all.

Vidyāraṇya, the author of the *Vivaraṇaprameyasaṃgraha*, rejects various views of the senses which were held by the Buddhists, the Mīmāṃsakas, and others, and he defines the senses as the instruments (*karaṇa*) of perception, their existence being no more than inferred. According to him, the senses are neither sense-orifices (*golaka*), nor a peculiar capacity (*śakti*) of the organ, nor a different substance (*dravya*) having its locus in the visible sense-organ.[11] Such discussions concerning the nature of the senses are apparently absent from Śaṅkara's works. It is likely that he made no attempt to investigate the nature of the senses, simply accepting what was commonly or traditionally known about them in his time. He strongly emphasized that they were different from *Ātman*.

Śaṅkara's concept of the internal organ is not so clear. In his *Brahmasūtrabhāṣya* he says that "the internal organ which constitutes the limiting adjunct (*upādhi*) of *Ātman* is called in different places by different names, such as *manas, buddhi, vijñāna*, and *citta*."[12] With regard to the *manas* (mind) he also makes the following comments: ". . . finally there is the *manas* which has all things for its objects and extends to the past, the present and the future; it is one only but has various modifications (*anekavṛttika*)." We find it designated by different terms in different places, as *manas* or *buddhi* or *ahaṃkāra* or *citta*, according to the differences of its modifications (*vṛttibheda*). And the *Śruti* also, after having enumerated its various modifications (*vṛtti*), such as desire, says at the end: "All this is *manas* only" (Bṛh. Up. I,5,3).[13] On the basis of the above passages Deussen considers that for Śaṅkara the two expressions *antaḥkaraṇa* and *manas* are completely interchangeable.[14] In fact Śaṅkara sometimes interprets the word "*manas*" as *antaḥkaraṇa* (GBh V,19, p. 267; PBh I,2, p. 13; I,6, p. 24, etc.).

Deussen further remarks that for Śaṅkara there is only one *antaḥkaraṇa*, the *manas*; even the *buddhi* is for him not a distinct faculty. But Śaṅkara uses the expression "twofold *antaḥkaraṇa*" (*antaḥkaraṇadvaya*, Upad I,3,116), so it is possible for us to infer that Śaṅkara may recognize the existence of two *antaḥkaraṇas*, though it is not clear what they would be. When Śaṅkara comments on the word *manas* in the *Kena Up*. (I,2 and 6), he interprets it as *antaḥkaraṇa* and says that the word *manas* in this case comprises both the *manas* and the *buddhi*. If so, the "twofold *antaḥkaraṇa*" might indicate the *buddhi* and the *manas*. Moreover, Śaṅkara describes *Ātman* as "Witness of all the *antaḥkaraṇas*" (*kṛtsnāntaḥkaraṇekṣaṇa*, Upad I,18,176). This expression might suggest that each of the modifications of the *antaḥkaraṇa* such as *manas*, *buddhi, vijñāna*, and *citta* is called *antaḥkaraṇa*: these *antaḥkaraṇas* may be represented by the two words *buddhi* and *manas*. Śaṅkara points out a self-contradiction in the Sāṃkhya system, saying that it describes the *antaḥkaraṇa* as three in one place and as one in another place (BSBh II,2,10, p. 425), but Śaṅkara himself does not make his own position clear with regard to whether the *antaḥkaraṇa* is one or more.

In most of the cases in Śaṅkara's works the *manas* is merely another name of the *buddhi*, or at least it is indistinguishable from the latter. He also indiscriminately uses the terms *citta* and *dhī* as synonyms of the *manas* and the *buddhi* without specification.[15] When for some unknown reason Śaṅkara seeks to distinguish the *buddhi* from the *manas*, he, like the Sāṃkhya, attributes the function of *niścaya* (BSBh II,3,32, p. 541; Upad I,16,4; GBh III,42, p. 180) or *adhyavasāya* (Upad I,16,21) to the *buddhi*, and that of *vikalpa* (Upad I,16,3) or *saṃkalpa* (Upad I,16,21) or *saṃkalpavikalpa* (GBh III, 42, p. 179; X,22, p. 456) or *vivekabuddhi* (GBh V,13, p. 257) or *saṃśaya* (BSBh II,3,32, p. 541) of the five senses and five organs of action to the *manas*. Relying probably upon the *Kaṭha Up.* (III,10) and the *Bhagavadgītā* (III, 42), he says that the *buddhi* is superior to the *manas* since the *buddhi* conveys the objects of experience to *Ātman* (BSBh I,4,1, p. 294).[16] In these instances the *manas* and the *buddhi* are distinct from each other as in the Sāṃkhya system.

According to Dharmarājādhvarīndra, the *antaḥkaraṇa* is one and has four different modifications (*vṛtti*), namely *manas, buddhi, ahaṃkāra*, and *citta*, the respective objects of which are *saṃśaya, niścaya, garva*, and *smaraṇa* (VP.I,58).[17] Śaṅkara's concept of *antaḥkaraṇa* is still unorganized and ambiguous, but it points to the systematized Vedāntic concept of *antaḥkaraṇa*.

It is a controversial problem for later Advaita philosophers whether or not the *manas* is an *indriya* (sense).[18] The Nyāya-Vaiśeṣika, the Mīmāṃsā, and the Sāṃkhya commonly assert that the *manas* is an *indriya*. In the *Brahmasūtrabhāṣya* (II,4,6, p. 572) the *manas* is one of the life organs (*prāṇa*),[19] but nowhere in Śaṅkara's writings does he explicitly affirm or deny that it is an *indriya*. However, he briefly refers to this problem as follows:

nanu manaso 'py evaṃ sati varjanam indriyatvena prāṇavat syāt, "manaḥ sarvendriyāṇi ca" (Muṇḍ. Up. II,1,3) *iti pṛthagvyapadeśadarśanāt/ satyam etat/ smṛtau tv ekādaśendriyāṇīti mano 'pīndriyatvena śrotrādi-*

vat saṃgṛhyate| prāṇasya tv indriyatvaṃ na śrutau smṛtau vā prasiddham asti. ([Objection] If it is so, the *manas* also would have to be excluded from the class of *indriya*, like the [*mukhya*] *prāṇa*, because it is found [in *Śrutis*] that in the passage "The *manas* and all the *indriyas*" (Muṇḍ. Up. II,1,3) [the *manas* and the *indriyas*] are being mentioned separately. [Answer] True, but in *Smṛtis* eleven *indriyas* are mentioned; so the *manas* also, like the auditory sense and so forth, is comprised in the class of *indriyas*. It is, however, established, neither in the *Śrutis* nor in the *Smṛtis* that the [*mukhya*] *prāṇa* is an *indriya*.—(BSBh II,4,17, p. 586)

When Vācaspatimiśra comments on this particular passage in his *Bhāmatī*, he tries to interpret Śaṅkara's argument as favorable to the view that the *manas* is an *indriya*. If Vācaspatimiśra is right, it would follow that Śaṅkara accepts the view of the *Smṛtis*, rejecting that of the *Śrutis*. This is contrary to the attitude of Śaṅkara and other Vedāntins towards the *Śrutis* and the *Smṛtis*. Though Dharmarājādhvarīndra does not refer to this passage of the *Brahmasūtrabhāṣya*, he contradicts the view of those who assert on the basis of the *Smṛtis* that the *manas* is an *indriya* (VP I,12).

As D.M. Datta remarks, Śaṅkara may "simply notice the difference of opinion, without trying either to reconcile the two opinions or reject one in favor of the other."[20] Śaṅkara's purpose in introducing the two views is not to point out that they are different, but rather to show that the *mukhyaprāṇa* is regarded as an *indriya* neither in the *Śrutis* nor in the *Smṛtis* whereas the *manas* is considered to be an *indriya* in the *Smṛtis*, though not so in the *Śrutis*. From this fact he concludes that the eleven *prāṇas* including the *manas* are different in essence from the *mukhyaprāṇa*. It is, therefore, not possible from the quoted passage to draw any conclusion concerning Śaṅkara's opinion on the problem in question.

However, in his argument mentioned above Śaṅkara does not deny but rather admits the validity of that evidence from which the opponent has come to the conclusion that the *manas* should be excluded from the class of *indriyas*; the evidence is the fact that the *manas* is mentioned separately from the *indriyas* in the passage "the *manas* and all the *indriyas*" (*manaḥ sarvendriyāṇi ca,* Muṇḍ. Up. II, 1,3). If so, he may intentionally or unintentionally be differentiating the *manas* from the *indriyas* conceptually, when he uses the expression "the *manas* and the *indriyas*" (*manaś cendriyāṇi ca*, Upad I, 1, 22). But the expression is being used to maintain that both the *manas* and the *indriyas* consist of name-and-form (*nāmarūpātmaka*, Upad I,1,22) and that they are, therefore, by nature different from *Ātman*. It is not important at all to Śaṅkara whether or not the *manas* is an *indriya*: what he wishes to emphasize is that neither the *manas* nor the *indriyas* are *Ātman*.

Since Name-and-Form as the primary material of the universe in Śaṅkara's doctrine corresponds to *prakṛti* in the Sāṃkhya,[21] his concept of the *manas* seems to be close to that of the Sāṃkhya and far removed from that of the Nyāya-Vaiśeṣika, according to which the *manas* is an eternal substance (*dravya*) distinct from the physical substances such as earth and water.[22] Śaṅkara is in agreement with the Sāṃkhya in regarding the *manas* as material and unconscious. In contrast with the Nyāya-Vaiśeṣika, he denies that the *prāṇas* including the *manas* are of atomic size (*paramāṇutulyatva*) and maintains that they are subtle and limited in size (*saukṣmyaparicchedа*) (BSBh II,4,7, p. 574).

The *Brahmasūtra* (II,3,32) attempts to prove the existence of the *antaḥkaraṇa* on the ground of an argument similar to that of the Vaiśeṣika.[23] Commenting on the *sūtra*, Śaṅkara says that if the existence of the *antaḥkaraṇa* were not accepted, either perpetual perception would result, whenever the three means (*sādhana*) of perception—*Ātman*, the senses, and their objects—were in proximity; or else, if perception were not to follow on the conjunction of the three causes, there would be no perception at all. The existence of some *manas*, therefore, has to be accepted, by attention or non-attention of which, perception and non-perception take place. He quotes a passage from *Bṛhadāraṇyaka Up.* (I,5,3) as scriptural evidence.[24]

Śaṅkara's concepts of the senses and the *antaḥkaraṇa* have so far been dealt with. *Ātman* not only occupies the most important position among the means of perception (*upalabdhisādhana*, BSBh II, 3,32, p. 541) but also constitutes the whole of Śaṅkara's doctrine. Here I will focus on its role in perception.

2. Psychology of External Perception

Although there is a divergence of opinion about the definition of perception among the different schools of Indian philosophy, it is generally defined as knowledge produced by the contact of sense and object. But this definition is not acceptable to the Advaita nor to the Prabhākara Mīmāṃsā and the Jaina system.[25] Śaṅkara does not make any attempt to define perception. According to Dharmarājādhvarīndra, the defining feature (*prayojaka*) of perception is not the sense-object contact but the identity (*abheda*) between the consciousness (*Ātman*) limited by an object like a jar (*viṣayacaitanya*) and the consciousness limited by the modification (*vṛtti*) of the *antaḥkaraṇa* (*pramāṇacaitanya*) (VP I,16). In the case of the perception of a jar, the *antaḥkaraṇa* goes out toward it through the visual sense and is transformed so as to assume the form of the jar. Such transformation (*pariṇāma*) is called "modification" (*vṛtti*) of the *antaḥkaraṇa*. The two limiting conditions of *Ātman*-consciousness, which are the jar and the modification, occupy the same locus, and thus do not show themselves as different. The identity of the two is the defining feature which distinguishes perception from inference, where the *antaḥkaraṇa* does not go out to the object (VP I,18–19).[26]

Like the Nyāya and other schools of Indian philosophy, Dharmarājādhvarīndra recognizes two classes of perception: one is *savikalpa* perception, which is the knowledge of a thing as qualified by an attribute (*vaiśiṣṭyāvagāhin*), and the other is *nirvikalpa* perception, which is the knowledge of a thing as unrelated to anything else (*saṃsargānavagāhin*) (VP I,59).[27] According to another classification which he makes, perception is again twofold: one is the perception due to *jīvasākṣin* which is the consciousness having the *antaḥkaraṇa* as its limiting adjunct (*antaḥkaraṇopahitaṃ caitanyam*), and the other is that due to *īśvarasākṣin* which is the consciousness having *māyā* as its limiting adjunct (*māyopahitaṃ caitanyam*) (VP I,66–73).[28] No such classifications appear in Śaṅkara's works.

Dharmarājādhvarīndra classifies perception in yet another way. Perception is twofold, namely the knowledge arising from the senses (*indriyajanya*) and that not so arising (*indriyājanya*), as for example the perception of pleasure, etc. (*sukhādipratyakṣa*) (VP I,120).[29] This classification corresponds to that of external (*bāhyapratyakṣa*) and internal perception (*mānasa-* or *āntarapratyakṣa*) in the Nyāya. Śaṅkara does not classify perception in any way, but he discusses problems of both external and internal perception.

How are external objects perceived? What is the mechanism of perception? According to Śaṅkara, external objects of perception such as sound and touch are material and unconscious; they do not have any knowledge of themselves nor of others (Upad I,14,41;

II,2,74; 3,113). The five senses are necessary for the perception of external objects. They serve the purpose of discerning the special object of each sense, such as smell (*gandhādiviṣayaviśeṣaparicchedārthatva*, BSBh II,3,18, p. 530). It is, however, not certain whether or not Śaṅkara, like Vidyāraṇya and other Advaitins,[30] holds that for perception to take place, the senses have to go out, reach their objects, and have contact with them. He merely says that the senses are directed toward external objects (*bahirmukha*, BUBh IV,3,6, p. 551).

The *antaḥkaraṇa* plays a vital role in external perception. Sound and other external objects, which are not self-established (*svataḥsiddhyasaṃbhava*), are established (*siddhi*) through the rise of *pratyayas* (notions) of the *buddhi* or *antaḥkaraṇa*, which take the form of external objects such as blue and yellow. These *pratyayas*, which in Śaṅkara's works[31] are sometimes preceded by the adjective *bauddha*, are nothing but modifications (*bheda*) of the *buddhi*, caused by the forms of external objects (*bāhyākāranimittatva*) and having mutually exclusive attributes (Upad II,2,74). Like later Advaitins Śaṅkara also uses the term *vṛtti* in the sense of modification of the *antaḥkaraṇa*,[32] a usage which is probably based upon that of *vṛtti* in *cittavṛtti* as in the *Yogasūtra*.[33] But Śaṅkara seems to prefer the term *pratyaya* to *vṛtti*.[34] In order to explain this mechanism of perception, Śaṅkara uses the similes of copper and its mold, light and its object. He says as follows:

> *mūṣāsiktaṃ yathā tāmraṃ tannibhaṃ jāyate tathā* /
> *rūpādīn vyāpnuvac cittaṃ tannibhaṃ dṛśyate dhruvam* //
> (Just as [molten] copper appears in the form of the mold into which it was poured, so it is certainly experienced that the *citta*, when pervading [the external objects] such as form-color, appears in their forms.—Upad I,14,3 [= *Pañcadaśī* IV,28])
> *vyañjako vā yathāloko vyaṅgyasyākārātām iyāt* /
> *sarvārthauyañjakatvād dhīr arthākārā pradṛśyate* //
> (Or, just as light, the illuminator, assumes the forms of what it illuminates, so the *dhī* is seen to have the forms of its objects, since it is the illuminator of all the objects.—Upad I,14,4 [= *Pañcadaśī* IV,29])

It has been maintained by N. K. Devaraja that the two elements in the Vedāntic theory of perception, "the going out of the *antaḥkaraṇa* to the object" and "the *antaḥkaraṇa* assuming the form of the object," are missing in Śaṅkara's discussion of perception as well as in Padmapāda's.[35] However, the two stanzas above show clearly that the second element is contained in Śaṅkara's view of perception. The idea may not be original to Śaṅkara. Already in Vyāsa's *Yogasūtrabhāṣya* (I,7) it is mentioned that the *citta* is colored by external things through the senses.[36] It is to be noted here that the two stanzas under discussion are quoted in Vidyāraṇya's *Pañcadaśī* (IV,28 and 29) as the authority for his own view of perception.

The stanzas also show that in Śaṅkara's view, the first element too is present to a considerable extent. Unlike Dharmarājādhvarīndra, Śaṅkara does not explicitly say that the *antaḥkaraṇa* goes out to the place of the object through the senses,[37] but he says that the *citta* or *antaḥkaraṇa* pervades (*vyāpnuvat*, Upad I,14,3; *saṃvyāpti*, Upad I,18,115) the external object such as form-color. It would be natural to take it that the *antaḥkaraṇa*, which is located internally and is not omnipresent, would have to go out in order to pervade its object which is external.

When the *antaḥkaraṇa* pervades its object, the object is called "the one which is seated in the *buddhi*" (*buddhyārūḍha*, Upad I,7,1; 18,94; II,2,70).[38] Śaṅkara explains this as follows:

ālokastho ghaṭo yadvad buddhyārūḍho bhavet tathā |
dhīvyāptiḥ syād ghaṭāroho dhiyo vyāptau kramo bhavet ||

(Just as a jar [when pervaded by light] becomes something situated in the light, so does it [when pervaded by the *buddhi*] become something seated in the *buddhi*. It is the *buddhi*'s pervasion [of the jar] that is the jar's being seated [in the *buddhi*]. In the pervasion by the *buddhi* there would be sequence [of stages].—Upad I,18,156, cf. Upad I,18,155 and 157)

It is thus necessary for perception of external objects that the *antaḥkaraṇa* assume the forms of those objects located in the *buddhi*. It is, however, not sufficient since the *antakḥaraṇa* and its *pratyayas* are both unconscious and material like the external objects and the senses. The *antaḥkaraṇa* and its *pratyaya* are merely objects perceptible (*grāhya*) by a perceiver (*grāhaka*) different from themselves (Upad II,2,74). This perceiver, according to Śaṅkara, is *Ātman*.[39] His discussion now tends to be metaphysical rather than psychological.

According to Śaṅkara, *Ātman* is transcendentally changeless (*kūṭastha*) and constant (*nitya*). Now if *Ātman*, as perceiver, were taken as perceiving the *pratyayas* having the forms of the external objects, *Ātman* itself could not be free from change and destruction (Upad II,2,74). In other words, if *Ātman*'s perceivership consisted in pervading the *buddhi* which is appearing in the forms of the external objects (Upad I,14,6), *Ātman*, like the *buddhi*, would also be subject to change, and the basis of Śaṅkara's doctrine would be destroyed. In order to get round this theoretical difficulty, which is a problem common to the Advaita and the Sāṃkhya[40] and the Yoga,[41] Śaṅkara introduces the concept of *ābhāsa*.[42] As I have pointed out elsewhere,[43] he uses this term to mean both "reflection" and "false appearance." When *ābhāsa* means simply reflection and no more, the terms *pratibimba* (Upad I,5,4), *praticchāyā* (BUBh IV,3,7, p. 561),[44] and *chāyā* (Upad I,12,6; 14,33) are its synonyms. When the reflection (*ābhāsa*) of self-effulgent *Ātman*-consciousness (*caitanyapratibimba*, Upad I,5,4) pervades the *buddhi*, which is by nature unconscious but endowed with action, the *buddhi* falsely appears (*ābhāsa*) as perceiver because of *Ātman*'s consciousness (*bodha*, Upad I,5,4) in it, together with the fact of its own action, just as torches and other things appear to be possessed of the power of burning on account of the fire in them (Upad I,18,71). After pervading, and taking the forms of, external objects, the *buddhi* becomes, as it were, an illuminator on account of the reflection of *Ātman* in it, and thus perceives external objects (Upad I,18,155 and 157). Just as the face is different from its reflection in the mirror, *Ātman* is different from its reflection in the *buddhi* (Upad I,18,32 and 33), and the reflection is by nature unreal (Upad I,18,40–46; 18,87). The appearance (*ābhāsa*) and disappearance (*abhāva*) in the *buddhi* is due to the Seeing (*dṛṣṭi* = *Ātman*, Upad I,18,84). *Ātman*'s perceivership means not that *Ātman* is the agent of an action of perceiving, but that the reflection of self-effulgent *Ātman* whose nature is perception is in the *pratyayas* of the *buddhi*. *Ātman* does not do anything but simply exist.[45]

There is no doubt that the exposition of *ābhāsavāda* in the *Pañcadaśī* is largely indebted to Śaṅkara's view. Vidyāraṇya himself clearly admits that the difference between the *Brahman*-consciousness and the fruit (*phala*)—*i.e.*, the reflection of consciousness (*cidābhāsa*)—is stated in Śaṅkara's *Upadeśasāhasrī*.[46] It is worthy of note that Vidyāraṇya, like Śaṅkara, regards the reflection as wholly unreal, whereas according to the *pratibimbavāda* of the Vivaraṇa,[47] it is real.

3. Semantic Analysis of Perception

There are various opinions among Indian philosophers about the essential nature of knowledge. According to the Nyāya-Vaiśeṣika, knowledge is a quality of *Ātman*-substance. The Buddhist and the Mīmāṃsā systems commonly characterize knowledge as an activity. Śaṅkara and other Advaitins, however, stand on the Upaniṣadic axiom that knowledge or perception is *Ātman* itself. But the word "perception" (*upalabdhi*)[48] is generally conceived to mean an "action" of perceiving which is indicated by the verbal root (*dhātu*) *upa-labh*[49]; action is nothing but change (Upad II,2,76).[50] It would thus be contradictory to assert that *Ātman* is transcendentally changeless and yet that perception is *Ātman*. Śaṅkara defends his position by maintaining that this ordinarily accepted sense is merely a figurative meaning (*upacāra*) of the word "perception." A verbal root can directly refer only to some *pratyaya* of the *buddhi*, which does have "action" as its nature. As mentioned before, it is when the reflection of *Ātman* is in it that the *buddhi* falsely appears as perceiver. In other words, the *buddhi* becomes consciousness-like (*cinnibha*) and is called *jña* (= *Ātman*), when the *Ātman*-consciousness (*caitanya*, *cit*) is superimposed upon it (Upad I, 18, 65; 68). When the reflection of *Ātman* is in the *buddhi* and the doership (*kartṛtva*) of the *buddhi* is superimposed upon *Ātman*,[51] *Ātman* falsely appears as the perceiver, and it is said that the *jña* knows (Upad I,18,65; cf. Upad I,18,70). Therefore, the entire process of perception, including all the perceiving activities of the *pratyaya* of the *buddhi*, such as pervading its objects and assuming their forms and colors, comes down to the fact that *Ātman*-perception, transcendentally changeless, falsely appears (*ābhāsa*) as perceiver (*ātmanaḥ upalabdhyābhāsaphalāvasānaḥ*, Upad II,2,77); however, this does not entail any change in *Ātman*-perception. At the end of the perceiving process taking place in the *buddhi*,[52] there is *Ātman*-perception falsely appearing as perceiver. In this sense the perceiver is nothing but constant perception (*nityopalabdhimātra*, Upad II,2,79). The word "perception" is, therefore, being used only figuratively when it has the sense of an "action" of perceiving. For example, the "action" of cutting (*chidikriyā*) results, at the end of the whole process of the cutting "action," in the static situation where the object that was to be cut has been separated into two parts (*dvaidhībhāva*); the word "cut" is figuratively used in the sense of the "action" of cutting which is signified by the verbal root, though primarily it means the static situation which has resulted from the "action" of cutting (Upad II,2,76–85).[53] It is, therefore, reasonable to assert that *Ātman* is perception.

One expresses one's experience of perception by means of language and says, *jānāmi* (I know) or *jānāti* (He knows).[54] According to the ordinarily accepted understanding of this sentence, "I" or "he," who is the subject of knowledge, "knows" some object of knowledge, just as, in case of the sentence *devadattaḥ karoti*, Devadatta, who is the agent of action, performs a certain action by himself. The verbal root denotes action while the verbal suffix indicates an agent. Thus the meanings of the verbal root (*prakṛti*) and the verbal suffix (*pratyaya*) are different from each other, but they have a common substratum (*āśraya*, Upad I,18, 51 and 52), namely Devadatta. Therefore, the two meanings belong to one and the same subject; Devadatta is the agent who actually performs an action. Likewise the verbal root *jñā* refers to the action of perceiving while the verbal suffix *-ti* or *-mi* indicates the agent.[55] Therefore, "I" or "he," like Devadatta, is the agent who actually perceives the object of perception. Ordinary people consider this "I" or "he" to be *Ātman* and think of themselves as different from *Brahman*, which is actionless (*akriya*) and constant (*nitya*).

Rejecting this ordinary understanding, Śaṅkara asserts that the verbal suffix indicates merely the reflection (*ābhāsa*) of *Ātman* which is in the *buddhi*, and that the verbal root means action (*kriyā*) of the *buddhi*. People say *jānāti* because they fail to distinguish *Ātman* from its reflection and the *buddhi* (Upad I,18,53). Perception (*avabodha*) does not belong to the *buddhi* and action does not belong to *Ātman*. For this reason the expression *jānāti* is applicable neither to the *buddhi* nor to *Ātman* (Upad I,18,54). Neither *Ātman* nor the *buddhi* can be the subject of the sentence *jānāti*, which requires the subject to be possessed of both perception and action.

Then what is the subject of this sentence? When consciousness (*caitanya*), the nature of *Ātman*, is superimposed upon the *buddhi* which is unconscious and of the nature of action, the *buddhi* becomes consciousness-like (*cinnibha*, Upad I,18,65; 68), assuming the form of *Ātman*. Then the notion (*dhī*) that "I am the Seeing (*Dṛśi* = *Ātman*)" occurs to the *buddhi* (Upad I,18,84; 89). This notion is called *ahaṃdhī* (Upad I,2,2) or *ahaṃpratyaya* (Upad II,2, 52; 2,53. etc.), *i.e.*, "I"-notion. It is also called *ahaṃkriyā* (Upad I,14,43), *ahaṃkāra* (Upad I,1,24; II,1,6, etc.), or simply *aham* as neuter (Upad I,5,5; 18,203). *Ātman* is said to be the object of this *ahaṃpratyaya* (*ahaṃpratyayaviṣaya*, Upad II,2,52; 2,53; BSBh II,3,38, p. 545; *asmatpratyayaviṣaya*, BSBh, Introduction, p. 17). The *buddhi* as the bearer of *ahaṃkāra* is called *ahaṃkartṛ* (Upad I,14,24; 18,20, etc.). This *ahaṃkartṛ* is the subject of the sentence *jānāmi* or *jānāti* (Upad I,18,65), since the meanings both of the verbal root and of the verbal suffix belong to it. Words are applicable to the *ahaṃkartṛ* but not to *Ātman*, since the former has generic attributes (*jāti*), action (*karman*), etc., which are absent in *Ātman*.

Thus, from a semantic and psychological analysis of perception, which seems to be unique among Advaitins, Śaṅkara rejects the ordinary concept of *Ātman* and, while doing so, refutes the act theory of knowledge according to which knowledge is a kind of activity or function (*kriyā*). It may not be out of place to note here that Jayanta finds the origin of act theory in a grammatical prejudice, a confusion between knowledge as manifestation and the verb "to know" as denoting an action.[56]

4. Psychology of Internal Perception

With regard to so-called internal perception, Śaṅkara refers to such mental or psychological events as the feelings of pleasure and pain (*sukhaduḥkhavedanā*), passion (*rāga*), aversion (*dveṣa*), desire (*kāma*, *icchā*), and fear (*bhaya*). All these mental events are perceived as objects of perception just as are jars and other external objects. They are, therefore, different from their perceiver, *Ātman* (Upad II,2,70). All these impurities (*aśuddhi*) are in the object of perception and never in *Ātman*, the subject of perception (Upad II,2, 36). They have the same substratum (*āśraya*) as the impressions (*saṃskāra*) of pain, of form-color, and so forth (Upad I,15,13; II,1,35). Their substratum is the *antaḥkaraṇa*. Even the discriminating notion (*vivekī pratyayaḥ*), "I am the knower, not the object of knowledge, pure, always free," also belongs to the *buddhi* (Upad I,12,14). Śaṅkara's view is based chiefly upon *Bṛhadāraṇ-*

yaka Up. I,5,3; "Desire, volition, doubt, faith, lack of faith, steadfastness, lack of steadfastness, shame, meditation, fear . . . all this is truly mind."[57] This *Śruti* passage also constitutes the basis of Dharmarājādhvarīndra's theory of *indriyājanya* perception (VP I,120).

Śaṅkara refutes the Nyāya-Vaiseṣika position that not only knowledge but also pleasure, pain, desire, aversion, and volition are qualities (*guṇa*) which inhere in *Ātman*-substance (Upad I,16, 51–66).[58] He says that if the position is accepted, then pleasure, for example, cannot be an object of knowledge, since knowledge and pleasure are qualities of one and the same *Ātman*-substance (Upad I,16,57). Furthermore, according to the Nyāya-Vaiśeṣika, pleasure, pain, etc., as particular facts are perceived when they come in contact with the *manas* through their inherence (*samavāya*) in *Ātman* which is conjoined (*saṃyukta*) with the *manas*. However, pleasure and knowledge cannot come in contact with the *manas* simultaneously. Therefore, pleasure cannot be an object of knowledge (Upad I,16,52 and 53) as they assert it is.

Śaṅkara maintains that pain is an object (*viṣaya*) of *buddhis*,[59] which are in turn objects of the inner *Ātman* (Upad I,18,201). He considers desire, aversion, and so on to be attributes (*dharma*) of the "*kṣetra*" (*i.e.*, the object of knowledge) and not those of *Ātman* (Upad II,1,36). His view is based upon *Bhagavadgītā* XIII, 6: "Desire, hatred, pleasure, pain, the aggregate, intelligence (*cetanā*), and steadfastness—this is *kṣetra* briefly described with its modifications."[60] In his commentary on this stanza Śaṅkara interprets "*kṣetra*" as the *antaḥkaraṇa*[61] which is an object of perception (*jñeya*). Dharmarājādhvarīndra also regards desire and the others as attributes of the *manas* (*manodharma*, VP I,7). Furthermore, Śaṅkara interprets the word *cetanā* in the above stanza as *antaḥkaraṇavṛtti* or "a modification of the *antaḥkaraṇa*" which manifests itself in the aggregate of the body and the senses, filled with the juice of the reflection of the *Ātman*-consciousness (*ātmacaitanyābhāsarasaviddha*, GBh XIII,6, p. 543): desire and so on are modifications (*vṛtti*) of the *manas* (BSBh II,4,6, p. 572). Dharmarājādhvarīndra says that desire (*kāma*) and other attributes of the *manas* are knowledge taking on the form of *vṛtti* (*vṛttirūpajñāna*, VP I,7).

According to Śaṅkara desire and other psychological events are perceived as objects just as a jar and other external objects are perceived as objects (Upad II,2,70). There is no essential difference between external and internal perception, since in the process of perception objects of external perception are transformed into *pratyayas* or *vṛttis* of the *buddhi* which are in the form of those external objects, and objects of internal perception are also transformed into *pratyayas* which are in the form of pleasure, pain, and other objects of internal perception:

yā tu syān mānasī vṛttiś cākṣuṣkā rūparañjanā /
nityam evātmano dṛṣṭyā nityayā dṛśyate hi sā //

(The modification of the *manas*, which is caused by the visual sense and is depicted by form-color [of its object], is certainly always seen by the constant Seeing of *Ātman.*—Upad I,13,6)

tathānyendriyayuktā yā vṛttayo viṣayāñjanāḥ /
smṛtī rāgādirūpā ca kevalāntar manasy api //

(In like manner the modifications [of the *manas*] which are connected with the senses other [than the visual one] and are depicted by [external] objects; also [the modification of the *manas*] in the form of memory and in the forms of passion and the like, which is unconnected [from the senses], located in the *manas.*—Upad I,13,7)

mānasyas tadvad anyasya dṛśyante svapnavṛttayaḥ /
draṣṭur dṛṣṭis tato nityā śuddhānantā ca kevalā //

(and the modifications of the *manas* in the dreaming state are also seen to be another's. The Seeing of the Seer is, therefore, constant, pure, infinite and alone.—Upad I,13,8)

The only difference in mechanism between external and internal perception lies in the fact that the modifications of the *manas* are connected with the senses in case of external perception and not in case of internal perception (Upad I,13,7). Though Śaṅkara does not try to analyze perception and though it is not clear whether or not he considers the *manas* to be an *indriya*, the above distinction easily leads one to Dharmarājādhvarīndra's division of perception into the two types, *indriyajanya* and *indriyājanya.* Pleasure and the like, which have the *buddhi* as their substratum, differentiate the *buddhi*, which, being illumined by the constant light of *Ātman*, appears as *Ātman* in the aggregate of the body and the senses (Upad I,16,7). Thus it is through immovable consciousness (Upad II,2,73) that one perceives everything, external and internal, seated in the *buddhi* (*buddhyārūḍha*, Upad II,2, 70).

Śaṅkara does not seek to go beyond this point with regard to perception. However, Dharmarājādhvarīndra finds here the defining feature of perception which is common to the *indriyajanya* and *indriyājanya* perception. In both cases the consciousness limited by the *vṛtti* of the *antaḥkaraṇa* (*pramāṇacaitanya*) is identical with that limited by the object (*viṣayacaitanya*) such as a jar in the *indriyajanya* and pleasure in the *indriyājanya* (VP I,21–22).

Dharmarājādhvarīndra seems primarily to aim at the completion of the Vedāntic theory of means of knowledge. On the other hand, Śaṅkara is primarily concerned not with the establishment of any epistemologically or philosophically perfect system but with the salvation of people suffering from transmigratory existence here in the present world. The only truth that Śaṅkara intends to arrive at from his analysis of perception is that of the identity of *Ātman* and *Brahman*.

In his book *A History of Indian Philosophy*, Dasgupta considers that Padmapāda, one of Śaṅkara's disciples, was probably the first to attempt to explain from a Vedāntic point of view the process of perception, which was elaborated by Prakāśātman (tenth century) and later writers, and that Padmapāda's views were all collected and systematized in the exposition of the *Vedāntaparibhāṣā* of Dharmarājādhvarīndra in the sixteenth century.[62] However, my investigation has shown that Śaṅkara's view of perception, which has so far been overlooked and seems to depend considerably upon the Sāṃkhya and the Yoga views,[63] already displays the essential characteristics of the later Advaita theory of perception.

5. Four States of Ātman

The previous sections have been concerned with our daily mental and psychological experiences in the waking state (*jāgrat*). But Indian thinkers were not contented with the investigation of the waking state. They also speculated on the dreaming state (*svapna*) and deep sleep (*suṣupta*) and discovered metaphysical significance in those states. Their speculation even extended to a fourth state (*caturtha*, *turya*, *turīya*) which transcends the above three.

Philosophic speculation on the four states started with Upaniṣadic thinkers,[64] and its most systematic exposition is seen in the *Māṇḍūkya Up.*, on which Śaṅkara wrote a commentary.[65] The *Brahmasūtra* also discusses the four states (BS III,2,1–9) as well as the state of swooning (*mugdha*, BS III,2,10),[66] which is not examined in the Upaniṣads. It is, however, to be noted here that the *Brahmasūtra*, which stands in the line of *bhedābheda*, neglects or perhaps may not know of this fourth, which could properly fit into a non-dualistic system alone.[67]

According to Śaṅkara, *Ātman* is the only one, eternal and changeless. Nevertheless, it appears in many ways because of the limiting adjunct (*upādhi*), just as one and the same gem appears different when blue or yellow color is put near it (Upad I,17,16; 17,26; 17,27). *Ātman* appears and is designated differently according to the three states. When *Ātman* is in the waking state and external (*bāhya*)—in other words, perceiving external objects—it is called *virāj* or *vaiśvānara* (Upad I,17,64, cf. *Vedāntasāra* [XVII] 36). In the waking state both the five senses (Upad I,17,24) and the internal organ are at work and, according to the *Māṇḍūkya Up.* and *Gauḍapādīyakārikā*, it is conscious of external objects (*bahiṣprajña*, Māṇḍ. Up. 3; GK I,1).

When *Ātman* is in the dreaming state, the five senses cease to function and only the internal organ is functioning. The *Ātman* in this state is called *taijasa* (Upad I,15,24, cf. *Vedāntasāra* [XVII] 117) or *prajāpati* (Upad I,17,64), and it is conscious of things internal (*antaḥprajña*, Māṇḍ. Up. 4; GK I,1). In other words, the object of perception in this state is not an external object but a residual impression (*vāsanā*) of something grasped through the senses in the waking state (Upad I,11,10; 15,24); this is like recollection of a memory in the waking state (Upad I,14,1; 17,24). Since in the dreaming state *Ātman* is free from limiting adjuncts such as the body and the senses, *Ātman* appears in a purer form and is seen to be self-effulgent (*svayaṃprabha*), just as a sword is seen to shine when drawn from its sheath (Upad I,11,11).

In the state of deep sleep everything vanishes (Upad I,17,64); even the internal organ ceases to function. The *Ātman* in this state is called *prājña* (Upad I,15,25; 17,64); it sees nothing else (*ananyadṛś*, Upad I,15,25). Deep sleep is usually regarded as the entire cessation of consciousness. The *Vaiśeṣika* thinks that consciousness is adventitious because *Ātman* does not have this quality in deep sleep.[68] In the Vedāntic theory, however, the *Ātman* in this state is a mass of mere consciousness (*prajñānaghana*, Muṇḍ. Up. 5; *ghana-prajña*, GK I,1). Nobody sees anything in the state of deep sleep, but this does not mean that in deep sleep Pure Consciousness ceases to be (Upad I,18,97). It is only because there is no object of sight that nothing is seen in the deep sleep, and not because sight—*i.e.*, Pure Consciousness—ceases to be. It is by Pure Consciousness that one denies the existence of the objects of sight (Upad II,2,90–93). This *Ātman* is free from the pain which is experienced in the waking and dreaming states (Upad II,2,45). It is in a purer form, but not yet perfect. Just as one goes from the waking state to the states of dream and deep sleep, one comes back from the state of the deep sleep to the dreaming and waking states. In this sense this state is, so to speak, the seed (*bīja*) of the two other states (Upad I,16,18). Therefore, the *Ātman* in this state is called *avyākṛta* (unmanifest, Upad I,17,64). The state of deep sleep is also called *tamas* (darkness) or *ajñāna* (ignorance). When this seed has been burnt up by the knowledge of *Ātman*, it is like a seed that has been scorched, without power of germinating (Upad I,17,25).

The above three states are only adventitious and not one's own nature, since they perish like clothes and wealth (cf. Upad II,2, 86–89). The triad is a verbal handle (*vācārambhaṇa*) and consequently unreal (Upad II,17,65). *Vaiśvānara*, *taijasa*, and *prājña* are all merely *Ātman* with limiting adjuncts (*sopādhi*, Upad I,15, 29). "The *Ātman* without limiting adjuncts (*anupādhika*) is indescribable, without parts, attributeless and pure; neither mind nor speech reach it" (Upad I,15,29). This *Ātman* is *turīya* (Upad I,10,4). This *Ātman* cannot be expressed by any words.

Since this *turīya* (Upad I,10,4) is nothing but *Brahman*, it is, though indescribable, indicated by means of all the possible negative adjectives which are used to describe *Brahman*: "non-dual" (*advaya*), "free from desire" (*akāma*), "unborn" (*aja*), "free from evils" (*apahatapāpman*), "fearless" (*abhaya*). Adjectives such as "absolutely changeless and constant" (*kūṭasthanitya*), which are affirmative in form but really negative in intention, are also employed to characterize it.

This *Ātman* is always the same in all beings (Upad I,8,3; 10,9); though perfectly stainless and non-dual, it is covered by inverted knowledge (*viparyaya*) which is *avidyā* (nescience, Upad I,10,8).

This last is the reason why the highest truth, that *Ātman* is *Brahman*, is not generally recognized.

C. Exegetical Approach

1. The Means of Knowledge

Early Vedānta philosophers did not pay much attention to problems concerning the means of knowledge (*pramāṇa*) by which valid knowledge (*pramā*) is attained, although to other schools of Indian philosophy these were important, even essential, topics. The Materialists (Cārvāka) accepted only sense-perception (*pratyakṣa*) as the means of knowledge, rejecting all others. Some Vaiśeṣikas and the Buddhists recognized both sense-perception and inference (*anumāna*), to which the Sāṃkhyas added a third means: statement by an authority (*āptavacana* or *śabda*). The Naiyāyikas accpeted comparison (*upamāna*) in addition as a fourth means.

In the *Brahmasūtra* (I,3,28; III,2,24; IV,4,20) "*pratyakṣa*" and "*anumāna*" are accepted as means of knowledge, but the words have a quite special meaning and merely stand for "*Śrutis*" and "*Smṛtis*," respectively.[1]* The *Brahmasūtra* does not discuss problems of *pramāṇa*. Early Advaita writers are interested only in demonstrating the illusory nature of the world and engaged in discussing the metaphysical aspect of knowledge (*jñāna*) which is the nature of *Brahman-Ātman*, and not in examining the means of knowledge. In the tenth century, Prakāśātman employs four means of knowledge in his philosophical discussion: sense-perception, inference, postulation (*arthāpatti*) and verbal testimony (*śabda*).[2] In the sixteenth century, Dharmarājādhvarīndra enumerates six means of knowledge, the above four and two additional ones, comparison and non-cognition (*anupalabdhi*) (VP, *Upodghāta* 10); he devotes the first six chapters of his *Vedāntaparibhāṣā* to the establishment of a Vedāntic theory.

Śaṅkara himself does recognize the significance of the means of knowledge, remarking that everything (*sarvapadārtha*) is established through verbal testimony (*śabda*), inference (*anumiti*), and other means of knowledge, and not otherwise (Upad I,18,

*Footnotes to section III, C begin on p. 65.

133). It is true that Śaṅkara's doctrine is on the whole illusionistic, but his arguments are strikingly realistic and not idealistic. He maintains that knowledge (*jñāna*) results from the means of knowledge (*pramāṇajanya*) which have existing things as their objects (*yathābhūtaviṣaya*) and that knowledge, therefore, depends upon existing things (*vastutantra*) and not upon Vedic injunction (*codanātantra*) nor upon man (*puruṣatantra*) (BSBh I,1,4, p. 83).[3] He rejects the Vijñānavādin's position that there is no difference whatever between knowledge and the object of knowledge, the latter being nothing but the former, since for Vijñānavāda no external objects exist.[4]

In his arguments he often takes it for granted that the means of knowledge are generally accepted.[5] There is no doubt that he was well acquainted with *nyāya* (logic). In his writings he refers to at least three means of knowledge: sense-perception, inference, and verbal testimony.[6] In no place in his works, however, does he give any systematic account of them, though he is aware of the relative importance of the various means of knowledge. His disregard or deliberate avoidance of the point is largely based upon his religio-philosophical standpoint. *Ātman-Brahman*, the knowledge of which is the means to final release (*mokṣa*), is self-evident (*svapramāṇaka*, Upad I,18,203) and self-established (*svataḥsiddha*, Upad II,2,93, etc.). Therefore, *Ātman-Brahman* is by nature independent of the means of knowledge; *Ātman-Brahman* is established neither by sense-perception nor by other means of knowledge (Upad II,2, 60). An investigation of the means of knowledge is of no use for attainment of final release.

Then how is the knowledge of *Ātman-Brahman* obtained? It is attained only through the *Śrutis* (Upad I,11,9; 18,217, etc.), which are not to be doubted (*anatiśaṅkyatva*, Upad I,17,67) and are the right means of acquiring knowledge (*pramāṇa*, Upad I,17,8. Cf. Upad I,18,216; BS I,1,7). Śaṅkara's firm conviction that the *Śruti* is infallible is seen here and there in his works. No argument or justification is necessary for the validity of the *Śruti*. This is not peculiar to Śaṅkara but is the basic standpoint of the Vedānta and the Mimāṃsā.[7] His absolute reliance on the *Śruti* leads to the denial of the validity of the other means of knowledge (Upad I,18, 7; 18,183; 18,223). Nevertheless, use is made of the other means in order to know *Ātman-Brahman* (Upad I,18,134) as well as the objects of knowledge (*prameya*) different from *Ātman* (Upad II,2,93). However, it is only before the attainment of the knowledge of *Ātman* that sense-perception and other means of knowledge are valid (Upad I,11,5). It is to be noted here that Dharmarājādhvarīndra, who systematized the Advaita theory of the means of knowledge, also carries on his discussion of the means of knowledge under the same condition. He says: " 'In your [= Advaitin's] view, a jar etc. are sublated since they are unreal. So how can knowledge of them be valid knowledge?' We [= Advaitins] reply, 'Because a jar, etc., are sublated after the realization of *Brahman*. . . . but they are not sublated in the state of transmigration.' "[8] An investigation of the means of knowledge is after all in the sphere of nescience (*avidyā*) for Śaṅkara.

Like the author of the *Brahmasūtra* Śaṅkara recognizes the authority of the *Smṛtis*. To support his argument he often quotes *Śruti* passages, especially Upaniṣadic passages, and then *Smṛti* passages which are not incompatible with the former (Upad II,1, 8).[9] However, Śaṅkara is endowed with too much creativity and reasoning power to remain a simple traditionalist. Furthermore, the time did not allow him to rest his case entirely on the *Śrutis* and *Smṛtis*. He has to defend his position, and to meet the opposition of those who do not accept the authority of these scriptures. Śaṅkara salutes his teacher's teacher, who defeated hundreds of enemies of the *Śrutis* by means of sword-like words supported by thunderbolt-like reasoning (*yukti*) and protected the treasure of the meaning of the *Vedas* (Upad I,18,2). He himself declares: "Thus both the false assumption based upon dualism and the view that *Ātman* does not exist have been rejected through reasoning (*yukti*)" (Upad I,16,68). As in Buddhism and other systems of Indian philosophy, so in Śaṅkara, not only scriptural testimony (*śruti*, *śāstra*) but also rational proof (*yukti*, Upad I,16,65; 18,43; 18,88; 19,25; *nyāya*, Upad II,1,44; *anumāna*, Upad I,12,18; 18,14) constitutes an essential part of the arguments.[10] It is also noteworthy that, to refute objections, Śaṅkara frequently resorts to arguments based on *prasaṅga* (*reductio ad absurdum*), in which he first admits an opponent's thesis for argument's sake, and then points out how, if it were accepted, a conclusion which is not desired by the opponent would be arrived at.[11] This type of argument was often employed by Nāgārjuna and his disciple, Āryadeva, of the Mādhyamika school of Buddhism. It is probable that they influenced the *Brahmasūtra*, which also utilizes this type of argument.[12]

However, no matter how reasonable an argument may be, it cannot be accepted by the Vedāntins if it is incompatible with the *Śrutis*. The Vedānta, which may be styled "a positive theology based upon scripture,"[13] began originally as an exegesis of the *Vedas*, especially the Vedānta, *i.e.*, the Upaniṣads, which resulted in the composition of the *Brahmasūtra*. The *Brahmasūtra* records differences in interpretation of many places of the *Śrutis* but unfortunately it does not discuss systematically any methodological problems concerning the exegesis of the *Vedas*. In his many commentaries Śaṅkara does not deal with these problems; he presents only the results of applying his exegetical and theological method.[14] But some of Śaṅkara's exegetical principles are recognized in the *Upadeśasāhasrī*.

2. The Sentence "Tat Tvam Asi"

An Indian syllogism begins with a proposition named *pratijñā* (thesis) which contains a minor (*pakṣa*) and a major term (*sādhya*) and which is restated in the fifth and last proposition, called *nigamana* (conclusion). The *pratijñā* shows what the subject of inference is and what is to be proved.[15] The author of the *Brahmasūtra*, Śaṅkara, Bhāskara, Rāmānuja, and other Vedānta exegetes also seem to have begun with their own philosophical or theological viewpoints, the validity of which was to be proved or justified by means of their skilful exegetical techniques.[16] This is clear from the fact that founders and important philosophers of minor schools of the Vedānta wrote commentaries on the *Brahmasūtra* from their own philosophical or theological standpoints in order to give authoritative standing to their doctrines or theological systems by demonstrating that these could successfully and consistently be used to interpret the *Brahmasūtra*.

Whatever standpoint an exegete may adopt, he has to work with the conviction that all the *Śrutis* and other works regarded as authoritative are coherent and consistent in every respect and do not contradict one another,[17] though this is absolutely impossible for modern philologists to admit. From his standpoint of non-dualism, Śaṅkara states his view of the *Vedas* as follows:

As [the *Vedas*] are devoted to one object [only], *i.e.*, the knowl-

> edge [of *Brahman*], [the wise] know that they [consist of] one sentence [only]. The oneness of *Ātman* [and *Brahman*] should indeed be known through the understanding of the meaning of [this one] sentence. (Upad I,17,9)

Thus the huge bulk of the *Vedas* is equated with a single sentence, "*tat tvam asi*" (Thou art That), which was uttered nine times by the Upaniṣadic philosopher Uddālaka Āruṇi to his son, Śvetaketu, in their famous dialogue in the *Chāndogya Up*. (VI,8–16). This sentence is looked upon as imparting the essence of the entire *Vedas*, namely the identity of *Brahman* and *Ātman*. Tremendous efforts to interpret the sentence were made by Śaṅkara and his followers. One other *Śruti* sentence—"*aham brahmāsmi*" (I am *Brahman*) (Bṛh. Up. I,4,10) also was assigned great importance. These celebrated sentences came to be designated *mahāvākya* (great sentences)[18] by later Advaitins such as Sadānanda.[19] In the *Upadeśasāhasrī* the term "*aham*" in the *aham brahmāsmi* sentence is explained alongside the interpretation of "*tat tvam asi*" (cf. Upad I,18,96; 18,101, etc.), but the meaning of the former sentence is not specifically analyzed, probably because an examination of "*aham*" is nothing but that of "*tvam*," and the two sentences are syntactically the same. Therefore, our attention will first be focused on the sentence "*tat tvam asi*."

3. An Exegetical Method: *Anvaya* and *Vyatireka*

An interpretation of an Upaniṣadic sentence involves a semantic analysis. How is the meaning of a sentence apprehended? When one hears the words of a sentence, one gets a unitary sense which is the meaning of the sentence. How is this possible? The Mīmāṃsakas proposed two different solutions to this problem. According to the *anvitābhidhāna* theory of the Prabhākara school of Mīmāṃsā, the meaning of a sentence can be known only through memory, since both the individual word-meanings and their syntactic mutual relationship, which constitute the meaning of a sentence, are conveyed by the words themselves which are remembered to possess certain meanings. This theory was severely criticized by the Bhāṭṭa school of Mīmāṃsā, who asserted the *abhihitānvaya* theory: that the meaning of a sentence can be understood indirectly through the recollection of the individual word-meanings since, although the words can convey their individual meanings, their mutual relationship cannot be conveyed by the words but by the word-meanings; the knowledge of the logical connection between the remembered individual word-meanings precedes that of the sentence-meaning.[20]

Śaṅkara does not positively take one side or the other,[21] but in the *Upadeśasāhasrī* he expresses his idea fragmentarily:

> There is no fixed rule in the *Veda* to the effect that in a sentence a [particular] word should be placed first and another [particular] word should be placed next. (Upad I,18,175)

And then he continues to assert in the same stanza:

> The syntactical relation of words (*padasāṃgatya*) is based upon [their] meanings.

He further says:

> The knowledge that one is ever-free arises from the sentence and not from anything else. The knowledge of the meaning of the sentence is also preceded by recollecting the meaning of the words. (Upad I,18,188)

His view is that nobody can know the sentence-meaning without recollecting the word-meanings (Upad I,18,178). These remarks are not sufficient for us to infer any definite conclusion, but it seems to me that he takes the *abhihitānvaya* theory as a basis, or at least that he holds a similar opinion. His followers are divided among themselves on this problem, but almost all important Advaita writers such as Vācaspatimiśra support the theory of the Bhāṭṭa school.[22]

If, in order to understand the sentence-meaning, the word-meanings have first to be recollected, the next problem is: How can word-meanings be recollected? In this connection Śaṅkara refers to the *anvayavyatireka* method.[23] His failure to give an explanation of this method, which he seems to assume is well known, prevents us from getting a clear understanding of it. He describes it as the logical means (*yukti,* Upad I,18,96) by which, when hearing the words in a sentence, one can recollect (*saṃsmṛti,* Upad I,18,176: *smaraṇa,* Upad I,18,178; *smaryate,* Upad I,18,189), discriminate (*viveka,* Upad I,18,180) or ascertain (*avadhāraṇa,* Upad I,18,96) their meanings.

In his *Naiṣkarmyasiddhi* (II,8,9; III,31, etc.), Sureśvara also applies the *anvayavyatireka* method to an interpretation of the sentence "*tat tvam asi.*" Though the method is not defined in his work, either, it is treated not only as an exegetical method but also as a term signifying logical thinking or logical method. It is used as a synonym for *nyāya* and *anumāna.*[24] However, Śaṅkara says that the *anvayavyatireka* method is mentioned only for the purpose of discriminating the meaning of the word "Thou" and for no other purpose (Upad I,18,180). Therefore, the usage of the method is limited and serves only an exegetical purpose, though it is used as a synonym of *yukti* in the *Upadeśasāhasrī* (I,18,96). Furthermore, it seems to be a meditational method rather than an exegetical method. An attempt will be made to reconstruct the method as far as possible.

In Śaṅkara's view, in the sentence "Thou art That," the meanings of the two words "That" (*tat*) and "art" (*asi*) are already known (Upad I,18,193). For him, the word "That" means *Brahman*, or Existent (*sat*, Upad I,18,169) or Painless One (*nirduḥkha*, Upad I,18,169).[25] The word "art" means that the words "That" and "Thou" have the same referent (*tulyanīḍatva*, Upad I,18,169; 18,194).[26] Therefore, the sentence "Thou art That" is taken to be an identity judgment and not a universal positive judgment. Śaṅkara compares it to the sentence, "The horse is black" (*nīlāśvavat*, Upad I,18,169) since, like "horse" and "black," "Thou" and "That" have the same referent. Although the meanings of these two words are known, the sentence-meaning is still not understood since help is needed for the recollection of the meaning of the word "Thou" (Upad I,18,179; 18,193). Here it is that the *anvayavyatireka* method is applied, to ascertain the meaning of the word "Thou" (Upad I,18,180). When the meaning of the word "Thou" has been discriminated clearly, the sentence-meaning "I am ever-free" becomes manifest (Upad I,18,179; 18,180; 18,181; cf. Naiṣ II,1).

Now in the sentence "Thou art That," through the word "art" indicating an identity judgment, the word "Thou" comes to be used in connection (*yoga*) with the word "That" which refers to the Painless One (*nirduḥkhavācin*, Upad I,18,169). Therefore, the word "Thou" must also refer to that Painless One (Upad I,18, 169; 194). The word "Thou" has various meanings. But, among them, "the inner *Ātman*" (*pratyagātman*) is the only meaning that is compatible with "the Painless One." And through the word "art" indicating an identity judgment, the word "That" comes to be used in connection with the word "Thou." Therefore, the word

"That" refers to the inner *Ātman* (Upad I,18,170; 18,194). This is the meaning which is present (*anvaya*) in, or compatible with, the two words. This is the *anvaya* method, that of positive formulation. On the other hand, the word "Thou" ordinarily means "a sufferer of pain" (*duḥkhin*, Upad I,18,181; *duḥkhitva*, Upad I,18,195). This is the meaning absent (*vyatireka*) in, or incompatible with, the word "That." Therefore, this meaning is excluded (*apoha*, Upad I,18,181) or removed (*vārayetām*, Upad I,18,195) from the word "Thou." Further, the word "That" may mean here "something other than the inner *Ātman*" (*apratyagātman*, Upad I,18,195),[27] but this meaning is absent (*vyatireka*) in, or incompatible with, the word "Thou." For this reason the meaning "something other than the inner *Ātman*" must be removed from the word "That" (Upad I,18,195). This is the *vyatireka* method, a negative formulation used to exclude all the incompatible meanings. In this sense the two words "Thou" and "That" are said to mutually convey the meaning of the sentence, "Not this. Not so" (Upad I,18,195). The above is a tentative outline of Śaṅkara's *anvayavyatireka* method.

4. Later Advaitins' Exegetical Method

In later Advaitins' works, Śaṅkara's *anvayavyatireka* method came to be replaced by another method, *jahadajahallakṣaṇā*. It is usual to distinguish three kinds of *lakṣaṇā*[28] (transfer or metaphor), according to how closely the primary meaning is retained in the actual meaning:

1. *Jahallakṣaṇā* (or *Jahatsvārthā lakṣaṇā*). For example, in the sentence *gaṅgāyāṃ ghoṣaḥ* (the village is on the Ganges), the primary meaning of the word *gaṅgā* (Ganges) is abandoned and the secondary meaning "the bank (*tīra*) of the river Ganges" is taken. In this case the primary meaning is rejected since it is contrary to fact that the village should be situated actually on the Ganges. A secondary meaning, connected with the primary meaning, is adopted to suit the context.

2. *Ajahallakṣaṇā* (or *Ajahatsvārthā lakṣaṇā*). In the sentence *kuntāḥ praviśanti* (the lances enter), the word "*kuntāḥ*" refers to the lances themselves and the men who carry them. In this example the secondary meaning includes the primary sense as well.

3. *Jahadajahallakṣaṇā*. This is a *lakṣaṇā* in which a word expres-

sive of the qualified abandons part of its meaning and denotes another part. In a sentence like "*so 'yaṃ devadattaḥ*" (This is that Devadatta) the word "that" (*sas*) refers to Devadatta as qualified by the past time and space whereas the word "this" (*ayam*) points at the same Devadatta as qualified by the present time and space.[29] Though this sentence is an identity judgment, it does not mean that the two incompatible qualifiers "this" and "that" are identical, nor does it signify that the person qualified by "this" is identical with the same person when qualified by "that." The sentence should be understood to mean the identity of the substantive Devadatta by abandoning the incompatible elements. In this case only a part or an aspect of the primary meaning is retained; the rest, which is incompatible, is abandoned.

Rejecting the first two *lakṣaṇās*,[30] the later Advaitins accept the third and apply it to the sentence "Thou art That" as an exegetical method. "That" is qualified by all-knowingness (*sarvajñatva*), and "Thou" is qualified by the inner organ (*antaḥkaraṇa*). But the sentence indicates the identity of "That" and "Thou" in their essence, excluding one mutually incompatible elements (VP IV, 26). "That" and "Thou" cannot be identical with each other in their meanings which are universal consciousness and an individual consciousness, respectively. The sentence means the identity of consciousness common to both only by abandoning the two incompatible qualifiers "universal" and "individual."[31]

5. Discontinuance of Śaṅkara's Method

As I have mentioned, Śaṅkara's *anvayavyatireka* method was inherited by his disciple Sureśvara. Though Sureśvara has tried to theoretically strengthen it, his use of the method does not seem to be very much different from that of his *guru*.[32] Śaṅkara compares "*tat tvam asi*" with "*nīlāśva-*" (The horse is black) (Upad I,18,169), while Sureśvara employs the sentence "*nīlotpala-*" (The lotus is blue) (Naiṣ III,2). Padmapāda,[33] another of Śaṅkara's disciples, compares the same sentence with "*so 'yam*"[34] (This is that) which becomes the stock-instance of *jahadajahallakṣaṇā*. Sarvajñātman (900 A.D.), who is traditionally regarded as a disciple of Sureśvara, refers in his *Saṃkṣepaśārīraka* (I,154–157) to the threefold transfer (*lākṣaṇikavṛtti*) and compares the sentence with "*so 'yaṃ pumān*" (This is that person) (Sś I,149;151).[35] These facts may allow us to suppose that Śaṅkara's method was already neglected at the time of his own pupils, or at any rate of Sureśvara's.[36]

Why was Śaṅkara's method dropped by later Advaitins? One reason is that the method contains a defect in logical exactitude, and the other is that his technical terms are loanwords from Grammarians or Naiyāyikas. The logical defect occurs where he compares the sentence "*tat tvam asi*" with "*nīlāśva-*." There are two theories, *saṃsarga* and *bheda*, concerning the problem of how a sentence can have a single meaning, when the words forming it have definite meanings of their own. According to the first, the meaning of a sentence is *saṃsarga* or the mutual association of the word-meanings. In an example like "*gauś śuklā*" (The cow is white), this sentence denotes the association of cowness and whiteness, and the words constitute a syntactic unity. In the theory of *bheda,* on the other hand, which is mutual exclusion by the word-meanings, the word "white" excludes all colors other than "white" and the word "cow" excludes all white things other than cows. Since Kumārila refers to the latter theory,[37] Śaṅkara might be expected to have known it. But his comparison of "*tat tvam asi*" with "*nīlāśva-*" does not deal with this problem, as it is only concerned with showing the identity of the referent. When Sureśvara, however, compares the sentence with "*nīlotpala-*", he definitely has the above discussion in mind and rejects an opponent's assertion that the meaning of the sentence is the mutual association of the two word-meanings as in the case of "*nīlotpala-*" (Naiṣ III,76). Furthermore, he seems to take the second view.[38] Through the statement "*nīlotpala-*," non-blueness and non-lotushood are immediately ruled out. Likewise, through the sentence "*tat tvam asi*," non-Brahmanhood and otherness are excluded from the individual *Ātman* and *Brahman* respectively. But "*nīlotpala-*" is not in essence comparable to the sentence "*tat tvam asi*" since "*tat*" and "*tvam*" are incompatible in parts of their meanings whereas "*nīla*" and "*utpala*" are not incompatible in their meanings.[39] This is true of the example "*nīlāśva-*." Sentences such as "*nīlotpala-*" and "*nīlāśva-*" are suitable for the theories of *bheda* and *saṃsarga*, but not for an Advaitic interpretation of "*tat tvam asi*." This may be at least one of the reasons why Padmapāda uses the example "*so 'yam*" instead of "*nīlāśva-*," abandoning the example used by his *guru* and fellow disciple. The sentence "*so 'yam*" shows that the subject and its predicate have the same substratum and at the same time indicates that they are mutually incompatible in some aspect of their meanings. It has opened the way for the later stock-instance "*so 'yaṃ devadattaḥ.*" This is one reason why the method of *anvayavyatireka* used in conjunction with the "*nīlāśva*" example may have come to be dropped.

The terms *anvaya* and *vyatireka* are used by the Naiyāyikas and the Grammarians, but in a different way from the way they are used by Śaṅkara and Sureśvara. The Naiyāyikas use the *anvayavyatireka* for establishing an invariable concomitance (*vyāpti*) between *hetu* and *sādhya.* The Grammarians use it "to demonstrate that certain meanings are justifiably attributed to certain linguistic items." Śaṅkara's usage, which is concerned with the problem of word-meanings, is closer to that of the Grammarians than to that of the Naiyāyikas, but it is not identical to it.[40] His *anvayavyatireka* method is not used for the sake of determining "the constant co-occurrence (*sāhacarya*) of a linguistic item (*śabda*) and a meaning (*artha*),"[41] but only for the purpose of discriminating the meanings of words in the sentence "*tat tvam asi,*" especially "*tvam*" (Upad I, 18,178; 180). When we examine it more closely, we find that the *anvayavyatireka* method is a means of realizing the true *Ātman,* excluding non-*Ātman* and, in essence, a kind of meditation and on the same line with *parisaṃkhyāna* meditation (Upad II,3), which Śaṅkara urges. He uses a well-known term *nāmarūpa* in a peculiar sense of his own, *i.e.*, to mean the material cause of the world, but his usage was disregarded even by his disciples. It seems to me that his *anvayavyatireka* method shared the fate of *nāmarūpa.*

Śaṅkara's *anvayavyatireka* method has thus been supplanted by *jahadajahallakṣaṇā.* Although his method was not yet well systematized, it was the first attempt at a methodological approach to the *mahāvākya* sentence. He was the first to give an exegetical and logical foundation for the non-dualistic interpretation of that sentence. Moreover, when he says, "Without abandoning their own meanings (*svārtha*) [the words "Thou" and "That"] convey a special meaning (*viśiṣṭārthasamarpaka*) and result in the apprehension of the inner *Ātman*" (Upad I,18,171), he suggests the essential characteristic of *jahadajahallakṣaṇā*, namely that the two words retain part of their meanings. It should be emphasized that for Śaṅkara, the part of their meanings which is retained is determined by the *anvaya* method, and the other part, which is incompatible and to be abandoned, is determined by the *vyatireka* method. Therefore, Śaṅkara's method can be said to be essentially the same as *jahad-ajahallakṣaṇā*. The fundamental principles of the exegetical method concerning the sentence "*tat tvam asi*" were set up by Śaṅkara and systematized by Sarvajñātman.[42]

6. The Sentence "*Ahaṃ Brahmāsmi*"

As for the sentence "*ahaṃ brahmāsmi*" (I am *Brahman*), Śaṅkara like Sureśvara[43] tries to clarify only the meaning of the word "*aham*" (I) in the sentence alongside the clarification of "*tvam*," since "*aham*" in the sentence is identical with "*tvam*."[44]

Ordinary people wrongly think of "*aham*" as the body (*dehābhimānin*, Upad I,12,5), as an experiencer (*bhoktṛ*, Upad I,12,7, etc.), or as an agent (*kartṛ*, Upad I,12,17), and justify themselves as follows:

> The meaning of verbal root and verbal suffix, though different [from each other], are seen to have one and the same subject as in "*karoti*" (he does), "*gacchati*" (he goes), etc. according to universally accepted opinion. (Upad I,18,51)

This is the reason why they cannot understand the meaning of the sentence "*ahaṃ brahmāsmi*." Taking the example of a sentence "*jānāmi*" (I know) or "*jānāti*" (he knows), we have already seen how such a grammatical presupposition is wrong.[45] According to Śaṅkara, the subject of the sentence "*jānāmi*" is merely the *ahaṃkartṛ* which is the *buddhi* as the bearer of *ahaṃkāra* ("I"-notion), since the meanings of both verbal root and verbal suffix can belong to it. The words are capable of expressing the *ahaṃkartṛ* which has generic attributes (*jāti*) and action (*karman*), but not of expressing *Ātman* devoid of them (Upad I,18,28). *Ātman* is said to be the object of *ahaṃpratyaya* (*ahaṃpratyayaviṣaya*, Upad II,2,52; 2,53. cf. BSBh II,3,38, p. 545; *asmatpratyayaviṣaya*, BSBh, Introduction, p. 17). Therefore, words referring to the *ahaṃkartṛ*, in which there is the reflection of the inner *Ātman*, can indicate the latter indirectly but never designate it directly (Upad I,18,29). As the *ahaṃkartṛ* has the reflection of *Ātman* and appears to be *Ātman*, it is expressed by words which are used in the sense of *Ātman*, just as words which mean fire are not directly used in the sense of, for example, a torch, but only indirectly, since they mean something different from a torch (Upad I,18,30–31). *Ātman* can neither be expressed by words nor cognized (Upad I,18,57). Therefore, the primary meaning of "I" or "Thou" is not the inner *Ātman* but the *ahaṃkartṛ* which ordinary people mistake for the inner *Ātman* through *avidyā*. If the *anvayavyatireka* method is applied to the sentence "I am *Brahman*" here, it is determined that "I" means the inner *Ātman* and not the *ahaṃkartṛ*.

For this reason the sentence "*ahaṃ brahmāsmi*" also shows the identity of the inner *Ātman* and *Brahman*. One of the ten boys who crossed the river, when counting the party, failed to count himself and thought that one boy was missing. When he was told, "You are the tenth," he immediately realized that he was the tenth. Similarly, through such sentences as "Thou art That," right knowledge concerning the inner *Ātman* will become clearer (Upad I,18,190) and one comes to know one's own *Ātman*, the Witness of all the internal organs (Upad I,18,174). Unless and until one can realize, "I am the existent," the sentence "Thou art That" will still be meaningless (Upad I, 18,90).

Notes to Introduction III, A

[1]Cf. Nakamura II, p. 424.

[2]Śaṅkara does not accept *ānanda* as a positive character of *Brahman-Ātman*. See Eigen, p. 276; Mayeda Upad, pp. 39–40. Cf. D.H.H. Ingalls, "The Study of Śaṁkarācārya," *Annals of the Bhandarkar Oriental Research Institute*, vol. 33 (1952), p. 7.

[3]Cf. Nakamura II, p. 426.

[4]Cf. Nakamura II, p. 424. Bādarāyaṇa's *Brahman* is the Highest One who is above the deities. He is the supporter (*dhṛti*) of the world (BS I,3,16). He is also conceived as the cause of the fruits of action (BS III, 2,38; 41).

[5]BS II, 3,46.

[6]Cf. Mayeda Upad, pp. 38–39.

[7]Cf. S. Radhakrishnan, *Indian Philosophy*, vol. II (New York: The Macmillan Co., 1958), p. 437; Nakamura II, pp. 427–437.

[8]Cf. S. Radhakrishnan, *Indian Philosophy*, vol. II, p. 437.

[9]BS II,1,24; Nakamura II, p. 435.

[10]BS II, 1,4 and 6.

[11]This is the problem of evil. Cf. Nakamura II, pp. 439–440; R. Otto, *Mysticism East and West* (New York: Collier Books, 1962), pp. 125–126.

[12]Reply to the first question: *Brahman* Himself can create the world, just as milk spontaneously becomes curd, and just as gods create various things without any instruments (BS II,1,24–25). Reply to the second question: It needs no discussion. In this

world, there are many cases where things material come forth from things conscious. For example, hair and nails grow from humans. There are also cases where things conscious come forth from things material. For example, worms come out from cowdung. Therefore, it is not unreasonable that things material come out from *Brahman* (BS II, 1,6). Reply to the third question: Even though *Brahman* creates the universe for the sake of Its sport (*līlā*), there are no faults of unfairness and absence of compassion (*nairghṛṇya*) in *Brahman,* since It creates various conditions for each individual in accordance with the merits and demerits which each individual has created in the past lives; therefore, even though an individual may suffer more or suffer less, we cannot say that *Brahman* is without compassion. And even though one individual does not have the same amount of pleasure and pain as others, we cannot say that *Brahman* is unfair (BS II,1,34. cf. BS II,1,33; 3,42). Cf. Nakamura II, pp. 435–441.

[13]*nāmarūpe vyākaravāṇi,* Chānd. Up. VI,3,2 (cf. BS II,4,20) and *nāmarūpayor nirvahitā,* Chānd. Up. VIII,14,1 (cf. BS I,3,41).

[14]Eigen, pp. 258–259; Mayeda Upad, pp. 31–34.

[15]For example, Taitt. Ā. III,11,1; 12,7; Taitt. Up. II,6,1; Bṛh. Up. I,4,7, etc.

[16]For example, Manu XII,119; BhG V, 13; XIII,2, etc.

[17]By the expression *tattvānyatvābhyām anirvacanīya-*,Śaṅkara indicates indeterminacy of the primary material *nāmarūpa* which is to be transformed into something. There is no implication here as to the ontological status of the primary material. Instead of *tattvānyatvābhyām,* the term *anirvacanīya* associated with *sadasadbhyām,* which expresses an ontological judgment, is, in later Advaitins' works, used as an adjective of *avidyā* or *māyā,* which is regarded as the primary material. See Eigen, p. 261–264; D. H. H. Ingalls, "The Study of Śaṁkaracārya," *Annals of the Bhandarkar Oriental Research Institute,* vol. 33 (1952), p. 7; Mayeda Upad, pp. 32–34. The term *anirvacanīya* as an attribute of *avidyā* appears first in Maṇḍanamiśra's *Brahmasiddhi.* See S. Kuppuswami Sastri, *Brahmasiddhi by Ācārya Maṇḍanamiśra with Commentary by Śaṅkhapāṇi* (Madras Government Oriental manuscripts series, no. 4, 1937), p. 9, line 14; S. Dasgupta, *A History of Indian Philosophy,* vol. II, p. 89; Eigen, p. 255, note 1. Therefore, this new truth-value of *avidyā, anirvacanīyatva,* seems to have existed in Śaṅkara's time. The association of the term with *avidyā* occurs in the doctrine of all Advaitins except Śaṅkara, Sureśvara, and Toṭaka. Cf. D. H. H. Ingalls, "Śaṁkara on the Question: Whose Is Avidyā?" *Philosophy East and West,* vol. 3 (1953), no. 1, pp. 69 ff.

[18]*Upadeshasāhasrī von Meister Shankara* (Bonn: Ludwig Röhrscheid Verlag, 1949), p. 19, note 71.

[19]Eigen, p. 264–267.

[20]Cf. S. Dasgupta, *A History of Indian Philosophy,* vol. I (Cambridge, 1951), p. 258, note 1 and p. 468.

[21]Nakamura IV, pp. 328–332 and p. 430; *The Indian Development of Philosophical Speculations* (in Japanese; Tokyo: Genrisha, 1949), pp. 240–244.

[22]P. Hacker, *Vivarta* (Mainz: Verlag der Akademie der Wissenschaften und der Literatur, 1953), pp. 208–213.

[23]Cf. P. Hacker, *Vivarta,* pp. 220–225 and pp. 234–236.

[24]"eine Art illusionistischer Pariṇāmavāda," *Vivarta* p. 210.

[25]The idea of *trivṛtkaraṇa* first appears in Chānd. Up. VI,3–4. This is the theory that gross elements are triply mixed from the three subtle elements, fire (*tejas*), water (*ap*), and food (*anna*); a preponderance of one of the three subtle elements over the two others brings about the differences among fire, water, and other gross elements. Śaṅkara discusses this problem in the BSBh II,4,20–22. Cf. P. Deussen, *The System of the Vedânta,* pp. 240–241; S. Dasgupta, *A History of Indian Philosophy,* vol. II, p. 74, note 1.

[26]The fully developed theory of *pañcīkaraṇa*, the oldest reference to which may be Mbh XII,9089 and XII,244,2 (Poona Critical ed.), asserts that the five subtle elements—ether (*ākāśa*), air (*vāyu*), fire (*agni*), water (*ap*), and earth (*pṛthivī*)—are first divided into two halves; then one of the two halves of each subtle element is combined with one-fourth of each remaining half of all the other subtle elements. Thus one half of each gross element (*e.g.* earth) is made from itself and the other half of it is constituted of four equal parts of each of the other elements (ether, air, fire, and water); *i.e.*, one-eighth of it is from each of the other four elements. The Upad seems to be based upon Taitt. Up. II,1 and BS II,3,1–12. Cf. *Pañcadaśī* I, 27; *Vedāntasāra* [XV] 123–128; P. Deussen, *Allgemeine Geschichte der Philosophie*. I.3 (Leipzig: F. A. Brockhaus, 1908), p. 446; S. Dasgupta, *History of Indian Philosophy*, vol. II, p. 74, note 1; P. Hacker, *Upadeshasāhasrī von Meister Shankara*, p. 20, note 72; H. Nakamura, *The Vedāntasāra* (Kyoto: Heirakuji Shoten, 1962), pp. 152–153.

[27]S. Dasgupta, *A History of Indian Philosophy*, vol. II, p. 74, note 1.

[28]*Vedāntasāra* [XV] 124. Cf. *Pañcadaśī* I,27. It is to be noted here that Sadānanda defends *pañcīkaraṇa* by asserting that the *Śruti* which sets forth *trivṛtkaraṇa* indirectly refers to it (*Vedāntasāra* [XV] 126).

[29]VP VIII, 30.

[30]See note 2, above.

[31]A work entitled *Pañcīkaraṇa*, which treats *pañcīkaraṇa* as a way of meditation (*samādhividhi*), is traditionally ascribed to Śaṅkara, but it may not be authentic. There is the following negative evidence: (1) *Brahman* is described as "*paramānandādvaya*" although Śaṅkara as the author of the BSBh avoids using *ānanda* as the nature of *Brahman* (see note 2). (2) In its colophon the work is attributed to Śaṅkarācārya and not to Śaṅkarabhagavadpāda, as would be expected if it were a genuine work (cf. P. Hacker, "Śaṅkarācārya and Śaṅkarabhagavadpāda," *New Indian Antiquary*, vol. 9, 1947, pp. 176–178 and pp. 182–183). (3) The whole text, which is an independent and non-commentary work, is colored by Sāṃkhyan doctrine and sets forth a *pañcīkaraṇa* theory different from the one mentioned above; it is said that from *Brahman* there arose *avyakta*; from *avyakta*, *mahat*; from *mahat*, *ahaṃkāra*; from *ahaṃkāra*, *pañcatanmātra*; from *pañcatanmātra*, *pañcamahābhūta*. Such a theory of evolution is not advanced in any of his works which can be regarded as genuine, except the GBh. The BhG, which has Sāṃkhya as one of its doctrinal bases, refers to a very similar idea of evolution (VII, 4 and XIII, 5). Consequently Śaṅkara as its commentator seems to be forced to comment on it, just as he refers to the term *ānanda* only when the text to be interpreted forces him to do so. Moreover, his idea of evolution in his GBh is slightly different from that of the *Pañcīkaraṇa*: in the latter *avyakta* evolves from *Brahman* (*brahmaṇo 'vyaktam*), while in the former *avyakta* is regarded as *īśvaraśakti* (GBh XIII,5) and as *mama īśvarī māyāśaktiḥ* (GBh VII, 4).

Notes to Introduction, III, B

[1]See P. Deussen, *The System of the Vedânta* (Reprint ed.; New York: Dover Publications, Inc., 1973), pp. 325–327; Nakamura II, pp. 457–463.

[2]BS I,4,2; III,3,30; IV,2,9–11.

[3]*dehabījair bhūtasūkṣmair*, BSBh III,1,1, p. 594.

[4]BS II,4,8–19.

[5]For a detailed account of the principal vital air, see P. Deussen, *The System of the Vedânta*, pp. 333–336.

[6]Cf. P. Deussen, *The System of the Vedânta*, pp. 336–337.

[7]Cf. S. Chatterjee, *The Nyāya Theory of Knowledge* (Calcutta: University of Calcutta, 1950), pp. 138–139.

[8] *viṣayālocanahetutvaṃ cendriyāṇām*, BSBh II,4,19,p. 587. Śaṅkara refutes the Vaiśeṣika position that the Consciousness of *Ātman* is adventitious, but maintains that though Consciousness is *Ātman*'s constant nature, still the senses are of use since they serve the pupose of discerning their special respective objects *nityasvarūpacaitanyatve ghrāṇādyānarthakyam iti cet, na, gandhādiviṣayaviśeṣaparicchedārthatvāt/ tathā hi darśayati*——"*gandhāya ghrāṇam*" (Chānd. Up. *VIII,12,4*)*ityādi*, BSBh II,3,18, p. 530.

[9] Cf. *Nyāyasūtra* 3,1,52–61.

[10] Cf. *Nyāyasūtra* 3,1,62–73; S. Chatterjee, *The Nyāya Theory of Knowledge*, pp. 133–135.

[11] *Vivaraṇaprameyasaṃgraha* (Acyutagraṃthamālā 8, Saṃvat 1996), pp. 613–620. Cf. T. M. P. Mahadevan, *The Philosophy of Advaita* (Madras: Ganesh & Co., 1957), pp. 22–24; D. M. Datta, *The Six Ways of Knowing* (Calcutta: University of Calcutta, 1960), pp. 39–40.

[12] *tac cātmana upādhibhūtam antaḥkaraṇaṃ mano buddhir vijñānaṃ cittam iti cānekadhā tatra tatrābhilapyate*, BSBh II, 3,32, p. 541.

[13] *sarvārthaviṣayaṃ traikālyavṛtti manas tv ekam anekavṛttikam/ tad eva vṛttibhedāt kvacid bhinnavad vyapadiśyate*—"*mano buddhir ahaṃkāraś cittaṃ ca*" *iti/ tathā ca śrutiḥ kāmādyā nānāvidhā vṛttīr anukramyāha*—"*etat sarvaṃ mana eva*" (Bṛh. Up. *I.5.3) iti*, BSBh II,4,6, p. 272.

[14] P. Deussen, *The System of the Vedânta*, p. 330.

[15] For example, *citta*, Upad I,12,1; II,2,75; etc.; *dhī*, Upad I,9,6; 14,4; 14,5; II,1,35; etc. Sureśvara, like Śaṅkara, uses these terms as synonymous with *buddhi* and *manas*. See P. Hacker, Unters, p. 1950.

[16] *viṣayebhyaś ca manasaḥ paratvaṃ, manomūlatvād viṣayendriyavyavahārasya/ manasas tu parā buddhiḥ/ buddhiṃ hy āruhya bhogyajātaṃ bhoktāram upasarpati/ buddher ātmā mahān paraḥ*, . . ., BSBh I,4,1, p. 294.

[17] Cf. D. M. Datta, *The Six Ways of Knowing*, p. 48.

[18] Cf. T. M. P. Mahadevan, *The Philosophy of Advaita*, pp. 29–31; D. M. Datta, *The Six Ways of Knowing*, pp. 53–59.

[19] Cf. P. Deussen, *The System of the Vedânta*, p. 327.

[20] D. M. Datta, *The Six Ways of Knowing*, pp. 53–55. Cf. T. M. P. Mahadevan, *The Philosophy of Advaita*, pp. 29–31.

[21] See Introduction, III,A,1, pp. 18–21.

[22] Cf. S. Chatterjee, *The Nyāya Theory of Knowledge*, pp. 144–145.

[23] Cf. S. Chatterjee, *The Nyāya Theory of Knowledge*, p. 145; D. M. Datta, *The Six Ways of Knowing*, p. 47 and pp. 52–53.

[24] Cf. P. Deussen, *The System of the Vedânta*, p. 326 and pp. 331 – 332; BUBh I,5,3.

[25] Cf. S. Chatterjee, *The Nyāya Theory of Knowledge*, pp. 116–130.

[26] Cf. S. Radhakrishnan, *Indian Philosophy*, vol. II (New York: Macmillan Co., 1958), pp. 488–489; S. Chatterjee, *The Nyāya Theory of Knowledge*, pp. 122–124.

[27] Cf. S. Radhakrishnan, *Indian Philosophy*, vol. II, p. 490; S. Chatterjee, *The Nyāya Theory of Knowledge*, pp. 190–191; D. M. Datta, *The Six Ways of Knowing*, pp. 93–102.

[28] Cf. S. Radhakrishnan, *Indian Philosophy*, vol. II, p. 490.

[29] Cf. S. Radhakrishnan, *Indian Philosophy*, vol. II, pp. 489–490.

[30] *Vivaraṇaprameyasaṃgraha*, pp. 621–623; T. M. P. Mahadevan, *The Philosophy of Advaita*, pp. 26–28; D. M. Datta, *The Six Ways of Knowing*, pp. 40–42; S. Chatterjee, *The Nyāya Theory of Knowledge*, pp. 138–144. VP (I,122–123) says that all the senses produce perceptual knowledge (*pratyakṣajñāna*) only when they are connected with their respective objects and that *ghrāṇa*, *rasana* and *tvac* produce perceptions of *gandha*,

rasa and *sparśa*, while remaining in their own places, whereas *cakṣus* and *śrotra* go to the place of their objects by themselves and perceive their respective objects.

[31]For example, *bauddhais . . . pratyayair*, Upad I,18,68; *bauddhaḥ pratyayaḥ*, Upad II, 2,77; *bauddhapratyaya*, Upad II,2,78; *śabdādyākārabauddhapratyaya*, Upad II,2,84; *bauddhāḥ pratyayāḥ*,PBh II,4,42, p. 34. This expression is also found in the *Yogasūtrabhāṣyavivaraṇa* (Madras Gov. Oriental Series no. XCIV, 1952, p. 354) which is ascribed to Śaṅkara. Cf. note 62.

[32]For example, *vṛtti*, Upad I,13,7; 18,1; *antaḥkaraṇavṛtti*, GBh XIII,6,p.543; *dhiyo vṛttiḥ*, Upad I,17,35; *buddhivṛtti*, BUBh IV,3,7,p. 561 (cf. *Yogasūtrabhāṣyavivaraṇa*, p. 355); *manaso vṛttiḥ*, Upad I,17,36; *mānasī vṛttiḥ*, Upad I,13,6. Instead of *vṛtti, vṛtta* is also used, for example, *manaso vṛttam*, Upad I, 11,3; *manovṛttam*, Upad I,11,4. Cf. VP I,4.

[33]*Yogasūtra* I,2; IV, 18. Cf. *Yogasūtra* I, 4; 5; IV, 23. *cittavṛtti* in the *Yogasūtra* and its *Bhāṣya* seems also to be synonymous with *cittapracāra* in the Upad (II,2,75; 82). The following argument about *Ātman*'s changelessness in the Upad resembles the *Yogasūtra* (IV, 18) and its *Bhāṣya* to the extent that we have to admit Śaṅkara's indebtedness to the *Yogasūtra* and its *Bhāṣya*: *yatas teṣāṃ pratyayānāṃ niyamena aśeṣataḥ upalabdher eva apariṇāmitvāt kūṭasthatvasiddhau, niścayahetum eva aśeṣacittapracāropalabdhiṃ saṃśayahetum āttha/ yadi hi tava pariṇāmitvaṃ syāt, aśeṣasvaviṣayacittapracāropalabdhir na syāt, cittasyeva svaviṣaye, yathā cendriyāṇāṃ svaviṣayeṣu/ na ca tathātmanas tava svaviṣayaikadeśopalabdhiḥ/ ataḥ kūṭasthataiva taveti*. Upad II,2,75.

Yogasūtra IV, 18 reads: *sadājñātāś cittavṛttayas tatprabhoḥ puruṣasyāpariṇāmitvāt.*

Cf. *sarveṣāṃ manaso vṛttam aviśeṣeṇa paśyataḥ /*
tasya me nirvikārasya viśeṣaḥ syāt kathaṃcana // Upad I,11,3.

Cf. . . . *dṛśimātreṇa puruṣena dṛśyānāṃ cittavṛttīnāṃ cidātmanā vyāpyamānatvāt, draṣṭā puruṣa iti . . .* , *Yogasūtrabhāṣyavivaraṇa* I,4, p. 15.

The idea that the *buddhi* assumes the forms of external things through the senses is also expressed in Vyāsa's *Yogasūtrabhāṣya* I,7: *indriyapraṇālikayā cittasya bāhyavastūparāgāt tadviṣayā sāmānyaviśeṣātmano 'rthasya viśeṣāvadhāraṇapradhānā vṛttiḥ pratyakṣaṃ pramāṇam.* In his *Yogasūtrabhāṣyavivaraṇa* (p. 19) Śaṅkara comments on this sentence as follows:. . . *indriyam eva praṇāḍikayā dvāraṃ śabdādyākāravṛttirūpeṇa pariṇāmamānasya cittasya/ atas tat tenendriyadvāreṇa sāmānyaviśeṣātmakabāhyavastvākāratayā pariṇamamānam uparajyate/ tasya taduparāgād dhetoḥ "cittasya" yā mudrāpratimudrāvat "vṛttiḥ" sāmānyaviśeṣātmakavastūparāge 'pi "viśeṣāvadhāraṇapradhānā" saiva "pratyakṣaṃ pramāṇam."* He expresses the same idea elsewhere in his *Vivaraṇa*, for example: *indriyamārgeṇa cittaṃ bāhyākāreṇa pariṇamamānaṃ hi saṃbadhyati . . . ato viṣayā ātmākāreṇa pariṇataṃ "cittam abhisaṃbadhyoparañjayanti,"* IV, 17, p. 347; *svasya bauddhasya pratyayasyopalabdhir bhavati/ tadartham eva hi sā buddhiḥ śabdādipratyayarūpeṇa pariṇamate*, IV, 22, p. 354. Furthermore, it is significant for the later Advaita theory of *pramāṇa* that Vyāsa and his interpreter Śaṅkara define *pratyakṣa* on the basis of the concept of *vṛtti*. Śaṅkara further says in his *Vivaraṇa* (I, 7, p. 19): *pramāṇākhyā vṛttis tridhaiva bhidyate/ tatra pramāṇākhyāyāś cittavṛtteḥ prathamo bhedaḥ pratyakṣam.*

[34]Śaṅkara as the author of the *Yogasūtrabhāṣyavivaraṇa* also uses *pratyaya* as a synonym of *vṛtti* (IV,22, p. 354): *bauddhaḥ pratyayo jāyamāna eva tasyāḥ (=citeḥ) karmatām āpadyate/ taṃ bauddhaṃ pratyayaṃ vṛttim "anupatanty" upalabhamānā "bhoktṛśaktiḥ."*

[35]N. K. Devaraja, *An Introduction to Śaṅkara's Theory of Knowledge* (Varanasi: Motilal Banarsi Dass, 1962), pp. 99–102. Cf. S. Dasgupta, *A History of Indian Philosophy*, vol. II (Cambridge: University Press, 1952), pp. 105–106. Radhakrishnan regards this theory as crude from the scientific point of view in his *Indian Philosophy*, vol. II (New York: Macmillan Co., 1958), pp. 492–493. Cf. N. K. Devaraja, *An Introduction to Śaṅkara's Theory of Knowledge*, p. 100. D. M. Datta has tried to defend this theory on the

ground of theories of the Gestalt school of psychology in his book, pp. 60–70. Cf. T. M. P. Mahadevan, *The Philosophy of Advaita*, pp. 32–33.

[36]See note 33, above. This idea may be traced back to the Bṛh. Up. I,5,3.

[37]*antaḥkaraṇam api cakṣurādidvārā nirgatya ghaṭādiviṣayadeśaṃ gatvā* . . . , VP I,18.

[38]Judging from the illustration "*ālokastho ghaṭo yadvad buddhyārūḍho bhavet tathā*" (Upad I,18,156), *-ārūḍha* is probably synonymous with *-stha*. Rāmatīrtha, a commentator of the Upad, interprets the term as *buddhivṛttikoḍīkṛta* (*Padayojanikā* II,7,1; 18,94). However, Dignāga uses the term in a different sense; in his usage it is synonymous with *kalpita* or *vikalpita*. See Th. Stcherbatsky, *Buddhist Logic*, vol. II (Reprint ed. New York: Dover Publications, Inc., 1962), p. 19 and p. 143. Vācaspatimiśra, the author of the *Bhāmatī*, interprets as *buddhiparikalpita* the term *buddhyārūḍha* which is used in the BSBh II,2,28, p. 467, when Śaṅkara mentions a Buddhist doctrine.

[39]For example, "*bodha*"-*śabdena bauddhāḥ pratyayā ucyante/ sarve pratyayā viṣayībhavanti yasya sa ātmā sarvabodhān pratibudhyate sarvapratyayadarśī*, PBh II,4,42, p. 34; *svabuddhyārūḍham eva sarvam upalabhase* . . . *kūṭasthanityacaitanyasvarūpeṇa*, Upad II,2,73; *ahaṃ hi tato 'nyaḥ samastam arthaṃ jānāmi buddhyārūḍham*, Upad II,2,70.

[40]Cf. *Sāṃkhyakārikā* 20 and *Gauḍapādabhāṣya* 20.

[41]Cf. *Yogasūtra* IV,17–18 and *Yogasūtrabhāṣya* IV,17–18.

[42]Vācaspatimiśra says in his *Tattvakaumudī* (Poon Oriental Series, no. 10, 1957, p. 10): *so 'yaṃ buddhitattvavartinā jñānasukhādinā tatpratibimbitas tacchāyāpattyā jñānaśukhādimān iva bhavatīti cetano 'nugṛhyate/ citicchāyāpattyā 'cetanā 'pi tadadhyavasāyo 'py acetanaś cetanavad bhavatīti*. The *Sāṃkhyakārikā* lacks the concept of *pratibimba*, though Vi jñānabhikṣu often refers to it. Cf. R. Garbe, *Die Sâṃkhya-Philosophie* (Leipzig: H. Haessel, 1917), pp. 84–85 and pp. 376–378. As far as I know, Vācaspati is the first writer to introduce the concept into the Sāṃkhya system as an elaborate form of *saṃyoga* in *Sāṃkhyakārikā* 20 in order to explain the relationship between *ātman* and the *buddhi*. *Saṃyoga* has a realistic connotation which is suitable for the classical Sāṃkhyan doctrine, but *pratibimba* is an illusionistic term. It is probable that the Sāṃkhya borrowed this idea from the Advaita Vedānta. On the other hand, Śaṅkara's *ābhāsa* seems to be based partly upon the Buddhist usage of the term. See S. Mayeda, "The Meaning of *Ābhāsa* in Śaṅkara's Upadeśasāhasrī" (in Japanese), *Journal of Indian and Buddhist Studies*, vol. VI (1958), no. 1, pp. 174–177.

[43]S. Mayeda, "The Meaning of *Ābhāsa* in Śaṅkara's Upadeśasāhasrī."

[44]*praticchāyā* is synonymously used: *buddhis tāvat svacchatvād ānantaryāc cātmacaitanyajyotiḥpraticchāyā bhavati/ tena hi vivekinām api tatrātmābhimānabuddhiḥ prathamā/ tato 'py ānantaryān manasi caitanyāvabhāsatā buddhisaṃparkāt/ tata indriyeṣu/ manaḥ saṃyogāt/ tato 'nantaraṃ śarīre/ indriyasaṃparkāt. pāramparyeṇa kṛtsnaṃ kāryakaraṇasaṃghātam ātmā caitanyasvarūpajyotiṣāvabhāsayati/ tena hi sarvasya lokasya kāryakaraṇasaṃghāte tadvṛttiṣu cāniyatātmābhimānabuddhi yathāvivekaṃ jāyate*, BUBh IV,3,7, p. 561.

[45]Cf. Upad I,18,154–155.

[46]*brahmacitphalayor bhedaḥ sahasryāṃ viśruto yataḥ*, *Pañcadaśī* VIII, 12.

[47]Cf. T. M. P. Mahadevan, *The Philosophy of Advaita*, p. 225.

[48]In the Nyāya-Vaiśeṣika system *upalabdhi* and *jñāna*, which are considered to be the nature of *Ātman* by Śaṅkara, are treated as synonyms of *buddhi* and *pratyaya*: *buddhir upalabdhir jñānam ity anarthāntaram*, *Nyāyasūtra*, I.1,15; *buddhir upalabdhir jñānaṃ pratyaya iti paryāyāḥ*, *Vaiśeṣikopaskāra*, 8,1,1. Cf. *Nyāyakośa* (Bombay Sanskrit & Prakrit Series no. XLIX, 1928), pp. 604–608.

[49]For example, *Mahābhāṣya* III,2,84 defines *dhātvartha* as *kriyā*. Cf. L. Renou, *Terminologie Grammaticale du Sanskrit* (Bibliothèque de l'Ecole des Hautes Etudes no. 280–282). pp. 168–169.

[50]Cf. R. C. Pandeya, *The Problem of Meaning in Indian Philosophy* (Varanasi: Motilal Banarsidass, 1963), pp. 118–120.

[51]According to Śaṅkara, *avidyā* is superimpostion (*adhyāsa, adhyāropa*). See Introduction, IV, D, 1, pp. 76–79.

[52]Probably Śaṅkara does not conceive the idea that "as soon as the *antaḥkaraṇa* has assumed the shape or form of the object of its knowledge, the ignorance (*ajñāna*) with reference to that object is removed, and thereupon the steady light of the Pure Consciousness (*cit*) shows the object which was so long hidden by ignorance" (Dasgupta, *A History of Indian Philosophy*, vol. I, p. 472).

[53]The Indian grammarians' defintion of a verb varies. The *Mahābhāṣya* (I,3,1) discusses whether a verb denotes action (*kriyāvacana*) or state (*bhāvavacana*). Cf. L. Renou, *Terminologie Grammaticale du Sanskrit*, p. 244; R.C. Pandeya, *The Problem of Meaning in Indian Philosophy*, pp. 118–120. In *Nirukta* I,1 Yāska defines a verb as *bhāvapradhāna*; *bhāva* as the result of action is predominant in the meaning of a verb and action is only secondary. Śaṅkara's concept of a verb seems to be close to Yāska's. It is worthy of note that in this respect Śaṅkara's position is different from that of Maṇḍanamiśra who is a senior contemporary of Śaṅkara. Cf. R. C. Pandeya, *The Problem of Meaning in Indian Philosophy*, pp. 117–123.

[54]According to the Naiyāyikas there is first the cognition of an object, "This is a pot" which is technically called *vyavasāya*. Then another cognition, "I know the pot," which is called *anuvyavasāya*, takes place after the second cognition cognizes the first. Cf. *Nyāvasiddhāntamañjarīprakāśa* 69; VP I,50–51; S. Chatterjee, *The Nyāya Theory of Knowledge*, pp. 187–188. The Advaitins do not accept this theory. According to the *Pañcadaśī* (VIII, 15–17), the expression "This is a pot" is based upon *ābhāsa* whereas the expression "The pot has been known" comes from *Brahman*.

[55]The meaning of the verbal suffixes is a controversial problem. Cf. R. C. Pandeya, *The Problem of Meaning in Indian Philosophy*, pp. 123–128.

[56]*Nyāyamañjarī* (Vizianagara Sanskrit Series vol. 8, no. 10), p. 20. Cf. S. Chatterjee, *The Nyāya Theory of Knowledge*, pp. 11–12.

[57]*kāmaḥ saṃkalpo vicikitsā, śraddhāśraddhā, dhṛtir adhṛtir hrīr dhīr bhīr ity etat sarvam mana eva*, Bṛh. Up. I,5,3.

[58]In BSBh II,2, 17 Śaṅkara refutes the Vaiśeṣika position that the six categories, namely substance, quality, action, generality, particularity, and inherence, are absolutely different from one another and have different characteristics and that quality, action and the like have the attribute of depending on substance. According to Śaṅkara a quality is essentially of the nature of the substance (*dravyātmakatā guṇasya*, BSBh II,1,17, p. 444). Cf. N. K. Devaraja, *An Introduction to Śaṅkara's Theory of Knowledge*, p. 93.

[59]*buddhi* in a plural form in the present case probably means *pratyaya* of the *buddhi*.

[60]*icchā dveṣaḥ sukhaṃ duḥkhaṃ saṃghātaś cetanā dhṛtiḥ/*
etat kṣetraṃ samāsena savikāram udāhṛtam//

[61]GBh XIII,6, p. 542–544.

[62]Vol. II, pp. 105–106. As for the theory of knowledge of Padmapāda and Prakāśātman, see P. Hacker, Unters, pp. 2047–2055 and K. Camman, *Das System des Advaita nach der Lehre Prakāśātmans* (Wiesbaden: Otto Harrassowitz, 1965), pp. 132–155.

[63]I have already pointed out some similarities of Śaṅkara's view to that of the Sāṃkhya and the Yoga. See notes 30, 31, 32, 33, 39, 40, 41. In the BSBh Śaṅkara quotes the *Nyāyasūtra*, the *Vaiśeṣikasūtra*, the *Sāṃkhyakārikā*, the *Yogasūtra*, and the *Mīmāṃsāsūtra* among the texts belonging to the six systems of Indian philosophy. He quotes these texts in order to attack their tenets except the *Nyāyasūtra* (I,1,2; 18) and the *Yogasūtra*

(I,6; II, 44). It is, however, only the *Yogasūtra* (I,6) that he quotes concerning the problem of perception. He says: *evaṃ tarhi 'paramatam apratiṣiddham anumataṃ bhavati' iti nyāyād ihāpi yogaśāstraprasiddhā manasaḥ pañcavṛttayaḥ parigṛhyante "pramāṇaviparyayavikalpanidrāsmṛtayaḥ"* (*Yogasūtra* I,6) *nāma/bahuvṛttitvamātreṇa vā manaḥ prāṇasya nidarśanam iti draṣṭavyam/jīvopakaraṇatvam api prāṇasya pañcavṛttitvān "manovad" iti yojayitavyam*, BSBh II,4,12, p. 581. In this context it is significant that there is a commentary on Vyāsa's *Yogasūtrabhāṣya* which is ascribed to Śaṅkara. The authenticity of this text has not yet been established, but as far as I can see now, there is no conclusively negative evidence. As I have already pointed out (see especially notes 30, 32, and 33), the text reveals similarities to Śaṅkara's view of perception. This fact may point to this authorship of the text. Cf. P. Hacker, "Śaṅkara der Yogin and Śaṅkara der Advaitin: Eine Beobachtungen" WZKSO, vol. XII-XIII (1968/1969), pp. 117–148; H. Nakamura, "Notes on Śaṅkara's *Yogasūtrabhāṣya vivaraṇa*" (*Prof. J. Okuda Felicitation Volume*. Kyoto: Heirakuji Shoten, 1976), pp. 1219–1229; *do*, "Śaṅkara's *Yogasūtrabhāṣyavivaraṇa* [I]" (*Journal of Indian and Buddhist Studies* 25–1, 1976), pp. 70–77; [II] (*Journal of Indian and Buddhist Studies* 26–1, 1977), pp. 119–127; Trevor Leggett, *The Chapter of the Self* (London and Henley: Routledge & Kegan Paul, 1978), pp. 173–175.

[64]Cf. P. Deussen, The *Philosophy of the Upaniṣads* (Reprint ed. New York: Dover Publications, Inc., 1966), pp. 296–312; T.M.P. Mahadevan, *Gauḍapāda: A Study in Early Advaita* (University of Madras, 1960. 3rd ed.), pp. 95–106.

[65]This is one of his authentic works. See S. Mayeda, "On the Author of the Māṇḍūkyopaniṣad- and the Gauḍapādīya-Bhāṣya," *Prof. V. Raghavan's Felicitation Volume of the Adyar Library Bulletin*, vols. 31–32, 1967–68, pp. 73–94.

[66]This state is not regarded as an independent state. Cf. Nakamura II, pp. 468–469; P. Deussen, *The System of the Vedânta*, pp. 352–353.

[67]Some scholars think that the three states are investigated by the *Māṇḍūkyopaniṣad* and the GKBh to establish the non-duality of *Ātman*. See T.M.P. Mahadevan, *Gauḍapāda*, p. 95; R. D. Karmarkar, *Gauḍapāda-Kārikā* (Poona: Bhandarkar Oriental Research Institute, 1953), p. li.

[68]Cf. M. Hiriyanna, *Outlines of Indian Philosophy* (New York: Macmillan Co., 1932), p. 230; Chandradhar Sharma, *A Critical Survey of Indian Philosophy* (London: Rider & Co., 1960), p. 177.

Notes to Introduction, III, C

[1]P. Deussen, *The System of the Vedânta*, pp. 23–24 and p. 90; Nakamura II, pp. 409–419.

[2]K. Camman, *Das System des Advaita nach der Lehre Prakāśātmans* (Wiesbaden: Otto Harrassowitz, 1965), pp. 4–8.

[3]Cf. BSBh I,1,1, p. 35; PBh, Introduction, p. 6; Upad I,1,13; P. Hacker, Unters, p. 2047; J. F. Staal, *Advaita and Neoplatonism* (Madras: University of Madras, 1961), pp. 101–102.

[4]Cf. BSBh II,2,28; Upad I,16,10–14; 18,141–152.

[5]P. Deussen, *The System of the Vedânta*, pp. 89–90.

[6]S. Radhakrishnan, *Indian Philosophy*, vol. II, p. 488. Śaṅkara uses the term *anupalabdhi* (cf. Upad II,2,59; 2,90) but it is probably not a technical term.

[7]In order to show the absolute authority of the *Veda*, the Mīmāṃsakas assert that the *Veda* is not the work of any person (*apauruṣeya*). See *Mīmāṃsāsūtra* I,1,27–32; *Sarvadarśanasaṃgraha* (Poona: Bhandarkar Oriental Research Institute, 1924) XII, *ll*. 128–216; P. V. Kane, *History of Dharmaśāstra*, vol. V, pt. 2, pp. 1202–1204; G. Jha, *Pūrvamīmāṃsā*

in Its Sources, pp. 126–127. Śaṅkara also accepts their view (*apauruṣeya*, BSBh I,2,2, p. 163). Cf. P. Deussen, *The System of the Vedânta*, pp. 94–96.

[8]*nanu siddhānte ghaṭāder mithyātvena bādhitatvāt tajjñānaṃ kathaṃ pramāṇam? ucyate—brahmasākṣātkārānantaraṃ hi ghaṭādīnāṃ bādhaḥ,. . . na tu saṃsāradaśāyāṃ bādhaḥ,. . .*, VP, Upodghāta, 7–8.

[9]*Mīmāṃsāsūtra* I,3,3 reads:"When there is conflict [between *Veda* and *Smṛti*], the *Smṛti* should be disregarded because it is only when there is no such conflict that there is an assumption [of Vedic text in support of *Smṛti*]." Among the *Śrutis* Śaṅkara quotes the BhG most frequently and almost neglects the *Purāṇas* from which Rāmānuja cites profusely.

[10]Cf. BS II,1,36; III,2,38–40; Nakamura II, p. 414.

[11]See Upad I,16,50; 18,61; 18,75; 18,88; II,2,56, etc.

[12]BS II,1,1; 1,8; 1,11; 1,21; 1,26; II,3,32. Cf. Nakamura II, pp. 418–419.

[13]J.A.B. van Buitenen, *Rāmānuja's Vedārthasaṃgraha* (Poona: Deccan College, 1956), p. 48.

[14]Cf. R. V. de Smet, *The Theological Method of Śaṃkara* (Thesis Rome, Pontifical Universitas Gregoriana, 1953), which has not yet been published; R. V. de Smet, "Langage et connaissance de l'Absolue chez Çaṃkara" (*Revue Philosophique de Louvain*, Tome 52, 1954), pp. 31–74; J.A.B. van Buitenen, *Rāmānuja's Vedārthasaṃgraha*, pp. 48–69.

[15]*Nyāyasūtra* I,1,33 and its *Bhāṣya*. Cf. S. Chatterjee, *The Nyāya Theory of Knowledge*, p. 274.

[16]I have shown elsewhere how Śaṅkara advaitinized *Gauḍapādīyakārikā*, an extremely Buddhistic text. See S. Mayeda, "On the Author of the Māṇḍūkyopaniṣad- and the Gauḍapādīya-Bhāṣya," *Dr. V. Raghavan Felicitation Volume, The Adyar Library Bulletin*, vols. 31–32, 1967–68, pp. 73–94.

[17]Cf. R. V. de Smet, "Langage et connaissance de l'Absolue chez Çaṃkara," p. 50.

[18]It is said that there are 11 or 12 sentences called "*mahāvākya*." See Colonel G. A. Jacob, *The Vedāntasāra of Sadānanda, together with the Commentaries of Nṛsiṅhasarasvatī and Rāmatīrtha* (Bombay: Nirṇaya-Sāgar Press, 1934), pp. 155–156.

[19]*Vedāntasāra* [IX] 65; [XXIII] 166. Rāmānuja calls these sentences *śodhakavākya*. Cf. J. A. B. van Buitenen, *Rāmānuja's Vedārthasaṃgraha*, p. 58.

[20]Cf. *Le Tattvabindu de Vācaspatimiśra: Edition critique, Traduction et Introduction*, par M. Biardeau (Publications de l'Institut Français d'Indologie N°3. Pondichéry, 1956), pp. xxvi-xxvii; D. M. Datta, *The Six Ways of Knowing*, pp. 296–307; K. Kunjunni Raja, *Indian Theories of Meaning* (Adyar Library Series, vol. 91, 1963), pp. 191–227; G. Jha, *Pūrva-Mīmāṃsā in Its Sources* (Benares Hindu University, 1942), pp. 151–152.

[21]Cf. D. M. Datta, *The Six Ways of Knowing*, p. 302.

[22]Cf. *ibid.*, p. 301.

[23]Śaṅkara does not mention this method when he comments on the sentence "*tat tvam asi*" (Chānd. Up. VI, 8–16) in his *Chāndogyopaniṣadbhāṣya*. As far as I know, the Upad is the only work of his that refers to it.

[24]*anvayavyatirekanyāya*, Naiṣ III,54 (cf. *yukti*, Naiṣ II,21); *liṅga*, Naiṣ III,33; *anumāna*, Naiṣ III,34. Cf. Unters, p. 1999.

[25]Cf. Śaṅkara ad Chānd. Up. VI,8,7.

[26]Theoretically strengthening Śaṅkara's method of *Anvaya-Vyatireka*, Sureśvara points out a threefold relationship in the sentence "*tat tvam asi*": (1) the identity of referents (*sāmānādhikaraṇya*) of the two words, *tat* and *tvam*, (2) the subject-predicate relation (*viśeṣaṇaviśeṣyatā*) between the two word-meanings, and (3) the relation of indirectly indicated and indirect indicator (*lakṣyalakṣaṇasaṃbandha*) between the inner

Ātman and the two word-meanings (*sāmānādhikaraṇyaṃ ca viśeṣaṇaviśeṣyatā / lakṣyalaṣaṇa-saṃbandhaḥ padārthapratyagātmanām //* Naiṣ III,3). Sadānanda adopts it in his *Vedāntasāra* ([XXIII] 167–169). The first relationship seems to correspond to Śaṅkara's *tulyanīḍatva,* which probably means not only the grammatical apposition but also the identity of referents.

[27]This meaning seems to correspond to "*pārokṣya*" or "*parokṣatva*" (remoteness, otherness) which is regarded as the meaning of "*tat*" in Naiṣ III,77; 78 and *Vedāntasāra* [XXIII] 170.

[28]For a detailed explanation, see K. K. Raja, *Indian Theories of Meaning*, pp. 249 ff.; R. V. de Smet, "Langage et connaissance de l'Absolue chez Çaṃkara", pp. 38–40; H. Nakamura, *The Vedānta-Sāra*, pp. 160–163.

[29]"*sa*" indicates something remote either in space or time while "*ayam*" points to something near to the speaker or his time. See J. S. Speijer, *Sanskrit Syntax* (Reprint ed., Delhi: Motilal Banarsidass, 1973), pp. 202–203.

[30]Cf. *Vedāntasāra* [XXIV] 175; [XXV] 176 (= *Pañcadaśī* VII, 75); [XXVI] 183.

[31]D. M. Datta, *The Six Ways of Knowing*, pp. 319–320.

[32]P. Hacker explains Sureśvara's *anvayavyatireka* as: "Reflexion darüber, dass der Inhalt der Wörter und setzes wohlbegründet und das Gegenteil logisch unmöglich ist" (Unters, p. 1980). Cf. Naiṣ II,8–9; Unters, p. 1999, note 2.

[33]*Pañcapādikā* (Madras Government Oriental Series No. CLV), IX, pp. 345–346.

[34]Cf. J.A.B. van Buitenen, *Rāmānuja's Vedārthasaṃgraha*, pp. 62–64. The *Vākyavṛtti*, which is traditionally attributed to Śaṅkara and devoted to an interpretation of the sentence "*tat tvam asi*," compares it with "*so 'yam*" and treats it as *bhāgalakṣaṇā* (partial transfer, 48), which is a synonym for *jahadajahallakṣaṇā*. Sadānanda uses the term *bhāgalakṣaṇā* in his *Vedāntasāra*[XXXIII] 172. Appayadīkṣita styles it *bhāgatyāgalakṣaṇā* in his *Siddhāntaleśasaṃgraha* (ed. by S. S. Suryanarayana Sastri, vol. II, Madras, 1937, p. 55). The *Vākyavṛtti* shows some more non-Śaṅkaran characteristics: (1) the term *ānanda* is used as a positive characteristic of *Brahman-Ātman* (11, 12, 30, 39; 40, 53); (2) the work is attributed to Śaṅkarācārya or Śaṅkarabhagavat; and (3) the terms *jaḍa* and *ajaḍa* are used (20). As for the authorship problem of the *Vākyavṛtti*, see my article "On the Vākyavṛtti" (in Japanese. *Dr. H. Nakamura Felicitation Volume: Indian Thought and Buddhism.* Tokyo: Shunjūsha, 1973, pp. 57–69). The *Vivekacūḍāmaṇi*, which is also traditionally ascribed to Śaṅkara, refers to *jahati* (= *jahallakṣaṇā*) and *ajahati* (= *aja hallakṣaṇā*) (247) and compares the sentence with "*sa devadatto 'yam*" (248). This work is also not genuine.

[35]Cf. J.A.B. van Buitenen, *Rāmānuja's Vedārthasaṃgraha*, p. 64.

[36]The *Pañcadaśī* (I,37–47; IV, 74) adopts the *anvayavyatireka* method while using "*so 'yam*" as a sample sentence.

[37]*Tantravārtika* (Ānandāśrama S. S. No. 97), p. 447. Cf. K. Kunjunni Raja, *Indian Theories of Meaning*, p. 193.

[38]*tatpadaṃ prākṛtārthaṃ syāt tvaṃpadaṃ pratyagātmani /*
nīlotpalavad etābhyāṃ duḥkhyanātmatvavāraṇe // Naiṣ III, 2. Cf. Unters, pp. 1981–1983.

[39]Although Sureśvara does not state explicitly, he seems to be well aware of this defect for he rejects application of the two theories, *bheda* and *saṃsarga*, to the sentence "*tat tvam asi*" on the ground that "*tat*" and "*tvam*" are incompatible in their ordinary meanings and asserts that the sentence "*tat tvam asi*" expresses *avākyārtha* (non-sentence-meaning) beyond either mutual association or exclusion of the two word-meanings (Naiṣ III,23–28). He also points out the difference between the identity of *Brahman* and *Ātman* and that of the lotus and blue (*tādāmyam anayos tasmān nīlotpalavilakṣaṇam, Saṃ-*

bandhavārtika, 905). It may be due to his extraordinary devotion to his *guru* (cf. Mayeda Upad, pp. 44–49) that he did not abandon it though he knew its defect. However, Padmapāda, who was a more independent thinker than Sureśvara, could give it up. P. Hacker remarks about his personality: "*Im ganzen können wir sagen, daß Padmapāda ein schlechter Kommentator, dafür aber ein um so selbständigerer Denker ist*" (Unters, p. 1933).

[40]G. Cardona, in his article "Anvaya and Vyatireka in Indian Grammar" (*The Adyar Library Bulletin*, vols. 31–32, 1967–78, p. 347), seems to take Śaṅkara's usage as the same as that of the Grammarians. D.S. Ruegg (*Contributions à l'histoire de la philosophie linguistique indienne*. Paris, 1959, p. 32), J. F. Staal (*Philosophy East and West*, vol. 10, 1960, pp. 54–55), H. Scharfe (*Die Logik im Mahābhāṣya*. Berlin, 1961, pp. 93–96) and others have discussed *anvaya-vyatireka*, but they have taken into consideration only the usage of the term in Indian logic and grammar. It was probably P. Hacker who first pointed out its Advaitic usage (Unters, p. 1980 and pp. 1999–2000). After him J.A.B. van Buitenen, in his *Rāmānuja's Vedārthasaṃgraha* (Poona, 1956, pp. 62–64) paid some attention to it.

[41]G. Cardona, "Anvaya and Vyatireka in Indian Grammar," p. 345.

[42]Dharmarājādhvarīndra introduces *jahadajahallakṣaṇā* as the traditional view, but denies that the sentence "*tat tvam asi*" is a *lakṣaṇā* (VP IV, 27–30).

[43]See Unters, p. 1980.

[44]See Unters, p. 1983.

[45]Introduction, III,B,3, pp. 38–40.

IV. TRANSMIGRATION AND FINAL RELEASE

A. Transmigration

In a dialogue in the *Upadeśasāhasrī* (II,1,9–12) a teacher says to his pupil who wishes to get out of the ocean of transmigratory existence:

> When you are dead your body will be eaten by birds or will turn into earth right here. How then do you wish to get out of the ocean of transmigratory existence? Because if you turn into ashes on this bank of the river you cannot get across to the other side of the river. (II,1,11)

The pupil answers:

> I am different from the body. The body is born, dies, is eaten by birds, turns into earth, is destroyed by weapons, fire, and so forth, and suffers from disease and so on. I have entered this body as a bird enters a nest, by force of the merit and demerit accumulated by myself. Again and again, by force of the merit and demerit, when this body perishes, I shall enter another body as a bird enters another nest when its previous one has been destroyed. Thus I am in beginningless transmigratory existence. I have been abandoning [old] bodies which have been obtained one after another in the spheres of gods, animals, men, and hells by force of my own *karman* and I have been getting other new bodies over and over again. I am forced by my own *karman* to rotate in the incessant cycle of birth and death as in a water-wheel. I have obtained this body in the course of time. I am tired of this rotation in the wheel of transmigratory existence, so I have come to you, Your Holiness, in order to end the rotation

in the wheel of transmigratory existence. Therefore I am eternal and different from the body. The bodies come and go like a person's garments. (II,1,12)

In another dialogue a pupil, tired of transmigratory existence characterized by birth and death and seeking after final relaese, asks his Brahmin teacher:

Your Holiness, how can I be released from transmigratory existence? I am aware of the body, the senses and [their] objects; I experience pain in the waking state, and I experience it in the dreaming state after getting relief again and again by entering into the state of deep sleep again and again. Is it indeed my own nature or [is it] due to some cause, my own nature being different? If [this is] my own nature, there is no hope for me to attain final release, since one cannot avoid one's own nature. If [it is] due to some cause, final release is possible after the cause has been removed. (II,2,45)

What is transmigratory existence (*saṃsāra*)? What is its cause? This is an important problem for Śaṅkara to clear up. In the *Upadeśasāhasrī* it seems that two types of transmigratory existence are distinguished. One is the transmigratory existence characteristic of birth and death (*janmamaraṇalakṣaṇa,* Upad II,1,45) which takes place in past, present, and future existences. It is expressed in the answer of the first pupil, who is just a novice and still at the first Vedāntic stage of his training or *śravaṇa* ("hearing").[1]* It may be called "external transmigratory existence" and can be traced back to the Upaniṣadic concept of transmigration.

The other type is the one which is characterized by the waking and dreaming states (*jāgratsvapnalakṣaṇa,* Upad II,2,110; cf. I,16, 18) or by agency and experiencership (*kartṛbhoktṛtvalakṣaṇa,* Upad I,18,49; *kartṛtvabhoktṛtvalakṣaṇa,* Upad II,2,51). This type of transmigratory existence, which is shown in the answer of the second pupil, who has reached the second stage of his Vedāntic training or *manana* ("thinking"),[1]* may be called "internal transmigratory existence" which is experienced in this present world.

By the word "*saṃsāra*" is generally meant the first type of transmigration, which lays stress on the existence after death.[2] Of course it includes the second type, but the latter focuses attention chiefly on the present daily life. The author of the *Upadeśasāhasrī,*

***Notes to section IV, A are on p. 94.**

however, is primarily concerned with the second one and pays no attention to what happens after death. He is not interested in the future life, which is anyway nothing but transmigratory existence. His immediate task is to lead a seeker after final release, who is tired of transmigratory existence, to the final goal, namely the cessation of the future life. What concerns Śaṅkara most is final release (*mokṣa*) from the transmigratory existence which we are experiencing every moment in this present world.

Śaṅkara analyzes the nature of transmigratory existence as follows:

> *Karmans* [as the results of actions, good or bad, in the past existence] produce association with a body. When there is association with a body, pleasant and unpleasant things are inevitable. From these result passion and aversion [and] from them actions (*kriyā*). (Upad I,1,3)
>
> [From actions] merit (*dharma*) and demerit (*adharma*) result [and] from merit and demerit there results an ignorant man's association with a body in the same manner again. Thus this transmigratory existence rolls onward powerfully forever like a wheel. (Upad I,1,4)

The term *karman* has various meanings in Śaṅkara's works as in other Indian texts. The term in the first stanza quoted above means the results of actions, good or bad, in the past existence.[3] The term *kriyā* in the same stanza seems to be used in the sense of actions, good or bad, which require verbal, physical, and mental activities,[4] including the Vedic rituals.[5] When Śaṅkara takes up *karman* to discuss its nature and value as the means to final release (*mokṣa*), he often uses the term synonymously with *kriyā* in the sense mentioned above.

It appears from what Śaṅkara says that he conceives of transmigratory existence as the following cycle: (1) *karmans* or works as the results of actions in the previous existence—(2) one's connection with the body—(3) experience of pleasure and pain—(4) passion and aversion (= *doṣa*, Upad I,1,7)—(5) actions (*kriyā*)—(6) merit and demerit (= *karmans*). In other words, transmigratory existence is the continuously recurring process of the performance of actions (*karman* or *kriyā*) and the experience of their fruits. In this sense it is possible to replace the above cycle of transmigratory existence by another, that of doership (*kartṛtva*) and experiencership (*bhoktṛtva*):

> Their view is that the transmigratory existence exists as a real substance characterized by doership and experiencership (Upad I,18,49).

> The pupil said, "Even though I exist [eternally], still I am not the highest *Ātman*. My nature is transmigratory existence which is characterized by doership and experiencership, since it is known by sense-perception and other means of knowledge." (Upad II,2,51)

Transmigratory existence can also be described as the waking and dreaming states (Upad I,16,18; II,2,110) since the performance of actions and the experience of their fruits take place in the waking and dreaming states. The seed (*bīja*) of the two states is the state of deep sleep and consists of darkness (*tamas* = *avidyā*, Upad I,17,25; GK I, 13). Similarly, the ultimate cause of this transmigratory existence is *ajñāna* or ignorance (Upad I,1,5; II, 2,110), which is also called the controller of transmigratory existence (*niyāmaka*, Upad I,16,17).

In another place (Upad II,3,112) the cycle of transmigratory existence is described as: (1) nescience (*avidyā*)—(2) faults (*doṣa*)—(3) verbal, physical, and mental activities—(4) accumulation of *karmans* the results of which are desirable, undesirable, and mixed. In this way transmigratory existence can be traced back to ignorance or nescience.[6] This cycle reminds us of the Buddhist theory of dependent origination (*pratītyasamutpāda*), which also has nescience as its first factor.[7]

> As knowledge is the very nature of *Ātman* it is constantly applied figuratively to the intellect. And the absence of discriminating knowledge (*aviveka*) is beginningless; this and nothing else is taken to be transmigratory existence. (Upad I,16,61)

> Therefore let transmigratory existence be nothing but nescience (*avidyāmātra*) due to the absence of discriminating knowledge. Because of [the existence of] the immovable *Ātman*, transmigratory existence is always existent in *Ātman* as it were. (Upad I, 18,45)

Thus transmigratory existence is said to be nothing but the absence of discriminating knowledge (*aviveka*) concerning *Ātman* and non-*Ātman*, or to be nothing but nescience (*avidyā*) due to the absence of discriminating knowledge.

B. Final Release

Almost all systems of Indian philosophy have final release as their final goal; for the Hindus it is man's fourth and final aim, the culmination of the other three, which are *dharma* (virtue), *artha* (material gain), and *kāma* (love). However, there is considerable variety in the way it is conceived. The author of the *Upadeśasāhasrī* refers to the following various ideas of final release:

(1) It is a change of state (*avasthāntara*).

(2) It is *Ātman*'s connection (*saṃyoga*) with *Brahman*.

(3) It is *Puruṣa*'s disconnection (*viyoga*) from *Prakṛti*.

(4) It is for *Ātman* to go to *Brahman* or for *Brahman* to come to *Ātman*.

(5) It is the destruction of *Ātman*.

The first view, which includes the fifth, is refuted as follows:

> Likewise, as the nature of *Ātman* is changeless, It has no change of state, for if It had any change of state, Its destruction would no doubt occur. (Upad I,16,38)
>
> To him who [asserts that] final release is a change of state, final release is artificial; therefore, it is perishable (Upad I,16,39ab).
>
> Likewise, it is also unreasonable that [final release] is a change of state [in *Ātman*], since [It] is changeless. If there were change [in *Ātman*], [It] would have parts; consequently [It] would perish like a jar, etc. (Upad I,16,63)

The second, third, and fourth views are criticized as follows:

> It is by no means reasonable that final release is [*Ātman*'s] connection [with *Brahman*] or disconnection [from *Prakṛti*], since [Its] connection [with *Brahman*] and disconnection [from *Prakṛti*] are not permanent. And [it is by no means reasonable that final release is for *Ātman*] to go (*gamana*) [to *Brahman* or for *Brahman*] to come (*āgamana*) [to *Ātman*]. (Upad I,16,39cd-40abc)

The last view is denied:

> But one's own nature is not abandoned, since one's own nature has no cause, the others (= a change of state, etc.) indeed have their causes. One's own nature is indeed neither accepted nor abandoned by oneself [or by any others]. As [It] is the nature of all, It cannot be abandoned nor grasped, since It is not different [from anything]. Therefore, It is eternal, since [It] is not an

object and not separated [from anything]. (Upad I,16,40d-42)

Among the above five opinions the second one attracts our attention. Śaṅkara does not make clear who advocates it, but it is in line with the *Brahmasūtra*, according to which final release is the connection (*yoga*) of the individual Self with *Brahman* (BS I,1,19); when they are united, the individual Self enters into the relation of non-division (*avibhāga*) from *Brahman* (Upad IV,2, 16).[1]* It is very likely that Śaṅkara is here rejecting the traditional Vedāntic concept of final release. And it may be remarked that when he comments on the term "*yoga*" in the *Brahmasūtra*, he interprets it in the sense of identity,[2] probably in order to avoid direct contradiction of the *Brahmasūtra*.

There is no change of state in *Ātman*. There is nothing which binds *Ātman*. There is no bondage in *Ātman* (Upad I,16,57). *Ātman* is ever-free, ever-released, pure, transcendentally changeless, invariable, immortal, imperishable (Upad I,13,3). There is no ignorance (*ajñāna*) in *Ātman* which has eternal knowledge as its nature, just as there is no darkness in the sun which has light as its nature (Upad I,16,37). If *Ātman*, our true nature, is really such, then what is bondage? If there were no bondage, there would be no release from it. If so, the *Śrutis* and other scriptures, which teach us bondage and liberation from it, would be meaningless.

According to Śaṅkara, bondage is a confused idea (*bhrānti*) of the intellect and final release is the cessation thereof (Upad I,16, 59). When illumined by the light of *Ātman*, the intellect thinks that there is knowledge in itself and that there is no other knower than itself. This is the confused idea which is in the intellect (Upad I,16,60). It is the absence of the discriminating knowledge of *Ātman* and non-*Ātman*, which absence is nothing but the transmigratory existence (Upad I,16,61; 18,45). Just as when, in the twilight, a rope is mistaken for a snake, the snake, though unreal, exists in the rope by the fact of the existence of the rope until the moment when the two are differentiated, so transmigratory existence, although not real, always exists in *Ātman* by virtue of the existence of the immovable *Ātman*, but only until the two are differentiated (Upad I,18,45; 18,46).

For this reason final release is merely the attainment of the discriminating knowledge of *Ātman* and non-*Ātman*. Or, it may

*Notes to section IV, B are on p. 95.

be said that final release is to attain the view of *Brahman-Ātman* identity (Upad II,1,28; 1,29), abandoning that of *Brahman-Ātman* difference (Upad II,1,27; 1,28; 1,29; 1,42). In other words, it is the cessation of *avidyā* (Upad I,17,7) or the cessation of false superimposition (*mṛṣādhyāsa,* Upad I,16,30) upon *Ātman* which is ever-released. In this respect Śaṅkara's concept of final release is very similar to the Mahāyāna Buddhist view of *nirvāṇa,* characterized by Candrakīrti as "being of the nature of destruction of all false assumptions" (*sarvakalpanākṣayarūpa*).[3]

C. Transmigrator

The concept of transmigration presupposes the existence of the transmigrator or the subject of transmigratory existence. The author of the *Upadeśasāhasrī* mentions several different views of the transmigrator:

(1) It is the reflection (*ābhasā*) in the bearer of the "I"-notion (Upad I,18,33).
(2) It is part of the Knower (*Jña* = *Ātman*) (Upad I,18,34).
(3) It is a modification (*vikāra*) of the Knower (Upad I,18,34)
(4) It is the bearer of the "I"-notion (*ahaṃkartṛ*) which bearer is the locus of *Ātman* (Upad I,18,34).
(5) It is the independent (*svatantra*) bearer of the "I"-notion (*ahaṃkartṛ*) (Upad I,18,35).[1]*
(6) It is the individual continuity of the "I"-notion, (*ahaṃkārādisaṃtāna*) (Upad I,18,35).[2]

Among these five different opinions Śaṅkara explicitly mentions only the name of the holder of the sixth view, that is to say, the Buddhists (*saugata*). The second is the theory which is found in the *Brahmasūtra* (II,3,43) and the *Bhagavadgītā* (XV,7) and which is also asserted by Bhartṛprapañca, Śaṅkara's predecessor in Vedānta.[3] The third also is said to have generally been advocated by early Vedānta philosophers such as Bhartṛprapañca.[4]

Śaṅkara opposed all the above theories. The reflection of *Ātman* cannot be a transmigrator as in the first theory, since it is unreal (*avastu,* Upad I,18,44). Naturally the second, third, and sixth are quite unacceptable to Śaṅkara's Advaitism, although no verse

*Notes to section IV, C are on p. 95.

is specifically devoted to their refutation. The fourth and fifth are rejected on the ground that the bearer of "I"-notion is non-conscious (Upad I,18,44).

What then is his view of the transmigrator? *Ātman* cannot be a transmigrator since It is transcendentally changeless (Upad I, 18,44). Furthermore, in Śaṅkara's philosophy, *Ātman* is the only existent; there exists nothing else. Then Śaṅkara says:

> Therefore, let transmigratory existence be nothing but nescience due to the absence of discriminating knowledge. Because of [the existence of] the immovable *Ātman*, the transmigratory existence is always existent in *Ātman* as it were. (Upad I,18,45)

Ātman is ever-released and transcendentally changeless, and It does not transmigrate. Nevertheless, It is regarded as a transmigrator, but only because of *avidyā*. In fact, there exists no transmigrator anywhere, as the transmigratory existence itself is unreal. Then what is *avidyā*? This must now be considered.

D. *Avidyā*[1]*

1. Nature of *Avidyā*

As we have seen in the previous pages, our inner *Ātman* is transcendentally changeless (*kūṭastha*), constant (*nitya*), eternal, pure, nondual, unborn, free from desire, fear, and evils, and not subject to transmigration; as the Upaniṣadic passages such as "*tat tvam asi*" say, our inner *Ātman* is nothing but the universal Self, *Brahman*. However, we do in fact experience pleasure and pain, and sink into transmigratory existence in our daily life. Our actual life is just the reverse of the above-mentioned original and true state of man.

The *Upadeśasāhasrī* (II,2,45) relates the following dialogue between a teacher and his pupil, who is tired of transmigratory existence and is seeking after final release:

> Your Holiness, how can I be released from transmigratory existence? I am aware of the body, the senses and [their] objects; I experience pain in the waking state, and I experience it in the dreaming state after getting relief again and again by entering into the state of deep sleep again and again. Is it indeed my

*Notes to section IV, D begin on p. 95.

> own nature or [is it] due to some cause, my own nature being different? If [this is] my own nature, there is no hope for me to attain final release, since one cannot avoid one's own nature. If [it is] due to some cause, final release is possible after the cause has been removed.

When the teacher replies to him that transmigratory existence is due to some cause, he asks his teacher what its cause is and what his own nature is (Upad II,2,47). In reply to him the teacher asserts that the cause is *avidyā*, which is removed by knowledge (*vidyā*) (Upad II,2,48). Then the pupil asks his teacher again:

> What is that *avidyā*? And what is its object? And what is knowledge, remover of *avidyā*, by which I can realize my own nature? (Upad II,2,49)

Śaṅkara in another work gives a similar example of questions to be put to teachers:

> How does bondage come about? How does release come about? What is knowledge? What is *avidyā*?" (GBh IV, 34, p.232)

In reply to this question, the teacher says:

> Though you are the highest *Ātman* and not a transmigrator, you hold the inverted view, "I am a transmigrator." Though you are neither an agent nor an experiencer, and exist [eternally], [you hold the inverted view, "I am] an agent, an experiencer, and do not exist [eternally]"—this is *avidyā*. (Upad II,2,50)

In other words *avidyā* is the superimposition of the qualities of one thing upon another (Upad II,2,51).[2] In his *Brahmasūtrabhāṣya* Śaṅkara defines superimposition (*adhyāsa*) as "the appearance, in one thing, of another thing previously perceived, in the form of a memory." In his philosophy *avidyā* is mutual superimposition of *Ātman* and non-*Ātman* such as the body, the senses, and the inner organ (*antaḥkaraṇa, buddhi*). For example, mistaking a rope for a snake in twilight, people are frightened. Or they are delighted when they mistake mother-of-pearl for silver. In these examples, when they see a rope or mother-of-pearl, they remember in it a snake or a piece of silver which they have previously perceived. In other words, they superimpose the qualities of a snake or of silver upon a rope or a piece of mother-of-pearl. They are frightened or delighted to see a snake or silver falsely projected onto a rope or mother-of-pearl through this kind of psychological process.

Likewise, people superimpose upon *Ātman* qualities of non-*Ātman* which is merely material product of the Unevolved Name-and-Form, and they wrongly conceive of *Ātman* as different from *Brahman*. Without discriminating *Ātman* from non-*Ātman*, they continue in transmigratory existence. Ordinary people think of the bearer of "I"-notion as *Ātman*. But this is not right since the bearer of "I"-notion is merely the bearer of the notion that "I am *Ātman*" which arises by error in the inner organ, when the Pure Consciousness, *i.e.*, the nature of *Ātman*, is superimposed upon the inner organ. The *ātman* which they conceive to be *Ātman* is not true *Ātman* but the bearer of "I"-notion—that is, the inner organ upon which the nature of *Ātman* is superimposed through *avidyā*.

As is clear from the above examination, *avidyā* in Śaṅkara's view is a kind of psychological and perceptual error, or an innate psychological and epistemological defect. *Avidyā* is identical with the original error of all beings, and *mithyājñāna* (false knowledge) is a synonym of it. In the case of Śaṅkara's followers, however, *avidyā* is the material from which all forms of *mithyājñāna* come; *avidyā* is not *mithyājñāna* but the cause of *mithyājñāna*.[3] In Śaṅkara's works, *avidyā* is sometimes treated, like sexual desire (*kāma*), as a kind of psychic affection (*kleśa*), as in the Yoga system.[4] Psychic affection is regarded as a wider concept to which *avidyā* belongs. As is seen in such instances as *avidyā-kāma-karman* (*avidyā*, desire and action, Upad I,15,21; BSBh I,2,17, p. 181), *avidyā* is the first and most dangerous member of a series of psychic affections that causes the others.

However, later Advaitins materialized and raised *avidyā* to the status of a metaphysical and eternal substance or a cosmic power (*śakti*). They regarded it as the primary material cause of the universe (*upādāna*), abandoning Śaṅkara's Unevolved Name-and-Form. In order to save monism, they characterized *avidyā* as indefinable as real or unreal (*sadasadbhyām anirvacanīya-*),[5] belonging neither to the category of being nor to that of non-being. It is given a lower reality than *Brahman* and a higher reality than the unreal.

The philosophy of Śaṅkara and his followers has generally been called *māyāvāda* (illusion theory).[6] And the term *avidyā* is often taken as a synonym of *māyā* by later Advaitins. However, in Śaṅkara's philosophy the concept of *avidyā* is different from that of *māyā*, and moreover, *māyā* has little terminological significance.[7] It is peculiar to Śaṅkara that two different historical starting points are recognized in the usage of the term *māyā*: one is the *Māyā* of the Vaiṣṇavism of the *Bhagavadgītā* which means the miraculous and veiling power of the god Viṣṇu, and the other is the *māyā* of Mahāyāna Buddhism in the sense of illusion or magical illusion, to which the void or unreal appearance of things illusory is compared. The *māyā* of Śaṅkara's followers loses its theistic element and is regarded as the material cause of the universe.[8]

2. The Locus and the Object of Avidyā

When *avidyā* is accepted, another question arises: Whose is *avidyā*? What is the locus (*āśraya*) of *avidyā*? In other words, who is the transmigrator? Śaṅkara hold that everything except *Brahman-Ātman* is unreal and falsely constructed by *avidyā*. Presumably then *avidyā* should belong to *Brahman-Ātman*. If so, *Brahman-Ātman* Itself should be in transmigratory existence, and Śaṅkara's position becomes untenable. But he in fact declares that there is no ignorance (*ajñāna*) in *Ātman* which has eternal knowledge as its nature, just as there is no darkness in the sun which has light as its nature (Upad I,16,37). Śaṅkara is quite aware of the difficulty in finding a logical solution to the whole question. He says:

> If you ask, "Whose is *avidyā*?" we reply, "It belongs to you who ask." [If you ask,] "Is it not declared by the Upaniṣads, ⟨I am *Brahman*⟩?" [we reply,] "If so, you are enlightened; *avidyā* does not belong to anybody." (BSBh IV,1,3,p. 833)[9]

In the *Upadeśasāhasrī*, the same question is put to the teacher by his pupil:

> Your Holiness, is the mutual superimposition of the body and *Ātman* made by the composite of the body and so on or by *Ātman*? (Upad II,2,62; cf. Upad I,18,20)

This question appears different, but is almost the same. It may be paraphrased as: "Your Holiness, which is the locus of *avidyā*, the composite of the body and so on, or *Ātman*?" To this question the teacher answers as follows:

> What would happen to you, if [the mutual superimposition] is made by the composite of the body and so on, or if [it] is made by *Ātman*? (Upad II,2,63)

In reply to this question the pupil says:

> If I am merely the composite of the body and so on, then I am non-conscious, so I exist for another's sake; consequently, the mutual superimposition of body and *Ātman* is not effected by me. If I am the highest *Ātman* different from the composite [of the body and so on], then I am conscious, so I exist for my own sake; consequently, the superimposition [of body] which is the seed of every calamity is effected upon *Ātman* by me who am conscious. (Upad II,2,64)

Quite unexpectedly the teacher retorts:

> If you know that the false superimposition is the seed of [every] calamity, then do not make it!

In the above conversation the teacher would not make clear which of the two, the composite or *Ātman*, is responsible for the mutual superimposition. The questions and answers continue further with the teacher skillfully leading his pupil to the realization, through psychological and epistemological argument, that he himself is transcendentally changeless (Upad II,2,66–83). Finally, the pupil says:

> If so, Your Holiness, I am of the nature of transcendentally changeless and eternal perception whereas the actions of the intellect, which have the forms of [external objects] such as sound, arise and end with the result that my own nature which is perception falsely appears [as perceiver]. Then what is my fault? (Upad II,2,84)

Then the teacher concludes:

> You are right. [You] have no fault. The fault is only *avidyā* as I have said before. (Upad II,2,85)

Śaṅkara knows what the questioner is really asking, but he deliberately does not give him the sort of answer that he is actually looking for.[10] Instead of dwelling on futile arguments, he leads the questioner directly to true realization. Like Gotama Buddha who avoided metaphysical speculation because of its uselessness for *nirvāṇa*, Śaṅkara too refrains from engaging in endless and profitless speculation on *avidyā*. He is a religious teacher who has before him an aspirant actually suffering in transmigratory existence and seeking final release. Indulgence in profitless speculation is nothing but the result of *avidyā*.

Similarly, the object of *avidyā* also is not discussed by Śaṅkara in his *Brahmasūtrabhāṣya* partly because he avoids in general the use of purely theoretical concepts.[11] He does however in the *Upadeśa-sāhasrī* pay some attention to this problem.

After the teacher gives a definition of *avidyā* (Upad II,2,50), his pupil raises an objection:

> Even though I exist [eternally], still I am not the highest *Ātman*. My nature is transmigratory existence which is characterized by agency and experiencership, since it is known by sense-perception and other means of knowledge. [Transmigratory existence] has not *avidyā* as its cause, since *avidyā* cannot have one's own *Ātman* as its object.

Then, on the basis of his idea of a general rule that mutual superimposition is possible only when two things are fully known, as in the case of silver and mother-of-pearl, the pupil denies that mutual superimposition takes place between non-*Ātman* and *Ātman*, which is not fully known. His teacher rejects the proposed general rule and explains how the mutual superimposition of body and *Ātman* occurs (Upad II,2,51–54). In this discussion the teacher affirms only the possibility of the mutual superimposition of *Ātman* and non-*Ātman*. It is not possible for us to judge whether Śaṅkara affirms or rejects the pupil's statement quoted above that *avidyā* cannot have one's own *Ātman* as its object. As in the case of the locus of *avidyā*, Śaṅkara refrains from giving a clear-cut reply to the problem of the object of *avidyā*, although he is well aware that it is theoretically important.

However, even Śaṅkara's personal pupils were already unwilling to shelve the question, and Sureśvara, one of them, further develops the concept of *avidyā* (= *ajñāna*):

> And that *ajñāna* cannot be self-existent. Therefore, it must be admitted that it is *ajñāna* of someone about some object.
> *tac cājñānaṃ svātmamātranimittaṃ na saṃbhavatīti kasyacit kasmiñścit viṣaye bhavatīty abhyupagantavyam.* (Naiṣ III, Introduction)

In other words, Sureśvara stresses the locus and the object of *avidyā* and logically concludes that *Ātman* is both the locus and the object of *avidyā*. His view is accepted by Sarvajñātman, and further by Prakāśātman of the Vivaraṇa school of the Avaita Vedānta.

On the other hand, Maṇḍanamiśra, the author of the *Brahmasiddhi*,[12] assertes that the locus of *avidyā* is *jīva*, the individual *ātman*, and that the object of *avidyā* is *Brahman*, which is concealed by it. His view is accepted by Vācaspatimiśra, the author of the *Bhā-*

matī, and forms the fundamental standpoint of the Bhāmatī school of the Advaita Vedānta. This is one of the basic differences between the two schools.

3. A Theoretical Defect in *Avidyā*

Certainly the most crucial problem which Śaṅkara left for his followers is that of *avidyā*. If the concept of *avidyā* is logically analyzed, it would lead the Vedānta philosophy toward dualism or nihilism and uproot its fundamental position.

As we have seen above, *avidyā* is mutual superimposition (*anyonyādhyāsa*) between *Ātman* and non-*Ātman*. If so, *avidyā* would come to be logically untenable. Śaṅkara himself is aware of this fact and points it out in the pupil's question to his teacher:

> Is it not experienced that the thing which is superimposed [upon something else] through *avidyā* does not exist [in the latter]?—for example, silver [does not exist] in a mother-of-pearl nor a person in a tree-trunk nor a snake in a rope? . . . Likewise, if the body and *Ātman* are always mutually superimposed in the form of constantly non-distinct notions, then they cannot exist in each other at any time. Silver, etc., which are superimposed through *avidyā* upon mother-of-pearl, etc., do not exist [in the latter] at any time in any way and *vice versa*; likewise the body and *Ātman* are mutually superimposed through *avidyā*; this being the case, it would follow as the result that neither the body nor *Ātman* exists. And this is not acceptable, since it is the theory of the Nihilists. . . . For this reason the body and *Ātman* are not superimposed upon each other through *avidyā*." (Upad II,2,55)

With the above objection the pupil has put forward a cogent argument striking at the very basis of the Advaita doctrine. If mutual superimposition is accepted, not only the body but *Ātman* as well would come to be non-existent. The teacher well understands what the pupil wants to say but does not answer directly. Deliberately side-stepping the sharp thrust of the question, the teacher asks instead what the relationship is between the body and *Ātman*. The pupil answers that they are permanently connected with each other like the interconnected bamboo and pillars of the structure of a house. The teacher rejects this by means of Sāṃkhyan arguments and then concludes:

> Not so; because it is accepted that *Ātman*, like space, is by nature

not composite. Although *Ātman* exists as connected with nothing, it does not follow that the body and other things are without *Ātman*, just as, although space is connected with nothing, it does not follow that nothing has space. Therefore, there would not arise the fault that [I shall] arrive at the Nihilists' position. (Upad II,2,58)

Thus the teacher does not give any definite answer to the point raised by his pupil that a further examination of *avidyā* as mutual superimposition results in nihilism. As far as I know, Śaṅkara's own pupils did not take up this problem; it was Sarvajñātman who first tired to treat it.

Sarvajñātman is traditionally said to be a pupil of Sureśvara.[13] In his *Saṃkṣepaśārīraka* he has further developed the concept of *avidyā* on the basis of the ideas of his teacher and of Padmapāda, and tried to tackle the problems left unsolved by Śaṅkara.

In Sarvajñātman's opinion *avidyā* is beginningless (*anādi*, Sś I, 454); it is not simply a negative entity like the absence of knowledge but a positive entity (*bhāvarūpa*, Sś I,320–322). He identifies it with *māyā* (Sś II,190; 191; III,94; 105; 108–9). Following his teacher's opinion that *Ātman* is both the locus and the object of *avidyā* (Sś I,316; 318; 319; III,15), he rejects Maṇḍana's view (Sś II,174). His *avidyā* is the cause (*nimitta*) of superimposition (*adhyāsa*, Sś I,27). He says:

The idea that by [accepting] mutual superimposition, this world would turn out to be without a basis and void, is a great confusion of thought, arising out of the obstinacy of certain "Great Men" who are [actually] in a total ignorance; thus it has nothing to support it

. . . . *mahān saṃbhramaḥ*/
keṣāṃcin mahatām anūnatamasāṃ nirbandhamātrāśrayād
anyonyādhyasane nirāspadam idaṃ śūnyaṃ jagat syād iti // Sś I,31bcd

To justify his statement, he proposes two new technical terms: one is *adhiṣṭhāna* and the other is *ādhāra*.[14] *Adhiṣṭhāna* is the object of *moha* (= *avidyā*) with its products (*savilāsamohaviṣaye vastuni*, Sś I,31. Cf. Sś I,32). *Avidyā* has two faculties: one is an obscuring faculty (*āvaraṇaśatki*) and the other is a projecting faculty (*vibhramaśakti* = *vikṣepaśakti*, Sś I,20). *Avidyā* works on its object, *i.e.*, *Ātman*, and projects it in various forms illusorily. It is *adhiṣṭhāna* that is *Brahman-Ātman*, the object of *avidyā*. On the other hand *ādhāra* is the locus of superimposition (*ādhāre 'dhyasanasya vastuni*, Sś I,31). In the case of the false knowledge of a piece of mother-of-pearl ("This is silver"), the mother-of-pearl is *adhiṣṭhāna* and the *ādhāra* is the referent of the term "this" which is the locus of superimposition.

The *adhiṣṭhāna* is essentially different from *ādhāra*. If they were to be the same, or if a pair of things unreal were to be mutually superimposed, this world would indeed be void without any substrate (Sś I,32; 33), but his position is that if two things, one real and the other unreal, are mutually superimposed,[15] the above criticism does not hold good (Sś I,33). Thus Sarvajñātman, introducing two new concepts *adhiṣṭhāna* and *ādhāra* into the system, has tried to demonstrate the reality of the mother-of-pearl as *adhiṣṭhāna*, *i.e.*, *Ātman*, translating mutual superimposition between a mother-of-pearl or *adhiṣṭhāna* and silver into one between "this" or *ādhāra* and silver.

However, as I have discussed elsewhere,[16] Sarvajñātman's solution is not satisfactory, and if we examine the nature of "this" more closely, we find that his position leads into *regress ad infinitum*. He succeeded to some extent in making the theory of mutual superimposition look logically tenable, but he could not demonstrate any real solution. After him arguments about *avidyā* continued, but, as far as I know, no one attempted to solve this problem.

E. The Means to Final Release

According to Śaṅkara's concepts of transmigratory existence and final release, the means to final release must necessarily be something which leads the aspirant to the cessation of nescience, the nature of which is the mutual superimposition of *Ātman* and non-*Ātman*.

Action (*karman*) arises from the innate conviction "I am an agent. This is mine" (Upad I,1,13), which results from a false superimposition of non-*Ātman* —such as the body, senses, and inner organ—upon the actionless *Ātman*. As is clearly shown in the above cycle of transmigratory existence, action has as its cause ignorance (Upad I,11,15) which has to be removed in favor of final release. With regard to rituals, Śaṅkara says:

> . . . it is prohibited [by the *Śrutis*] to hold the view that [*Ātman*] is different [from *Brahman*]; use of the rituals is [made] in the sphere of [the view] that [*Ātman*] is different [from *Brahman*]; and the sacred thread and the like are requisites for the rituals. Therefore, it should be known that the use of rituals and their requisites is prohibited, if the identity [of *Ātman*] with the highest *Ātman* is realized, since [the use of] rituals and their requisites such as the sacred thread is contradictory to the realization of the identity [of *Ātman*] with the highest *Ātman*. [The use of] rituals and their requisites such as the sacred thread is indeed enjoined upon a transmigrator [but] not upon one who holds the view of the identity [of *Ātman*] with the highest *Ātman*, and the difference [of *Ātman*] from It is merely due to the view that [*Ātman*] is different [from *Brahman*]. (Upad II,1,30)

Use of all the rituals and their requisites such as the sacred thread is made by those who hold that *Ātman* is different from *Brahman*. The compound *avidyā-kāma-karman* is sometimes used in Śaṅkara's works:[1]* *avidyā* causes *kāma* (desire) from which *karman* (action) results.[2] Action does not contradict nescience but is of the same nature. Therefore, action cannot be the means to final release. Furthermore, any result of action is not final release but something non-eternal (Upad I,17,8), either to be produced, to be obtained, to be changed, or to be purified (Upad I,17,50).[3] Thus action of any kind should be abandoned.

> [The *Śrutis*] would not declare that [*Ātman*] is by nature unrelated to the rituals, by nature unconnected with the class and other factors of rituals, if it were not desirable that the rituals and such requisites of the rituals as the sacred thread be abandoned completely. Therefore, the seeker after final release should abandon the rituals together with their requisites since [they] are contradictory to the view of the identity [of *Ātman*] with the highest *Ātman*. (Upad II,1,32)

> Because of the incompatibility [of knowledge with action] a man who knows thus, being possessed of this knowledge, cannot perform action. For this reason action should be renounced by a seeker after final release. (Upad I,1,15; cf. Upad I,1,21; 18,222)

*Notes to section IV, E are on p. 96.

Thus there is no hope of attaining immortality through action, which has ignorance as its cause (Upad I,11,5).

According to Śaṅkara, it is only knowledge of *Brahman* and nothing else that by nature contradicts knowledge. Only the knowledge of the identity of *Ātman* with *Brahman* can be the means to final release:

> Only knowledge [of *Brahman*] can destroy ignorance; action cannot [destroy it] since [action] is not incompatible [with ignorance]. Unless ignorance is destroyed, passion and aversion will not be destroyed. (Upad I,1,6)

Knowledge of *Brahman* is called the supreme purification (*paramaṃ pāvanam*, Upad I,16,71), since it enables the aspirant to be free from every kind of evil. Śaṅkara enthusiastically advises the aspirant to be firmly established in the path of knowledge (*jñāna-patha*):

> Thus both the false assumptions based upon dualism and the views that *Ātman* does not exist have been rejected through reasoning; seekers after final release, being free from doubts which arise from the views of others, become firm in the path of knowledge. (Upad I,16,68)

Knowledge of *Brahman* is incompatible not only with ignorance but also with action. The realization of the nature of *Ātman* comes about only when there is cessation of actions (Upad I,17,48). When actions have been renounced, the nature of *Ātman* is realized. The renunciation of all actions becomes the means for discriminating the meaning of the word "Thou" in the sacred sentence "Thou art That" (Upad I,18,219). From this viewpoint Śaṅkara also vehemently refutes *jñānakarmasamuccayavāda*, the opinion that knowledge must be combined with the performance of actions in order to attain final release.[4]

> [Objection]: Should not [certain] action too be always performed while life lasts? For this [action], being concomitant with knowledge [of *Brahman*], leads to final release. Action, like knowledge [of *Brahman*, should be adhered to], since [both of them] are equally enjoined [by the *Śrutis*]. As the *Smṛti*[5] also [lays it down that] transgression [results from the neglect of action, so], action should be performed by seekers after final release. [If you say that] as knowledge [of *Brahman*] has perma-

> nent fruit, and so does not depend upon anything else, [we reply:] Not so! Just as the *Agniṣṭoma* sacrifice, though it has permanent fruit, depends upon things other than itself, so, though knowledge [of *Brahman*] has permanent fruit, it always depend upon action. Thus some people think.
>
> [Reply]: [We say] Not so, because action is incompatible [with knowledge]. In fact action is incompatible with knowledge [of *Brahman*], since [it] is associated with misconception [of *Ātman*]. And knowledge [of *Brahman*] is declared here [in the Vedānta] to be the view that *Ātman* is changeless. (Upad I,1,8–12)

Knowledge of *Brahman* depends upon the real (*vastvadhīna*), whereas the Vedic injuction to perform actions depends upon an agent (*kartradhīna*, Upad I,1,13) whose very existence is a result of superimposition of non-*Ātman* upon *Ātman* through nescience. Śaṅkara further says:

> Because of the incompatibility [of knowledge with action], therefore, one who knows so, being possessed of this knowledge, cannot perform action. For this reason action should be renounced by a seeker after final release. (Upad I,1,15)
>
> Those who know, "I am Brahman" (Bṛh. Up. I,4,10) and [yet think], "I am doer and experiencer" are deprived of both knowledge and action; they are materialists (*nāstika*) without a doubt. (Upad I, 11,8)

Thus Śaṅkara will not allow that action has any value as a means to final release, and even *jñānakarmasamuccayavāda* is also rejected by him. From his philosophical standpoint even ethical or moral actions are still based upon nescience and must therefore be rejected, since their incompatibility with knowledge must hinder the aspirant in attaining knowledge of *Brahman*. When Śaṅkara explains how one knows one's own *Ātman* from a sentence of the *Śrutis*, he relies upon the well-known illustration of the ten boys who crossed a river. Counting the party after the crossing to make sure none was missing, the leader failed to count himself and thought that one boy was mising. But when he was told, "You are the tenth," he realized immediately that he himself was the tenth.[6] In like manner one attains true knowledge of *Brahman-Ātman* from such sentences of the *Śrutis* as "Thou art That." This is a logical conclusion from Śaṅkara's position.

F. Śaṅkara's View of Ethics

As we have seen in the previous section, Śaṅkara accepts the knowledge of *Brahman* as the only means to final release, rejecting action in any form. In fact, however, Śaṅkara does not one-sidedly teach only the knowledge of *Brahman*, but here and there in his works recommends certain ethical and moral actions. In the *Upadeśasāhasrī*, though he says that knowledge is the realization of the identity of *Brahman* and *Ātman* and states that this is affirmed most emphatically in the *Śruti*, he goes on to prescribe: (1) the observance of abstention (*yama*), which consists of abstinence from injury (*ahiṃsā*), from falsehood (*satya*), from theft (*asteya*), from incontinence (*brahmacarya*) and from possessions (*aparigraha*); (2) austerities (*tapas*); (3) the concentration of the mind (*samādhāna*) and (4) the emaciation of the body (*dehaviśoṣaṇa*); as well as (5) the performance of the regular permanent rites (*nityakarman*) and sacrifices (*yajña*) (Upad I,17,21–23). He rejects the opinion of those who assert *jñānakarmasamuccayavāda* that *prasaṃkhyāna* meditation should be observed until *Ātman* is apprehended (Upad I,18,9 ff.), but in the chapter entitled "Parisaṃkhyāna" in the *Upadeśasāhasrī* (II,3,112–116) he prescribes *parisaṃkhyāna* meditation for those seekers after final release who are devoting themselves to the destruction of their acquired merits and demerits (*puṇyāpuṇya*) and do not wish to accumulate more of them. And he advises the wise man to perform *parisaṃkhyāna*.[1]* Whatever difference Śaṅkara may recognize between *prasaṃkhyāna* and *parisaṃkhyāna*—a difference which he does not explain in his writings—it is unquestionable that both of them are not knowledge but a kind of action. If the Upad were a commentary on some text like the *Bhagavadgītā*, which stresses *karmayoga* (performance of actions) and *bhaktiyoga* (loving faith),[2] it might have been that Śaṅkara reluctantly had to recommend action, in order to conform to his text. But the *Upadeśasāhasrī* is not a commentary on any text. Thus when Śaṅkara insists on a complete renunciation of action and at the same time recommends the aspirant to perform some action, this must certainly be an expression of his own view.

Thus our examination has revealed that Śaṅkara's treatment of

*Notes to section IV, F begin on p. 96.

action is self-contradictory. Bhāskara (c. 750–c. 800) in his own *Gītābhāṣya* (III, 4) has already severely criticized Śaṅkara's self-contradiction in this respect.[3] How should we understand this self-contradiction? It is not likely that Śaṅkara contradicts himself unknowingly. It can hardly be other than intentional. For what purpose does he knowingly sacrifice logical and theoretical consistency?

One of the most influential schools of philosophy at Śaṅkara's time was the Mīmāṃsā to which belonged Kumārila (c. 650–c. 700) and Prabhākara (c. 700).[4] Maṇḍanamiśra in particular (c. 670-c. 720),[5] who must have been a younger contemporary of Kumārila and Prabhākara and an elder contemporary of Śaṅkara, was recognized by Advaitins and Mīmāṃsakas both as a high authority on the Mīmāṃsā. As the author of the *Brahmasiddhi* he played a significant role in the history of the Advaita doctrine.[6] Sureśvara, who was the most faithful exponent of Śaṅkara's philosophy and seems to have attacked Maṇḍanamiśra's position,[7] is traditionally said to have been converted from the Mīmāṃsā school to Advaita by Śaṅkara.[8] Judging from Śaṅkara's writings, the Mīmāṃsā was unquestionably a chief target of his severe attack.

Radhakrishnan remarks: "His (= Śaṅkara's) denial of the adequacy of works to salvation is a reaction against the exaggerated emphasis which Mīmāṃsakas place on Vedic ritualism." This is of course true, and by this theory "Śaṅkara's unnecessary emphasis on the futility of the *karmamārga* for the final end of perfection"[9] may be explicable. However, this theory is not enough to explain why Śaṅkara dares to contradict himself with regard to the problem of action.

Eliot Deutsch explains why Indian philosophy in general, and Advaita Vedānta in particular, "turns its back on all theoretical and practical considerations of morality and, if not unethical, is at least 'a-ethical' in character" and points out two reasons: one is that "the entire Advaita system is permeated with value questions, and in such a way, that an independent, separate treatment of them is unnecessary"; the other is that the neglect of ethics, which is quite purposive, is "based on the belief that *Brahman* transcends all moral distinctions and that man, being essentially not different from *Brahman*, is likewise in his essence 'beyond good and evil.' "[10] Neither does this theory seem to be satisfactory for explaining the above-mentioned self-contradiction. We must adopt another point of view.

The Mīmāṃsā school had experienced significant development and changes in its doctrine by Śaṅkara's time. Jaimini (200–100 B.C.) and Śabarasvāmin (c. 550) did not pay attention to the problem of final release, but later writers of the school had to take it into consideration. Jaimini and Śabarasvāmin pointed out only the way to life in heaven and stressed the performance of the Vedic rites. Kumārila,[11] Prabhākara,[12] and Maṇḍanamiśra[13] advocated their respective *jñānakarmasamuccayavāda* theories about the way to final release. Though not much is known of theories concerning this problem which were proposed by Vedāntins before Śaṅkara, the *Brahmasūtra* itself stands in the tradition of *jñānakarmasamuccayavāda*. Ṭaṅka (Brahmānandin)[14] and Bhartṛprapañca[15] were *jñānakarmasamuccayavādins*. Bhāskara also expounded *jñānakarmasamuccayavāda*, probably soon after Śaṅkara's death. It is highly probable that *jñānakarmasamuccayavāda* in many varieties was prevalent among Mīmāṃsakas and Vedāntins while Śaṅkara was active. Śaṅkara, therefore, seems to have taught his teachings to, or fought against, mostly thinkers holding various types of *jñānakarmasamuccayavāda*. The Sāṃkhya had already lost their vitality and Buddhism also was on the wane.

In the *Upadeśasāhasrī* (II,1,2), Śaṅkara sets forth the following qualifications required in a seeker before he is initiated into the knowledge of *Brahman-Ātman* by his teachers[16]:

1. He must be dispassionate toward all passing objects attainable as they are by means other than knowledge.
2. He must have abandoned the desire for sons, wealth, and worlds and reached the state of a *paramahaṃsaparivrājaka* ascetic.[17]
3. He must be endowed with tranquillity, self-control, and the like.
4. He must be possessed of the qualities of a student, which are well known from the scriptures.
5. He must be a Brahmin[18] who is internally and externally pure.
6. His caste, profession, behavior, knowledge, and family must have been examined.
7. He must approach his teacher in the prescribed manner.

Judging from the above requirements, it is a prerequisite that those who come to Śaṅkara for his instruction have some knowledge about *Ātman* and *Brahman* and have fulfilled, or are at least seriously practicing, a number of ethical and moral laws prescribed by the *Dharmaśāstras* for their particular castes, stages of life (*āśrama*), and the like.[19] Some of the candidates must have been Mīmāṃsakas, others Vedāntins following *jñānakarmasamuccaya-vāda*, and yet others Yogins or followers of different creeds.

Thus when the aspirant started receiving Śaṅkara's teaching of the knowledge of *Brahman-Ātman*, his burning concern must previously have been with the performance of action; he might also have acquired, from the study of the *Veda*, some knowledge of *Brahman* and *Ātman* different from Śaṅkara's. His attachment to action, which is based on a conviction of *Brahman* and *Ātman* as separate, must sometimes have been too strong for him to understand Śaṅkara's doctrine of the complete identity of *Brahman* and *Ātman*. In the Prose Part of the *Upadeśasāhasrī* Śaṅkara illustrates his teaching method, using the example of a pupil and his teacher. The pupil is a Brahmin's son who has become a *paramahaṃsaparivrājaka* ascetic (Upad II,1,10). After he has been taught, by means of many *Śruti* and *Smṛti* passages, that he (= *Ātman*) is identical with *Brahman* and that he himself is free from caste, family, and purificatory ceremonies, he put to his teacher the objection:

> I am one [and] He is another; I am ignorant, experience pleasure and pain, am bound and a transmigrator [whereas] he is essentially different from me, the god not subject to transmigration. By worshipping Him with oblation, offerings, homage and the like through the [performance of] the actions prescribed for [my] class and stage of life, I wish to get out of the ocean of transmigratory existence. How am I He? (Upad II,1,25)

It is highly probable that this was a typical pupil of the time, and Śaṅkara's teaching required such pupils to make a total change in their views of life. In such a case one of the most effective teaching methods was to give them a great shock by the radical negation of action, which they had been considering their most important duty and which is based on the view that *Ātman* is different from *Brahman*. They then could be led to the realization of the oneness of *Brahman* and *Ātman*. Śaṅkara's drastic denial of action and of *jñānakarmasamuccayavāda* was apparently effective in shocking his pupils into an insight into the true nature of *Ātman*.

Śaṅkara's view is essentially different from antinomianism in Christianity.[20] He does not intend to nullify the moral laws through his teaching of the knowledge of *Brahman* and *Ātman*. In various places he affirms, though admittedly with reservations, that the performance of actions, including the observance of the moral laws, is indispensable for final release. In the *Upadeśasāhasrī* (I,17,44) Śaṅkara says that action can take place only before acquisition of knowledge of *Ātman*, since a firm belief that "Thou art That" removes any notions of belonging to a certain caste and so on, which are prerequisites to the performance of action. This statement is indeed negative, but it implies paradoxically the positive meaning that action should be performed before one can achieve cessation of nescience. Before the cessation of nescience, abstinence from injury (*ahiṃsā*) and other abstentions (*yama*), the regular rites, and even sacrifice (*yajña*) should be observed to purify the mind, since knowledge appears when the mind becomes pure like a mirror (Upad I,17,22). According to Śaṅkara, the cessation of nescience is nothing but final release. Practically speaking, therefore, the aspirant should perform actions until his attainment of final release.

Śaṅkara explains what teachers should do when they have begun to teach knowledge to their pupils and see signs that they do not grasp it. The causes which prevent them from attaining knowledge are demerit, worldly laxity, absence of firm preliminary learning concerning the discrimination between eternal and noneternal things, care about what other people think, pride of caste, and the like. He instructs teachers to remove those causes by means of non-anger (*akrodha*), abstinence from injury and other abstentions, and the observances (*niyama*), which consist of purity (*śauca*), contentment (*saṃtoṣa*), self-mortification (*tapas*), study (*svādhyāya*), and devotion to the lord (*īśvarapraṇidhāna*). He considers these means to be compatible with knowledge, though they are unquestionably actions.[21] And he further tells them to help their pupils properly achieve the virtues, such as modesty (*amānitva*), which are described as means to attain knowledge (Upad II,1,4–5). Moreover, he prescribes that teachers should be endowed with tranquillity (*śama*), self-control (*dama*), compassion (*dayā*), kindness (*anugraha*), and the like and that they should lead blameless lives (*abhinnavṛtta*), free from faults such as deceit (*dambha*), pride (*darpa*), trickery (*kuhaka*), wickedness (*śāṭhya*), fraud (*māyā*), jealousy (*mātsarya*), falsehood (*anṛta*), egotism (*ahaṃkāra*), self-interest (*mamatva*); their knowledge is used for the purpose of helping others (Upad II,1,6).

In his famous work *Mysticism East and West,* Rudolf Otto attempts to get to the heart of mysticism by comparing Eastern and Western mysticism with reference to Śaṅkara and Meister Eckhart. After showing striking similarity between the two great masters, he turns to the differences between them, and remarks:

> It is because the background of Śaṅkara's teaching is not Palestine but India that his mysticism has no ethic. It is not immoral, it is a-moral. The Mukta, the redeemed, who has attained ekatā or unity with the eternal Brahman, is removed from all works, whether good or evil. Works bind man. He leaves all activity and reposes in oneness. . . . With Eckhart it is entirely different. . . . His wonderfully liberating ethic develops with greater strength from the ground of his mysticism.[22]

The same criticism has been made of Śaṅkara's ethical views as well as the ethics of Indian philosophy in general and the Advaita Vedānta in particular. S. Radhakrishnan devotes a chapter of his *Indian Philosophy* to the defense of Śaṅkara's position against some objections put to him by P. Deussen and other Western scholars.[23] In his *Advaita Vedānta: A Philosophical Reconstruction,* Eliot Deutsch also takes up this problem for consideration and gives a favorable interpretation of the ethics of the Advaita Vedānta.[24]

Śaṅkara's teaching is neither "immoral" nor "a-moral." Moral and ethical perfection is not his chief topic, not because he denies it nor because he is indifferent to it, but because he considers it to be a matter of course. He says:

> Having been awakened from the ignorance as to the meanings of the words, and seeking for the realization of the meaning of the sentence, how should one come to follow his desires, when renunciation etc. have been enjoined [on such a man]? (Upad I,18,226)[25]
>
> Even if suffering from hunger, one certainly does not want to

take poison. Nobody whose hunger has been appeased by sweet food knowingly wants to take poison unless he is a fool. (Upad I,18,229)

These words clearly show Śaṅkara's view of ethics. His radical denial of actions by means of a penetrating analysis is the most effective way to lead to a higher level those who are suffering in transmigratory existence, who are already fully committed to the ethical and moral laws and other requirements for admission to Śaṅkara's teachings. He brings about in his pupils a sudden revolutionary change of world view by uprooting the foundation of their present convictions, so that they may easily be led into a totally new vision. He says:

. . . when knowledge is firmly grasped, it conduces to one's own beatitude (*śreyas*) and to the continuity [of knowledge]. And the continuity of knowledge is helpful to people as a boat is helpful to one wishing to get across a river. (Upad II,1,3)

As in the case of other great religious teachers like the Buddha, Śaṅkara is primarily concerned with the salvation of people who are suffering from transmigratory existence here in the present world and not with the establishment of a consistent philosophical or ethical system.[26] Śaṅkara's view of ethics may be vague or self-contradictory, but this is because its real aim is the highest possible effectiveness in leading his pupils to the final goal.

Notes to Introduction IV, A

[1]Preface, p. xi.

[2]Cf. P. Deussen, *The System of the Vedânta*, pp. 357 ff.; Nakamura II, pp. 483–489.

[3]*Karman* is said to constitute the efficient cause (*nimittakāraṇa*) for the origination of a new body (BSBh III,1,2, p. 597).

[4]*Kriyā* here corresponds to *vāṅmanaḥkāyapravṛtti* (verbal, mental, and physical activities) in Upad II,3,112.

[5]Cf. The expression *kriyāḥ sarvā dārāgnyādhānapūrvikāḥ* in the immediately preceding stanza (Upad I,1,2).

[6]Cf. BSBh I,1,1, p. 41; II,3,50, p. 561; GBh XVIII,12, p. 691; PBh, Introduction, 4, p. 4; VBh, Introduction, 1, p. 61. *Ajñāna*, in Śaṅkara's usage of the term, is almost but not entirely synonymous with *avidyā*. His concept of *avidyā* is wider than that of *ajñāna*.

[7]In his *Naiṣ* (I,1) and *Vārtika* on Śaṅkara's *Taittirīyopaniṣadbhāṣya* (I,7 and II,125), Sureśvara also gives a similar causal cycle. See J. M. van Boetzelaer, *Sureśvara's Taittirīyopaniṣadbhāṣyavārtikam Translated into English with an Introduction and Notes* (Leiden: E. J. Brill, 1971), pp. 7–8.

Notes to Introduction IV, B

[1]Cf. Nakamura II, pp. 489–493.

[2]*tadātmanā yogas tadyogaḥ, tadbhāvāpattiḥ*, BSBh I,1,19, p. 124.

[3]*sarvakalpanākṣayarūpa, Prasannapadā* (Louis de La Vallée Poussin, *Mūlamadhyamakakārikā de Nāgārjuna, avec la Prasannapadā, commentaire de Candrakīrti*. St-Pétersbourg, 1903–1913 [Bibl. Buddhica, IV]), p. 524, line 6.

Notes to Introduction IV, C

[1]Ānandajñāna and Rāmatīrtha attribute this opinion to the Bhāṭṭa school of Mīmāṃsā.

[2]According to Ānandajñāna and Rāmatīrtha this is the theory of the Prāsaṅgikas.

[3]Cf. Nakamura III, p. 172. This theory is refuted in GK III,7.

[4]See Śaṅkara *ad* Bṛh.Up. IV,3,7, p. 560; Nakamura III, pp. 632–633. This view is rejected in GK III,7.

Notes to Introduction IV, D

[1]I have already examined Śaṅkara's *avidyā* in detail in connection with the authorship problem of the Upad in Mayeda Upad, pp. 23–30. Here I have tried to avoid overlapping with that essay as far as possible.

[2]Cf. BSBh, Introduction, p. 19; Eigen, pp. 248–249; Mayeda Upad, pp. 23–24.

[3]Eigen, pp. 248–249. Cf. S. Mayeda, "The Authenticity of the Bhagavadgītābhāṣya Ascribed to Śaṅkara," pp. 159–160. As I have shown in Mayeda Upad, pp. 24–25, the term *mithyājñāna* is used only once in the Upad (II,3,116), and it is difficult to determine its exact meaning there. But it should be so interpreted as in the BSBh since the Upad can safely be attributed to Śaṅkara (see Mayeda Upad, pp. 22–64).

[4]*avidyādīn kleśān*, BSBh IV,2,7, p. 861. Cf. *Yogasūtra* II,3; Eigen, p. 249; Mayeda Upad, pp. 25–26.

[5]See Introduction, III, A, 2, p. 22; Mayeda Upad, pp. 29–30 and pp. 32–34.

[6]For example, *History of Indian Literature by M. Winternitz*, tr. by S. Jhā, vol. III, pt. II (Delhi: Motilal Banarsidass, 1967), p. 493. He explains it as "the Māyā-theory, according to which the world is merely a deceptive vision, an illusion (*māyā*)" (*ibid*, p. 483). Cf. Mayeda Upad, p. 35.

[7]Cf. Y. Kanakura, *A Study of the Vedānta Philosophy* (in Japanese. Tokyo: Iwanami Shoten, 1932), pp. 225–286; Eigen, pp. 268–269; Mayeda Upad, p. 35.

[8]Cf. Eigen, pp. 271–272; Mayeda Upad, pp. 61–62.

[9]A similar dialogue is also seen in GBh XIII,2, p. 537.

[10]Cf. Eigen, pp. 254–256; D. H. H. Ingalls, "Śaṅkara on the Question: Whose Is Avidyā?" *Philosophy East and West*, vol. 3 (1953), no. 1, pp. 69–72.

[11]Eigen, pp. 258–259.

[12]Cf. S. Kuppuswami Sastri, *Brahmasiddhi by Ācārya Maṇḍanamiśra with Comm. by Śaṅkhapāṇi* (Madras Government Oriental Manuscripts Series no. 4, 1937), p. xxviii and pp. 10–11; S. Dasgupta, *A History of Indian Philosophy*, vol. II, pp. 89–90 and pp. 101–102.

[13]It is generally thus admitted according to Rāmatīrtha, a commentator on Sś (cf. S. Dasgupta, *A History of Indian Philosophy*, vol. II, p. 111) but not unanimously (cf. N. Veezhinathan, *The Saṁkṣepaśārīraka of Sarvajñātman Critically Edited with Introduction, English Translation, Notes and Indexes*. Madras: University of Madras, 1972, pp. 4–5).

[14]Cf. S. Dasgupta, *A History of Indian Philosophy*, vol. II, pp. 113–114.

[15]Cf. BSBh, Introduction, p. 9. He demonstrates that superimposition must be mutual and not one-sided (Sś I,34–38).

[16]S. Mayeda, "The Development of the Concept of *Avidyā* in the Advaita Vedānta System: Śaṅkara and Sarvajñātman." *Journal of Indian and Buddhist Studies* 24–1 (1975), pp. 78–83.

Notes to Introduction IV, E

[1]For example, Upad I,15,21; BSBh I,2,17, p. 181; GBh XIV, 3, p. 589; PBh IV,9, 67, p. 60; Śaṅkara *ad* Muṇḍ. Up. III,1,11. Cf. Eigen, p. 249.

[2]Cf. S. Radhakrishnan, *Indian Philosophy*, vol. 2, p. 623.

[3]Cf. T. M. P. Mahadevan, *The Philosophy of Advaita* (Madras: Ganesh & Co., 1957), pp. 257–258.

[4]Cf. S. Dasgupta, *A History of Indian Philosophy*, vol. II, pp. 99–100.

[5]Manu XI,41–71, especially XI,44.

[6]For this illustration, see Upad I,12,3. and note 2, p. 129.

Notes to Introduction IV, F

[1]*Parisaṃkhyāna* is mentioned as something which Śaṅkara recommends in PBh I,5, 29, p. 24, as well.

[2]Rudolf Otto remarks about Śaṅkara's GBh as follows: "With an almost appalling persistency and obduracy Śaṅkara uses all the powers of his dialectic and his penetrating intellect to cloud and twist the clear meaning of the Gītā which praises the deed dedicated to Īśvara, and to reduce this action to a lower level than the stage of complete cessation of all willing and doing." (*Mysticism East and West*, tr. by B. L. Bracey and R. C. Payne. New York: Collier Books, 1962, p. 225).

[3]Cf. S. Mayeda, "The Authenticity of the Upadeśasāhasrī Ascribed to Śaṅkara," *Journal of the American Oriental Society*, vol. 85, no. 2, pp. 190–191; Mayeda Upad, pp. 50–51; V. Raghavan, "Bhāskara's Gītābhāṣya," *Festschrift für Erich Frauwallner, WZKSO*, Bd. XII-XIII, 1968/69, p. 287.

[4]For the date of Kumārila, see Nakamura I, pp. 107–115. H. Nakamura, *A History of Indian Thought* (in Japanese. Tokyo: Iwanami Shoten, 1956), p. 179 is relied upon for the date of Prabhākara. Cf. S. Kuppuswami Sastri, *Brahmasiddhi by Ācārya Maṇḍanamiśra*, pp. lvii-lviii.

[5]Nakamura I, p. 114. M. Biardeau places Maṇḍanamiśra chronologically between Kumārila and Śaṅkara and assigns him the dates 7th-8th century (*La Philosophie de Maṇḍana Miśra vue à partir de la Brahmasiddhi*. Paris: École Francaise d'Extrême-Orient, 1969), p. 1. According to T. Vetter. Maṇḍanamiśra lived in about 700 A.D. (*Maṇḍanamiśra's Brahmasiddhiḥ, Brahmakāṇḍaḥ, Übersetzung, Einleitung und Anmerkungen*. Veröffentlichungen der Kommission für Sprachen und Kulturen Süd- und Ostasiens, Heft 7, Wien, 1969, p. 15).

[6]Cf. S. Kuppuswami Sastri, *Brahmasiddhi*, pp. lvii-lxxv. In his *Brahmasiddhi* Maṇḍanamiśra attacks a view of the relation between knowledge and action which may well be Śaṅkara's.

[7]Sureśvara repeatedly refutes *prasaṃkhyānavāda*, which may have been advocated by Maṇḍanamiśra. See Naiṣ I,67; III,123–126; *Sambandhavārttika* 818–849; S. Kuppuswami Sastri, *Brahmasiddhi*, pp. xxviii-xxxi; xxxiii-xxxvi.

[8]The Maṇḍana-Sureśvara equation has been denied by such able scholars as M.

Hiriyanna, S. Kuppuswami Sastri, and S. Dasgupta, but they do not deny that Sureśvara was once a Mīmāṃsaka. Cf. T. M. P. Mahadevan, *The Saṃbandha-Vārtika of Sureśvarācārya* (Madras University Philosophical Series No. 6), pp. xi-xii; M. Biardeau, *La Philosophie de Maṇḍana Miśra*, p. 2.

[9]S. Radhakrishnan, *Indian Philosophy*, vol. 2, pp. 627–628.

[10]Eliot Deutsch, *Advaita Vedānta: A Philosophical Reconstruction* (Honolulu: East-West Center Press, 1969), pp. 99–100.

[11]Cf. S. Radhakrishnan, *Indian Philosophy*, vol. 2, pp. 423–424; M. Hiriyanna, *The Naiṣkarmyasiddhi of Sureśvarācārya* (Bombay Sanskrit and Prakrit Series No. XXXVIII, 1925), p. xxii (note 1); G. Jha, *Pūrva-Mīmāṃsā in Its Sources* (Benares: Benares Hindu University, 1942), pp. 37–38.

[12]Cf. S. Radhakrishnan, *Indian Philosophy*, vol. 2, p. 423; G. Jha, *Pūrva-Mīmāmsā*, pp. 36–37.

[13]Cf. M. Hiriyanna, *Naiṣkarmyasiddhi of Sureśvarācārya*, pp. xxv-xxvii; S. Kuppuswami Sastri, *Brahmasiddhi*, pp. xxvii-xxxi; xxxiii-xxxvi. Maṇḍanamiśra refers to seven different theories of the problem of the relation of *jñāna* and *karman* in his *Brahmasiddhi* (p. 26, line 24–p. 28, line 7). It is said that Brahmadatta was also a *samuccayavādin* and was criticized by Sureśvara. Cf. Naiṣ I,67; M. Hiriyanna, *The Naiṣkarmyasiddhi of Sureśvara*, pp. xxiii-xxv.

[14]Nakamura III, pp. 116–117.

[15]Nakamura III, pp. 183–187; M. Hiriyanna, "Fragments of Bhartṛprapañca," Proc. III OC (Madras, 1924), pp. 439–450; do, *The Naiṣkarmyasiddhi of Sureśvarācārya*, pp. xvii-xxx; Y. Kanakura, *A Study of the Vedānta Philosophy*, pp. 24–102.

[16]Cf. Upad I,13,27; 16,7; 17,53; 17,86; 17,87; BSBh I,1,1; *Vedāntasāra* [IV] 4–31.

[17]Cf. P. V. Kane, *History of Dharmaśāstra*, vol. II, pt. II (Poona, 1941), pp. 983 ff. However, when Śaṅkara illustrates the teaching method in the second chapter of the Prose Part of the Upad, he gives an example of a *brahmacārin* and his teacher (Upad II,2, 45). The requirement of being a *paramahaṃsaparivrājaka* might not be very strict.

[18]In his commentary on the Bṛh.Up. III,5,1 and IV,5,15 Śaṅkara affirms that only the Brahmin can be *saṃnyāsin*. Most of the medieval writers on *Dharmaśāstras* support this opinion. But Sureśvara is against Śaṅkara's position in this respect. Cf. P. V. Kane, *History of Dharmaśāstra*, vol. II, pt. II, pp. 943–944.

[19]The *Dharmaśāstra* in Hinduism corresponds to the *Vinaya* in Buddhism. Śaṅkara himself is the author of the commentary on the *Adhyātmapaṭala* of the *Āpastamba-Dharmasūtra* (cf. P. Hacker, "Śaṅkara der Yogin und Śaṅkara der Advaitin," *WZKSO*, vol. XII-XIII, 1968/69, p. 147; T. Leggett, *The Chapter of the Self*. London and Henley: Routledge & Kegan Paul, 1978. pp. 166–173.

[20]Among the Hindus it may be the Teṅgalai of the Śrīvaiṣṇava Sect who hold a view similar to antinomianism.

[21]In his BSBh (I,1,4, p. 83) Śaṅkara refutes the opinion that *jñāna* itself is an activity of the mind (*mānasī kriyā*).

[22]*Mysticism East and West*, p. 225.

[23]*Indian Philosophy*, vol. II, pp. 621–634.

[24]*Advaita Vedānta*, pp. 99–102.

[25]Cf. BS III,4,31; BSBh II,3,48.

[26]Eigen, p. 256; D. H. H. Ingalls, "Śaṁkara on the Question: Whose is Avidyā?" *Philosophy East and West*, vol. III (1953), no. 1, pp. 69–72.

A THOUSAND TEACHINGS

PART I. *THE METRICAL PART*

CHAPTER 1
PURE CONSCIOUSNESS

1. Salutation to the all-knowing Pure Consciousness[1] which pervades all, is all, abides in the hearts of all beings, and is beyond all objects [of knowledge].

2. Having completed all the rituals, preceded by the marriage ceremony and the ceremony of installing the sacred fire,[2] the *Veda* has now begun to utter knowledge of *Brahman*.

3. *Karmans* [as the results of actions, good or bad, in the past existence] produce association with a body.[3] When there is association with a body, pleasant and unpleasant things are inevitable. From these result passion and aversion [and] from them actions.

4. [From actions] merit and demerit result [and] from merit and demerit there results an ignorant man's association with a body in the same manner again. Thus this transmigratory existence rolls onward powerfully forever like a wheel.[4]

5. Since the root cause of this transmigratory existence is ignorance, its destruction is desired. Knowledge of *Brahman* therefore is entered on. Final beatitude results from this knowledge.

6. Only knowledge [of *Brahman*] can destroy ignorance; action cannot [destroy it] since [action] is not incompatible [with ignorance]. Unless ignorance is destroyed, passion and aversion will not be destroyed.

7. Unless passion and aversion are destroyed, action arises inevitably from [those] faults.[5] Therefore, for the sake of final beatitude, only knowledge [of *Brahman*] is set forth here [in the Vedānta].

8. [Objection:][6] "Should not [certain] action[7] too always be performed while life lasts? For this [action], being concomitant with knowledge [of *Brahman*], leads to final release.

9. "Action, like knowledge [of *Brahman*, should be adhered to], since [both of them] are equally enjoined [by the *Śrutis*]. As the *Smṛti*[8] also [lays it down that] transgression [results from the neglect of action, so] action should be performed by seekers after final release.

10. "[If you say that] as knowledge [of *Brahman*] has permanent fruit, and so does not depend upon anything else, [we reply:] Not so! Just as the *Agniṣṭoma* sacrifice,[9] though it has permanent fruit, depends upon things other than itself,

11. "so, though knowledge [of *Brahman*] has permanent fruit, it always depends upon action. Thus some people think." [Reply:] Not so, because action is incompatible [with knowledge].

12. In fact action is incompatible with knowledge [of *Brahman*], since [it] is associated with misconception [of *Ātman*]. And knowledge [of *Brahman*] is declared here [in the Vedānta] to be the view that *Ātman* is changeless.

13. [From the notion,] "I am agent; this is mine" arises action. Knowledge [of *Brahman*] depends upon the real, [whereas] the Vedic injunction depends upon an agent.[10]

14. Knowledge destroys the factors of action[11] as [it destroys] the notion that there is water in the salt desert. After accepting this true view, [how] would one decide to perform action?

15. Because of the incompatibility [of knowledge with action] a man who knows thus, being possessed of this knowledge, cannot perform action. For this reason action should be renounced by a seeker after final release.

16. It is the innate assumption of people that *Ātman* is not distinct from the body and the like. This arises from nescience. So long [as they have it], the Vedic injunction to perform actions would be [valid].

17. [The *Śruti* passage,] "Not thus! Not so!" (Bṛh. Up. II,3,6), excluding the body and the like, leaves *Ātman* unexcluded so that [one] may know *Ātman* free from distinction. Thereby nescience is removed.

18. Once nescience has been removed through the right means of knowledge, how can it arise again, since it does not exist in the one alone, the inner *Ātman* free from distinction?

19. If nescience cannot arise again, how can there be the notions, "[I am] an agent, [I am] an experiencer," when there is

the knowledge, "I am the Existent"? Therefore knowledge has no helper.

20. Renunciation is therefore said by the *Śruti* to "be superior" (M.N. Up. 21,2) to the actions [there enumerated, beginning with truth and] ending with mental activity.[12] "[Only] this much," says the Vājins'[13] *Śruti*,

21. "[is, verily, the means to] immortality"[14] (Bṛh. Up. IV,5, 15). Therefore action should be abandoned by seekers after final release. [You] said that, as with the *Agniṣṭoma* sacrifice, [knowledge depends upon action].[15] To this the following reply is given:

22. Because action has to be accomplished through various factors of action and varies in its result, knowledge is the opposite of it. Therefore the example is not applicable.

23. Since the *Agniṣṭoma* sacrifice, like agriculture, etc., has as its object a result [to be accomplished through various factors of action], it requires support from other actions [than itself]. But what else does knowledge depend upon?

24. The transgression [resulting from neglect of action][16] is imputed only to one who has "I"-notion. A knower of *Ātman* has neither "I"-notion nor desire for the result [of action].

25. Therefore, in order to destroy ignorance, end transmigratory existence, and set forth knowledge of *Brahman*, this Upaniṣad has been commenced.

26. And the word "Upaniṣad" may be derived from the verbal root "*sad*" preceded by the prefix "*upa-*" and "*ni-*" and followed by the suffix "*kvip*,"[17] since it diminishes and destroys birth and the like.[18]

Notes

[1]The Sanskrit term "*caitanya*" translated here as "Pure Consciousness" is used as a synonym for *Brahman-Ātman*, indicating the nature of It (see Introduction, III,A,1, p. 19).

[2]*Agnyādhāna*, which is the same as the *Agnyādheya*, is a Vedic sacrifice performed by a sacrificer and his wife with the help of four priests. Cf. P. V. Kane, *History of Dharmaśāstra*, vol. II–III (Poona: Bhandarkar Oriental Research Institute, 1941), pp. 986–998.

[3]See Upad I,15,6 (*dehayogaḥ kriyāhetuḥ*).

[4]On *karman* and transmigration, see Introduction, IV,A, pp. 69–72.

[5]"Faults" (*doṣa*) here means passion and aversion. Cf. Upad II,3,112. Rāmatīrtha

interprets it as passion (*rāga*), aversion (*dveṣa*), and delusion (*moha*) in his commentary *Padayojanikā*.

[6]Commentators Rāmatīrtha and Bodhanidhi (see Preface, note 4) take this objection (I,8–11) as made against the Advaitins by those who assert that knowledge must be combined with the performance of religious actions and duties (*jñānakarmasamuccayavādins*). As I have pointed out, Śaṅkara vehemently rejects this position. Cf. S. Dasgupta, *A History of Indian Philosophy*, vol. II (Cambridge: University Press, 1952), p. 100; S. Mayeda, "Ādi-Śaṅkarācārya's Teaching on the Means to Mokṣa: Jñāna and Karman", *Felicitation Volume in honour of Śaṅkarācārya of Kāñcī*, *Journal of Oriental Research* (Madras), vols. XXXIV-XXXV, 1964–1966, pp. 66–75.

[7]In his English translation (see Preface, note 4) Jagadānanda seems to take "*karma . . . nityaṃ kartavyam*" as "*nityakarma kartavyam*" and translates it as "Obligatory duties should be performed." But, from the context, it seems to me that *karman* here is used in a wider sense which includes *nityakarman; karman* probably means action as a means to final release which is in contrast with knowledge as such, and *nityam* is an adverb which modifies *kartavyam*.

[8]Cf. Manu XI,41–71, especially XI,44.

[9]This is one of the Vedic sacrifices, in which *Soma* is used as the offering. It is a one-day sacrifice and an integral part of the *Jyotiṣṭoma* sacrifice, which generally occupies five days. It is to be performed in spring (*vasanta*) every year and on a new moon or full moon day. See W. Caland and V. Henry, *L'Agniṣṭoma*, 2 vols. (Paris: Ernest Leroux, Éditeur, 1906–1907); P. V. Kane, *History of Dharmaśāstra*, vol. II-III, pp. 1133–1203.

[10]Cf. BSBh I,1,1,p. 35; I,1,4, p. 83; PBh, Introduction, p. 6.

[11]*Kāraka*, which is here translated as "factors of action," is a case-form of a noun dependent upon a verb. This term comprises the notions of ablation (*apādāna*), of giving (*saṃpradāna*), of instrument (*karaṇa*), of location (*adhikaraṇa*), of object (*karman*), of agent (*kartṛ*), but the notion expressed by the genitive case is excluded from *kāraka*. It is also defined as something instrumental in bringing about the action (*kriyānimitta*, *Sarasvatīkaṇṭhābharaṇa*, I,1,32). Cf. L. Renou, *Terminologie grammaticale du Sanskrit* (Paris: Librairie Ancienne Honoré Champion, 1957), pp. 127–128.

[12]M. N. Up. 21 refers to truth (*satya*), penance (*tapas*), self-control (*dama*), tranquility (*śama*), giving (*dāna*), and so forth, and concludes that renunciation (*nyāsa*) is superior to all those lower austerities (*etāny avarāṇi tapāṃsi nyāsa evātyarecayat*).

[13]Vājin = Vājasaneyin, a Vedic school, to which the Bṛh.Up. belongs.

[14]Bṛh. Up. IV,5,15 reads: *etāvad are khalv amṛtatvam*. According to Śaṅkara's commentary on this passage (Ānandāśrama S. S. No. 15, 1936, p. 714), the complete knowledge of *Ātman* which is obtained through "Not thus, not so" and renunciation of everything are the means to immortality. In order to sum up this meaning, the *Śruti* says "*etāvad are khalv amṛtatvam*," which means that the means to Immortality is this much, and only this much—*i.e.* this view of the non-dual *Ātman* which is arrived at through "Not thus, not so" and which does not depend upon any other cause cooperative with it. My translation of this quotation is based upon the above-mentioned interpretation of Śaṅkara which fits here in our present context. Cf. Upad I,11,2.

[15]See the preceding stanzas 10 and 11.

[16]See the preceding stanza 9.

[17]*Kvip* is a suffix which disappears after having been added to several verbal roots, including *sad*, preceded by a preverb. See Pāṇini III,2,61; 76, etc.

[18]Śaṅkara gives similar etymological explanation of the word "*upaniṣad*" in his commentaries on Upaniṣads. He takes the verbal root *sad* to mean (1) destroy (*viśa-*

raṇa), (2) go, reach (*gati*) and (3) mitigate (*avasādana*), and interprets the word "*upa-ni-ṣad*" as: (1) "destroy the seeds of transmigratory existence such as nescience," (2) "make seekers after final release go to the highest *Brahman*," or (3) "mitigate such a multitude of miseries as living in the womb, birth and old age (*garbhavāsajanmajarād-yupadravabṛnda*, Śaṅkara *ad* Kaṭh. Up., Introduction [Śrī Śāṃkaragranthāvaliḥ 3. Śrīraṃgam, n.d.], pp. 101–102). In another place he explains the word as: (1) "destroy (*niśātayati*) such numerous evils as birth, old age and disease (*garbhajanmajarāro-gādyanarthapūga*)," (2) "lead to the highest *Brahman*," or (3) "mitigate (*avasādayati*) completely, i.e. annihilate (*vināśayati*) nescience and other causes of transmigratory existence" (Śaṅkara *ad* Muṇḍ. Up., Introduction [Śrī Śāṃkaragranthāvaliḥ 3. Śrīraṃgam, n.d.], p. 304). Today it is generally accepted by scholars that the word Upaniṣad derived from the verb *upa-ni-sad* means "sit (*sad*) down (*ni*) near (*upa*) [some one]," the verbal root *sad* being taken to mean "sit." Cf. Max Müller (tr.), *The Upaniṣads*, pt. 1 (The Sacred Books of the East, vol. 1. Reprint ed. New York: Dover Publications, Inc., 1962), pp. lxxix-lxxxiv; P. Deussen, *The Philosophy of the Upanishads* (Reprint ed. New York: Dover Publications, Inc., 1966), pp. 10–15; M. Winternitz, *A History of Indian Literature*, tr. by S. Ketkar (Reprint ed. New Delhi: Oriental Books Reprint Corporation, 1972), pp. 243–244; S. Dasgupta, *A History of Indian Philosophy*, vol. 1, p. 38.

CHAPTER 2
NEGATION

1. As [*Ātman*] cannot be negated, [It] is left unnegated [by the *Śruti*,] "Not thus! Not so!" (Bṛh. Up. II,3,6). One attains [It] in some such way as "I am not this. I am not this."

2. The notion "[I am] this" arises from the *ātman* [which is identified with] "this" (= non-*Ātman*)[1] and is within the range of a verbal handle.[2] As it has its origin in the negated *ātman*, it could not become [accepted as] a right notion again [as before].

3. Without negating a previous notion, a following view does not arise. The Seeing (= *Ātman*) is one alone, self-established. As It is the result [of the right means of knowledge],[3] It is not negated.

4. When one has traversed the forest of "this" (= non-*Ātman*) which is contaminated with anxiety, delusion, and so on, one arrives at one's own *Ātman*, just as the man from the land of Gandhāra [arrived at Gandhāra] through the forest.[4]

Notes

[1]Commentators Ānandajñāna, Bodhanidhi, and Rāmatīrtha interpret "*idamātman*" as "*ahaṃkartṛ*" or "the bearer of 'I'-notion" (*i.e.* the intellect), which ordinary people regard as their *Ātman* (see Introduction, III,B,3, pp. 39–40). But "this" (*idam*) means here the object of knowledge which should be negated as non-*Ātman* in some such way as, "I am not 'this,' I am not 'this'" (cf. the previous stanza). Therefore, "*idamātma-*" is the same as "*niṣiddhātma-*" or "the negated *ātman*" in the next line. *Ātman* is always the subject of knowledge and not the object of knowledge. It is not indicated by any words, since *Ātman* has no universals (*jāti*), action (*karman*) etc. which non-*Ātman* like the intellect possesses. (Cf. "*idamaṃśa*," Upad I,12,11.) Śaṅkara also uses "*yuṣmad-*" in the sense of "the object" or "non-*Ātman*" in contrast to "*asmad-*" or "the subject" or "*Ātman*." (Cf. BSBh, Introduction, p. 4.)

[2]Cf. Chānd. Up. VI,1,4–6.

[3]Cf. Upad II,2,77; 93; 103; 108 (*avagatiḥ pramāṇānāṃ phalam*).

[4]This simile is used in a famous dialogue between Uddālaka and his son Śvetaketu in Chānd. Up. VI,14,1–2 so that Uddālaka may explain to his son how *Ātman*, though subtle and imperceptible, can be realized. A man who is led, with his eyes covered, away from the Gandhāras and left in a place where there are no human beings, will at last arrive at Gandhāra by asking his way from village to village. In the same way one who meets a teacher to instruct him obtains true knowledge.

CHAPTER 3

THE LORD

1. If the Lord is non-*Ātman*, one ought not to dwell upon [the knowledge] "I am He." If He is *Ātman*, the knowledge "I am the Lord" destroys the other [knowledge].[1]

2. If, being different from *Ātman*, [He] is taken to have characteristics such as "not coarse,"[2] what is the use of them when He is not an object of knowledge? If He is *Ātman*, the notion of difference[3] is destroyed [by them].

3. Understand, therefore, that [that predication of qualities] such as "not coarse" are meant to negate false superimposition[4] [upon *Ātman*]. If [they] were meant to negate [false superimposition] upon something other [than *Ātman*], this would indeed be a description of emptiness (*śūnyatā*).[5]

4. And if it is thought [that they are meant to negate false superimposition] upon something other than the inner *Ātman* of a man who wishes to know, the words [of the *Śruti*], "[He is . . .] without breath, without mind, pure [, higher than the high Imperishable]" (Muṇḍ. Up. II,1,2), would also be meaningless.

Notes

[1]"*Anyanivartikā*" may be in the sense of "*anya-dhī-nivartikā*" if the compound "*anyadhīhnuti*" in the next stanza is taken into consideration. "*Anyadhī*" is synonymous with "*avidyā*" according to Upad I,17,21 (cf. *anyadṛṣṭi*, Upad I,17,6; 56). If so, this sentence can be translated as: ". . . the knowledge 'I am the Lord' destroys the [notion] of difference."

[2]See Bṛh. Up. III,8,8.

[3]See note 1.

[4]According to Śaṅkara, "*avidyā* is the superimposition of the qualities of one upon the

other" (*avidyā nāmānyasminn anyadharmādhyāropaṇā*, Upad II, 2,51). In other words, *avidyā* is mutual superimposition of *Ātman* and non-*Ātman* such as the body, the senses, and the inner organ.

[5]This is an important term in Mahāyāna Buddhism, especially the Mādhyamika School founded by Nāgārjuna (150–250). The term "*śūnyatā*" is sometimes translated as "emptiness," "voidness," or "nothingness" and mistaken for absolute negation of existence, which Śaṅkara also seems to mean by the term here. Buddhists are called nihilists (*vaināśika*) by Śaṅkara (cf. Upad II,2,55; 2,57; 2,58) and other writers of the orthodox schools of Indian philosophy. *Śūnyatā*, however, means that nothing has any intrinsic nature of its own (*niḥsvabhāvatva*); it denotes the unreality of the foundation of the phenomenal appearance but not the unreality of the appearance as such. The idea of *śūnyatā* is not a philosophical concept but, rather, a method which leads to the penetration into true reality. Cf. E. Conze, *Buddhist Thought in India* (Reprint ed. Ann Arbor: The University of Michigan Press, 1967), pp. 242–243.

CHAPTER 4
"I"-NOTION

1. When action, which has the "I"-notion as its seed and is in the bearer of the "I"-notion (= the intellect),[1] has been burnt up by the fire of the notion that "I am not [an agent or an experiencer],"[2] how can it produce a result?

2. If [you say:] "[Even after the action has been burnt up,] production of a result [of action] will take place as previously experienced," [we reply:] No; it (= production of a result) is based upon other action. [If you say,] "When the "I"-notion [as the seed of action] has been destroyed, we ask you, How can there be that [action beyond that which has been burnt up]? Answer that,"

3. [we reply:] As [action] can fashion the body and so on, it can overpower knowledge in you concerning the Existent and produce a result. When action comes to an end, knowledge will arise.

4. As experience [of the result of action] and knowledge are both results of action which has already begun to produce a result, it is reasonable that they (= knowledge and action) are not contradictory to each other. But other [action, namely that which has not yet begun to produce a result,] is different in nature.

5. A man who has knowledge of *Ātman*, which negates the notion that the body is *Ātman* and is as [firm] as [ordinary people's] notion that the body is *Ātman*, is released even without wishing.

[5'. Therefore, all this is established. The reasoning is as stated by us.] [3]

Notes

[1]See Introduction, III,B,3, pp. 39–40.

[2]Ānandajñāna and Rāmatīrtha interpret "*nāhampratyaya-*" as "*nāhaṃ kartā bhoktā vā kiṃ tu brahmaivāsmīti (yaḥ pramāṇajanitaḥ) pratyayaḥ.*" Bodhanidhi also interprets in the same way but with a slight difference in expression.

[3]This line may be a later interpolation. See Mayeda Upad, p. 221.

CHAPTER 5
SUSPICION OF URINE

1. Just as the sage Udaṅka did not accept the nectar, thinking that it was urine,[1] so people do not accept the knowledge of *Ātman* out of fear that action will be destroyed.

2. *Ātman*, abiding in the intellect, is seen as it were moving and meditating [when the intellect moves and meditates]. The mistake about transmigratory existence is like that of a man in a [moving] boat who thinks that it is the trees [along the shore which are moving].

3. Just as to a man in the boat the trees [appear to] move in a direction opposite [to his movement],[2] so does *Ātman* [appears to] transmigrate, since the *Śruti* reads, "[He, remaining the same, goes along both worlds,] appearing to think [, appearing to move about]" (Bṛh. Up. IV,3,7).

4. Intellect being pervaded by the reflection[3] of Pure Consciousness, knowledge arises in it; and so sound and other [objects of the sense-organs] appear.[4] By this people are deluded.

5. The "I"-notion appears to be as it were Pure Consciousness and exists for Its sake. And it does not do so, when the "this"-portion has been destroyed. [So] this Pure Experience[5] [which is other than "this"-portion] is the highest [*Ātman*].

Notes

[1]This story appears in the *Mahābhārata, Aśvamedhaparvan*, Sec. 54, pp. 208–212. It runs as follows: When Viṣṇu allowed the sage Udaṅka to ask him for some boon, he asked for water and Viṣṇu told him to think of him whenever he wanted water. One day, wandering over the desert, he became thirsty and thought of Viṣṇu. Then he saw, in the

desert, a naked hunter of the Caṇḍāla class, all besmeared with dirt, surrounded by a pack of dogs. Extremely fierce-looking, he carried a sword and was armed with bow and arrows. Udaṅka saw a copious stream of water issuing from the urinary organs of that hunter. The hunter offered the water repeatedly but Udaṅka did not accept it, and finally became angry. But later Viṣṇu explained to him that the hunter was Indra and that he had appeared before him to give him nectar.

[2]Cf. Naiṣ II,63.

[3]See Introduction, III,B,2, pp. 36–37.

[4]Rāmatīrtha in his commentary suggests here the two ways of reading: one is "*buddheḥ śabdādibhir bhāsas*" and the other is "*buddheḥ śabdādinirbhāsas*" which I have used.

[5]Ānandajñāna, Bodhanidhi and Rāmatīrtha take this "*anubhava*" (Pure Experience) as "*Sākṣin.*"

CHAPTER 6
HAVING CUT

1. *Ātman* Itself is not qualified by a hand which has been cut off and thrown away. Likewise, none of the rest [of the body] qualifies [*Ātman*].[1]

2. Therefore, every qualification is the same as a hand which has been thrown away, since it is non-*Ātman*. Therefore, the Knower (= *Ātman*) is devoid of all qualifications.[2]

3. This whole [universe] is qualification, like a beautiful ornament, which is superimposed [upon *Ātman*] through nescience. Therefore, when *Ātman* has been known, the whole [universe] becomes non-existent.[3]

4. One should always grasp *Ātman* alone as the Knower, disconnected [from all qualifications],[4] and abandon the object of knowledge. One should grasp that what is called "I" is also the same as a part which has been abandoned.[5]

5. As long as the "this"-portion is a qualification [of *ātman*], that ["I"-portion] is different from [*Ātman*] Itself. When the qualification has been destroyed, the Knower is established [independently from it], as a man who owns a brindled cow [is established independently from it].

6. The learned should abandon the "this"-portion in what is called "I," understanding that it is not *Ātman*. ["I" in the sentence of the *Śruti*] "I am *Brahman*" (Bṛh. Up. I,4,10)[6] is the portion which has been left unabandoned in accordance with the above teaching.

Notes

[1]This stanza appears as Naiṣ IV,26.

[2]This stanza appears as Naiṣ IV,28.

[3]This stanza appears as Naiṣ IV,27.

[4]Cf. stanza 2.

[5]This stanza appears as Naiṣ IV,29.

[6]The Upaniṣadic sentence "*ahaṃ brahmāsmi*" (I am *Brahman*) is one of the *Mahāvākyas* (Great Sentences) which the Advaitins consider to be best indicative of the Advaita doctrine. There are said to be eleven or twelve *Mahāvākyas*, but among them this sentence and "*tat tvam asi*" (Thou art That) are best known.

CHAPTER 7
LOCATED IN THE INTELLECT

1. Everything located in the intellect[1] is always seen by Me in every case [of cognition]. Therefore, I am the highest *Brahman*; I am all-knowing and all-pervading.

2. Just as [I] am the Witness of the movements in My own intellect,[2] so am I [also the Witness of the movements] in others' [intellects]. I can be neither rejected nor accepted. Therefore, I am indeed the highest [*Ātman*].

3. There is no change in the *Ātman*, nor impurity, nor materiality, and because It is the Witness of all intellects, there is no limitation of its knowledge, as there is in the case of knowledge of intellect.

4. Just as in a jewel the forms such as red color are manifested in the sunshine,[3] so in my presence everything becomes visible [in the intellect]. Therefore through Me [everything becomes visible] as [the forms such as red color become visible] through sunshine.

5. The object of knowledge in the intellect exists when the intellect exists; otherwise it does not exist. Since the Seer is always seer, duality does not exist.

6. Just as the intellect, from absence of discriminating knowledge, holds that the highest [*Ātman*] does not exist, just so when there is discriminating knowledge, nothing but the highest [*Ātman*] exists, not even [the intellect] itself.

Notes

[1]*Pāda* a of this stanza appears again as *pāda* a of stanza 18.94. When the intellect per-

vades its object of knowledge, the object is called "the one which is seated in the intellect" (*buddhyārūḍha*). See Introduction, III,B,2, p. 36. Cf. Upad I,18,155–157.

[2]*Buddhicāra* is synonymous with *cittapracāra* (Upad II,2,75; 82), which is again synonymous with *cittavṛtti* in *Yogasūtra* I,2; IV,18. See Introduction, III,B,2, p. 35, and note 32.

[3]Cf. Upad I,17,16; 18,122.

CHAPTER 8

THE NATURE OF PURE CONSCIOUSNESS

1. I Myself have the nature of Pure Consciousness, O Mind; [My apparent] connection with taste, etc., is caused by your delusion. Therefore no result due to your activity would belong to Me, since I am free from all attributes.

2. Abandon here activity born of illusion and come ever to rest from search for the wrong, since I am forever the highest *Brahman*, released, as it were, unborn, one alone, and without duality.

3. And I am always the same to beings,[1] one alone; [I am] the highest [*Brahman*] which, like the sky, is all-pervading, imperishable, auspicious, uninterrupted, undivided and devoid of action. Therefore no result from your efforts here pertains to Me.

4. I am one alone; No other than that [*Brahman*] is thought to be Mine. In like manner I do not belong to anything since I am free from attachment. I have by nature no attachment. Therefore I do not need you nor your work since I am non-dual.

5. Considering that people are attached to cause and effect, I have composed this dialogue, making [them] understand the meaning of the truth of their own nature, so that they may be released from [their] attachment to cause and effect.

6. If a man ponders on this dialogue, he will be released from ignorance, the origin of great fears. And such a man is always free from desire; being a knower of *Ātman*, he is ever free from sorrow, the same [to beings], and happy.

Note

[1]Cf. *samo 'haṃ sarvabhūteṣu*, BhG IX,29.

CHAPTER 9

SUBTLETY

1. It is to be known that [in the series] beginning with earth[1] and ending with the inner *Ātman*, each succeeding one is more subtle and more pervasive than the preceding one which has been abandoned.

2. The means of knowledge show that external earth is the same as the bodily earth. [External] water and all the other elements should be known to be the same as [bodily elements].

3. Just as the [clear] sky is all-pervading before the origination of air and other [elements], so am I always one alone, all, Pure Consciousness only, all-pervading and non-dual.

4. It is said that all beings from Brahmā down to the plants are my body. From what else can the faults such as desire and anger arise in Me?

5. Although I am always untouched by the faults of beings, being the Lord who abides in all beings, [yet] people look upon Me as contaminated [by the faults of beings] just as an ignorant person looks upon the sky as blue.

6. As the intellects of all beings are always to be illuminated by My Pure Consciousness, all beings are the body of Me who am all-knowing and free from evils.

7. The object of knowledge [in the waking state] is looked upon as having an origin, as is [the object of] knowledge in the dreaming state. [True] knowledge is constant and without object; hence duality does not exist.

8. The Knower's Knowing[2] is indeed said to be constant, for nothing else exists in the state of deep sleep. Knowing in the waking state results from nescience; therefore the object of knowledge should be looked upon as unreal.

9. Just as the Infinite[3] lacks form-and-color, etc., and is not the object of sight, etc., so it is not to be taken to be an object of knowledge.

Notes

[1]The text reads "*gandhāder*" here, but Ānandajñāna comments on it: *pṛthivī gandhaśabdenocyate*, and Rāmatīrtha also says: *gandhaśabdaḥ pṛthivīśabdārthaḥ*.

[2]The word *jñāti* means "relative" in the Upaniṣads (for example, Chānd. Up. VI,15,1; VIII,12,3; Kauṣ. Up. I,4). Bodhanidhi and Rāmatīrtha interpret it as *jñapti*. Ānandajñāna's interpretation on this term is not clear but seems to take it as *caitanya*.

[3]The word *bhūman* is sometimes translated as grandeur, the superlative, acme, and plenum. The *bhūman* in Chānd. Up. VII,23 is interpreted in BS I,3,8, which takes it as *paramātman* according to BSBh I,3,8, p. 213.

CHAPTER 10
SEEING

1. The highest [*Brahman*]—which is of the nature of Seeing, like the sky, ever-shining,[1] unborn, one alone, imperishable, stainless, all-pervading, and non-dual—That am I and I am forever released. Om.[2]

2. I am Seeing, pure and by nature changeless. There is by nature no object for me. Being the Infinite,[3] completely filled in front, across, up, down, and in every direction, I am unborn, abiding in Myself.

3. I am unborn, deathless, free from old age, immortal, self-effulgent, all-pervading, non-dual; I am neither cause nor effect, altogether stainless, always satisfied and therefore [constantly] released. Om.

4. Whether in the state of deep sleep or of waking or of dreaming, no delusive perception appears to pertain to Me in this world. As those [three states] have no existence, self-dependent or other-dependent, I am always the Fourth,[4] the Seeing and the non-dual.

5. The continuous series of pains due to the body, the intellect and the senses is neither I nor of Me, for I am changeless. And this is because the continual series [of pain] is unreal; it is indeed unreal like an object seen by a dreaming man.

6. It is true that I have neither change nor any cause of change, since I am non-dual. I have neither good nor bad deeds, neither final release nor bondage, neither caste nor stages of life, since I am bodiless.

7. Since I am beginningless and attributeless,[5] I have neither action nor result [of action]. Therefore I am the highest [*Ātman*], non-dual. Just as the ether, though all-pervading, is not stained,

so am I not either, though abiding in the body, since I am subtle.[6]

8. And I am always the same to [all] beings,[7] the Lord, for I am superior to, and higher than, the perishable and the imperishable.[8] Though I have the highest *Ātman* as my true nature and am non-dual, I am nevertheless covered with wrong knowledge[9] which is nescience.

9. Being perfectly stainless, *Ātman* is distinguished from, and broken by, nescience, residual impression, and actions. Being filled with powers such as Seeing, I am non-dual, standing [perfect] in my own nature and motionless like the sky.

10. He who sees *Ātman* with the firm belief "I am the highest *Brahman*" "is born no more" (Kaṭh. Up. I,38), says the *Śruti*. When there is no seed, no fruit is produced. Therefore there is no birth, for there is no delusion.

11. "This is mine, being thus," "That is yours, being of such kind," "Likewise, I am so, not superior nor otherwise"—[such] assumptions of people concerning *Brahman*, which is the same [to all beings], non-dual and auspicious, are nothing but their stupidity.

12. When there is completely non-dual and stainless knowledge, then the great-souled experiences neither sorrow nor delusion. In the absence of both there is neither action nor birth. This is the firm belief of those who know the *Veda*.

13. He who, in the waking state, like a man in the state of deep sleep, does not see duality, though [actually] seeing, because of his non-duality, and similarly he who, though [in fact] acting, is actionless—he [only]is the knower of *Ātman*, and nobody else. This is the firm conclusion here [in the Vedānta].

14. This view which has been declared by me from the standpoint of the highest truth is the supreme [view] as ascertained in the Vedānta. If a man has firm belief in it, he is released and not stained by actions,[10] as others are.

Notes

[1]*Sakṛdvibhāta*. "*Sakṛt*" has two meanings: one is "sudden" (for example, *sakṛdvidyutta*, Bṛh. Up. II,3,6) and the other is "always" (for example, *sakṛdvibhāto hy evaiṣa brahmalokaḥ*, Chānd. Up. VIII,4,2). Śaṅkara interprets "*sakṛdvibhāta*" in Chānd. Up. VIII,4,2

as "*sadā vibhātaḥ*" in his *Bhāṣya* on it. When he comments on the GK, he interprets "*sakṛdvibhāta*" as "*sadaiva vibhātaṃ, sadā bhārūpam*" (GKBh III,36) and as "*sadaiva vibhāte*" (GKBh IV,81). In his commentary on this stanza, Bodhanidhi interprets "*sakṛdvibhāta*" as "*sadābhāsasvarūpam ādityavat prakāśasvarūpatvāt na kadācid api tamasābhibhūyate.*" Rāmatīrtha interprets it as "*ekadaiva visphuritam, sadaiva spaṣṭam bhāsamānam.*"

[2]This whole stanza is quoted in *Vedāntasāra* [XXX] 210. *Om* is the sacred syllable called *praṇava* and sometimes compared with *Amen*. It is used at the opening of most Hindu works and as a sacred exclamation may be uttered at the beginning and end of Vedic recitation or before any prayer.

[3]See Upad I,9,9.

[4]The *ātman* in the waking state is called *vaiśvānara* (Upad I,17,65), that in the dreaming state *taijasa* (Upad I,15,24), and that in the state of deep sleep *prājña* (Upad I,15,25; I,17,65) or *avyākṛta* (Upad I,17,65). These three kinds of *ātman* are not the true *Ātman*; they are only the *ātman* limited by adjuncts (*sopādhi*, Upad I,15,29). Free from all limiting adjuncts (*anupādhika*, Upad I,15,29), the true *Ātman* transcends all these three, and It is called *Turīya* (Upad I,10,4; Bṛh. Up. V,14,3–7), which is also called *Caturtha* (Māṇḍ. Up. 7) or *Turya* (Maitri Up. VI,19; VII,11,7–8). See Introduction, III,B,5, pp. 43–46.

[5]Cf. *anāditvān nirguṇatvān*, BhG XIII, 31.

[6]Cf. BhG XIII,32, which probably is the basis of this stanza.

[7]Cf. BhG IX, 29; Upad I,8,3.

[8]Cf. BhG XV, 16–18.

[9]*Yogasūtra* I,8 defines "*viparyaya*" as "*mithyājñānam atadrūpapratiṣṭham.*" According to Śaṅkara's usage of the term *mithyājñāna*, it is a synonym of *avidyā* (cf. Mayeda Upad, pp. 24–25; Introduction, IV,D,1, p. 78). In GBh XIII,2, p. 529, Śaṅkara refers to three kinds of *avidyā*: (1) *viparītagrāhaka*, (2) *saṃśayopasthāpaka*, and (3) *agrahaṇātmaka*. Among those three, (1) seems to correspond to "*viparyaya.*" Thus, though *viparyaya* is not a synomym of *avidyā*, it is probable that *avidyā* is a wider concept to which *viparyaya* belongs. All three commentators take *avidyā* as the cause of *viparyaya* or *mithyājñāna*: (1) Ānandajñāna, *avidyāmūlena mithyājñānenāvṛta ātmā*, (2) Bodhanidhi, *viparyayena mithyājñānenābhivṛtaḥ ācādita iva tuśabdo ivārthe mithyājñānaṃ kena hetuneti ced avidyayā anirvacanīyayā . . . yad viparyayajñānaṃ tenābhivṛta iva svataḥśuddhasvabhāvo 'pi,* and (3) Rāmatīrtha, *avidyāvilasita eva viparyaya ity arthaḥ*. The term "*abhivṛta*" is of interest, since later Advaitins characterize *avidyā* as *āvaraṇaśakti*, though Śaṅkara does not do so in his works.

[10]Cf. *na māṃ karmāṇi limpanti*, BhG IV,14; Upad I,16,71.

CHAPTER 11

THE QUALITY OF BEING THE BEHOLDER

1. The quality of being the Beholder is self-established as belonging to beings, and their [apparent] difference from this [Beholder] arises from ignorance. Therefore, the difference is removed by the words, "You are the Existent."

2. The scripture rejects action with the subtle body,[1] saying that, since "[The means to] immortality" is "[Only] this much" (Bṛh. Up. IV,5,15),[2] nothing else accompanies knowledge.

3. I see the modification[3] of the mind in all beings without exception. [But] how can I, who am changeless, have differentiation in any respect?

4. I am the Beholder of modification of the mind and also of the mind [itself], [in beings] in the waking state as in the dreaming state; since neither [the mind] nor [its modification exists] in the state of deep sleep, [I am] Pure Consciousness only, all-pervading and non-dual.

5. Just as a dream is true until awakening, so would the identity of the body with *Ātman* be [true, as well as] the authoritativeness of sense-perception and the other [means of knowledge] and the waking state until [the attainment of] knowledge of *Ātman*.

6. Like ether, though abiding in all beings, I am free from [all] the faults of beings; I am the Witness, the Observer, the pure, attributeless *Brahman*; so I am alone.[4]

7. Being different from name, form, and action[5] and by nature constantly free, I am *Ātman*, *i.e.*, the highest *Brahman*; I am Pure Consciousness only and always non-dual.

8. Those who know "I am *Brahman*" (Bṛh. Up. I,4,10) and [yet think] "I am doer and experiencer" lose both knowledge and action; they are materialists (*nāstika*) without a doubt.

9. Just as it is [ordinarily] assumed that *Ātman* is connected with the results of merit and demerit,[6] although this [connection] is invisible, so the scripture[7] says it should be admitted that *Ātman* is *Brahman* and that final release results from knowledge.

10. The residual impressions [enumerated in the *Śruti*,][8] beginning with a saffron-colored robe, are perceived here only by those who see dreams. The Seeing (= *Ātman*) is different from those [residual impressions], alone.

11. Just as it is seen that a sword [shines] when it is drawn from its sheath,[9] so the Knower, separated in the dreaming state from cause and effect, is seen to be self-effulgent.

12. The natural state of the Knower who was awakened by being pushed [with the hand][10] has been declared [in the *Śruti*] by the sentences such as "Not thus" (Bṛh. Up. II,3,6, etc.), which remove [everything] falsely constructed [upon Him].

13. Just as a great king and other worlds [that I become, as it were, in the dreaming state according to the *Śruti*][11] are things falsely constructed upon Me in the dreaming state, so the double form [of *Brahman*] and the residual impression should be known [as falsely constructed].

14. Action is performed by *Ātman* identified with the gross and subtle body [and] in the form of residual impression. As My own nature is "Not thus! Not so!" (Bṛh. Up. II,3,6, etc.), action is not performed anywhere by Me.

15. Therefore there is no hope of immortality from action which has ignorance as its cause. Since the cause of final release is knowledge, it does not depend upon anything else but knowledge.

16. The immortal is fearless and not injured. *Ātman* [which was left unnegated by the *Śruti*,] "Not thus! [Not so!]" (Bṛh. Up. II, 3,6, etc.)[12] is dear to Me.[13] Therefore, along with action, one should abandon anything [else] which is contrary [to *Ātman* or] different from It.

Notes

[1]Jagadānanda translates "*saliṅga*" as "with their accessories" (*i.e.*, the accessories of Vedic actions): the sacred tuft of hair on the head, the sacred thread, etc., according to his footnote 2, p. 116. His translation seems to be based upon Rāmatīrtha's interpretation, according to which "*saliṅga*" means "*sasādhana*." According to Ānandajñāna,

however, "*liṅga*" means "*hetu*" or "*saṃsārahetu*," which may be associated with the usage of *liṅga* in the Nyāya. The term "*liṅga*" is used three more times in the Upad (I,11,14; 15,10; II,1,4). In Upad I,11,14 and 15,10 the word means "the subtle body," and Upad I,11,14 especially suggests that the word "*liṅga*" here also means "subtle body." Bodhanidhi supports this, interpreting it as "*sūkṣmaśarīra*."

[2]See Upad I,1,20–21.

[3]For a fuller explanation of the modification (*vṛtta, vṛtti* or *pratyaya*) of the mind or the internal organ (*antaḥkaraṇa*), see Introduction, III,B,2, pp. 35–37.

[4]This stanza is probably based upon the following passages of the Upaniṣads: (1) *eko devas sarvabhūteṣu gūḍhas . . . sākṣī cetā kevalo nirguṇaś ca*, Śvet. Up. VI,11, and (2) *aham brahmāsmi*, Bṛh. Up. I,4,10.

[5]This stanza is probably based upon Bṛh. Up. I,6,1 (cf. I,6,2 and 3): *trayaṃ vā idam, nāma rūpaṃ karma*. According to Śaṅkara's commentary on Bṛh. Up., the universe consists of these three, but all of them are non-*Ātmans*. Therefore, one should turn away from them. Śaṅkara holds that this is the import of this section of the Upaniṣad. Cf. Upad II,1,18 ff.; Śaṅkara *ad* Bṛh. Up. II,3,6, p. 334.

[6]Cf. *puṇyo vai puṇyena karmaṇā bhavati pāpaḥ pāpena*, Bṛh. Up. III,2,13 (cf. Bṛh. Up. IV, 4,5).

[7]Rāmatīrtha quotes Muṇḍ. Up. III,2,9 and Śvet. Up. III,8; 6,15.

[8]Cf. Upad I,14,48. Bṛh. Up. II,3,1–6 describes two forms of *Brahman*: the formed and the formless, the mortal and the immortal. In Bṛh. Up. II,3,6, the form of the formless is said to be like a saffron-colored robe (*mahārajanaṃ vāsas*), white wool (*pāṇḍvāvika*), the [red] Indragopa beetle (*indragopa*), a flame of fire (*agnyarci*), the [white] lotus flower (*puṇḍarīka*), a sudden flash of lightning (*sakṛdvidyutta*). According to Śaṅkara's commentary on Bṛh. Up. II,3,6, p. 333, the formless is the subtle body, the particular forms of which are residual impressions (*vāsanā*); the saffron-colored robe and the like are residual impressions.

[9]The simile of a sword appears in Śaṅkara *ad* Bṛh. Up. IV,3,10, p. 584.

[10]Bṛh. Up. II,1 contains a dialogue on *Brahman* between Gārgya Dṛptabālāki and Ajātaśatru, a king of Benares. Dṛptabālāki, though a Brahmin, had only imperfect knowledge of *Brahman*, worshipping It as the Person in the sun, the Person in the moon, etc. On the other hand, Ajātaśatru, though a king, had perfect knowledge of *Brahman* and knew It as *Ātman*. In the beginning of their dialogue Dṛptabālāki explained his ideas of *Brahman* but the king rejected them all. So he had to request the king to receive him as a pupil. Then the king acceded to his request, saying, "It is contrary to usual practice that a Brahmin should come to a *Kṣatriya*, thinking 'He will tell me *Brahman*' " (Bṛh. Up. II,1,15). The two of them went up to a man who was asleep and called him by various titles. But he did not awaken. Then the king woke him by pushing (or rubbing) him with his hand. After that, the king taught Dṛptabālāki with reference to the states of dreaming and deep sleep that all vital airs, all worlds, all gods, and all beings come forth from *Ātman*.

[11]This is referred to in the dialogue between Gārgya Dṛptabālāki and Ajātaśatru (Bṛh. Up. II,1,18. See note 10 above). When the person consisting of consciousness (*vijñānamaya*) (= *ātman*) is in the dreaming state, he becomes, as it were, a great king (*mahārājan*), a great Brahmin (*mahābrāhmaṇa*), and the like. To be, as it were, a great king—to be, as it were, a great Brahmin, and so forth—are his worlds (*loka*) which are consequences (of his action) (*karmaphala*), according to Śaṅkara's commentary.

[12]Cf. Upad I,2.2.

[13]Cf. Bṛh. Up. I,4,8 and II,4,5.

CHAPTER 12

IN THE SUNLIGHT

1. Just as a man thinks that a body in sunlight is [itself] bright, so he thinks that the mind[1] which appears to be the Seer is[indeed] "I, the Seer."

2. Whatever is seen in this world, *Ātman* comes to be identified with it. Consequently [a man] is deluded and so he does not recognize *Ātman*.

3. Just as [the lad who] was himself the tenth thought that he was among the nine [others],[2] so these deluded folk [think that *Ātman* is] among the objects of knowledge [such as the intellect] and do not [understand] otherwise.

4. Explain reasonably how the two incompatible notions, "You should act" and "You are That,"[3] can exist at the same time and have the same locus.

5. He who misconceives the body as *Ātman* has pain; he who has no body[4] has by nature no [pain], as in the sleeping state. In order to remove pain from the Seeing, [the *Śruti*] says, "Thou[art]That" (Chānd. Up. VI,8,7, etc.).

6. A *Yogin*, seeing the notion [of the intellect] on which the reflection of the Seeing (= *Ātman*) is mounted like the reflection of a face in a mirror, thinks that *Ātman* is seen.

7. Only if he knows that the various deluded notions do not belong to the Seeing, is he beyond doubt the best of *Yogins*. No one else can be.

8. "Understander of understanding"[5] is what is meant by the word "Thou" [in the sentence, "Thou art That" (Chānd. Up. VI, 8,7, etc.)].[6] Therefore this is the [right] apprehension of this word; any other apprehension is false.

9. Since I am always of the nature of the Seeing and constant, how is it possible for Me [sometimes] to see and [sometimes] not to see?[7] Therefore any apprehension [of the word] different from that is not accepted.

10. Just as the body, the site of the sun's heat, is an object to the Seeing, so the intellect[8] here is the site [of pain—corresponding to heat in the example]; therefore, the intellect is the object to the Seeing.

11. The Knower whose "this"-portion[9] has been negated is homogeneous like ether, non-dual, ever-free and pure. He is Myself; I am *Brahman*, alone.

12. There can never be another understander superior to the Understander; therefore, I am the highest Understander, being always released in all beings.

13. He who knows that *Ātman*'s Seeing is undiminished and that [*Ātman*] is not a doer, abandoning the [very] notion that he is a knower of *Brahman*, [he alone] is a knower of *Ātman* and no one else.[10]

14. The discriminating notion, "I am the Knower, not the object of knowledge, pure, always released," also belongs to the intellect, since it is the object of cognition and perishable.

15. Since *Ātman*'s Seeing is undiminished and not produced by factors of action,[11] the false assumption that this Seeing can be produced is made by another seeing which is [Its] object.

16. [The notion that] *Ātman* is a doer is false, since [it] is due to the belief that the body is *Ātman*. The belief, "I do not do anything," is true and arises from the right means of knowledge.

17. [The notion that *Ātman*] is a doer is due to factors of action [whereas the notion that It] is not a doer is due to Its own nature. It has been fully ascertained that the understanding, "[I am] a doer," "[I am] an experiencer," is false.

18. When one's own nature has thus been understood by means of the scripture and inference, how can this understanding, "I am to be enjoined [to act]," be true?

19. Just as ether is within all, so am I within even ether itself; I am always changeless, motionless, pure, free from old age, released, and non-dual.

Notes

[1]In Śaṅkara's writings the terms *buddhi, manas, citta,* and *dhī* are used synonymously in most cases. See Introduction, III,B,1 pp. 30–31.

[2]This illustration, which is employed by Śaṅkara and his followers to show how people are deluded, and how they realize that they are *Brahman-Ātman*, is probably based upon folktales. One of a group of ten boys, who had swam across a river, counted their number. Failing to count himself who was the tenth, he counted only nine boys and thought that one boy was missing. But when he was told, "You are the tenth," he realized immediately that he was the tenth. See Upad I,18,170; 172; 173; 174; 187; 190; 199; Śaṅkara *ad* Bṛh. Up. I,4, 7; Śaṅkara *ad* Taitt. Up. II, 1; Naiṣ III,64–71; *Saṃbandhavārtika*, 206–216; *Pañcadasī* VII,57 ff. and VII, 247 ff. For parallel stories in Indian folktales, see S. Thompson and W. E. Roberts, *Types of Indic Oral Tales* (FF Communications No. 180), Type No. 1287: *Numskulls Unable to Count Their Own Number.*

[3]This is based upon "*tat tvam asi*" (Chānd. Up. VI,8,7, etc.).

[4]*Ātman* is described as bodiless. Cf. Chānd. Up. VIII,12,1; Upad I,15,6; 15,7; 18, 164.

[5]This is based upon Bṛh. Up. III,4,2.

[6]For a detailed explanation of the sentence "*tat tvam asi*," see Introduction, III,C, 2–5, pp. 49–57.

[7]Cf. Upad I,13,2 and 5.

[8]The term *sattva* is a synonym for *buddhi* in Śaṅkara's works. Cf. Upad I,15,2.

[9]Cf. Upad I,2,2; 5,5; 6,5; 6,6.

[10]Stanza 12,13cd is quoted in *Vedāntasāra* [XXXVI] 236.

[11]See Upad I,1,14.

CHAPTER 13

EYELESSNESS[1]

1. As I am eyeless, I do not see. Likewise, as I am earless, how shall I hear? As I have no organ of speech, I do not speak. As I am mindless, how shall I think?

2. As I am devoid of the life principle,[2] I do not act. Being without intellect, I am not a knower. Therefore I have neither knowledge nor nescience, having the light of Pure Consciousness only.

3. Ever-free, pure, transcendentally changeless,[3] invariable, immortal, imperishable, and thus always bodiless.[4]

4. [All-]pervading like ether, I have neither hunger nor thirst, neither sorrow nor delusion, neither decay nor death, since I am bodiless.

5. As I have no sense of touch, I do not touch. As I have no tongue, I do not perceive taste. As I am of the nature of constant knowledge, I never have [either] knowledge or ignorance.

6. The modification of the mind,[5] which is caused by the eye and takes on form-and-color [of its object], is certainly always seen by the constant Seeing of *Ātman.*

7. In like manner the modifications [of the mind] which are connected with the senses other [than the eye] and are colored by [external] objects; also [the modification of the mind] in the form of memory and in the forms of passion and the like, which is unconnected [from the senses], located in the mind[6];

8. and the modifications of the mind in the dreaming state are also seen to be an other's. The Seeing of the Seer is, therefore, constant, pure, infinite, and alone.

9. The Seeing is [wrongly] taken to be inconstant and impure

because of the absence of discriminating knowledge with regard to It. Similarly, I experience pleasure and pain through [a seeing] which is the object and adjunct [of the Seeing].

10. Through deluded [seeing] all people think, "[I am] deluded," and again through a pure [seeing] they think, "[I am] pure"; for this reason they continue in transmigratory existence.

11. If one is a seeker after final release in this world, he should always remember *Ātman* which is ever-free, described in the scripture as eyeless, etc.[7] [which] includes the exterior and the interior, and is unborn.[8]

12. And as the scripture says that I am eyeless, etc., no senses at all belong to Me. And there are the words in the [Muṇḍ. Up. (II,1,2)] belonging to the *Atharvaveda*, "[He is. . .] breathless, mindless, pure."

13. As it is stated in the Kaṭh. Up. (I,3,15) that I do not have sound, etc., and [in the Muṇḍ. Up. (II,1,2) that I am] "without breath, without mind," I am indeed always changeless.

14. Therefore, mental restlessness[9] does not belong to Me. Therefore, concentration does not belong to Me. Both mental restlessness and concentration belong [only] to the changeable mind.

15. As I am without mind and pure, how can those two (= restlessness and concentration) belong to Me? Freedom from mind and freedom from change belong to Me who am bodiless and [all-]pervading.

16. Thus, as long as I had this ignorance, I had duties to perform, though I am ever-free, pure, and always enlightened.

17. How can concentration, non-concentration, or anything else which is to be done belong to Me? For, having meditated on and known Me, they realize that they have completed [all] that had to be done.

18. "I am *Brahman*" (Bṛh.Up. I,4,10). I am all, always pure, enlightened and unfettered, unborn, all-pervading, undecaying, immortal, and imperishable.

19. In no being is there any Knower other than Myself; [I am] the Overseer of deeds, the Witness, the Observer, constant, attributeless, and non-dual.[10]

20. I am neither existent nor non-existent[11] nor both, being

alone and auspicious. To Me, the Seeing, there is neither twilight nor night nor day at any time.

21. Just as ether is free from all forms, is subtle and non-dual, so am I devoid even of this [ether], I am *Brahman*, non-dual.

22. My separatedness, *i.e.*, in the form "my *ātman*," "his *ātman*," and "your *ātman*," is what is falsely constructed [on Me], just as the difference of one and the same ether arises from the difference of holes [in various objects].

23. Difference and non-difference, one and many, object of knowledge and knower, movement and mover—how can these [notions] be falsely constructed on Me who am one alone?

24. Nothing to be rejected or accepted belongs to Me, for I am changeless, always released and pure, always enlightened, attributeless, and non-dual.

25. Thus, with concentrated mind, one should always know everything as *Ātman*.[12] Having known Me to be abiding in one's own body, one is a sage, released and immovable.

26. If a *Yogin* thus knows the meaning of the truth, he is one who has completed all that was to be done,[13] a perfected one and knower of *Brahman*. [If he knows] otherwise, he is a slayer of *Ātman*.[14]

27. The meaning of the *Veda* herein determined, which has been briefly related by me, should be imparted to serene wandering ascetics by one of disciplined intellect.[15]

Notes

[1]See Upad II,3, which is entitled "*Parisaṃkhyāna*" and is similar to this chapter. Cf. Unters, p. 1925, n. 2.

[2]According to Śaṅkara, the individual consists of the following six components: (1) the body, gross (*sthūla*) and subtle (*sūkṣma*), (2) the five senses (*buddhīndriya*), (3) the five organs of action (*karmendriya*), (4) the internal organ (*antaḥkaraṇa*), (5) the principal vital air (*mukhya prāṇa*), and (6) *Ātman*. The term *prāṇa* in its wider sense comprises (2)–(5), and the term is probably used here in this wider sense. In the first stanza, (2) (eye and ear), (3) (organ of speech), and (4) (mind) are referred to. See Introduction, III,B,1, pp. 28–33. Cf. P. Deussen, *The System of the Vedânta*, pp. 324–332; Nakamura II, pp. 451–463.

[3]The word "*kūṭastha*," which is translated as "transcendentally changeless," is unknown to the classical *Upaniṣads* but used in the BhG (VI,8; XII, 3; XV, 16). Though the precise interpretation of this word is not entirely clear, Śaṅkara interprets it as

aprakampya (not to be caused to tremble or shake) in his commentary on the BhG (VI, 8). In another place (BhG XII,3) Śaṅkara interprets "*kūṭa*" as indicating *avidyā* and the many other seeds of *saṃsāra*, and so "*kūṭastha*" means "standing on this *kūṭa*" (see S. Mayeda, "The Authenticity of the Gītābhāṣya Ascribed to Śaṅkara," WZKSO, vol. IX, 1965, pp. 182–183). In Pāli the word "*kūṭaṭṭha*" is used in the sense of "not subject to change" or "immovable" and interpreted as "*pabbatakūṭaṃ viya ṭhita*" (see *The Pali Text Society's Pali-English Dictionary*, p. 53). Cf. F. Edgerton (tr.), *The Bhagavad Gītā* (Harvard Oriental Series vol. 38. Cambridge: Harvard University Press, 1952), vol. 1, note 2 on BhG VI,8, p. 183. In the Upad, Śaṅkara uses "*kūṭastha*" as an antonym of "*vikriyāvat*" (Upad II, 2,74) and "*pariṇāmin*" (Upad II,2,75). See note 22 of Upad II,2.

[4]See note 4 of Upad I,12.

[5]See Upad I,11,3.

[6]According to Śaṅkara, desire and other psychological facts are perceived as objects just as a jar and other external objects are perceived as objects (see Upad II,2,70). There is no essential difference between external and internal perception, since in the process of perception objects of external perception are transformed into *pratyaya* (notion) or *vṛtti* (modification) of the *buddhi* (or *manas*) which are in the form of external objects, and objects of internal perception are also transformed into those which are in the form of pleasure, pain, and other objects of internal perception. For a fuller account of perception, see Introduction, III,B,2–4, pp. 33–43.

[7]Cf. Bṛh. Up. III,8,8; Śvet. Up. III,19.

[8]Cf. Muṇḍ. Up. II,1,2; Upad I,14,18; II,1,7.

[9]In later Advaitins' works the term *vikṣepa* has the technical sense of projection and *avidyā* (or *māyā*) is said to have the projective power (*vikṣepaśakti*) and the obscuring power (*āvaraṇaśakti*). Cf. T. M. P. Mahadevan, *The Philosophy of Advaita* (Madras: Ganesh & Co., 1957), pp. 240–242. However, Śaṅkara's concept of *avidyā* (or *māyā*) does not have such attributes. The term *vikṣepa* here means "moving about" or "restlessness" of the mind. This usage of the term is in accordance with that in *Yogasūtra* I,30 and 31 (*cittavikṣepa*), which Śaṅkara interprets as "*cittaṃ vikṣipanti viṣayeṣv iti cittavikṣepāḥ*" in his *Yogasūtrabhāṣyavivaraṇa* (Madras Government Oriental Series, XIV), p. 82. It also agrees with that in Buddhist texts. For example, *Abhidharmakośabhāṣya* (ed. by P. Pradhan. Tibetan Sanskṛt Works Series vol. VIII. Patna, 1967), p. 56, line 13; p. 339, line 21; p. 340, line 1. Cf. *U. Wogihara: Sanskrit-Chinese-Japanese Dictionary* (Tokyo: Suzuki Research Foundation, 1940–1974), p. 1202; Mayeda Upad, p. 29.

[10]This stanza is probably based upon Śvet. Up. VI,11. See Upad I,11,6.

[11]Cf. Upad I,19,19.

[12]Cf. Bṛh. Up. IV,4,23: *iti tasmād evaṃvit, . . . samāhito bhūtvā, . . . sarvam ātmānaṃ paśyati.*

[13]Cf. *kṛtakṛtya*, BhG XV,20; Ait. Up. IV,4.

[14]Cf. *ātmahan*, *Īśā Up.* III.

[15]As for the conditions for admission to Śaṅkara's teachings, see Upad II,1,2. Cf. Upad I,16,72; 17,53; 17,86; 17,87; BSBh I,1,1; P. Deussen, *The System of the Vedânta*, pp. 60–82.

CHAPTER 14

DREAM AND MEMORY

1. Since the form-and-color of a jar, etc., is seen appearing in dream and memory, it is certainly to be inferred that the intellect has previously been seen in that form.

2. Just as one oneself is not the body which is seen wandering about begging alms in the dreaming state, so is he different from the body which is seen in the waking state, since he is the seer [of the body].

3. Just as [molten] copper appears in the form of the mold into which it was poured, so it is certainly experienced that the mind, when pervading [the external objects] such as form-color, appears in their forms.[1]

4. Or, just as light, the illuminator, assumes the forms of what it illuminates, so the intellect is seen to have the forms of its objects, since it is the illuminator of all the objects.[2]

5. And the intellect in the form of [certain] objects must have been seen by the [dreaming] man before [also]. If not, how could he see [these forms] in the dreaming state? Again, when a form is being recalled, whence would it come to him?

6. [To say] that [the intellect] is an illuminator means that it is seen in the guise of [illuminable objects such as] form-and-color. In like manner [when we say] that the power of Seeing is the Seer, it means that It pervades [the intellect] when the intellect is appearing [in the form of objects].

7. Since all intellects in all bodies are illumined by Me, who have Pure Consciousness only as [My] light, I am therefore indeed the *Ātman* of all.

8. The intellect becomes instrument, object, agent, action, and

result in the dreaming state. Since [the intellect] is also seen in the same way in the waking state, the Seer is different from it.

9. The intellect and so on are non-*Ātman* since they are by nature [objects] to be rejected or accepted. *Ātman* is the agent which rejects or accepts; [*Ātman*] is neither to be abandoned nor taken.

10. Since [*Ātman*] includes the exterior and the interior,[3] is pure and a homogeneous mass of intelligence, how can there be falsely constructed upon [It] an exterior, an interior, and anything else to be rejected?

11. When the *Brahman*-knower realizes that the *Ātman* has been left through the exclusion of [every-]thing else by saying, "Not thus! Not so!"(Bṛh. Up. II,3,6), then why should he make any further effort?

12. Being beyond hunger, etc.,[4] I am constantly *Brahman*; how can I have duties to perform? Thus one should rightly consider.

13. A knower of *Ātman*, if he wishes to perform some other duty here, is like a man who has reached the further bank of a river and, on being there, wishes to go back to the other bank.

14 If a knower of *Ātman* were [an object] to be rejected or accepted, he should not be considered to be worthy of final release. He is certainly thrown out by the mouth of *Brahman*.

15. As the vital air[5] is the universe including the sun, there is neither day nor night for a knower of the vital air. How can there be [day or night] for a knower of *Brahman*, since He is non-dual?

16. Indeed *Ātman* neither remembers nor forgets Itself, since [Its] Pure Consciousness is not impaired. The knowledge that it is the mind that remembers has also its origin in nescience, the cause.

17. As it is said traditionally that if the highest *Ātman* is the object of a knower, this [*ātman*] would be something falsely constructed through nescience; when [this *ātman*] has been excluded like a snake [falsely constructed] on a rope, [the highest *Ātman*] is non-dual.

18. Since there exists neither agent nor object nor result[6] and since [*Ātman*] includes both the exterior and the interior and is unborn,[7] how can anyone have the notion about It (*Ātman*), "This is mine" or "This is I"?

19. The notions "oneself" and "one's own" are indeed falsely

constructed [upon *Ātman*] through nescience. When there is [the knowledge of] the oneness of *Ātman*, these notions certainly do not exist. If the seed does not exist, whence shall the fruit arise?

20. The Imperishable is the Seer, the Hearer, the Thinker, and the Understander. As It is not different from the Seer, etc., I, the Seer, am the Imperishable.[8]

21. As everything, whether stationary (inanimate) or movable (animate), is possessed of seeing or some other activity, everything is the Imperishable. Therefore I, the Imperishable, am the *Ātman* of all.

22. Whoever sees *Ātman* as devoid of duties remaining [undone], devoid of action itself and of the result of the action, and free from the notions "mine" and "myself," he [really] sees [the truth].

23. If you have come to know that the notions "mine" and "myself," efforts and desires are by nature void in *Ātman*, continue to be self-abiding. What is the use of efforts?

24. Whoever looks upon the *Ātman* as the bearer of the "I"-notion and as the knower is not a knower of the *Ātman*. He who looks upon it as not so is a knower of the *Ātman*.

25. Just as *Ātman*, though different, is thought to be identical with the body, etc., in like manner, since *Ātman* is not recognized as a non-agent, It [is thought to] consist of action and its result.

26. Seeing, hearing, thinking, and understanding[9] are always experienced by people in the dreaming state. Since these are the nature of *Ātman*, therefore *Ātman* is directly perceptible.

27. To the knower of *Ātman* there is no fear of the other world nor any fear of death; to him even gods like Brahmā and Indra[10] are pitiable objects.

28. If his inauspicious desire, the cause of all afflictions, has been completely destroyed, what use is it to him to be a god, to be Brahmā and Indra?

29. He to whom both "I," the notion of "oneself," and "my," the notion of "one's own," have become meaningless, becomes a knower of *Ātman*.

30. For one who has come to know that *Ātman* is the same, whether adjuncts such as the intellect exist or not, how can there be anything which he ought to do?

31. Once one has understood that *Ātman* is [*Brahman*]—[like]

ether, clear, stainless, of homogeneous intelligence, and non-dual —what else, say, should such a one do?

32. He who sees *Ātman* abiding in all beings and [yet] also [sees] an enemy of *Ātman* surely wants to make fire cold.

33. *Ātman*, which acts as the intellect[11] and the life organs, is like the reflection [of the sun in the water],[12] within the range of sense-perception, etc., since it is said, "[He, remaining the same, traverses both worlds,] appearing to think [, appearing to move about]" (Bṛh. Up. IV,3,7), and is Itself pure and released.

34. I am devoid of the life organs and mind, unconnected [with anything], the Seeing, [all-]pervading like ether, how can there be anything for Me to do?

35. I never see non-concentration, nor anything else [needing] to be purified, belonging to Me who am changeless, the pure *Brahman* free from evil.

36. [Nor do] I [see] anything to be pursued as belonging to [Me] who am all-pervading and motionless, nor any upward, downward, or oblique direction as belonging to [Me] who am devoid of parts on account of being attributeless.

37. Being light of Pure Consciousness only, there is no darkness in It at all. I am ever-free; how is there now anything left for Me to do?

38. Since [It] is mindless, what does [It] think? Again, since [It] is devoid of organs [of action], what does [It] do? The words of the *Śruti*, "[He is . . .] certainly without breath, without mind, pure" (Muṇḍ. Up.II,1,2),[13] are true.

39. As *Ātman* is without time, without place, without direction, and without cause,[14] he who always meditates [on *Ātman*] never depends upon time and the like.[15]

40. Whoever bathes in that spiritual pilgrimage place, where gods and *Vedas* and every purification unite, becomes immortal.

41. Sound and the other [external objects of knowledge] are not perceived by themselves, nor are they perceived by each other. Since taste, etc., are perceived by something other than themselves, they are objects of perception, and therefore belong to the body.

42. In like manner, "I"-notion, "my"-notion, desire, effort, change, pleasures and the like are [perceived by something other

than themselves] since [they are] objects of perception in ordinary life. Moreover, since they are objects, they are not perceived by each other. It (= their perceiver = *Ātman*) is different from them.

43. Since every change such as the "I"-notion, etc. has its agent, it is connected with the result of actions, and is illumined, as by the sun, on all sides by [*Ātman*, which is] of the nature of Pure Consciousness. *Ātman* is therefore unfettered.

44. [*Ātman*,] which is of the nature of Seeing, having pervaded, like the sky, the minds of all embodied beings, abides [there]. Therefore, there is neither a knower lower than this one nor a [knower] higher than this one. Consequently there is only one Lord.

45. The body and the intellect being perceivable by something other than themselves, the doctrines that there is no *Ātman*[16] have been fully rejected by me, since it has been established that [*Ātman*] is beyond action which causes impurity, is completely stainless, all-pervading, unfettered, and non-dual.

46. If, in your view,[17] the mind in the form of a jar, etc., activated variously by its own modifications, is not cognized [by *Ātman* different from the mind], [then] it would not be possible to prevent [It] from having faults—*i.e.*, impurity, the nature of non-consciousness and change—as the mind has.

47. Just as ether, being pure and uninterrupted, is neither attached nor stained,[18] so is *Ātman* indeed always the same to all beings and always free from old age, death, and fear.

48. As the formless and the formed, actions and residual impressions[19] are through nescience falsely constructed upon *Ātman* by those whose seeing is deluded; therefore, by saying, "Not thus!" Bṛh.Up. II,3,6, etc.), they are excluded from [*Ātman*], which is of the nature of Seeing, and the Seeing [alone] is left unexcluded [by the *Śruti*].

49. The form of the mind in the waking state, which arises from its connection with [external] objects, is seen at the time of memory and to a man in the dreaming state, as [external] objects [are seen in the waking state]. This is also the case with regard to the residual impression of the body. The body and the mind are different from the Seeing since they are [Its] objects.

50. There are no distinctions in ether, which is by nature pure, whether there is any impurity such as a cloud, or whether [such impurity] has passed away; in like manner there is no distinction

at any time in the Seeing which is like ether, whether Its duality is negated by the *Śrutis* or not.

Notes

[1]This stanza is quoted in *Pañcadaśī* IV,28.

[2]This stanza is quoted in *Pañcadaśī* IV,29. Stanzas 14,3, and 4 are very important, since they reveal Śaṅkara's view of the psychology of perception. For a detailed discussion, see Introduction, III,B,2, pp. 33–37.

[3]Cf. Muṇḍ. Up. II,1,2; Upad I,13,11; 14,10, etc.

[4]The three commentators Ānandajñāna, Bodhanidhi, and Rāmatīrtha, take *aśanāyādi* as *ṣaḍūrmi* (the six waves of existence), *i.e.*, *aśanāyā* (hunger), *pipāsā* (thirst), *śoka* (grief), *moha* (delusion), *jarā* (old age), and *mṛtyu* (death). Cf. Bṛh. Up. III,5,1; Upad I,18,103; 18,206; 19,4.

[5]Cf. *prāṇo 'sau lokaḥ*, Bṛh. Up. I,5,4; *prāṇo hy evaitāni sarvāṇi bhavati*, Chānd. Up. V,1, 15 (= VII,15,4); *prāṇā vāvādityāḥ*, Chānd. Up. III,16,5 and 6; *ādityo ha vai prāṇaḥ*, Praś. Up. I,5 and III,8.

[6]Cf. stanza 8.

[7]Cf. Muṇḍ. Up. II,1,2; Upad I,13,11; II,1,7.

[8]This stanza is based upon Bṛh. Up. III,8,11.

[9]Cf. Bṛh. Up. III,8,11; Upad I,14,20.

[10]The gods Brahmā, Viṣṇu, and Śiva constitute the Hindu triad and represent the creative, preservative, and destructive principles, respectively. However, Brahmā never attained the popularity of the other two. Indra, an atmospheric god, is the most prominent divinity in the *Ṛg-Veda*. He is often identified with thunder and wields a weapon named "*vajra*" which means thunderbolt. In the later Hindu mythology, however, Indra has fallen into the second rank, being inferior to the triad.

[11]*Prajñā* is *buddhi* according to Rāmatīrtha.

[12]Rāmatīrtha says: *chāyeva sūryādipratibimbam iva jaleṣu.*

[13]Cf. Upad I,3,4; 13,12.

[14]Cf. *asya jagato . . . pratiniyatadeśakālanimittakriyāphalāśrayasya* . . . , BSBh I,1,2, p. 47.

[15]Cf. BS IV,1,11.

[16]This is probably to refute the Buddhist tenet (*nirātmavāda*). It is of interest that Śaṅkara uses Buddhistic terms such as *śūnya* (void, stanza 23) and *tṛṣṇā* (thirst, stanza 28) in this chapter.

[17]This interpretation is supported by all the three commentators. If the reading "*tena*" is adopted in the first line instead of "*te na,*" as Rāmatīrtha suggests in his commentary, the following translation is possible: "If the mind in the form of a jar, etc., activated variously by its own modifications, is perceived by this [*Ātman*], it is not possible to prevent [It] from having the faults, *i.e.*, impurity, the nature of nonconsciousness and change."

[18]Cf. Kaṭh. Up. V,11; Upad I,10,7; 10,14; 15,23; 16,58; 16,71; II,3,116.

[19]See Upad I,11,10; 13.

CHAPTER 15

ONE THING CANNOT BE ANOTHER

1. As one thing cannot be another, one should consider that no thing is anything else, since if one thing could be another, it would certainly perish.

2. [The locus] where a thing which has previously been seen is seen, like a picture painted on a canvas, by him who is remembering [it] and [the agent of knowledge] by whom it is seen to him should be known to be what are termed the intellect[1] and the Field-Knower[2] (= *Ātman*) [respectively].

3. That which was connected with factors of action, such as agent, which ended with results [such as pleasure and pain], and was perceived—that is now remembered as having been located in the object (= the intellect) [of the Field-Knower]. Therefore, it (= the intellect) was formerly the object [of the Field-Knower].

4. And the object is different from the Seer, since it is always the object like a jar. The Seer and the object are heterogeneous; otherwise [the Seer would be] like the intellect and not the Witness.

5. If one believes that one's own [lineage, etc.] is identical with *Ātman*,[3] lineage, etc., like a dead body, will prompt [one] to obey injunctions.[4] Therefore, lineage, etc., like a dead body is not [identical with *Ātman*]; otherwise [*Ātman*] would be non-*Ātman*.

6. As [the *Śruti*] says, "Pleasure and pain do not [touch one who is bodiless]" (Chānd. Up. VIII,12,1), bodilessness is not the result of actions. The cause of [one's] connection with the body is actions.[5] Therefore a man of knowledge should abandon actions.

7. If *Ātman* is independent with regard to actions, It should also be thought to be so with regard to the cessation of actions. If

bodilessness is known to be a result which cannot be attained through actions, why should one perform actions?

8. Having completely abandoned the cause of actions such as lineage, a wise man should remember from scripture his own nature, which is incompatible with the cause of actions.

9. *Ātman* is one and the same in all beings and these beings are in It as [they are] in the ether.[6] It is declared that like the ether [It] has brightly and radiantly pervaded everything.[7]

10. On account of the absence of any wound or sinew, one should negate the gross body. As [*Ātman*] is pure and free from evils, [one should negate] impurity, and as the *Śruti* says, "[He is] bodiless" (*Īśā Up*. 8), [one should negate] the subtle body.[8]

11. Just as Vāsudeva (= Kṛṣṇa) said [to Arjuna] that He himself was the same in the holy *aśvattha* fig-tree and in his own body,[9] he who knows himself to be the same is the best knower of *Brahman.*

12. Just as "I"- and "my"-notions are not considered to arise with regard to other bodies, they do not arise with regard to this body either, since [*Ātman*] is equally the Witness of the intellect [in both cases].

13. Passion and aversion have, and the latent impression of form-and-color, a common substratum, [the intellect], and what is perceived as fear has the intellect as its substratum; therefore, the Knower is always pure and free from fear.[10]

14. One [comes] to consist of that upon which one fixes one's mind, if [one is] different from [it]. [But] there is no action in *Ātman* through which to become *Ātman.* [It] does not depend upon [anything else] for being *Ātman*, since, if [It] depended upon [anything else], It would not Itself be [*Ātman*].

15. Consciousness[11] is homogeneous, undivided, free from old age and devoid of impurity, like the ether. Because of adjuncts such as the eye, etc., It is regarded as contrary [to what It is].

16. On account of being an object like a jar, etc., the "I"-notion is not an attribute of *Ātman.* Other notions and faults should be known in like manner. *Ātman* is therefore devoid of impurity.[12]

17. As [*Ātman*] is the Witness of all notions, It is changeless and all-pervading. If the Seer were to change, He would be of limited knowledge like the intellect, etc.[13]

18. The Seeing of the Seer, unlike [that] of the eye, etc., is not

interrupted, since [the *Śruti*] says, "For there is no [cessation of the Seeing of] the Seer" (Bṛh. Up. IV,3,23). Therefore, the Seer is always experiencer.

19. One should examine thus: Am I a composite of the elements [such as earth and water]? Am I a composite of the organs [, internal and external]? Or am I any single one [of them] separately? Or who am I?

20. I am neither an individual element nor all the elements; I am neither an individual sense-organ nor all the sense-organs, since they are [respectively] objects of knowledge and instruments of knowledge, as are the jar, etc. The Knower is different from these.

21. The fuel of the fire of *Ātman* is the intellect. Blazing up with nescience, desire, and action,[14] the intellect always burns through the gates such as the ear, etc.

22. When the intellect, inflamed by the oblation of objects, functions among [the sense-organs], which have the right eye as their chief, the fire of *Ātman* becomes the experiencer of gross objects.[15]

23. If, being devoid of passion and aversion, one remembers, at the time of perceiving form-and-color, etc., that oblations are being offered to the fire of *Ātman*, one is not stained by faults in the waking state.

24. The *Ātman*, which [in the dreaming state] sees the memory-impressions—which are caused by action due to nescience—manifested in the abode of the mind [and] illumined by the self-effulgent One, is called *Taijasa.*[16]

25. When [in the state of deep sleep] neither [external] objects nor [their] memory-impressions are aroused by actions [to appear] in the intellect, then *Ātman* should be known to be *Prājña,*[17] which beholds nothing else.

26. The states of the mind, the intellect, and the sense-organs,[18] which are aroused by actions, are illumined only by Pure Consciousness as a jar, etc., are illumined by the sun.

27. Since this is so, the Knower, which illuminates the notions [of the intellect] by Its own light, and of which they are the objects, is called the agent of those notions [of the intellect] only by the deluded.

28. [Only to the deluded], therefore, is [It] also all-knowing

since [It] illuminates everything by Its own light. In like manner, as [It] is the cause of all actions, *Ātman* is all-doing.

29. The *ātman* thus described is [the *ātman*] with adjuncts. [But] the *Ātman* without adjuncts is indescribable, without parts, attributeless and pure; neither mind nor speech reaches It.

30. [*Ātman* is conceived variously—] as intelligent or unintelligent, agent or non-agent, pervading or not pervading, bound or released, one or not one, pure or in some other way.

31. Without attaining [It], words turn back together with the notions [of the intellect],[19] since [It] is attributeless, actionless, and devoid of distinction.

32. Just as the ether pervades everywhere and is unconnected with anything formed, so here [in the Vedānta] one should know *Ātman* to be the pure and highest state.[20]

33. Just as the sun [drives away] the darkness, so the All-Seeing One endowed with light, having given up sense-perception [in the waking state] and its memory [in dream], drives away the all-devouring darkness [in deep sleep].

34. That *Ātman*, whose objects are the notions which have as their objects form-and-color [in the waking state], memory [in dream], and darkness [in the state of deep sleep], is the all-pervading Seer, the same in all beings.

35. From the contact of *Ātman* with intellect, mind, eye, objects, and light there arise the various notions of the intellect which are characterized by ignorance.[21]

36. Distinguishing one's own *Ātman* from the rest, one should know It to be the pure and highest state, the Seer abiding in all beings, the same, beyond all fears,

37. the whole, all-pervading, calm, devoid of impurity, existing firm like the ether, without parts, without actions, the all, constant and free from duality.

38. Having inquired, "Is the Knower, the Witness of all notions, knowable by me [or not]?", one should ascertain whether or not *Brahman* is known.

39. On account of teachings such as "[It is] the unseen Seer" (Bṛh. Up. III,7,23) and "[If you think 'I know well,' you know] but little" (*Kena Up.* II,1), the highest *Brahman* is not knowable by me or others by any means.

40. [It] is my own nature, uninterrupted; [It] has the light of

knowledge as Its nature; [It] does not depend upon anything else for [Its] knowledge. Therefore [It] is always known to me.

41. The sun does not need any other light for its illumination; Knowledge does not require any other knowledge than its own knowledge for its illumination.

42. Whatever one's own nature may be, it does not depend upon anything else, since no light is to be manifested by another light.

43. Something destitute of light is manifested through its contact with something else which has light as its nature. It is, therefore, certainly false to say that light is an effect of the sun.

44. That which did not exist previously and comes into existence from something else is declared to be its effect. Because light is the nature of the sun, it is not [the case] that light which did not previously exist arises from the sun.

45. The sun and the like [, which have light as their nature], though they merely exist, are thought to be agents of light (illumination), since jars, etc., are manifested [by them]. This should also be taken to be true of *Ātman* which is [by nature] knowledge.[22]

46. Just as, when a snake comes out of its hole, the sun becomes [its] illuminator without any effort, so *Ātman* becomes a knower since It has knowledge as Its nature.

47. Thus [fire], which is [by nature] hot, becomes a burner merely by existing. This should also be taken to be true of *Ātman* which is [by nature] knowledge, when Its adjunct is known, as [the sun becomes an illuminator] when a snake which has come out [of its hole] is known.

48. Just as the Knower becomes a knower even without any effort, so It becomes a doer like a magnet.[23] *Ātman* Itself, therefore, is by nature neither knowable nor not knowable.

49. As there is the teaching that It is different from the known and the unknown,[24] bondage, final release, and other states are those which are falsely constructed upon *Ātman*.

50. Just as there is neither day nor night in the sun, since there is no distinction in the nature of light, so is there neither knowledge nor ignorance in *Ātman*, since there is no distinction in the nature of knowledge.

51. He who has come to know *Brahman* as described above, free

from rejection and acceptance as described above, is truly never born [again].

52. He who has fallen into the rivers of births and deaths can never save himself from them by anything else but knowledge,

53. because the *Śruti* says, "The knot of the heart is loosened, all doubts are cut off and one's actions are destroyed, when He is seen" (Muṇḍ.Up. II,2,8).

54. If a man, having completely excluded "I"- and "my"-notions, has a firm belief in that ether-like state destitute of the body, which has been declared according to well-studied scripture and inference, he is released.

Notes

[1]Upad I,12,10.

[2]The body is called the field (*kṣetra*) and *Ātman*, which knows it, is called the Field-Knower (*kṣetrajña*). Cf. BhG XIII.

[3]See a dialogue between the teacher and his pupil which starts at Upad II,1,9. Cf. BSBh I,1,1, p. 24.

[4]According to the commentators Ānandajñāna, Bodhanidhi, and Rāmatīrtha, this means that on account of the belief that a dead body is my mother or my father, the dead body prompts one to perform purificatory rites (*saṃskāra*).

[5]Cf. Upad I,1,3.

[6]Cf. *Īśā Up.* VI; BhG VI,30.

[7]Cf. *Īśā Up.* VIII.

[8]The whole stanza seems to interpret *Īśā Up.* VIII.

[9]Cf. BhG X,19–42, especially X,26; 37. Vāsudeva, or son of Vasudeva, is another name for Kṛṣṇa who is the chief speaker and expounds his philosophical doctrine to Arjuna in the BhG.

[10]This stanza is quoted in Upad II,1,35.

[11]In Śaṅkara's GBh the highest *Ātman* is called *vijñapti* (III,29, p. 139), the nature of *Ātman* is described as *vijñaptimātra* (II,17, p. 81), and *Brahman* is identified with *jñaptimātra* (III,33, p. 141). These are technical terms characteristic of the Vijñānavādin school of Buddhism. In the Upad, Śaṅkara uses the term *jñapti* three times. In this stanza he uses it in the sense of *caitanya* of *Ātman*. But in Upad I,16,25, where he attacks the Bāhyārthavādins of Buddhism, he seems to treat it as a synonym of *dhī* (*i.e.*, *buddhi*), and in Upad I,18,55 he asserts that the term *jñapti* is not applicable to *Ātman*, since it indicates "becoming" (*bhāva*). Cf. Nakamura III, pp. 529–530; S. Mayeda, "On the Author of the Māṇḍūkyopaniṣad- and the Gauḍapādīya-Bhāṣya," *The Adyar Library Bulletin*, vols. 31–32, 1967–68, p. 92.

[12]This stanza is quoted in Naiṣ IV,30.

[13]Cf. Upad II,2,75.

[14]Cf. *avidyā-kāma-karman*, BSBh I,2,17, p. 181. *Kleśa* (a psychic affection) is regarded as a wider concept to which *avidyā* belongs. *Avidyā* is the first and most dangerous mem-

ber of a series of *kleśas* and it causes the other (cf. *Yogasūtra* II,3). Cf. Eigen, p. 249; Mayeda Upad, pp. 25–26.

15According to GK I,2a, *Viśva* (= *Vaiśvānara*), *i.e.*, *Ātman* in the waking state, which experiences things gross (*sthūlabhuj*, GK I,3), is in the right eye (*dakṣiṇākṣimukhe viśvaḥ*). Commenting on this line, Śaṅkara says that though *Viśva* exists equally in all the sense-organs, it is especially referred to as existing in the right eye, for in the right eye is noticed the faculty of perception at its best (*upalabdhipāṭavadarśana*, p. 27; *dakṣiṇam akṣyeve mukhaṃ tasmin prādhānyena . . . viśva 'nubhūyate*, p. 26). Cf. Kauṣ. Up. IV,17; Bṛh. Up. II,3,5; Nakamura III, p. 307, note 1; R. N. Hume, *The Thirteen Principal Upanishads* (4th impression. Madras: Oxford University Press, 1958), p. 297, note 4.

16See Introduction, III,B,5, pp. 43–46. Cf. Māṇḍ. Up. IV; *Vedāntasāra* [XIV] 117.

17See Introduction, III,B,5, pp. 43–46. Cf. Māṇḍ. Up. V.

18Rāmatīrtha interprets the states of the mind, the intellect, and the senses as the states of dreaming, deep sleep, and waking, respectively.

19Cf. Taitt. Up. II,9; Māṇḍ. Up. III,1,8.

20The last line of this stanza appears again in stanza 36b.

21Cf. Upad I,16,19.

22The last line of this stanza appears again in stanza 47b.

23The same simile is seen in Upad I,17,79.

24Cf. *Kena Up.* I,4; S. Mayeda, "Śaṅkara's Authorship of the Kenopaniṣadbhāṣya," *Indo-Iranian Journal*, vol. X (1967), no. 1, p. 54, note 63.

CHAPTER 16

CONSISTING OF EARTH

1. It is said [traditionally] that the hard element in the body consists of earth and that the liquid element consists of water. Digestion, activity, and space have their origin in fire, air, and ether, respectively.

2. [The five senses, *i.e.*,] olfactory [, gustatory, visual, cutaneous, and auditory, consist of earth, water, fire, air, and ether] and their [five respective] objects of perception [namely, smell, taste, form-and-color, touch, and sound] are qualities[1] of earth and the other [four elements], since [each] sense is taken to have as its object a thing of its [own] kind like light and color.[2]

3. These [five senses] are [traditionally] said to be for the purpose of perception and [the five organs or action] such as the larynx and hand are said to be concerned with action. The mind[3] within, the eleventh, is for the sake of discriminating those [senses and organs of action].

4. The intellect is for the purpose of determining [objects]. As by its light, its own nature, *Ātman* is always illumining the intellect which perceives all objects, It is called the Knower.[4]

5. Just as the illuminating light takes the forms of the objects to be illuminated and, though [apparently] mixed [with its object], it is not [really] mixed [with it], so the Knower, though [apparently] mixed with notions, is not [really] mixed with them[5] at any time.

6. Just as a light on a stand can illumine without any effort everything that its light reaches, so the Knower sees without any effort the notions [of the intellect] in the forms of sound, etc., which It reaches.

7. Pleasure, etc., differentiate the intellect which, being illumined by the constant light of *Ātman*, appears as *ātman* in the composite of the body and the senses.

8. One with the feeling "I am suffering" does indeed regard *Ātman* as suffering from headache, etc. The Seer is different from Its object, which is suffering pain, and as It is the Seer, It is not suffering pain.

9. One suffers pain because he mistakenly believes, "I am a sufferer of pain," and not because he perceives any [actual] sufferer of pain. In the composite of the limbs, etc., one is the Seer of pain and never the sufferer of pain.

10. If [you object,[6]] "Like the eye [*Ātman*] is both an object and an agent," [we reply:] No, [because] eyes are many and composite. Therefore, *Ātman* cannot become the object, since It is the Seer.

11. If [you][7] think that *Ātman* is also many on account of knowledge, effort, etc., [we reply:] As [It] is homogeneous knowledge, It, like light, is not an object.

12. Though light is an illuminator, it does not illumine itself, [since it has in itself no difference as between illuminator and illuminated]; even if [it] had [such a] difference, it would not illumine itself, since [both the parts, illuminator and illumined, would be] the same [in nature].[8] In like manner *Ātman* [which has homogeneous knowledge] never sees Itself.

13. Nothing which has something else as its nature can become an object of the latter, as fire can neither burn nor illumine itself.

14. For this very reason is refuted [the idea] that the intellect perceives itself by itself.[9] In like manner it is also unreasonable [to assume] parts [of *Ātman*],[10] since [both parts, viz. the cognizer and the cognized] would be the same [in their nature and *Ātman* has in Itself] no difference.

15. Similarly, it is also unreasonable [to assume] that [*Ātman*] is empty.[11] For this reason has it been said that the intellect, like a jar, is seen by [*Ātman*] as other than [Itself], since [*Ātman*] is established before the discrimination[12] of that [intellect].

16. Whatever may exist before the discrimination [of the intellect], if it is the cause [of the discrimination], it is free from discrimination, since it is the cause of the rise of the discrimination.

17. Abandoning ignorance, which is the root of false assumption

and which is the impeller of transmigratory existence, one should know *Ātman* to be the highest *Brahman*, which is released and always fearless.

18. One should abandon as non-existent the triad of the states of waking, dreaming, and their seed called the state of deep sleep and consisting of darkness[13]; for when one [of them] exists, the others do not.

19. From the [apparent] mixing up of *Ātman* with intellect, mind, eye, light, object, and so on,[14] actions arise; therefrom results the confused idea that *Ātman* acts.

20. The shutting and opening of the eye in [its] place (= the eye-socket) are related to the air and not to the eye, since [the eye ever] shines [with the power of perception]. Similarly, [they] are neither in the mind nor in the intellect since [the mind and the intellect ever] shine.

21. Thinking and determination belong to the mind and the intellect respectively, neither having the attributes of the other. And everything is [falsely] constructed on *Ātman*.

22. The perception of the senses is limited by the places [where they are located in the body]. The intellect comes to be identical with those senses. When the Knower sees this intellect, it is felt to be, as it were, of the same size as the body.[15]

23. [All] this[16] is indeed the mere *dharma* (element of life)[17] which indeed perishes every moment and arises without intervals. [Though all this is momentary,] there arises the recognition that this [is that past one] because of similarity, just as a lamp [at this moment is recognized to be the same as it was at the previous moment on account of similarity[18]]. The cessation of [all] this is the aim of life.[19]

24. According to some [Buddhists],[20] there exist [the external objects] such as form-and-color, the forms of which are manifested by one other than themselves. According to other [Buddhists][21] nothing else exists but this [consciousness]. [Now] the improbability of the former [theory] is explained.

25. As [in their view] consciousness takes the forms of external objects and perishes every moment, it [will] never have memory. And as the intellect itself perishes every moment, it [will] have nowhere to store any impression [of the past].[22]

26. As not even a receptacle [for the impression and memory]

exists, there will be no instrument [with which to ascertain] the similarity [of a thing at this moment to what it was at the previous moment[23]]; therefore, [the former theory is unreasonable]. If there were a receptacle [for the impression and memory], there would be abandonment [of the theory] that [everything] is momentary. [But] that is not acceptable [to them].

27. And since cessation [of all this] is accomplished without any effort, it will be useless to teach means for achieving it. As [all this] comes to an end at every [moment], cessation does not depend upon anything else [for its accomplishment].

28. Even if they seek to say that [cessation] should depend upon another stream of existence, though different [in essence therefrom], if everything is momentary, it does not depend upon anything else.

29. Because [if] the two exist at the same time and are connected with each other, each [of them], having been established through the connection [with the other], will depend upon the other.

30. It is our opinion that where there is false superimposition[24] there is [also] annihilation of it. Tell me to whom final release as the result belongs, if everything perishes.[25]

31. Truly [It] exists Itself; It may be called Knowledge, *Ātman*, or something else. As It is the Knower of the existence and non-existence [of things], it is not accepted that It is non-existent.[26]

32. It is Being by which the non-existence [of things] is accepted. If It were not Being, people would not become aware of the existence and non-existence [of things]. And this is not acceptable.

33. That which is taken to exist before the false assumptions of "being," "non-being," and "being and non-being" is non-dual, since It is the same [in all]; It is eternal and different from what is falsely assumed.

34. Duality should be taken to be unreal like the object of a dream, since it comes into being through false assumptions and does not exist before the false assumptions of "being," "non-being," and the like.

35. On the authority of the scripture, which says that modifications are a verbal handle,[27] they are indeed unreal, since [the *Śrutis*] say, "Death after death does he attain [who thinks he sees manifoldness in this world]" (Bṛh. Up. IV,4,19), and the *Smṛti*

also says, "[For this is . . .] my miraculous power [which is hard to go beyond]" (BhG VII,14).

36. So *Ātman* is pure, since [It] is different in nature from false assumptions. Therefore, [It] is neither to be accepted nor rejected. *Ātman* is not what is falsely assumed by something other than [Itself].

37. Just as darkness does not exist in the sun, since it has light as its nature, so there is no ignorance in *Ātman*, since It has constant knowledge as Its nature.

38. Likewise, as the nature of *Ātman* is changeless, It has no change of state,[28] for if It had any change of state, Its destruction would certainly occur.

39. To him who [asserts that] final release is a change of state, final release is something produced; therefore it is perishable. It is by no means reasonable that final release is a union [of *Ātman* with *Brahman*] or disunion [from *Prakṛti*],

40. since [any] union [with *Brahman*] or disunion [from *Prakṛti*] is not permanent. And [it is by no means reasonable that final release is for *Ātman*] to go [to *Brahman*, or for *Brahman*] to come [to *Ātman*]. But one's own nature is never lost,

41. since one's own nature has no cause, whereas the others (=a change of state, etc.)[29] indeed have their causes. One's own nature is indeed neither acquired nor lost by oneself [or by any others].

42. As [It] is the nature of all, It cannot be abandoned nor grasped, since [It] is not different [from anything]. Therefore it is eternal, since [It] is not an object and not separated [from anything].

43. As everything exists for *Ātman*'s sake, *Ātman* is eternal and isolated. Therefore the knower of final release should abandon all actions along with their accessories.[30]

44. The attainment of *Ātman* is the supreme attainment[31] according to the scriptures and reasoning. But the attainment of *Ātman* is not attaining something other [than *Ātman*]. Therefore one should [simply] give up [the misconception of *Ātman*] as non-*Ātman*.

45. The loss of equilibrium of the [three] *guṇas* is not possible,[32] since nescience, etc., are inactive [in this state], and no other cause is satisfactory [on the theory proposed].

46. If one [of the three *guṇas*] were the cause of another [*guṇa*], there would [either] always be activity or never activity at all. There would not be any necessity for activity either in the *guṇas* or in *Ātman* (= *Puruṣa*).[33]

47. If [the single *Prakṛti*] existed for the [*Puruṣas*],[34] the distinction between released and bound [*Puruṣas*] would not be reasonable. And the relation of an object and its seeker [is not possible between *Prakṛti* and *Puruṣa*], [since] neither the Knower (= *Puruṣa*) nor the other (= *Prakṛti*) is a seeker after an object.

48. Since in the Sāṃkhya system *Puruṣa* is changeless, even [there] it is not reasonable for *Pradhāna* (= *Prakṛti*) to exist for another's (= *Puruṣa*) sake. Even if there were changes [in It], it would still not be reasonable.

49. As no mutual relation between *Prakṛti* and *Puruṣa* is possible and as *Pradhāna* (= *Prakṛti*) is non-intelligent, it is not reasonable for *Pradhāna* to exist for *Puruṣa*'s sake.

50. If any action took place [in *Puruṣa*, It] would be perishable. If [action took place] only in knowledge [of *Puruṣa*, It would be perishable] in the same way. If [the functioning] of *Pradhāna* has no cause, it follows that there is no final release.

51. Just as heat [, a quality of fire,] is not to be manifested by [light, another quality of fire], pleasure and other [qualities of *Ātman*] are not to be cognized by cognition [*i.e.*, a quality of *Ātman*], as held by the followers of Kaṇāda[35] and others, since they have one and the same [substance (= *Ātman*)] as their basis.

52. Pleasure and cognition cannot inhere [in *Ātman*] at the same time, since a [single] contact of the mind [with *ātman*] causes one [quality only]; therefore, pleasure is not to be cognized by cognition.

53. And since the other [qualities] are different [from one another, their] simultaneous origination is not to be accepted. If [you say,] "It is the cognition of qualities that [they] are inherent [in *ātman*," we reply,] "No; because [cognition] distinguishes [qualities].

54. [Qualities] are to be apprehended by cognition, for [they are] to be distinguished by cognition, and there is memory, [e.g.,] "Pleasure was perceived by me"; [and,] according to you, [*ātman*] does not have cognition as its nature.

55. Pleasure and so on will not be qualities of *ātman*, since it is

changeless according to you. [Even if *ātman*, though changeless, could have different qualities,] as [qualities and *ātmans* are] different [from one another], why [do not the qualities of one *ātman*] belong to another or equally to the mind?

56. And if a cognition should become an object of cognition, a *regressus ad infinitum* would be inevitable. If some final [cognition] is admitted, the simultaneous origination [of all cognitions] is accepted.[36]

57. And as *Ātman* has no change of state,[37] there will be no bondage in It. Nor is there any impurity, for [It] has no attachment according to the *Śruti*, "[It] has no attachment, for [It does not get attached]" (Bṛh.Up.III,9,26).

58. And [this is also] because [*Ātman*] is subtle, one alone and imperceptible, according to the *Śruti*, "[The one . . .] is not stained [by the sorrow of the world]" (Kaṭh.Up. V,11 = II,2,11). [Objection:] "If that were so, there would be no final release at all, since there would be no bondage.

59. Thus the scripture would be meaningless." [Reply:] No; [because] bondage is taken to be a confused idea of the intellect, and final release is the cessation thereof. Bondage is what has been mentioned before[38] and nothing else.

60. Being illumined by Knowledge, the light of *Ātman*, the intellect thinks that there is Knowledge in Itself and that there is no other knower. This is indeed the confused idea which is in the intellect.

61. As Knowledge is the very nature of *Ātman*, It is constantly applied figuratively to the intellect. And the absence of discriminating knowledge is beginningless; this and nothing else is taken to be transmigratory existence.

62. Final release is its cessation and nothing else, since [every other view] is unreasonable. But final release is thought to be the destruction [of *Ātman*] by those according to whom final release is to become something else.

63. Similarly, it is also unreasonable that [final release] is a change of state [in *Ātman*],[39] since [It] is changeless. If there were change [in *Ātman*], [It] would have parts; consequently [It] would perish, like a jar, etc.

64. Therefore, assumptions concerning bondage, final release, etc., [which are] other than this are indeed confused ideas. The

assumptions of the Sāṃkhyas, of the followers of Kaṇāda, and of the Buddhists are lacking in profound consideration.

65. As [their assumptions] contradict the scriptures and reasoning, they should never be respected. Their faults can be pointed out hundreds and thousands of times.

66. And since it might also involve being culpable [under the text] "any other [of the manifold scriptures in the world] than this [should verily be doubted by the wise who wish for correct knowledge of the law],"[40] [they should not be respected at any time]. Therefore, having abandoned the teaching of other scriptures, a wise man should make firm his understanding

67. of the true meaning of the *Vedānta* (= *Upaniṣads*) and also of Vyāsa's thought,[41] with faith and devotion[42] and without any crookedness.

68. Thus both the false assumptions based upon dualism and the views that *Ātman* does not exist have been rejected through reasoning; seekers after final release, being free from doubts which arise from the views of others, become firm in the path of knowledge.

69. If one has attained the absolutely pure and non-dual Knowledge, which is self-witnessed and contrary to false assumptions, and rightly holds a firm belief, he will go to eternal peace, unaccompanied [by anything].

70. Having thoroughly examined this esoteric teaching, the supreme goal, people who are free from faults and devoid of any misconception [about *Ātman*] should always set their minds on rectitude.[43] Indeed, nobody who thinks himself different [from *Brahman*] is a seer of the truth.

71. Having come to know this highest means of purification, a man is released from the sins caused by nescience and accumulated in many other births; like the ether, he is unstained by actions[44] in this life.

72. This [highest means of purification] should be always taught to the seeker after final release whose mind has been calmed, whose senses have been controlled, whose faults have been abandoned, who is acting as prescribed [in the scriptures], who is endowed with virtues, and who is always obedient [to his teacher].[45]

73. Just as one does not falsely think that another's body [is

oneself or one's own], so having observed the highest truth and having attained this absolutely pure knowledge, he will then be released in all respects.

74. Certainly in this world there is no attainment more excellent than that of one's own nature,[46] since it comes from nothing else than this [*Vedānta*]. But the attainment of one's own nature, which is superior even to the kingdom of Indra, should not be given without examining [one's pupil] carefully.

Notes

[1]Bodhanidhi takes "*guṇa*" as "*pariṇāmaviśeṣa*" and Rāmatīrtha as "*kārya*." Both of them think that the five senses and their objects are special transformations or productions of the five elements. Jagadānanda follows Rāmatīrtha's interpretation. But such usage of the word "*guṇa*" is unusual. Moreover, like the Nyāya and the Mīmāṃsā, the Vedānta holds that the senses are constituted by earth and the other elements, to which smell, taste, etc., belong as qualities. Cf. S. Chatterjee, *The Nyāya Theory of Knowledge* (Calcutta: University of Calcutta, 1950), pp. 131–138; D. M. Datta, *The Six Ways of Knowing* (Calcutta: University of Calcutta, 1960), pp. 39–40. Taking into consideration the above facts and the previous stanza, I have translated the word "*guṇa*" as "quality."

[2]The commentators explain this simile as meaning that when there is brightness of color, it is because its illuminator (such as a lamp) is also bright.

[3]Śaṅkara's concept of *manas* is not clear. In most cases in his works the *manas* is merely another name for the *buddhi*, or at least it is indistinguishable from the latter. It is a controversial problem for later Advaita philosophers whether or not the *manas* is a sense (*indriya*), but Śaṅkara does not give any answer to this problem. See Introduction, III,B,1, pp. 30–33. Cf. T. M. P. Mahadevan, *The Philosophy of Advaita*, pp. 29–31; D. M. Datta, *The Six Ways of Knowing*, pp. 53–59.

[4]Ānandajñāna and Rāmatīrtha consider that this stanza is meant to refute Buddhism.

[5]Cf. BS II,3,30–31 and Śaṅkara's commentary on it.

[6]This probably refers to a tenet of the Vijñānavādins. See note 10.

[7]This probably refers to the Vaiśeṣika system, according to which *ātman* has qualities such as cognition (*buddhi*), pleasure (*sukha*), pain (*duḥkha*), desire (*icchā*), aversion (*dveṣa*), and effort (*prayatna*). According to Śaṅkara knowledge is the nature of *Ātman* and not Its quality. Cf. Upad I,16,51–56.

[8]Cf. Upad I,16,14.

[9]Stanzas 12–14 are probably meant to refute the Vijñānavādins. See note 10 below.

[10]In Upad I,18,142 Śaṅkara quotes a stanza from Dharmakīrti's *Pramāṇaviniścaya* which refers to the theory of the threefold part of consciousness, *i.e.*, the object (*grāhya*), the subject (*grāhaka*), and consciousness (*saṃvitti*). It is, therefore, very likely that here Śaṅkara refutes the above theory which was advocated by Vijñānavādins, Dignāga, and Dharmakīrti. According to Śaṅkara the Mādhyamakas consider the consciousness (*vijñāna*) to be free from the parts of subject and object (*grāhyagrāhakāṃśavinirmukta*) and empty (*śūnya*) (Śaṅkara *ad* Bṛh. Up. IV,3,7, p. 567).

[11]Stanzas 15–16 are probably meant to refute the Śūnyavādins.

[12]The function of *vikalpa* is attributed to the *manas* in other places. (Upad I,16,3. Cf. Upad I,16,21; GBh V,13, p. 257) but here it is regarded as belonging to the *buddhi*.

[13]Cf. Upad I,17,26; GK I,13.

[14]Cf. Upad I,15,35.

[15]Refutation of the Jain tenet. Cf. Upad I,16,22; 17,56; BSBh II,2,34, pp. 484–485.

[16]Refutation of Buddhism starts here. Stanza 24 suggests that stanza 23 may introduce doctrines which are commonly held by the Bāhyārthavādins and the Vijñānavādins. Cf. stanza 24 and notes 20 and 23. Ānandajñāna, Bodhanidhi, and Rāmatīrtha interpret "this" as knowledge (*jñāna*) and the object of knowledge (*jñeya*).

[17]"*Dharma*" here is used in a Buddhist technical sense. Rāmatīrtha interprets it as *vastumātra*.

[18]See Upad I,16,25 and 26; Śaṅkara *ad* Bṛh. Up. IV,3,7, pp. 574–575; BSBh II, 2,25, p. 462.

[19]See Upad I,16,27; Śaṅkara *ad* Bṛh. Up. IV,3,7, p. 567 and pp. 576–577.

[20]According to Ānandajñāna and Bodhanidhi, these are the Bāhyārthavādins or those who assert that there exist external objects. By this word Śaṅkara probably means both the Sautrāntikas and the Vaibhāṣikas of the Theravāda Buddhism in his BSBh (II,2,31, pp. 478–479) where he points out that both the Bāhyārthavādins and the Vijñānavādins hold the tenet of general momentariness (*kṣaṇikatva*) in common. Cf. Y. Kanakura, *A Study of the Vedānta Philosophy* (Tokyo: Iwanami Shoten, 1932), p. 138, p. 153, p. 179, and p. 201.

[21]According to Āanandajñāna, these are the Jñānamātravādins; according to Bodhanidhi, they are the Vijñānavādins.

[22]Cf. BSBh II, 2,25, pp. 461–464.

[23]Cf. stanza 23.

[24]Cf. Upad I,16,59; 17,7. Śaṅkara's concept of final release (*mokṣa*), which is the cessation of false superimposition (*mṛṣādhyāsa*), is very similar to Candrakīrti's, according to which *nirvāṇa* is of the nature of cessation of all false assumptions (*sarvakalpanākṣayarūpa, Prasannapadā*, Bibliotheca Buddhica IV, p. 524, line 6, etc.). Cf. Introduction, IV, B, pp. 73–75.

[25]Ānandajñāna and Rāmatīrtha attribute this tenet to the Śūnyavādins. Cf. Śaṅkara *ad* Bṛh. Up. IV,3,7, pp. 576–577.

[26]Cf. stanza 16.

[27]Cf. Chānd. Up. VI, 1,4.

[28]Cf. BSBh II,2,20, p. 457; stanzas 57; 63.

[29]See commentaries of Bodhanidhi and Rāmatīrtha.

[30]See Upad II,1,32.

[31]See *Āpastamba Dharmasūtra* I,8,22,2. Cf. Upad I,16,74; 17,4.

[32]Stanzas 45–50 are meant to refute the Sāṃkhya system. In contrast with the Vedānta, the Sāṃkhya advocates dualism, recognizing the two ultimate causes of the universe, namely *Puruṣa* (spirit) and *Prakṛti* (matter). *Prakṛti* (= *Pradhāna*) is nothing but the equilibrium of the three *guṇas*, namely *sattva, rajas* and *tamas*. When their equilibrium is broken, the evolution of the universe takes place. Cf. *Sāṃkhyakārikā* 16 and Gauḍapāda's commentary on it.

[33]Cf. note 32.

[34]Cf. *Sāṃkhyakārikā* 17; 31; 56; 57.

[35]Refutation of the Vaiśeṣika system starts here and seems to end with stanza 56. Kaṇāda or Ulūka (150–50 B.C.?) is the founder of the Vaiśeṣika school of philosophy. For the qualities of *ātman*, see note 7.

[36]The last two lines are not clear.

[37]Cf. stanzas 38; 39; 63.

[38]Stanza 30 and note 24.

[39]Stanzas 38; 39; 57.

[40]The three commentators quote a stanza, the source of which is not known:

yāny ato 'nyāni śāstrāṇi pṛthivyāṃ vividhāni vai /
śaṅkanīyāni vidvadbhir dharmaśuddhim abhīpsubhiḥ //

[41]See Mayeda Upad, pp. 40–41. In Śaṅkara's works Vyāsa indicates the author of the *Smṛtis* and not Bādarāyaṇa, the author of the BS.

[42]It is not certain in what sense the word *bhakti* is used here. In Upad II,3,116 "those who are devoted to Me" (*madbhakta*) are criticized. The word *bhakti* does not occur in the BSBh in the sense of "devotion," but only in the meanings of (1) "portion" or "division" (BSBh III,3,7, p. 682 and p. 683; III,3,9, p. 688) and (2) "figuratively" or "in a secondary sense" (as *bhaktyā*, BSBh I,3,14, p. 224; II,3,5, p. 502; III,2,4, p. 627). When Śaṅkara comments on the BhG, he treats it as almost synonymous with *jñāna*. Cf. GBh VIII,22, p. 273; XVIII, 54, p. 512; XVIII, 55, p. 513 – 514; O. Lacombe, *L'Absolu selon le Védānta* (Paris: Librairie Orientaliste Paul Geuthner, 1937), p. 353.

[43]Cf. Chānd. Up. III, 17,4; BhG XIII,7; XVI,1; XVII,14; XVIII,42.

[44]Cf. Upad I, 10, 14.

[45]This stanza is quoted in *Vedāntasāra* [IV] 27n and Rāmatīrtha *ad Maitri Up.* VI,29 (Ānandāśrama S. S. p. 476).

[46]Cf. Upad I,16,44; 17,4.

CHAPTER 17
RIGHT THOUGHT

1. Since nothing else exists, it is certainly the highest *Ātman*, all-knowing, all-seeing, and pure, which is the *Ātman* to be known. Salutation to this *Ātman* which one should know.

2. I ever bow down to those who, by their knowledge of words, sentences, and means of knowledge, have like lamps illumined *Brahman*, the secret doctrine of the *Vedas.*

3. Paying homage to those teachers whose words have reached [me] and destroyed [my] sins as the sunbeam reaching and destroying the darkness, I shall state the conclusion about the knowledge of *Brahman.*[1]

4. There is no other attainment higher than that of *Ātman*,[2] for the sake of which [attainment] exist the words of the *Vedas*[3] and of the *Smṛtis* as well as actions.

5. Whatever attainment may be desired for the sake of happiness, even though it be for one's own sake, is contrary [to happiness]. So the knowers of *Brahman* have declared the attainment of *Ātman* to be the highest one on account of its eternity.[4]

6. And as *Ātman* is by nature self-attained, attainment of It does not depend upon anything else. But any attainment which depends upon something else arises from seeing a difference [between *Ātman* and *Brahman*].

7. Seeing differnce is nescience. Its cessation is called final release.[5] And this cessation can arise not through action but through knowledge alone, since [that] is incompatible [with nescience].

8. A result of action is inconstant, since it has nescience and desire as its cause.[6] It is said that the *Vedas* alone are the right means to acquire knowledge with regard to *Ātman.*[7]

9. As [the *Vedas*] are devoted to one object [only], *i.e.*, the knowledge [of *Brahman*], [the wise] know that they [consist of] one sentence [only]. The oneness of *Ātman* [and *Brahman*] should indeed be known through the understanding of the meaning of [this one] sentence.

10. But difference between *Ātman* [and *Brahman*] is falsely assumed on the ground of difference of [meaning] which is understood [in the two different words, *Ātman* and *Brahman*]; even [the meaning] which is referred to is [falsely understood] on hearing [the word] *Ātman*. Therefore, this triad, *viz.* form, name, and action, is mentioned [as constituting the world in the *Śruti*].[8]

11. As this triad is falsely assumed to be interdependent, it is unreal like a figure which is described in word and painted elsewhere outside of the intellect.

12. And just as the form-and-color, which is seen [located outside of the intellect], is expressed in word through the intellect, so this whole is falsely assumed by the confused intellect.

13. Therefore it is reasonable that this triad is unreal; [*Ātman* which is] nothing but Being-Pure Consciousness only is not what is falsely assumed. *Ātman* is at once the primal knowledge and the object of knowledge,[9] but everything else is falsely assumed.

14. That [*ātman*] by which one knows everything in the dreaming state is knowledge but that [knowledge] is due to its *māyā*.[10] That by which one sees and hears [in the dreaming state] is called the eye and the ear respectively.

15. That by which one speaks in the dreaming state [is called] speech, and likewise, [it has the names] nose, tongue, sense of touch, other organs, and the mind.

16. On account of the limiting adjuncts which are falsely constructed [on *Ātman*], this very knowledge is different in many ways, just as difference appears in one and the same gem on account of difference of limiting adjuncts [such as blue and yellow].[11]

17. In like manner the knowledge of one when in the waking state is falsely assumed to have difference. [*Ātman* in the waking state] makes manifest the object in the intellect,[12] and because of this confused idea performs actions which arise from desire.

18. As in dream so in waking, something external and internal is produced by the notion of interdependence, just as a thing

written and the reading [of it come from the notion of their interdependence]:

19. His [*ātman*] falsely constructing the difference, desires it, and then wills [to obtain it]. Willing its desires,[13] it obtains [the results of] what it has done.[14]

20. Everything comes from nescience. This world is unreal, for it is seen by one who has nescience and is not perceived in the state of deep sleep.

21. It is indeed declared to us in the *Śruti* that knowledge is the notion of the oneness [of *Ātman* and *Brahman*] and nescience is the notion of the difference [of *Ātman* from *Brahman*]. Therefore knowledge is affirmed in the scripture with all vigor.

22. When the mind becomes pure like a mirror, knowledge shines forth; therefore [the mind should be purified]. The mind is purified by abstention,[15] the permanent rites,[16] sacrifices,[17] and austerities.

23. The best austerities of the body, etc.,[18] should be performed to purify the mind. The concentration of the mind, etc.[19] and the emaciation of the body in this and that [season][20] [should be performed].

24. Sense-perception should be known as the waking state, memory as the dreaming state, the absence of both as the state of deep sleep, and one's own *Ātman* as the highest state.[21]

25. The darkness called deep sleep is ignorance and [it is] the seed of the dreaming and waking states. If it is burned up by the knowledge of one's own *Ātman*, like a seed that has been scorched it has no power of germinating.[22]

26. That single *māyā* seed is to be known as repeatedly and successively [changing] in [these] three ways. *Ātman*, though one and changeless, is as the bearer of *māyā* [knowable] in many ways, like the sun in the water.

27. Just as one and the same seed becomes different in accordance with [differences of] vital air,[23] dreaming state, etc., so *Ātman* like the moon on the water becomes different in bodies in the dreaming and waking states.

28. Just as a magician comes and goes riding on an elephant created by his magic, so the *Ātman*, though motionless, is related to vital air, dreaming state, and the like.[24]

29. Just as there is neither elephant nor rider, but there stands

the magician different [from them], [so] there are neither vital air and the like, nor a seer of them, but the Knower, the Seeing, different [from them], always exists.

30. Neither for one whose sight is not bound, nor for the magician, is there any magical illusion. This magical illusion exists only for him whose sight is bound. Therefore in fact there is no magician at all.

31. *Ātman* should be directly known according to the *Śruti* which says that *Ātman* is directly present,[25] for the *Śrutis* say, "The knot of the heart is loosened . . . [when He is seen]" "(Muṇḍ.Up. II,2,8), "If[here he]does not[know It, there is great loss]" (*Kena Up.*II,5), and the like.

32. Because of Its being soundless, etc.,[26] It cannot be perceived by the sense-organs. Likewise, as [It] is different from pleasure, etc., how can [It be perceived] by the intellect?

33. Just as Rāhu, though he is invisible, [is perceived] in the moon [during an eclipse][27] and just as a reflection [of the moon, etc., is seen] in the water, so *Ātman*, though all-pervading, is perceived there in the intellect.

34. Just as the reflection and heat of the sun are perceived in the water but do not belong to the water, so knowledge [, though] in the intellect, is not a quality of it, since [it] differs in nature [from the intellect].

35. *Ātman*, whose Seeing never fails, sees a modification of the intellect[28] connected with the eyes, and is the Seer of seeing and [similarly] the Hearer of hearing—so says the *Śruti*.[29]

36. Seeing a modification of the mind which is isolated [from the senses], [It] is the Thinker of thinking, unborn. Likewise, [It is] the Understander [of understanding][30] since [It] has unfailing power. Therefore the scripture says, "For there is no [cessation of the Seeing of the Seer]" (Bṛh.Up.IV,3,23–30).

37. [It] is changeless, [from the *Śruti*,] "[It appears to] meditate"(Bṛh.Up.IV,3,7) and "[It appears to] move about" (Bṛh. Up.IV,3,7). [It] is pure, from the *Śruti*, "There a thief is [not a thief]" (Bṛh.Up.IV,3,22) and "[It is] not followed [by good, It is not followed by evil]" (Bṛh. Up.IV,3,22).

38. As [Its] power never fails, [It] is the Knower in the state of deep sleep as well as in the waking state, for it is changeless. But the distinction is supposed only as regards the object of knowledge

since the *Śruti* says, "Where there [seems to be another, there the one might see the other]" (Bṛh.Up.IV,3,31).

39. As mediated [by time, space, etc.], the ordinary seeing by non-*Ātman* [such as the eye] is indeed indirect. As Seeing is the nature of *Ātman* it has been said that *Brahman* is directly known.[31]

40. No second lamp is necessary for illuminating a lamp; similarly no knowledge other [than *Ātmun*] is required [for knowing *Ātman*], since Knowledge is the nature of *Ātman.*

41. It is not accepted that [*Ātman*] is an object, or changeable, or manifold. Therefore *Ātman* is not to be discarded or accepted by something other [than *Ātman*].

42. [*Ātman*] includes the exterior and the interior,[32] is unscathed, and beyond birth, death, and old age. What does one fear who knows, "I am *Ātman*"?

43. There is action (*karman*) only until injunction[to attain] *Ātman*, since notions of belonging to a caste, etc., are [then] removed; their removal results from the conclusion "Thou art That" (Chānd. Up. VI, 8, 7, etc.) based on the scriptural teaching "[It is] neither gross [nor subtle]" (Bṛh.Up.III,8,8), and the like.

44. Since in abandoning the body in the previous life one has given up lineage and the like, lineage and the like belong to the body. Thus the body is also non-*Ātman.*

45. Therefore the notions of "mine" and "I" which apply to the non-*Ātman* such as the body, etc., is nescience. It (= nescience) should be abandoned by means of knowledge of *Ātman* since the *Śruti* says, "[For this is the doctrine] of the demons" (Chānd. Up. VIII,8,5).

46. Just as the duties of observing ten-day periods of impurity[33] come to an end at the time of entering the life of a wandering ascetic, the actions based upon lineage and the like come to an end at the time of attaining knowledge.

47. But, willing his desires, an ignorant man obtains [the results of] what he has done.[34] When desires are cast off by him who sees his own *Ātman,* he becomes immortal.[35]

48. The injunction [to attain] the nature of *Ātman* results in the cessation of actions and the like. *Ātman* is neither an object to be accomplished nor a means of accomplishment; It is held to be eternally content as the *Śruti*[36] says.

49. Actions result in things being produced, obtained, changed, or purified. There are no results of action other than these. Therefore one should abandon [actions] together with [their] requisites.[37]

50. Concentrating upon *Ātman* the love which is [now set] on external things—for they end in suffering, are inconstant and exist for *Ātman*—a seeker after the truth should resort to a teacher

51. who is tranquil, wise, released, actionless, and established in *Brahman*, since the *Śruti* says, "One who has a teacher knows . . ." (Chānd.Up.VI,14,2) and the *Smṛti* also says, "Learn to know this [by obeisance, by questioning, by serving]" (BhG IV,34).

52. If a student is disciplined and properly qualified, the teacher should immediately transport him over his great interior ocean of darkness in the boat of the knowledge of *Brahman*.

53. Seeing, touching, hearing, smelling, thinking, knowing, and other powers, though they are of the nature of Pure Consciousness, are differentiated by limiting adjuncts.[38]

54. As the sun always shines, without destroying or creating [anything by its rays], so does [It] always know all, being all-pervading, all-seeing, and pure.

55. Through nescience [*Ātman*] abiding in the body is regarded as the Seeing of something other [than Itself], and as being the same size as the body[39] and possessed of the qualities of the body, by such comparisons as that of the moon in the water and the like.[40]

56. Having seen an external object, one shuts the eyes and remembers it [in the dreaming state] and [then] abandoning it [in the state of deep sleep], one opens up the Seeing of *Ātman*, reaches *Brahman*, and does not travel along any path.

57. He who has thus given up the triad, *viz.* the vital air (= the state of deep sleep)[41] goes across the great ocean of ignorance, for he is by nature abiding in his own *Ātman*, attributeless, pure, awakened, and released.

58. When he has realized, "I am unborn, undying, deathless, free from old age, fearless,[42] all-knowing, all-seeing, and pure," he is not born again.

59. He who knows the oneness of [*Ātman* and] *Brahman* concludes that the above-mentioned darkness-seed[43] does not exist. How should he be born [again] when it does not exist?

60. Just as clarified butter, extracted from milk, does not become the same as before if thrown back into it, [so] the Knower [once discriminated] from the untrue such as the intellect never becomes the same embodied *Ātman* as before.

61. One becomes free from fear realizing, " 'I am *Brahman*' (Bṛh.Up.I,4,10), which is 'the real, knowledge, and the infinite' (Taitt.Up.II,1), which is superior to the fivefold *ātman* such as [the *ātman* consisting of] the essence [of food], etc.,[44] and which is declared in the scripture to be 'invisible' (Taitt.Up.II,7)."

62. A man who knows the truth, *i.e.*, the bliss of that *Ātman*, from fear of which speech, mind, fire, and the like carry out their functions,[45] does not fear anything at all.[46]

63. If a knower of *Ātman* abides in his own infinite and non-dual kingdom, which is superior to name and the like,[47] then whom should he salute? Then, there is no need for action.

64. When [*Ātman*] is external [It is called] *Virāj* or *Vaiśvānara.* When [It] remembers within, [It is called] *Prajāpati.* But when everything vanishes [It] is called *Prājña* or *Avyākṛta.*[48]

65. As they are merely verbal handles,[49] however, the triad, namely, the state of deep sleep, etc., are unreal. A man who thus covers himself with the truth, "I am the True and the Knower," is released.[50]

66. As the sun has light as its nature, it has neither day nor night.[51] In like manner I have neither knowledge nor ignorance since I have Pure Consciousness as my nature, without distinctions [in It].

67. As the scripture is not to be doubted, one should remember, "I am always *Brahman*; as I am *Brahman*, I have nothing to reject or to accept."

68. He is not born [again] who sees thus, "I am the One in all beings just as the ether and all beings are in Me."[52]

69. There is nothing else but one's own [*Ātman*] anywhere, outside, within or inside, since the *Śruti* says, "[This *Brahman* is . . .] without an outside, without an inside" (Bṛh.Up.II,5,19); [It] is therefore pure and self-effulgent.

70. According to such scriptural passages as, "Not thus! Not so!" (Bṛh. Up.II,3,6, etc.), [*Ātman*] is "the quiescence of the pluralistic universe and non-dual"(GK II,35).[53] And according to such scriptural passages as, "[That Imperishable . . .is]

the unknown [Knower]" (Bṛh.Up.III,8,11), [It] should not be known in any way other than that.

71. If one has come to know the supreme *Brahman* realizing, "I am the *Ātman* of all," one becomes the *Ātman* of all beings, since the *Śruti* says, "[Whoever thus knows 'I am *Brahman*' becomes this all; even the gods have no power to prevent his becoming thus,] for he is their *Ātman*" (Bṛh. Up. I, 4,10).

72. If a living being clearly [knows] his *Ātman* as the highest *Ātman*, as God,[54] he is to be worshipped by the gods and ceases to be [domestic] animal for the gods.[55]

73. As a killer of the unreal thus covers himself with the truth,[56] "I am the Real-*Ātman* and the Knower, but, like ether, I am empty of anything else," he is not bound [again].

74. They are pitiable who know the supreme *Brahman* differently from this. "The gods would be under the power of him" (Taitt. Ā. 3,13,2d; *Vājasaneyi-Saṃhitā*, 31,21d) who is a self-ruler, a seer of non-difference and abiding in himself.[57]

75. Abandoning your relationship with lineage, etc., and other words along with actions and [saying,] "Om," you attain your own *Ātman*, which is all, pure,[58]

76. the bulwark of all that is established,[59] devoid of day, night, and the like,[60] and is to the sides, above, below, all, evershining, and free from disease.

77. One should know one's *Ātman* to be the highest One which is devoid of merit and demerit, free from past and future, free from cause and effect[61] and free from all bondage.

78. While being pure and not acting, [*Ātman*] does all; while standing, [It] goes past those who are running.[62] As It is almighty through Its *māyā*, It is thought to be manifold, though [really It is] unborn.[63]

79. While causing the world to turn around,[64] I, *Ātman*, am actionless, non-agent and non-dual for, like a king, I am merely the Witness [of the world], and like a magnet,[65] [merely] close [to it].

80. One should bear in mind, "I am that *Brahman* which is attributeless, actionless, eternal, free from the pairs [of opposites], free from disease, pure, awakened, and released."

81. Having properly known bondage, final release, and all [the causes] from which [all] this and both [bondage and final

release] result; the one (= the state of deep sleep) and the two (= the dream and waking states)[66] which are to be rejected; and the only, pure, and highest Truth which transcends the knowable and the unknowable, which has been studied and which is spoken of by the *Śrutis* and sages, —[having known all this] one would become a knower of *Brahman* who has transcended sorrow and delusion, who is all-knowing, all-doing, free from the fear of existence, and who has completed all that has to be done.

82. *Ātman* Itself does not become something to be rejected nor is It to be accepted by Itself or anything else. Nothing else becomes something to be rejected or to be accepted by Itself; this is true thought as has been mentioned [above, stanza 67].

83. This true thought leads [people] to understand *Ātman* and has all the *Upaniṣads* as its field; so, having come to know this, they are released from all the bonds of transmigratory existence.

84. As it is the supreme means of purification that is the secret doctrine of all the *Vedas* and is the highest [secret doctrine] even for the gods, it has been expounded here.

85. This secret and supreme knowledge should not be given to [a student] who is not tranquil but should be taught to a student who is dispassionate and obedient.

86. And there is no actionless one other than [the teacher] who is offering the knowledge of *Ātman*. Therefore, [a student] who is seeking after knowledge should always qualify himself with the qualities of a student.[67]

87. Salutation to that knowledge-*Ātman* which is all-knowing and almighty and besides which there is nothing else, neither knowledge, nor object of knowledge, nor knower.[68]

88. Salutation to the all-knowing teachers by whom through knowledge we have been led across the great ocean of birth and death filled with ignorance.

Notes

[1]Cf. BhG V,16; 17.
[2]See Upad I,16,44; 74.
[3]Śaṅkara interprets "*vedavāda*" (BhG II,42) as "*vedavākya*."
[4]Cf. the above note 2.
[5]See Upad I,16,30; 59.

[6]See Upad I,15,21.

[7]Cf. BS I,1,3.

[8]See Bṛh. Up. I,6,1.

[9]Cf. GK III,33; IV,1; Upad I,19,9. This idea is very similar to a tenet of the Vijñānavādins.

[10]In stanza 27 *Ātman* is compared to a magician (*māyāvin*). Cf. GK II,12; 19; III,24.

[11]This simile is employed here and there in Śaṅkara's works in order to illustrate the relation between *Brahman* and the phenomenal world. Cf. Upad I,7,4; 17,16; 18,122; BSBh I,3,19, p. 235; III,2,11, p. 641, etc. The simile is also used in Bhartṛhari's *Vākyapadīya* III,3,41.

[12]See Introduction, III,B,5, p. 44. Cf. GK II,13; 14; 15; 16.

[13]Cf. stanza 47.

[14]Cf. stanza 17.

[15]Abstention (*yama*) consists of non-injury (*ahiṃsā*), non-lying (*satya*), non-theft (*asteya*), non-incontinence (*brahmacarya*), and non-possession (*aparigraha*). See *Yogasūtra* II,30; *Vedāntasāra* [XXXI] 214; Upad II,1,4.

[16]Rāmatīrtha treats "*nitya*" as "*niyama*" while Bodhanidhi interprets it as "*avaśyānuṣṭheya*," which suggests that he treats it as "*nityakarman*" or "permanent rite." The reading "*niyama*" for "*nitya*" is not supported by manuscripts. In *Vedāntasāra* [IV] 7 "permanent rites" are defined as the rites which lead to disquiet (*pratyavāyasādhana*) when they are not performed. The ultimate object of the permanent rites is the purification of the intellect (*buddhiśuddhi*, *Vedāntasāra* [IV] 11) and their result is the attainment of the world of ancestors (*pitṛloka*, *Vedāntasāra* [IV] 13).

[17]For Śaṅkara's view of actions including sacrifice, see Introduction, IV,F, pp. 88–94.

[18]The BhG mentions the threefold austerity (*tapas*): (1) the austerity of the body (*śarīra*, XVII, 14), (2) of the speech (*vāṅmaya*, XVII, 15) and (3) of the mind (*mānasa*, XVII,16).

[19]According to Rāmatīrtha the senses are implied by the term "etc."

[20]Rāmatīrtha interprets "*tattaddehaviśoṣaṇam*" as "*teṣu teṣv ṛtuṣu dehaviśoṣaṇam* . . ."

[21]See Upad I,10,4.

[22]This stanza is quoted in Naiṣ IV,43. Cf. Upad I,16,18.

[23]The word "*prāṇa*" here may also imply the state of deep sleep. See stanza 57 below.

[24]With regard to stanzas 28–30, see Mayeda Upad, pp. 36–37.

[25]Cf. Bṛh. Up. III,4,1; 4,2; 5,1.

[26]Cf. Kaṭh. Up. III,15.

[27]According to an Indian tradition Rāhu is a demon who is supposed to seize the sun and the moon and swallow them, thus causing eclipses. When the gods had once produced the *amṛta*, water of life, by churning the ocean, he assumed a disguise and drank some of it. The sun and the moon detected him and informed Viṣṇu, who cut off his head. Thus Rāhu wreaks vengeance on the sun and the moon by occasionally swallowing them. Cf. Upad I,18,39–40 and note 26.

[28]See Upad I,11,3; 4.

[29]Bṛh. Up. III,4,2.

[30]Bṛh. Up. III,4,2.

[31]Cf. Upad I,14,26.

[32]Muṇḍ. Up. II,1,2; Upad I,13,11; 14; 18.

[33]It is believed that birth (*janāśauca*) and death (*mṛtakāśauca*) cause impurity to the members of the family or to relatives. The periods of impurity depend on many

circumstances. For a detailed explanation, see P. V. Kane, *History of Dharmaśāstra*, vol. IV, pp. 267 ff.

[34]Cf. Stanza 19.

[35]The author seems to have Bṛh. Up. IV,4,7 (Kaṭh. Up. VI,14) in mind.

[36]Rāmatīrtha quotes Bṛh. Up. IV,4,7 (*etasyaivānandasyānyāni . . . upajīvanti*) and another passage, "*nityatṛpto nirañjanaḥ*," the source of which is not known, but Rāmatīrtha says that it is a Śruti passage. Bodhanidhi quotes Bṛh. Up. III,9,28 (*vijñānam ānandam*). It is, however, to be noted here that BhG IV,20 reads "*nityatṛpto nirāśayaḥ*" and that there is a variant reading of *smṛter mataḥ* instead of *śruter mataḥ*.

[37]See Upad II,1,32.

[38]See stanzas 14–16.

[39]A tenet of Jainism. See Upad I,16,22.

[40]See stanzas 26, 33.

[41]In the state of deep sleep the mind and the senses enter into the vital air and *ātman* is submerged in the *Brahman*. In the waking state *ātman*, connected with the mind, exercises its influence throughout the body by means of the senses; in the dreaming state, the senses are absorbed into the mind, and their functions are extinguished. P. Deussen, *The System of the Vedânta*, p. 346. The expression "*prāṇādy . . . trikaṃ*" in question parallels "*suṣuptāditrikaṃ*" in stanza 65. It is, therefore, very probable that, as Rāmatīrtha interprets, "the vital air, etc." denotes "the states of deep sleep, dream, and waking."

[42]Cf. Bṛh. Up. IV,4,25.

[43]Cf. stanza 25.

[44]Taitt. Up. II,1–5 mentions the so-called fivefold sheath (*kośa*) in which *Ātman* is manifested as the individual *ātman*: (1) the sheath consisting of the essence of food (*annarasamaya*), (2) consisting of vital air (*prāṇamaya*), (3) consisting of mind (*manomaya*), (4) consisting of consciousness (*vijñānamaya*), and (5) consisting of bliss (*ānandamaya*). Cf. BSBh I,1,12–19; P. Deussen, *The System of the Vedânta*, pp. 137–138.

[45]Cf. Taitt. Up. II,8,1; Kaṭh. Up. VI,3; BhG II,23; XV,6. Rāmatīrtha points out another reading: *vāyvinau pāvakādayaḥ* for *vāṅmanaḥpāvakādayaḥ*.

[46]See Taitt. Up. II,9,1: *yato vāco nivartante aprāpya manasā saha ānandam brahmaṇo vidvān na bibheti kutaścana* (cf. Taitt. Up. II,4,1).

[47]See Chānd. Up. VII,1–26, where name (*nāman*), speech (*vāc*), mind (*manas*), etc., are enumerated as objects of meditation.

[48]See Upad I,10,4 and note 4.

[49]Chānd. Up. VI,1,4.

[50]This is based upon a famous dialogue between a Upaniṣadic thinker Uddālaka and his son Śvetaketu in which Uddālaka uses an illustration of the ordeal. When a man is seized on a charge of theft and put into an ordeal by a heated axe, he will be burned and killed by the axe if he is guilty and covers himself with untruth, but he will not be burned, and will be released, if he is innocent and covers himself with truth (Chānd. Up. VI,16,1–3). Cf. stanza 73.

[51]Cf. Upad I,14,15.

[52]Cf. *Īśā Up.* 6; BhG VI,30.

[53]The words "*prapañcopaśama*" and "*advaya*" are both Buddhistic. Nevertheless, *prapañcopaśama*, which already appears in the *Mādhyamikakārikā* (benedictory stanza and XXV,24), is used in Māṇḍ. Up. VII. In the Māṇḍ. Up. the term "*advaya*" is not used but *advaita*, which is a Vedāntic term, occurs twice, whereas in the GK the two terms are synonymously used at almost the same frequency. See Nakamura III, pp. 297–298, note 8; p. 510. In the Upad Śaṅkara uses *advaya* more frequently than *advaita*.

[54]See Bṛh. Up. IV,4,15.

[55]See Bṛh. Up. I,4,10.

[56]See stanza 65.

[57]Cf. Chānd. Up. VII,25,2.

[58]Cf. Muṇḍ. Up. II,2,5; 6.

[59]Cf. Bṛh. Up. IV,4,22.

[60]Cf. Chānd. Up. VIII,4,1; Upad I,14,15; 17,66.

[61]The first two lines seem to be based upon Kaṭh. Up. II,14. Hence the compound "*kṛtākṛta*" is translated as "cause and effect" according to Śaṅkara's commentary on Kaṭh. Up. II,14, where he interprets *kṛta* and *akṛta* as *kārya* and *kāraṇa* respectively.

[62]Cf. *Īśā Up.* 4.

[63]Cf. *Vājasaneyi-Saṃhitā* 31,19b; Taitt. Ā. 3,13,1b.

[64]Cf. BhG XVIII,61.

[65]See Upad I,15,48.

[66]What "*ekaṃ dvayaṃ ca*" means is not certain. According to Rāmatīrtha and Ānandajñāna, "*ekam*" denotes "*anuvṛttaṃ kāraṇam,*" and "*dvayam*" denotes "*vyāvṛttaṃ kāryam.*" But stanzas 24–30, 56, 57, 64, and 65 suggest that "*ekam*" denotes the state of deep sleep which is the only seed of the state of dream and waking (stanzas 25–26). If so, "*dvaya*" indicates the two states of dream and waking. In stanzas 57 and 65 these three states are called "*trika*" or triad.

[67]See stanzas 50–52.

[68]Cf. stanza 1.

CHAPTER 18

THOU ART THAT

1. Salutation to that *Ātman*, the Constant Awareness,[1] *Ātman* of the notions of the intellect, through which the modifications [of the intellect] disappear and arise.

2. Salutation to an Indra among ascetics, teacher of the teacher,[2] a man of great intellect, who defeated hundreds of enemies of the *Śrutis* by means of sword-like words supported by thunderbolt[3]-like reasoning and protected the treasure of the meaning of the *Vedas*.

3. If the understanding, "I am ever-free, the existent," could not arise, for what purpose does the *Śruti* teach thus zealously like a [devoted] mother?

4. From this [self-]established [*Ātman* which is indicated by the word] "I" the attribute "you"[4] is excluded—just as the notion of a serpent [is excluded] in application to a rope[5]—by means of reasoning and such teachings as "Thou art That" (Chānd. Up. VI,13,3, etc.) and so forth.

5. Just as the existence of merit, etc., is to be known on the evidence of the scriptures, [so is the existence of *Ātman*]. Just as poison is counteracted through meditation,[6] evil will be destroyed [through the scriptural sentence].[7]

6. The two [contradictory] notions, "I am the Existent-*Brahman*" and "I act," have *Ātman* as their Witness. It is considered more reasonable to give up only [that one] of the two [notions] which arises from ignorance.

7. The notion, "I am the Existent," arises from right means of knowledge [while] the other notion has its origin in fallacious means of knowledge; moreover, [the notion which has its origin

in] fallacious [means of knowledge] such as sense-perception[8] is negated like a mistake in orientation.

8. When the scripture says, "[I am] a doer,"[9] "[I am] an experiencer,"[10] that conforms to ordinary people's belief [concerning *Ātman*].[11] The notion, "I am the Existent," arises from the *Srutis*; the former notion is negated by it.

9. [Objection:][12] "Even when one is told, 'You are indeed the Existent,' one does not attain immovable final release of *Ātman*. Therefore, one should take up *prasaṃcakṣā* meditation[13] as well as reasoning.

10. "Even one who understands the meaning of the sentence does not grasp it from a single utterance. Therefore he needs further things; they are two, [*prasaṃcakṣā* meditation and reasoning],[14] as we have said [above].

11. "Since [the sentence] is not understood [immediately], there has to be an injunction to perform [Vedic] actions. Likewise the injunction [to meditate by *prasaṃcakṣā*] is not incompatible [with knowledge] as long as [that] is not firmly grasped.

12. "And [if][15]one did attain [*Ātman*] spontaneously, that activity would [it is true] be meaningless, [but as one does not] *prasaṃkhyāna* meditation should accordingly be performed until *Ātman* is grasped.

13. "And the firm impression which arises from sense-perception certainly negates the knowledge, 'I am the Existent,' which arises from the *Śruti*. And on account of faults one is attracted towards things external.

14. "[This is] because [the notion] which arises from sense-perception and has particulars (*viśeṣa*) as its objects would necessarily hinder the notions which arise both from the verbal testimony[16] and from inference, which have universals (*sāmānya*) as their objects.

15. "Nobody, even if he knows the meaning of the sentence, is found to be free from pain. If anybody is seen to become free from pain merely by hearing the meaning of the sentence,

16. "it is inferred that he must have performed [*prasaṃkhyāna* meditation] in past bodies. [If an injunction for *prasaṃkhyāna* meditation were not accepted,] the scripture would not be the authority for [right] conduct. If this be so, it is not desirable.

17. "After stating an end, 'You are the Existent,' the means [to it] should be enjoined. So it is *prasaṃkhyāna* meditation that is the means, and nothing else; the object of [*prasaṃkhyāna* meditation] is taken here to be the well-established [*Ātman*].

18. "Therefore, for the sake of apprehending [*Ātman*] one should perform *prasaṃkhyāna* meditation diligently, being endowed with tranquility, etc., and abandoning anything incompatible with [this] means and its object."

19. [Reply:] That is not so, for the secret doctrines (= Upaniṣads) end with "Not thus! Not so!" (Bṛh. Up. II,3,6, etc.). Ends to be attained by actions should be stated in the scripture before [these *Upaniṣadic* doctrines] and final release is not [an end to be attained by actions], since it is ever-existing.

20. Just as the pain of a son is superimposed upon himself by a father, though himself suffering no pain, so [pain] is superimposed by the bearer of the "I"-notion (=the intellect) upon its *Ātman* which is ever free from pain.

21. This superimposition is negated, as if it were a thing acquired, by the words, "Not thus! Not so!" (Bṛh. Up. II,3,6). Moreover no injunction based upon superimposition is at all reasonable.

22. As superimposition is [made] upon *Ātman*, so [its] negation is [made from *Ātman*], just as the superimposition of dust upon the sky and its negation therefrom are made by the unwise.

23. If a thing were [really] acquired and then negated, final release would certainly be [merely] temporary. Therefore this [negation of superimposition] is a negation of what has not been [in fact] acquired, like [the prohibition against] the building of a fire in the sky[17] [which is in fact impossible].

24. It is possible [to apply] a word or a notion to its object but not something else. It is not possible [to apply] either word or notion [to *Ātman*] since [It] is their own *Ātman* as well as the *Ātman* of the bearer of the "I"-notion.

25. [The *Śruti*,] "Not thus! Not so!" (Bṛh. Up. II,3,6, etc.) negates all things, including the notion of agency which is superimposed upon *Ātman*, Pure Consciousness, by the bearer of the "I"-notion, and it negates also the bearer of the "I"-notion.

26. [*Ātman*] is the self-effulgent Perception,[18] the Seeing, inter-

nally existing and actionless. [It] is the Witness which is directly cognized and in the interior of all, and the Observer which is constant, attributeless, and non-dual.[19]

27. The bearer of misconception [about *Ātman*] (= the intellect), because it is always near to *Ātman*, appears to be *Ātman*. From this arise the two [notions], "oneself" and "one's own," which are indicated by [the words] "I" and "my."

28. As this bearer of the "I"-notion has a universal, and is possessed of action, etc.,[20] it can be referred to by words. One's own *Ātman* cannot be referred to by any word since [It] neither has a universal nor is possessed of action, etc.

29. In the [bearer of the "I"-notion] there is the reflection[21] [of the internal Seeing], and words referring to the former could indicate the internal Seeing indirectly, [but] never designate It directly.

30. [This is] because that which is not a member of any genus and so on cannot be indicated by words. As the bearer of the "I"-notion has the reflection of *Ātman* [in it and appears to be *Ātman*],[22] it is the intellect that is referred to by the words for *Ātman*.

31. Just as [words] which mean fire are only indirectly used in the sense of a torch, etc.,[23] since they mean something different [from a torch, etc.]. Just as the reflection of a face is different from the face since it conforms to the mirror,

32. so the face is [different] from the reflection since it does not conform to the mirror. The reflection of *Ātman* in the bearer of the "I"-notion is thought to be like the reflection of a face [in a mirror].

33. *Ātman*, like the face, is always different [from Its reflection]; but as in the case of the face these two [*Ātman* and its reflection] are not discriminated [from each other]. Some there are who say that the reflection in the bearer of the "I"-notion is the transmigrator[24];

34. a shadow is a real substance according to [the authority of] the *Smṛti*,[25] and there are further reasons [for taking it to be a real substance]; for example, [the reason] that [one feels] cool [in a shadow].[26] [Some say that the transmigrator is] a part of the Knower[27] or a modification of It.[28] Others [think that the transmi-

grator] is [the bearer of the "I"-notion, *viz.*,] the locus of the reflection of *Ātman.*[29]

35. Some others say it is the independent bearer of the "I"-notion alone that is the transmigrator.[30] That transmigrator is the individual continuity of the "I"-notion and the like, and that there is no continuity apart [from that],—

36. so say the Buddhists.[31] It must be examined whether there is any truth among these [doctrines]. But an end should be put [for the time being] to the debate on what it is that transmigrates.[32] The topic of [the nature of the reflection] in question will now be discussed.

37. The reflection of the face in the mirror is not an attribute either [of the face or of the mirror.] If it were an attribute of either of the two, it would remain even if the other one were removed.

38. If it is proposed [by an objector] that [the reflection of the face is an attribute] of the face, since [it] is given the same name as the face, [we answer:] No, because [the reflection of the face] conforms to the mirror and because even when the face is there, no [reflection of it] exists [unless there is also a mirror].

39. If [you say] that [the reflection] is [an attribute] of both [the face and the mirror], [we answer:] That is not right since [it] is not seen even when both [are present unless they are properly placed]. [If you say that] Rāhu,[33] who is real though invisible, is seen against the sun and the moon,

40. [we answer:] Even before [he is seen in the sun and the moon] it has been established from the authority of the scriptures[34] that Rāhu is a real substance. However, if [you are of] the opinion that [he] is [merely] a shadow, then on the basis of the previous reasoning he would not be a real substance.[35]

41. The *Smṛti* [referred to in stanza 34] is a prohibition against stepping on the shadow [of a teacher, etc.][36] but does not prove that [it] is a real substance, since a sentence cannot [be taken to] express any other meaning than the one which it intends.[37]

42. It is from not using anything warm, etc., but not from the shadow that a feeling of coolness, etc. result,[38] for [coolness] is not observed [to be a property of shadows] though it is observed to be a property of water.

43. *Ātman*, [Its] reflection, and [Its] locus (= the intellect) are

comparable to the face, [its] reflection, and [its] locus (= the mirror). And the unreality of the reflection is understood by means of the scripture and reasoning.

44. [Objection:] "As the Seeing is changeless, [It] is not [the transmigrator], nor is the reflection [the transmigrator], for the reflection is unreal. Nor is the bearer of the "I"-notion [the transmigrator], since it is not conscious. Who could be the transmigrator?"

45. [Reply:] Therefore let transmigratory existence be nothing but nescience due to the absence of discriminating knowledge. Because of [the existence of] the immovable *Ātman*, transmigratory existence is always existent in *Ātman* as it were.

46. Just as a snake, [although not real], exists in a rope because of [the existence of] the rope until [the two] are discriminated, so it is because of [the existence of] the immovable *Ātman* that transmigratory existence, although not real, [exists in It, but only until the two are discriminated].

47. Some people think that *Ātman* is the locus of a reflection of *Ātman* which changes according to Its notions of Itself, and that It is [thus] a permanent transmigrator which experiences pleasure and pain.

48. These people, unguided by scripture, are deluded because they do not fully know *Ātman* and [Its] reflection as they really are, and think that *Ātman* is a bearer of the "I"-notion.

49. Their view is that transmigratory existence exists as a real substance[39] characterized by acting and experiencing. They undergo transmigratory existence since they do not know *Ātman*, [Its] reflection and [Its] locus, on account of their lack of discriminating knowledge.

50. If the intellect [, though appearing to be Pure Consciousness], has the reflection of Pure Consciousness, while *Ātman* has Pure Consciousness as Its nature, the *Vedas* are right to teach *Ātman* by means of words like "knowledge" (*jñāna*).

51. [Objection:] "The meaning of verbal root and verbal suffix,[40] though different [from each other], are seen to have one and the same subject as in '*karoti*' (he does), '*gacchati*' (he goes), etc., according to universally accepted opinion.

52. "Neither in ordinary life nor in the *Smṛti* is it seen that there are two separate subjects for these two [verbal root and verbal

suffix]. Explain why in construing '*jānāti*' (he knows) there should be two subjects."

53. [Reply:] It is the reflection of *Ātman* that is expressed by the verbal termination whereas the meaning of the root is the action of the intellect.[41] And it is on account of the absence of discriminating knowledge that the two [*Ātman* and intellect] are wrongly said to "know" (*jānāti*).[42]

54. Knowledge does not belong to the intellect and *Ātman* has no action. Therefore "to know" is not applicable to either of them.

55. Therefore the word "consciousness" (*jñapti*),[43] which implies action, has no application [to *Ātman*] either. For It is not anything changing, the doctrine being that *Ātman* is constant.[44]

56. It is the intellect but not [*Ātman*] that is expressed by [the word] "intellect" (*buddhi*) [which is an instrument], since [if *Ātman* were expressed by the word "intellect" which denotes an instrument, *Ātman* would Itself be an instrument and there would be no agent remaining, but] there can be no instrument without an agent. Nor again is [*Ātman*] expressed by words denoting an object, by saing [of It] "it is known" (*jñāyate*).

57. *Ātman* is never taken to be expressible by words or cognizable, according to those who [realize that] *Ātman* is only one, free from pain and changeless.

58. If the bearer of the "I"-notion were *Ātman*, then [*Ātman*] would be the primary meaning of a word.[45] But as [the bearer of the "I"-notion] has hunger, etc., it is not in the *Śruti*[46] taken to be *Ātman*.

59. [Objection:] "Unfortunately then there is no primary meaning [of the word] and neither is there any secondary meaning.[47] Nevertheless, the application of words like '*jānāti*' has to be accounted for.

60. "If words were false, the *Vedas* would not be an authority either. And this is not acceptable. Therefore the application of this word has to be taken according to the generally accepted way."

61. [Reply:] If what is generally accepted by deluded people is taken, it would entail the non-existence of *Ātman*, that is, the settled doctrine of the Lokāyatas,[48] and this is not acceptable.

62. If what is generally accepted by the learned [is taken], failure to discriminate [between *Ātman* and the intellect follows]

as before.[49] This *Veda* which is the authority does not make any useless [word].[50]

63. The face is indeed thought by men to be the same as the face in a mirror, for the reflection of the face is seen to be of the form of the face.

64. And because they do not discriminate between this [*Ātman*] which becomes falsely manifest in that [intellect] and that [intellect] in which this [*Ātman*] becomes falsely manifest, all people naturally use the verb "*jānāti*."[51]

65. Superimposing the agency of the intellect [upon *Ātman*], [they] say that the Knower (= *Ātman*) "knows" (*jānāti*). In like manner superimposing the Pure Consciousness [of *Ātman* upon the intellect], [they] say in this world that the intellect is knower.

66. As Knowledge is the nature of *Ātman* and is eternal Light, as the *Śruti* says,[52] It is never produced by the intellect, by *Ātman*, or by anything else.

67. Just as the "I"-notion arises with regard to the body and ordinary people say that [the body, *i.e.*, "I"] knows, so the intellect, and *Ātman* as well, are [regarded as] producers of knowledge.

68. Deluded thus by the notions of the intellect which are produced and appear to be Pure Consciousness, logicians say that knowledge is produced.

69. Therefore [the very existence of] a word like "*jānāti*," the notion [of it], and memory of it are from the absence of the discriminating knowledge of the Knower, [Its] reflection and the intellect.

70. The nature of the reflection [of the face], *viz.* conformity to the mirror, is superimposed upon the face. In like manner, the nature of the reflection of the Knower, *viz.* conformity to the attributes of the intellect, is taken to be [superimposed upon the Knower].

71. The notions of the intellect, therefore, on being illumined by the reflection of *Ātman*, appear, as it were, to be perceivers, just as torches, etc., appear to be burning [though in fact it is the fire in the torches, etc., that is burning].[53]

72. Saying that [the notions of the intellect] are manifest of themselves alone, and that [they] are of themselves alone perceivers, the Buddhists[54] deny the existence of a perceiver [other than the notions themselves].

73. If thus these notions of the intellect were not to be seen by anything else, tell [me] how are those Buddhists to be refuted?[55] [Even if it be said that] although their existence and non-existence are never perceived by anything else,

74. they have [among themselves] a continuous perceiver [apart from *Ātman*], [we reply:] It is also no more than a notion, since even if there is another perceiver, [it and the notions] are equally non-intelligent.

75. If [you] think that in the presence of the Overseer [the notions] would be established, [we answer:] No, because it would follow that even if [the notions were in the presence of] anything other [than the Overseer—for example, wood and clay—they would be established], since the Overseer, even though [they were in Its presence], does nothing to help establish them].[56]

76. Is the hearer who is suffering from pain and seeking after [final release] the Overseer or something else? It is not your view that it is the Overseer who is suffering from pain and seeking after [final release].

77. It can never be right to take it that I, a doer, am the Overseer and the Existent. Nor further is it proper that the statement of the *Śruti*, "You are the Existent," should also be false.

78. If the *Śruti* were making its statement [on the basis of] not discriminating the two ["I" (= *Ātman*) and "you" (= non-*Ātman*)], it would be comprehensible.[57] But if [the *Śruti*] were to say, "You [are the Existent]" [on the basis of] discriminating ["you"] from "I,"

79 & 80. [and "you"] refers to the continuum of the notions, there would be the defect already mentioned.[58] If [you[59] say that] "you" refers to the Overseer, [you] should explain here how any relation between the "I"-notion and the Overseer could exist through which "you" could indicate [the Overseer] indirectly. If [you say that] there is a relation of being seer and the object seen, how can there be [such a relation between the "I"-notion and the Overseer], when the Overseer is actionless?

81. If [you say], let the Overseer, though actionless, be in essence identical [with the "I"-notion], [we answer:] Unless it is grasped that the relationship is that the Overseer is the essence of "mine" (= the "I"-noton),[60] there will be no realization [of the identity of the "I"-notion and the Overseer].

82. If you think that the relationship can be grasped from the

scripture, [we answer:] No, because that would entail the threefold defects given already[61]; or else it would be an understanding of [the Overseer] as "mine" and [not the understanding of their identity].

83. While the intellect, [though] non-Seeing, is always appearing in the form of the Seeing (= *Ātman*), then from the intellect notions too appear, as sparks from a red-hot iron.[62]

84. It is [only on the assumption of] the ultimate Seeing that one can reasonably [account for the fact] that people [perceive the intellect's] false appearance [in the form of the Seeing of waking and dream, and] its disappearance [in deep sleep], and not otherwise [than on that assumption]. And as this is [in fact] the case, [the intellect] takes [itself] to be the Seeing.

85. [Objection:] "Can it not be that the Seeing enters [the intellect] as fire into a lump of iron?" [Reply:] That [contention] has been refuted by the illustration of the face and [its] reflection in a mirror.[63]

86. When the black iron appears red, that is considered to be an anology[64] [of the intellect appearing to be the Seeing].[65] An analogy, however, can never correspond in every detail.

87. In like manner, with the reflection of Pure Consciousness [in it], the mind appears to be Pure Consciousness. The reflection has been said to be false like the reflection of the face in a mirror.

88. It is not supported by the scriptures or reasoning that the mind is conscious. [If the mind were conscious,] it would follow that the body and the eye, etc., would also be so.

89. If [you say,] "Let them also be so," [we answer:] No, because [if it were so, you would have] become a materialist. And if there were no reflection in the mind, the notion that I am the Seeing would not arise."

90. If there were no notion, "I am the Existent," [the sentence], "Thou art That" (Chānd. Up. VI,8,7, etc.) would also be meaningless. To him who knows the distinction between "you" and "I" this sentence will be meaningful.[66]

91. It should be known that the two notions "my" and "this" inevitably denote "you" (= non-*Ātman*). [The notion] "I" is thought to denote "I" (= *Ātman*) and [the notion] "I am this" denotes both ["I" and "you"].

92. In regard to each other, a relation of principal and subordi-

nate is assumed, and it is reasonable that a relation of qualifying and qualified between them should be accepted.

93. These two [notions], "my" and "this," are both qualifying attributes of the [notion "I"] which is mentioned in the middle [of Upad I,18, 91], just as [the wealth and cows are qualifying attributes of a man in the case of] "a man possessed of wealth" and "a man possessed of cows": and similarly the body is [a qualifying attribute] of the bearer of the "I"-notion.

94. Everything seated in the intellect,[67] as well as the bearer of the "I"-notion, is [a qualifying attribute] of the Witness. Therefore the Knower makes everything manifest, though touching nothing.

95. All this, which has been set forth according to popular conviction, is inverted [thinking]. [Though] for those who are not intent upon discrimination, everything exists, [yet] it does not exist for those who have discriminating knowledge.

96. The logical means by which to ascertain [the meanings of] "this" [and] "I" should indeed be the method of agreement and difference[68] of the words and of the meanings of the words.[69]

97. In thinking, "I did not see anything else at all in this state of deep sleep," one does not deny his own Seeing but negates his own notions.[70]

98. [The scripture itself declares] the existence of Consciousness and Its immovability, saying, "[Then this person becomes] self-illumined" (Bṛh. Up. IV,3,9) [and] "For there is no [cessation of the Seeing of] the Seer [because of Its imperishability]" (Bṛh. Up. IV,3,23), but [declares] the perishability of the notions. [Thus] the scripture itself separates notions from Awareness.

99. When one has thus come to know, from the *Śruti* and from universally accepted usage, the meaning of the sentences, the *Śruti* says, "Thou art That" (Chānd. Up. VI,8,7, etc.) in order to remove the delusion of a hearer,[71]

100. just as Brahmā removed the ignorance of Daśaratha's son (= Rāma) merely by means of the declaration [, "You are the God Nārāyaṇa," and] did not mention any other effort whereby he was to know that he was Viṣṇu.[72]

101. [The sentence] that you are the Existence expresses only the basis of the word "I," which [rests] on the Light, *i.e.*, the inner *Ātman*. Thus the result of it is final release.[73]

102. If the result should not arise by merely hearing [the sen-

tence], then there would necessarily be some duty to be fulfilled. It is accepted that even before the verbal expression,[74] *Ātman* exists by Itself.

103. Right knowledge arises at the moment of hearing,[75] resulting in freedom from hunger, etc.[76] There is no doubt about the meaning of the sentences like "Thou art That" (Chānd. Up. VI,8,7, etc.), in the past, present, or future.

104. As the Awareness-*Ātman* is by nature free from obstacles, the right knowledge of one's own *Ātman* infallibly arises at the time of hearing.

105. Does one understand [at the time of hearing], "I am the Existent" or, "I am something else"? If [one understands, "I am] the Existent," the principal meaning of the word "I" should be regarded as being "the Existent."

106. If [one were to understand, "I am] something else," then it [would] be wrong to attain the knowledge, "I am the Existent." If the principal meaning is grasped, there is therefore no obstacle to the realization here.

107. The notion and its bearer (= the intellect), which have the reflection of [*Ātman* and appear to be *Ātman*], exist for Its sake. And since both are non-conscious, the result (= final release) is assumed to be in Pure Consciousness.[77]

108. The result (= final release) is proper to [*Ātman*] though [It is] immovable, just as victory, etc. are proper to a king,[78] since that result (*i.e.*, final release) is neither the nature nor the cause of either action or the notion.

109. Only in the sense that the mirror which has the reflection of a face and appears to be the face is the face, can the mirror of the intellect's notion which has the reflection of *Ātman* [and appears to be *Ātman* be what is called *ātman*]. In that sense the "I" is indeed [*ātman* but not in the true sense].

110. This is the way of realization that "[I] am the Existent." And [if] it were not so (= if there were no reflection), it would not be [realized]. If there were no medium, the teaching "Thou art That" (Chānd. Up. VI,8,7, etc.) would moreover be meaningless.

111. Thus, teaching is useful [only] when it is directed to a hearer. If the Overseer is not taken as the hearer, who would be the hearer?

112. If [you] suggest that in the presence of the Overseer the

intellect will be [a hearer], [we answer:] The Overseer does not do anything for [the intellect], any more than a piece of wood can be taken [to do anything for it].[79]

113. If the Overseer were to do anything for the intellect, would It not be subject to transformation? And what is wrong with [accepting] the reflection [theory] since it is supported by the *Śruti*[80] and other authority?

114. If [you say that to accept] a reflection entail changes [in *Ātman*], [we answer:] No, as already said, [it is unreal] just as a snake and so forth appears to be a rope[81] and so forth and just as a mirror [appears to be] a face.[82]

115. If [you say that] unless the appearance of [the intellect] as *ātman* is established apart from the perception of *Ātman*, there would arise the fallacy of mutual dependence,[83] [we answer:] The face and so on are established apart from [the appearance of the mirror as the face and like].

116. [You may say that] if the Overseer is established apart from [Its reflection], the reflection belongs to It, and if the reflection does belong to It, [the reflection] is distinct from the Overseer.

117. That is not so, since the notion [of the intellect] and the Seeing are in dream established each separately; since no chariot or other [external objects][84] exist in the dreaming state, [it is simply that] the notion [of the intellect] is being perceived by *Ātman*.

118. Pervaded by Awareness (= *Ātman*), the notion [of the intellect] assumes the form of an object [of perception]. The object [of perception] is taken to be that in whose form the notion arises.

119. As [the object of perception] is most desired, it is the object of an action.[85] One who is desirous of obtaining it is enjoined to perform the action. And that [notion of the intellect] to which the form [of the object] should be given is called an instrument.

120. That [*Ātman*] is called Knower[86] by the reflection of which [the notion of the intellect] is pervaded. He is a knower of *Ātman* who, having examined these three,[87] knows [which is *Ātman*] among them.

121. Since they are judged to be "right," "doubtful," or "false," the notions [of the intellect] are changeable. There is only the one Awareness in them but distinctions are made [in It] by the notions.

122. Just as the distinctions [in color, etc.] of a jewel are due to the distinctions of the limiting adjuncts,[88] so impurity and all

changes of the Awareness (= *Ātman*) are due to the notions [of the intellect].

123. The manifestation, perception, and establishment of the notions here [in this world] are due to another (= *Ātman*), since [it is *Ātman* that is] directly cognizable like a lamp. This is the inference which is being stated.[89]

124. Should one let the man ignorant [of It] grasp [*Ātman*] by some [accepted] means of knowledge, or [should it be] by negating [non-*Ātman*] so that [only] the other(= *Ātman*) remains,[90] without [using] any [of the accepted] means of knowledge?

125. If it is now said that [the method is that non-*Ātman*] is negated by verbal testimony which is a means of knowledge, it would follow that [*Ātman*] would be a void, since no Overseer would have been established.

126. If [you argue,] "You are a conscious being. How [can you be] the body?", [we answer:] Not [conclusive], because [it is] not established [through the mere negation that the conscious being is different from the body]. [Only] if a conscious being different [from anything else] had been established, would [the Overseer] be [established] in that way by abandoning something else."

127. [Objection:] "The Overseer simply exists of Itself and [our argument holds] since the conscious being is directly cognizable." [Reply:] Then the understanding of a man ignorant [of It] ought to be the same as [that of] the one [skeptic][91] who positively] asserts the non-existence [of *Ātman*].

128. [Objection:] "By the fact that people in ordinary life have the memory 'I knew this,' we may say that the instrument, object, and agent are established simultaneously."[92]

129. [Reply:] Even if [we admit for the sake of argument] that memory is a right means of knowledge,[93] it [only] appears to be simultaneous on account of its swiftness. The perceptions [of instrument, object, and agent arose originally] one after another before the memory [was laid down], and [now], after the memory [has been recalled, they come up] in the same manner.

130. One certainly assumes [distinctions like] "I knew this (= the object)" and "I knew me (= the agent)." Where distinctions are assumed there is no simultaneity.

131. And [a *regressus ad infinitum* follows] since the three [instrument, object, and agent] arise at the time of perceiving the na-

ture even [of one of them alone]; the agency associated with [the perception of] the nature [of the agent] is not [associated with the perception of the nature] of the instrument and the object.

132. The object of an action is declared to be that which it is intended should be always affected by the action of some agent.[94] Therefore it is accepted that the object of an action depends upon the agent [and] not upon anything else.

133. It is by verbal testimony, inference, or a means of knowledge other than these that anything becomes established for the man ignorant [of It], and not otherwise.

134. [Question:] "Is the Overseer too established by a means of knowledge, or without any?" [Reply:] One's own [Overseer] is [in fact] established without any [means of knowledge]; but this is not sufficient for the man ignorant [of It].

135. If the Overseer be taken to be the man ignorant [of It], there ought to be some evidence other than [Itself] for [It to be] known. And if anything other [than It] is the man ignorant [of It], there ought certainly to be [evidence other than Itself] for knowing [It].

136. Does "establishment"[95] mean "the state of being known,"[96] "coming into existence,"[97] or something else?[98] If [it means] "the state of being known," you must remember the two alternatives just mentioned [in the previous verse].

137. If "establishment" means "coming into existence," no effort would be of any avail for that, since it is well known to everyone that a thing [comes into existence] from its own causes.

138. In the doctrine, therefore, which accepts knowledge, object of knowledge, etc., "establishment" is said to be "the state of being known." The Overseer and the overseen are "established" [and] are "the object to be known," but they do not "come into existence."

139. If [you] assume that "establishment" means "distinctness"[99] of the object, agent, etc., [we say that] "distinctness" and "indistinctness" belong only to [the Overseer] different [from object, agent, etc.] and not to them.

140. And a jar does not become "distinct" to a blind man, an agent who has no faculty of seeing. If "distinctness" be supposed to belong to the agent, etc. [which have no faculty of seeing], the faculty of sight must have a bearer—the Overseer.

141. [Objection:][100] "Tell [us] what do you gain by [postulat-

ing] the dependence of knowledge upon something else (= *Ātman*)? [If you say,] '[The dependence of knowledge] upon the knower is accepted,' [we answer:] In our view the knower too is nothing but knowledge."

142. "It is certain that the nature of knowledge is devoid of distinction but yet is seen by those of distorted vision as if it had the distinction of object, knower, and consciousness."[101]

143. ["In our view knowledge is declared to be action and agent."][102] [Reply:] If [you admit that] knowledge is existent and perishable, [you should also] accept that it has a bearer. If [you say that] you accept no attribute [of knowledge], [you] give up [your own] position [that knowledge is existent and perishable].

144. [Objection:] "Surely an attribute such as existence is [really simply] the exclusion of non-existence, and so on?" [Reply:] Even then knowledge should not be perishable, for you hold that [it] has specific individuality.[103]

145. Destruction goes only up to specific individuality (= *Ātman*) [in our view. But you hold that] destruction is the exclusion of non-destruction. You say that sameness [perceived] as cow is the non-existence of non-cow, but that is not the specific individuality of a cow.

146. You say that the meaning denoted by the word "momentary" is also nothing but the non-existence of something else [than the momentary]. [Objection:] "Though non-existence is devoid of distinction, we take it that distinction arises because of names."

147. [Reply:] How in your view can one become many because of differences in names? If exclusion[104] is concerned with things other [than a cow], how does this [exclusion of them] indicate a cow?

148. Neither non-existences (negations) nor any particularities [could] ever distinguish [a cow from a non-cow], any more than names, generic properties, and the like [could distinguish] consciousness, since on your view [consciousness] is devoid of particularities.

149. If you accept sense-perception or inference[105] [as means of knowledge] in daily life, it must necessarily be admitted that it (sense-perception or inference) arises on the basis of differences between action and the agent.

150. Therefore blue and yellow or a jar and the like are qualifying attributes of consciousness; and so the [perceiver] which perceives [it] should be admitted.

151. There is the perceiver of form-color and other [external objects], which is different from them, since [they] are objects of perception. Likewise there is [the perceiver] of the notion [of the intellect] which is similarly different [from that notion], since [the perceiver] is the illuminator [of the notion], like a lamp.[106]

152. What kind of relationship other than that of the seer and the object of seeing will be possible between the Overseer who is the seeing and the object of the Overseer, which is the object of seeing?[107]

153. Being effected by the Overseer, seeing pervades the object of seeing, or rather, some help is given to the intellect by the permanent Overseer.[108]

154. It has previously been said[109] that the help is [for the intellect] to become Overseer-like [because of the reflection of the Overseer in it] and since the intellect [thus] becomes an illuminator, [it] pervades a jar and other [external objects], as light and the like pervade [their objects].

155. Just as a jar [when pervaded by light] becomes something situated in the light, so does it [when pervaded by the intellect] become something seated in the intellect.[110] It is the intellect's pervasion [of the jar] that is the jar's being seated [in the intellect]. In the pervasion by the intellect there would be sequence [of stages].

156. First the notion [of the intellect] pervades [objects]. Then there is the help of *Ātman*. [However] this sequence is not applicable to the Overseer of all, any more than to time, space and the like.

157. Something which, like the mind, perceives objects with the help of some factors, leaving some objects unperceived, is subject to transformation.

158. The knowledge "I am the Overseer" is merely a conviction pertaining to the intellect [but] not to the Overseer, since That is free from distinction, having no other [Overseer above It].

159. Even if the bearer [of the "I"-notion] were to realize final release, thinking thus, "I am [the Overseer]," it is not reasonable

that final release from pleasure and pain should take place in the bearer of the "I"-notion (= the intellect).

160. The notion "[I am] suffering pain" must arise from a misconception [of *Ātman*] as the body and so forth, like the notion that "[I am] owner of an earring." It is by the notion "I am the inner *Ātman*,"

161. namely by discriminating knowledge here [in our doctrine], that [the notion] devoid of discriminating knowledge is sublated. In the inverted view, [everything] would become nonexistent in the end since the valid means of knowledge would become invalid.

162. If [I,] *Ātman*, were burnt, cut, and destroyed, [I, *Ātman*] would suffer pain, but otherwise not; for though one [man] may be burnt, [cut, or destroyed], a different [man] never suffers the pain.

163. Being without touch and body,[111] I (= *Ātman*) can therefore never be burnt. Therefore [the notion "I suffer pain"] arises from false conception just as, when [one's] son is dead, [the notion "I am] dead" [arises from false conception].[112]

164. [The notion] "I am owner of an earring"[113] is certainly sublated by discriminating knowledge. Likewise the notion "[I] suffer pain" [is] always [sublated] by the notion "I am apart."

165. If it be established that [*Ātman*] suffers pain, it should be admitted that *Ātman* is always capable of suffering pain [but this is not the case]. [Therefore the notion "I] suffer" results from the false conception whereby the object [*i.e.*, pain] is produced and destroyed.

166. Just as, though [*Ātman* is] without touch and motion, [one feels] touch and motion, etc. [to be located in *Ātman*], so also because of lack of discriminating knowledge one feels pain to be located in *Ātman*, though it belongs to the mind.

167. By discriminating knowledge, namely the [right] notion of *Ātman*, pain is removed like motion, etc. Since the mind is by nature devoid of discriminating knowledge, it roams without desiring [to do so].

168. Then pain is experienced; [but it is] not [experienced] when the mind has become motionless. Therefore it is not reasonable that pain is located in the inner *Ātman*.

169. Since [in the sentence "Thou art That" the words]

"Thou" and "The Existent" (= That) have the same referent, this [sentence] is comparable to [the sentence] "The horse is black." Since the word "Thou" is [used] in apposition to [a word—"Existent"—which] refers to the Painless One (= *Brahman*), it [too] refers to that [Painless One].

170. Likewise, since the word "That" is [used] in connection with [the word which] denotes the inner *Ātman*, [it refers to the inner *Ātman*]. [Just like the sentence] "You are the tenth,"[114] the sentence ["Thou art That"] means the inner *Ātman*.

171. Without abandoning their own meanings [the words "Thou" and "That"] convey a special meaning and result in the realization of the inner *Ātman*. Therefore there is no other meaning contradictory to this meaning.

172. Since [the tenth boy] is included in the notion ["he must be among] the nine [others],"[115] [he] tries to know [which is the tenth boy], not counting himself as making up the ten. Similarly people [try to know] their own *Ātman*.[116]

173. Because their eyes are bound by nescience those people whose intellect is seized by desire do not clearly realize themselves to be the Seeing, just as [the tenth boy] does not realize himself to be the tenth.[117]

174. [Just as the boy knew himself to be the tenth through the sentence] "You are the tenth," so through such sentences as "Thou art That" one knows one's own *Ātman*, the Witness of all the internal organs.

175. There is no fixed rule in the *Veda* to the effect that in a sentence one [word] should be placed first and another word should be placed next; the syntactical relation of words is based upon [their] meanings.[118]

176. For when the meanings of the words in a sentence, while they are being listened to, are remembered by the method of agreement and difference,[119] then the meaning of the sentence is understood.

177. When the meanings of words in eternal sentences are clarified in order to convey the knowledge of the meaning of the sentences [to a pupil], then the question ["How am I *Brahman*?"] is out of place.

178. The method of agreement and difference has been mentioned for the purpose of remembering the meanings of the words,

for nobody can know the meaning of a sentence without remembering [the meanings of words].

179. In such sentences as "Thou art That," the meaning of sentences—[namely] "I am ever-free"—is not manifested from them because the meaning of the word "Thou" has not been analyzed.

180. The method of agreement and difference has been mentioned for the purpose of analyzing out the [meaning of the word "Thou"] and for no other purpose; for [it is only] when the meaning of the word "Thou" has been discriminated, like a *vilva* fruit[120] placed on the palm [of the hand],

181. the meaning of the sentence becomes manifest. And thus [the meaning of the sentence] is the One Apart,[121] since the inner *Ātman* is ascertained by the exclusion[122] of the [meaning] "experiencer of pain" from the meanings of the word "I."

182. Such being the case the [above-mentioned] meaning is possible; thus it is not reasonable for those versed in the meanings of words and sentences to abandon the [meaning] which is expressed in the *Śrutis* and to understand a meaning which is not expressed in the *Śrutis*.

183. [Objection:][123] "Sense-perception and other [means of knowledge] do sublate [knowledge arising from sentences], as [they do in the case of the sentence describing] cooking as applied to grains of gold[124] and so on." [Reply:] How can [knowledge arising from] sentences be sublated by that erroneous [knowledge] which arises from sense-perception and other [means of knowledge]?

184. [Objection:] "As long as there is the knowledge 'I suffer pain' [the knowledge] '[I am] free from pain' does not arise from the sentence, although [the former] is erroneous knowledge due to perception and other [means of knowledge]." [Reply:] Not so, because there are exceptions.

185. In the dreaming state I suffered pain today on account of burning, cutting, and the like [but the pain was sublated by the sentences]. Even if [the pain] be not sublated by the sentences in the dreaming state,

186. still it should be admitted that [pain] is sublated before [the beginning] of, and [after] the end of, the pain, since the persistence of pain or delusion is not seen anywhere.

187. If one knows that the inner *Ātman* is the [highest] *Ātman*

by sublating the [knowledge] that I suffer pain, just as [the boy knew he was] the tenth by sublating the knowledge that he was among the nine [others],[125] there is no contradiction.

188. The knowledge that one is ever-free arises from the sentence and not from anything else. The knowledge of the meaning of the sentence is also preceded by recollecting the meaning of the words.[126]

189. By the method of agreement and contrariety the meaning of words is certainly recollected. Thus one realizes that one is oneself free from pain and actionless.[127]

190. Through such sentences as "[Thou art] the Existent," like the [sentence] "You are the tenth," right knowledge concerning the inner *Ātman* will become clearer.[128]

191. Just as all pain in the dreaming state ceases by awakening so [the notion] that one suffers pain oneself is always [destroyed] by the [right] notion that the inner *Ātman* [is the highest] *Ātman.*[129]

192. In the case of grains of gold, etc., right knowledge does not arise since [grains of gold, etc.,] to which something other than [cooking] pertains, do not become soft.[130] But this is not true of such sentences as "Thou art That" since there is no contradiction.

193. In the sentence "Thou art That" the meaning of the two [words] "That" and "art" are already known. Because of the absence of any assistance to recollect the meaning of [the word] "Thou," the sentence will not produce right knowledge.

194. This word "art" means that [the words] "That" and "Thou" have the same referent.[131] The word "That" means inner *Ātman* and [the word] "Thou" has the meaning of the word "That."

195. The two [words] will remove [the notions] that [the word "Thou" (= the inner *Ātman*) means] a sufferer of pain and that [the word "That" (= *Brahman*) means] non-inner *Ātman.* And thus [the two words] will mutually convey the meaning of [the sentence] "Not thus! Not so!"

196. When the result of the [sentence] "Thou art That" is understood in such a way, how is it said that this [sentence] is not the means of knowledge and that it depends upon action?[132]

197. Therefore in the beginning, in the middle and in the end, the [injunction] "Perform action" is contradictory [to the sen-

tence]; so [it] should not be accepted since [it is] not stated in the *Śrutis*. And there [would] also [be] the meaningless abandonment of that which is stated in the *Śrutis*.[133]

198. [Objection:] "Satisfaction is felt from eating, but it is not experienced from the sentence. This analysis of the sentence is like [trying to] get boiled milk-rice from cow-dung."

199. [Reply:] It is true that [only] indirect knowledge arises from sentences referring to things other than *Ātman*. But it cannot be doubted that [direct knowledge arises from the sentence] which refers to the inner *Ātman*, just as the [true] number [ten] was obtained [from the sentence, "You are the tenth"].[134]

200. It has to be accepted that [the inner *Ātman*] is "self-evident," which is synonymous with "self-knowable." And the Awareness of one's own *Ātman* is established at the time of the cessation of the "I"-notion.

201. Pain is the object to intellects. How can this inner *Ātman*, the Seeing, have any connection with pain, when those [intellects themselves are in turn properly] taken to be merely objects to It?[135]

202. It is only Itself that is aware of the Seeing, for Its nature is Awareness. The Awareness of this [inner *Ātman*] is described as the intellect's coming into being as a possessor of Its reflection.

203. You here and now are final release, [self-]established and free from hunger, etc.[136] How can such a contradictory statement be made [in the *Śruti*] that [*Ātman*] is to be heard, etc., by you?[137]

204. If [you say] that [final release] has to be established, it might be so; then hearing and so forth would be necessary [to establish final release]. In that case final release would be non-eternal. Otherwise (*i.e.*, if it were eternal), the [injunctive] sacred word would be contradictory.

205. If the difference between a hearer and the object to be heard (= *Ātman*, or final release) were accepted, this [hearing, etc.] would be necessary. In that case, there would be a contradiction of the desired meaning [which is the identity of *Brahman* and *Ātman*]; the sacred word would be quite incoherent.

206. Once having known himself as "I am the [self-]established final release," any man who desires action would be foolish and would also betray the scripture.

207. For he who is [self-]established has no duty to perform;

he who has any duty to perform is not [self-]established. One who maintains both [ideas together] deceives himself.

208. [Objection:] "Only [the bare fact of] this reality is taught by the words, 'You are the [self-]established final release.' [But] what is the hearer to do so as to know that he is thus?

209. "It is experienced by means of perception that I am an agent and a sufferer of pain. Therefore there would be an effort [to know] that I am neither an agent nor a sufferer of pain.

210. "The *Śruti* has repeatedly affirmed agency, etc., when saying that reasoning, etc., should be employed in order to know that ['I must be neither an agent nor a sufferer of pain'] and to experience ['I am self-]established.' "

211. [Reply:] Once having understood "I am final release, painless, actionless, desireless, and [self-]established," how can one still accept such a contradictory meaning?

212. [Objection:] "You have to explain how it is that I experience that [I] have desire and action, and am not [self-]established, although I am not so."

213. [Reply:] That [point] may indeed be questioned about [but] not the experience that [one is] in final release. It is a thing which is contradicted by means of valid knowledge which is questionable.

214. The [experience] that I am in final release results from means of knowledge other [than perception, namely the sentence] "Thou art the Existent." It is [the experience] that [I] suffer pain which deserves to be questioned, arising as it does from fallacious perception.

215. One should be told what he asks and hopes for. The absence of pain is being asked for. How does this pain disappear from mind completely?

216. To meet this question, it must be stated what it is that removes pain. Since the *Śrutis* are the means of knowledge there is no doubt of one's own *Ātman*.

217. Therefore the sacred word of the *Śrutis* brings about the realization that one's *Ātman* is in final release. It should be accepted that [this sacred word] has this meaning, since there is no evidence to the contrary.

218. No Awareness of *Ātman* other than this is possible, since the *Śruti* says, "It is not known by those who [say they] understand

It" (*Kena Up.* II,3) [and] "[By what, my dear, should one know] the knower?" (Bṛh. Up. II,4,14).

219. The renunciation of all actions becomes the means for discriminating the meaning of the word "Thou"[138] since there is an [Upaniṣadic] teaching, "Having become calm, self-controlled, [. . . , one sees *Ātman* there in oneself]" (Bṛh. Up. IV, 4, 23).

220. In oneself should one see *Ātman*, the inner *Ātman* which is denoted by [the word] "Thou." Thence one sees all to be *Ātman*—that is, the One Apart which is meant by the sentence ["Thou art That"].

221. When the meaning of the sentence, *viz.* that all is *Ātman*, has become known to one through the right means of knowledge, how can any injunction enjoin him to perform [any action], since the other means of knowledge are untrue?

222. Therefore after the knowledge of the meaning of the sentence [has been realized], there cannot be any injunction to action, since two contradictory notions, "I am *Brahman*" and "I am an agent," do not [co-]exist.

223. The knowledge "I am *Brahman*" is not sublated by [the knowledge] "[I am] an agent" [and] "[I] have desire and am bound" which is derived from the fallacious means of knowledge.

224. When on the basis of the scripture the conviction "I am *Brahman* and no other" becomes firm, then the [above-mentioned erroneous] notion, like the notion that the body is *Ātman,* will become untenable.

225. Neither one who has come out to fearlessness from a state of fear, nor he who is still making efforts to do so, would seek, if he is independent, to go back to the state of fear.

226. Having been awakened from the ignorance as to the meanings of the words, and seeking for the realization of the meaning of the sentence, how should one come to follow his desires, when renunciation, etc., have been enjoined [on such a man]?

227.[139]Therefore everything has been established which we have said above.

228. Certainly nobody strives towards something in which he has no interest. Why should a seeker of final release make any effort, since he has no interest in the three worlds?[140]

229. Even if suffering from hunger, one certainly does not want to take poison. Nobody whose hunger has been appeased by sweet food knowingly wants to take poison unless he is a fool.[141]

230. Salutation to this good teacher who, like a bee, has collected for us from the flowers of the Upaniṣadic sentences the best honey of the nectar of knowledge.[142]

Notes

[1]Cf. Upad II,2,95 f.

[2]Rāmatīrtha interprets "*guror garīyas*" as "*paramagurave.*" The epithet "*paramaguru*" is traditionally applied to Gauḍapāda, the author of GK, whom the tradition regards as the teacher of Śaṅkara's teacher Govinda. Bodhanidhi interprets "*guror garīyas*" as "*sarvaguror api garīyase,*" which does not indicate any particular person.

[3]"*Vajra*" (thunderbolt) is a weapon of Indra who stands in the first rank among the gods in the *Veda*. Nearly one-fourth of the total number of hymns in the *Ṛg-Veda* are dedicated to him. Having drunk *soma* juice, he overcomes Vṛtra, the demon of drought and inclement weather, with his thunderbolts and forces the rain to pour down. Cf. A. A. Macdonell, *The Vedic Mythology* (Reprint ed. Varanasi: Indological Book House, 1963), pp. 54–66. The word *vajra* seems to be connected with the word *yatīndra* (an Indra of ascetics) in the present stanza (*pāda* d).

[4]"You" (*yuṣmad*) denotes the object, *viz.* non-*Ātman*, in contrast with "I" (*aham, asmad*), namely the subject, *Ātman*. See note 1 to Chap. 2, p. 108.

[5]Cf. Upad I,14,17; 18,46; 18,114; II,2,109.

[6]Rāmatīrtha interprets *dhyānāt* as *garuḍādimantrabījasmaraṇāt*; Ānandajñāna, as *mantrabījāder gāyatryā japāt*; Bodhanidhi, as *mantrabījākṣaradhyānād yathā gāyatryādijapāt.*

[7]Rāmatīrtha supplies here: *vākyād ātmatattvāvagamamātreṇa*; Ānadajñāna, *vākyaśaktiviśeṣāt.*

[8]Śaṅkara recognizes the significance of the means of knowledge (*pramāṇa*) but stresses that the knowledge of *Brahman-Ātman* is attained only through the *Śruti* (Upad I,11,9; 18,217, etc.). The *Śruti* is infallible, but any other means of knowledge than that is fallacious (*pramāṇābhāsajāta*, Stanza 223; *pratyakṣābhāsajanyatva*, Stanza 214). See Introduction, III,C,1, pp. 46–49.

[9]Cf. Bṛh. Up. IV,3,10.

[10]Cf. Kaṭh. Up. III,4.

[11]Cf. Upad I,12,17.

[12]This objection, which ends at stanza 18, seems to be made by the Mīmāṃsakas. See the next note. Cf. Upad I,1,8–11; 18,183.

[13]The word *prasaṃcakṣā* is used as a synonym of *prasaṃkhyāna* (see stanza 12). In his work Sureśvara makes an opponent define *prasaṃkhyāna* as: "Mentally going over the meaning of such *Śruti* sayings as 'Thou art That' and the reasoning based on the method of agreement and contrariety" (*tattvamasyādiśabdārthānuvayavyatirekayuktiviṣayabuddhyāmreḍanam*, Naiṣ III,90). It is also said that when properly performed, *prasaṃkhyāna* generates perfect knowledge through the increase of knowledge (*ibid*). Like Śaṅkara Sureśvara rejects *prasṃkhyāna*. Cf. Naiṣ I,67; III,88–93; 123–126; Bṛh. Up. Vārttika I,818–848; III,796–961; Unters, pp. 2005–2006; T.M.P. Mahadevan, *Saṃbandha-Vārtika of Sureśvarācārya* (Madras: University of Madras, 1958), pp. xxi-xxiii. In his *Brahmasiddhi*

Maṇḍanamiśra does not explicitly advocate the doctrine of *prasaṃkhyāna*. However, he uses the expression "*prasaṃkhyātāni karmāṇi*" (*Brahmasiddhi*, p. 33, line 11) and seems to hold the same idea, calling it *upāsanā* (see *Brahmasiddhi*, p. 35, and p. 134). It is said that the doctrine of *prasaṃkhyāna* is one of the instances in which Vācaspati, who is the author of the *Bhāmatī*, commentary on the BSBh, is made responsible by later Advaitins for a view which was originally set forth by Maṇḍanamiśra, which he simply revised and read into Śaṅkara's BSBh. See *Brahmasiddhi*, pp. xxvii-xxxi; S. S. Suryanarayana Sastri and C. Kunhan Raja, *The Bhāmatī of Vācaspati* (Madras: Theosophical Publishing House, 1933), pp. xxxix-xli and its footnote; A. J. Alston (tr), *The Naiṣkarmya Siddhi of Śrī Sureśvara* (London: Shanti Sadan, 1959), p. 197. As is clear in the Upad, Śaṅkara rejects *prasaṃkhyāna*, but he recommends *parisaṃkhyāna*, though how they differ from the former is not known; and an illustration of the latter appears in Upad II,3. Cf. PBh I,5,29, p. 24.

[14]Ānandajñāna interprets "two" (*dvaya*) as "*śabdānucintana*" and "*yuktyanucintana*"; Bodhanidhi, as "*yuktiśabdasāmarthya*"; Rāmatīrtha, as "*vākyānucintana*" and "*yuktyālocana*." Cf. the previous stanza. Śaṅkara recognizes the necessity of reasoning and *Vedic* teachings (see stanza 4) but not of *prasaṃkhyāna*.

[15]Ānandajñāna and Rāmatīrtha supply "*ced*" after "*pratipadyate*," but Bodhanidhi reads "*yato*" for "*tathā*."

[16]"What has been heard" (*śruta*) may stand for "*śabda*" (verbal testimony, especially *Śruti*), which constitutes one of the means of knowledge (*pramāṇa*).

[17]See Taitt. Saṃ. 5,2,7.

[18]In the Nyāya-Vaiśesika system "*upalabdhi*" (perception) and "*jñāna*" (knowledge) are synonyms for "*buddhi*" and "*pratyaya*" (*Nyāyasūtra* I,1,15; *Vaiśeṣikopaskāra* 8,1,1). According to them knowledge is a quality of *ātman*-substance. The Buddhist and the Mīmāṃsā systems commonly characterize knowledge as an activity. Śaṅkara rejects both theories and asserts that knowledge or perception is *Ātman* Itself or the nature of *Ātman*. See Introduction, III,B,3, pp. 38–40.

[19]Cf. Śvet. Up. VI,11; Upad I,11,6; 13,19.

[20]In GBh XIII,12, p. 553 (cf. Śaṅkara *ad* Māṇḍ. Up. 7 [Gītā Press, n. d.], pp. 50–51) Śaṅkara mentions "quality" (*guṇa*) and "relation" (*saṃbandha*) in addition to "universal" (*jāti*) and "action" (*kriyā*), and he styles them "*śabdapravṛttihetu*" in his commentary on Taitt. Up. II,1, p. 234 (cf. Śaṅkara *ad* Bṛh. Up. II,3,6, p. 334). But he enumerates "name" (*nāma*), "form-and-color" (*rūpa*), "action" (*karman*), "distinction" (*bheda*), "universal" (*jāti*), and "quality" (*guṇa*) in his commentary on Bṛh. Up. II,3,6, p. 334. Cf. Naiṣ III,103; Unters, p. 1962.

[21]In the Upad the word *ābhāsa* is used in the three meanings: (1) a fallacy (*pratyakṣābhāsa-*, Upad I,18,214; *pramāṇābhāsa-*, Upad I,18,223); (2) false appearance (Upad I,14,1; 18,84; 18,86, etc.); and (3) reflection (Upad I,18,43; 18,63, etc.). For a detailed discussion, see S. Mayeda, "The Meaning of Ābhāsa in Śaṅkara's Upadeśasāhasrī" (in Japanese. *Journal of Indian and Buddhist Studies*, vol. 6, no. 1, 1958), pp. 174–177; Introduction, III,B,2, pp. 36–37.

[22]Cf. Introduction, III,B,2, p. 36–37.

[23]See stanza 71.

[24]See Introduction, IV,C, pp. 75–76.

[25]See Manu IV,130; *Yājñavalkyasmṛti* I,152. This view is refuted later at stanza 41.

[26]This view is refuted at stanza 42. See Introduction, IV,C, pp. 75–76.

[27]Cf. BS II,3,43; BhG XV,7. It is reported that Bhartṛprapañca held this view. Cf. Nakamura III, p. 172. This theory is rejected in GK III,7. See Introduction, IV,C, pp. 75–76.

[28]The idea that the individual *ātman* is a modification (*vikāra*) of the highest *Ātman* is said to have been held generally by early Vedānta philosophers such as Bhartṛprapañca (see Śaṅkara *ad* Bṛh. Up. IV, 3,7, p. 560). See Nakamura III, pp. 632–633. See Introduction, IV,C, pp. 75–76. This theory is refuted in GK III,7.

[29]This opinion is refuted at stanzas 45, 47, and 48.

[30]Ānandajñāna and Rāmatīrtha attribute this opinion to the Bhāṭṭa school of Mīmāṃsā.

[31]According to Ānandajñāna and Rāmatīrtha this is the theory of the Prāsaṅgikas.

[32]This problem is taken up again in stanzas 44 f.

[33]See Upad I,17,33.

[34]Rāhu is said to be first referred to in the *Atharvaveda* (XIX,9,10). Chānd. Up. VIII,13 refers to the eclipse of the moon. This legend (see Upad I,17, 33) was developed especially in the *Purāṇas*.

[35]See stanzas 33–39.

[36]See stanza 34.

[37]This statement probably refers to the principle of *vākyabheda* (split of the sentence, or syntactic disunity), which is a fault (*doṣa*) emphatically disapproved in Mīmāṃsā as well as in *Dharmaśāstra*. According to this principle, one and the same sentence cannot be construed as laying down two separate injunctions (*vidhi*). Śaṅkara also refers to this principle in his BSBh III,3,14, p. 693; III,3,24, p. 711; III,3,42, p. 753. Cf. P. V. Kane, *History of Dharmaśāstra*, vol. V, pt. II, pp. 1299–1303; F. Edgerton, *The Mīmāṃsā Nyāya Prakāśa* (New Haven: Yale University Press, 1929), p. 46 and p. 293.

[38]See stanza 34.

[39]Bodhanidhi reads "*vastutas*" for "*vastusaṃs*." Cf."*avastusan*," stanza 46. Rāmatīrtha interprets "*vastusat*" as "*paramārthasat*."

[40]See Upad I,18,53; II,2,77–83. Cf. Introduction, III,B,3, pp. 38–40.

[41]See note 40 above.

[42]Cf. stanzas 64–67.

[43]Cf. Upad I,15,15 and note 11.

[44]Cf. Kaṭh. Up. II,18; V,13; Muṇḍ. Up. I,6.

[45]See stanza 29. Śaṅkara accepts two functions of words, primary (*mukhya*) and secondary (*guṇa*, *upacāra*), but does not give a full account of them. It may be Sarvajñātman who first set up a theory thereof in the Advaita Vedānta. See *Saṃkṣepaśārīraka* I,104; 154–157; T. Vetter, *Sarvajñātman's Saṃkṣepaśārīrakam. 1. Kapitel. Einführung, Übersetzung und Anmerkungen* (Wien: Kommissionsverlag der österreichischen Akademie der Wissenschaften, 1972), p. 19; N. Veezhinathan, *The Saṁkṣepaśārīraka of Sarvajñātman, Critically Edited with Introduction, English Translation, Notes and Indexes* (Madras: University of Madras, 1972), pp. 9–12; K. Kunjunni Raja, *Indian Theories of Meaning*, pp. 19–94 and pp. 231–273.

[46]Cf. Bṛh. Up. III,5,1.

[47]This is similar to Bhartṛhari's idea (*Vākyapadīya* III,8,13, p. 313). Cf. Nakamura IV, pp. 111–113.

[48]Lokāyata (or Cārvāka) is the materialism of India.

[49]See stanza 51 and following.

[50]Cf. stanza 60.

[51]See Introduction, III,B,3, pp. 38–40.

[52]Cf. Bṛh. Up. IV,4,16; IV,3,6; IV,3,9.

[53]See stanza 31.

[54]Probably the Vijñānavādins.

[55]Ānandajñāna and Rāmatīrtha take this objection as addressed to other Vedāntins (*svayūthya*).

[56]See stanza 112; *Sāṃkhyakārikā* 60.

[57]The first two lines are quoted in Naiṣ IV,20.

[58]Stanzas 76 and 77.

[59]According to Jagadānanda this is the refutation of the Sāṃkya. Cf. stanza 152.

[60]The word "*tādātmya*" which means identity is an abstract noun derived from a *bahuvrīhi* compound "*tad-ātman*" which means "what has this (*tat*) as its essence". Therefore the identity of A and B means that B has A as its essence or that A is B's essence. For this reason, without knowing the relationship that A is B's essence, nobody can tell that A is identical with B.

[61]See stanzas 74–80.

[62]As for this simile, see, for example, Bṛh. Up. II,1,20; Kauṣ. Up. III,3; IV,20; Muṇḍ. Up. II,1,1; *Maitri Up.* VI,26; *Yājñavalkyasmṛti* III,67.

[63]See stanzas 33 and 43.

[64]All the commentators take "*dṛṣṭa*" as "*dṛṣṭānta.*"

[65]See stanza 83.

[66]The last half stanza is quoted in Naiṣ IV,21.

[67]See Upad I,7,1 and note 1; Introduction, III,B,2, p. 36.

[68]*Anvayavyatireka*. For a detailed discussion, see Introduction, III,C,3, pp. 50–57.

[69]This stanza is quoted in Naiṣ IV,22.

[70]This stanza is quoted in Naiṣ IV,23.

[71]This stanza is quoted in Naiṣ IV,24.

[72]According to *Rāmāyaṇa* (Madras: M.L.J. Press, 1958), VI,120, 10 ff., in reply to Rāma (who has previously said that he considers himself to be merely a man, namely Daśaratha's son), Brahmā tells him, "You are the god Nārāyaṇa" (*bhavān nārāyaṇo devaḥ*, VI,120,13). Nārāyaṇa is another name for Viṣṇu.

[73]This stanza is quoted in Naiṣ IV,25.

[74]According to Bhartṛhari, all verbal expressions of *Brahman* are nothing but limiting adjuncts (*upādhi*) to the Absolute. Cf. *Vākyapadīya* III, 1,20; Nakamura IV, p. 185.

[75]See the previous stanza.

[76]Cf. Upad I,14,12 and note 4.

[77]There is a similar problem in the Sāṃkhya system: To which does final release (*mokṣa*) belong, Puruṣa or Prakṛti? Cf. Shinkan Murakami, "Mokṣa in the Sāṃkhya Philosophy" (in Japanese. *The Journal of Indian and Buddhist Studies*, vol. XXI, no. 1, 1972), pp. 74–79.

[78]Ātman is compared to a king who, without acting himself, makes others act by his mere presence. Cf. BSBh I,1,4, pp. 95–96.

[79]See stanzas 75; 154.

[80]Jagadānanda refers to Bṛh. Up. II,5,19, but in fact the idea of "*ābhāsa*" (reflection) of *Ātman* is not mentioned at all in the *Śrutis*. This is a case of Śaṅkara's discovering authority in the *Śrutis*, especially the *Upaniṣads*, for something which is not there. See S. Mayeda, "On the Author of Māṇḍūkyopaniṣad- and the Gauḍapādīya-Bhāṣya," pp. 92–93.

[81]The usual example is a rope appearing to be a snake. But it seems to be grammatically difficult to translate in this manner.

[82]See stanza 109.

[83]This probably means the vicious circle that the intellect's appearance as *ātman* depends upon *Ātman*'s perception while the latter depends upon the former.

[84]See Bṛh. Up. IV,3,10.

[85]See Pāṇini I,4,49. Cf. stanza 132 below.

[86]Cf. Upad I,15,48; 16,4; 18,65.

[87]The object of perception (*viṣaya*, stanza 118), the instrument (*karaṇa*, stanza 119), and the knower (*jñātṛ*, stanza 120).

[88]As for this simile, see Upad I,17,16.

[89]See stanza 151.

[90]Cf. the second and sixth chapters of the Metrical Part.

[91]Ānandajñāna and Rāmatīrtha regard this as referring to the Śūnyavādins.

[92]A. J. Alston suggests that this is a reference to Prabhākara or his school in his "*That Thou Art*," pp. 74–75.

[93]Apart from the Jaina, the Vaiśesika, and the Advaita Vedānta system, all the schools of philosophy are definitely opposed to memory (*smṛti*) being regarded as a distinct source of knowledge. Cf. Chatterjee, *The Nyāya Theory of Knowledge*, pp. 371–376.

[94]Stanza 119.

[95]*Siddhi*. Cf. stanzas 133, 134.

[96]*Jñātatā*. See stanza 135.

[97]*Svātmalābha*. Cf. stanza 137.

[98]Cf. stanza 139.

[99]Rāmatīrtha attributes this theory to the Bhāṭṭa school of the Mīmāṃsā.

[100]The Vijñānavādin's objection. K. B. Pathak takes this stanza, as well as the next one, as a quotation from a work of "Vijñānavādin Bauddha" (see "Dharmakīrti and Śaṃkarācārya," *Journal of the Bombay Branch of the Royal Asiatic Society*, XVIII, 1890–1896, p. 94). D. V. Gokhale also recognizes the possibility (*Shrî Shankarâchârya's Upadeshasâhasrî with the Gloss Padayôjanikâ by Shrî Râmatîrtha*. Bombay: The Gujarati Printing Press, 1917, p. 385, note (1)). But the point cannot yet be conclusively settled. Cf. Nakamura I, p. 103.

[101]This is a quotation from Dharmakīrti's *Pramāṇavārttika* II,354. This stanza is so famous that it is often quoted, with slight difference in reading, by other texts, for example, *Sarvadarśanasaṃgraha* II, lines 206–7; *Prakaraṇapañcikā*, p. 141; *Sarvasiddhāntasaṃgraha* IV,4; *Sāṃkhyapravacanabhāṣya* I,20; *Nyāyaratnākara* (*ad Ślokavārtika*), p. 272; *Nyāyamañjarī*, p. 540; Bṛh. Up. Vārttika IV,3,476; *Tattvavaiśāradī* IV,23, p.198. However, it seems to me that this stanza is a later interpolation or that, as Bodhanidhi's commentary suggests, copyists incorporated by mistake into the *mūla* text the stanza which a commentator originally quoted in his commentary for the purpose of clarifying stanza 141. This may also be true of half a stanza (*bhūtir yeṣām kriyā saiva kārakaṃ saiva cocyate*) which, in some manuscripts and printed editions (see variant readings of Mayeda Upad), constitutes the first two lines of the succeeding stanza, and which is also often quoted by other authors, for example, Bṛh. Up. Vārttika IV,3,494; *Bhāmatī* II,2,20; *Tattvavaiśāradī* IV,20, p. 195; *Bodhicaryāvatārapañjikā* IX,6 (cf. Louis de la Vallée Poussin, *Mūlamadhyamakārikās de Nāgārjuna*, St.-Pétersbourg, 1913, p. 116, note 1; D. V. Gokhale, *Shrî Shankarâchârya's Upadeshasâhasrî*, pp. 386–387, note 7). In this context the following two points should be noted here: (1) Manuscripts G4 and G8 (see Mayeda Upad) have between the stanzas 11 and 12 of Chapter 15 an additional stanza which in his commentary Bodhanidhi quotes from the Viṣṇu Purāṇa (VI,5,80); (2) Some manuscripts and printed editions (see variant readings of Mayeda Upad) have between the stanzas 23 and 24 of Chapter 17 an additional stanza which is a quotation from *Mahābhārata* 12,242,4 and which appears as a part of the *mūla* text in Rāmatīrtha's commentary and as a part of the commentary in Bodhanidhi's.

[102]See note 101.

[103]*Svālakṣaṇya*. According to Buddhism every element of existence (*dharma*. Cf. Upad

I,16,23) perishes momentarily and is separate in its existence, and carries its own specific individuality (*svalakṣaṇadhāraṇa*. Cf. *Prasannapadā*, xvii, 304; xxiii,456, etc.). Here Śaṅkara, however, seems to understand *svātman* by the term *svalakṣaṇa*.

[104]Cf. stanza 144. The theory of exclusion (*apoha*) was first maintained by Dignāga, a Buddhist logician, in the fifth chapter of his *Pramāṇasamuccaya*. There are three main views of the universal (*jāti* or *sāmānya*) in Indian philosophy: (1) the realistic view, (2) the conceptural view, and (3) the nominalistic view. According to (1), which was held by the Nyāya-Vaiśeṣika, the universal is a real entity which is distinct from, but inheres in, many individuals. The Jains and the later Advaita Vedāntins adopt (2) and reject the concept of the universal as a real, independent, and objective entity over and above the individuals; they assert that it is constituted by the essential common attributes of the individuals, and has existence not only in our mind but also in the particular objects of experience. The Buddhists hold the third view and also deny the existence of any independent reality of the universal. According to them universality attaches to names, and has no objective existence. Only the particular at a time point (*svalakṣaṇa*; see note 103) is ultimately real. There is no similarity between two particulars, such as two cows. They are, however, identified by disregarding the difference between them and attending to the contrast with, for example, horses; in this way "cows" are specified as non-horses, etc. The sameness as cow (see stanza 145) is really simply exclusion of all the non-cows (*apoha*). Cf. Th. Stcherbatsky, *Buddhist Logic*, vol. I, pp. 444–456; vol. II, pp. 405–432; K. Kunjuni Raja, *Indian Theories of Meaning*, pp. 317–318; S. Chatterjee, *The Nyāya Theory of Knowledge*, pp. 165–175; M. Hattori, "A Study of Mīmāṃsāślokavārttika, Apohavāda [I]" (in Japanese. *Kyōtodaigaku Bungakubu Kenkyū Kiyō*, No. 14, 1973), pp. 1–44; [II] (*ibid*, No. 15, 1975), pp. 1-63.

[105]From the time of Dignāga Buddhists have accepted two different means of knowledge, sense-perception (*pratyakṣa*) and inference (*anumāna*).

[106]See stanza 123.

[107]Cf. stanza 80.

[108]See stanzas 75, 87, 112–114, 154, and 156.

[109]See note 108.

[110]See Upad I,7,1 and note 1; 18,94; Introduction, III,B,2, p. 36.

[111]Cf. Kaṭh. Up. III,15; Chānd. Up. VIII,12,1; Upad I,15,6; 15,7.

[112]Cf. stanza 20.

[113]Cf. stanza 160; BSBh I,1,4, pp. 94–95.

[114]See Upad I,12,3.

[115]See note 114.

[116]This stanza appears as Naiṣ IV, 34.

[117]This stanza appears as Naiṣ IV, 35.

[118]See Introduction, III,C,3, p. 50–53.

[119]See stanza 96.

[120]*Vilva* or *Bilva* is Aegle marmelos, the wood-apple tree. Its delicious fruit when unripe is used medicinally.

[121]Cf. Upad I,17,9; 18,170; 18,172.

[122]Cf. note 104.

[123]Cf. stanzas 9–18; 192; Naiṣ II,5.

[124]*Kṛṣṇala* (*guñjā* or *raktikā*) is the black berry of the plant *Abrus precatorius* used as a weight. It also means a piece of gold of the same weight, which correponds to 0.122 grams or 1,875 grains. Cf. Manu VIII, 134–136; *Viṣṇudharmasūtra*, IV,6–10; VI,11–12; *Yājñavalkyasmṛti* I,363–365; P. V. Kane, *A History of Dharmaśāstra*, vol. II, pt. II, p. 1209; III, pp. 120–121 and footnote 162; G. Bühler, *The Laws of Manu* (SBE vol.

XXV, 1964), p. 277, note 134. According to Jagadānanda (p. 273, note 5) gold particles are cooked in order to sanctify them for use in certain sacrifices. If stanza 192 is taken into consideration, this simile probably means that even after cooking gold particles we do not perceive them as cooked, since they have not become soft; and so sense-perception denies the fact that they have been cooked. Cf. *Mīmāṃsāsūtra* X,1,1–3; 2,1–2; Śabara's commentary on these *sūtras*.

[125]See Upad I,12,3.

[126]This stanza appears as Naiṣ IV,31. See stanza 178; Introduction, III,C,3, p. 50–53.

[127]This stanza appears as Naiṣ IV,32.

[128]This stanza appears as Naiṣ IV,33.

[129]Cf. stanza 187.

[130]See stanza 183.

[131]Cf. stanza 169.

[132]See stanzas 9–18.

[133]See stanza 182.

[134]See Upad I,12,3; 18, 187.

[135]See Upad II,1,33–35.

[136]Cf. Upad I,14,12; 18,103.

[137]This probably refers to Bṛh. Up. II,4,5, according to which *Ātman* should be seen (*draṣṭavya*), heard (*śrotavya*), reflected on (*mantavya*), and meditated upon (*nididhyāsitavya*). Cf. stanza 205.

[138]The first two lines of this stanza are cited in Bhāskara's commentary on the BhG III,4 as quoted from the *Upadeśa Grantha*. See Mayeda Upad, pp. 50–51; V. Raghavan, "Bhāskara's Gītābhāṣya", WZKSO, vols. XII-XIII (1968–1969), p. 283 and p. 287. It is reported by D. V. Gokhale in his edition of the Upad (Bombay: The Gujarati Printing House, 1917), p. 415, note (3) that the first half stanza is quoted in *Vidvanmanorañjanīṭīkā* 4 (*vicārāya for vivekāya*), Madhusūdanasarasvatī's *Gūḍārthadīpikā* 3,6 and Viśveśvarasarasvatī's *Yatidharmasaṃgraha*, p. 72 and p. 156.

[139]Manuscripts of the text with the commentaries of Ānandajñāna and Bodhanidhi (see variants of Mayeda Upad) lack stanzas 227–230, and the two commentators do not refer to them at all. But stanzas 228 and 229 appear as Naiṣ IV,65 and 66. No conclusive evidence is available for any explanation of these facts.

[140]This stanza appears as Naiṣ IV,65. See note 139.

[141]This stanza appears as Naiṣ IV,66. See note 139.

[142]This *prakaraṇa* and the seventeenth open and end with benedictory stanzas. For a fuller discussion of the formation of the text, see Mayeda Upad, pp. 65–68.

CHAPTER 19
ANNIHILATION OF FEVER

1. Having taken the treatment by the medicines of knowledge and dispassion, which brings about the annihilation of the fever of desires, one does not [again] come to suffer pain from the delirium of that fever of desires and the connection with the series of hundreds of bodies.

2. You [O My Mind] seek to obtain valueless things, such as the notions of "I"- and "my"-notions. Other people[1] realize that your effort is for the sake of one other than yourself. You indeed have no knowledge of the objects, and I [who have it] have no desire to possess them. Therefore it is proper for you to be calm, O Mind!

3. As I am none other than the supreme and eternal One I am always satisfied [and] I have no desire. And being always released, I do not wish [My] welfare. O Mind, make more efforts for your tranquilization!

4. According to the *Śruti* it is the *Ātman* of both the world and us that transcends a series of the six waves of existence[2]; it is also known by Me from the [other] means of knowledge[3] as well. Therefore, O Mind, you make useless efforts.

5. When you have been calmed there is indeed no notion of difference, on account of which people fall into delusion through illusion, since the perception [of difference] is the cause of the rise of illusion; at the time of release from the perception [of difference], nobody has any illusion at all.

6. I am not deluded by your activity since I am by true nature enlightened, unfettered, and changeless. There is indeed no difference in our nature at an earlier and later time. Therefore, O Mind, your effort is useless.

7. As I am constant I do not become other [than I am]; if [I were] connected with changes, [I] would indeed be inconstant. I am always shining and therefore I am non-dual. Certain it is that what is falsely assumed is unreal.

8. In essence you are non-existent in this world, O Mind, since when scrutinized through reasoning [you] are [found to be] non-existent. Now there is no destruction of what is existent, and there is no origination of what is non-existent.[4] Both [destruction and origination][5] belong to you. Therefore you are not accepted as the existent.

9. The subject of seeing, the object of seeing, and seeing—all this is an error, since it is what you have falsely constructed. The object of seeing is not considered to be different from the Seeing. [The *ātman*] in the state of deep sleep is not different [from *ātman*] in the waking state.

10. And similarly false construction is also dual,[6] since it is not a real substance,[7] as in the familiar case of the torch circle.[8] As there is no difference of powers [of *ātman* such as seeing, etc.][9] nor of *ātman* [in different bodies], non-duality [of *ātman*] is ascertained to be as the *Śrutis*[10] say.

11. And if these conscious [*ātmans*] were different from one another, their destruction would certainly come about, since they would be limited and things which have differences are seen to be destructible. Moreover, the destruction of the world results from the final release of all.

12. Nobody belongs to Me and I do not belong to anybody, for I am non-dual and nothing that is falsely constructed exists. And I am not that which is falsely constructed but am established before the false construction. It is only duality that is falsely constructed.

13. Moreover, there is no false assumption of "being" or "difference" in regard to the Unborn (= *Ātman*); so [It] is not non-existent. Furthermore, that [*Ātman*] from which your false assumption proceeds is not falsely assumed since [It] was already established.

14. Whatever duality may be seen by you is certainly non-existent. That [*Ātman*] is not seen by you by no means shows [Its] non-existence. That from which the false assumption of "being" or "non-being" proceeds [must itself] exist. And just as an in-

vestigation [is accepted as the cause of a conclusion], so the Non-Dual and Existent [*Ātman* is to be accepted as the cause of the false assumption].

15. Since [It] is the cause of [your] investigation, the Existent is [in fact] accepted by you and supposed to exist. And if It were non-existent the investigation would be given up; so [It] would remain as such. If it is not desirable [that the investigation be given up] the Existent should by all means be accepted.

16. [Objection:][11] "Even if [we admit for the sake of argument] that there be the Existent I would be the same as the non-existent, since It has no practical efficiency,[12] any more than the [fabled] donkey's horn." [Reply:] But the absence of practical efficiency does not constitute a criterion of the non-existence [of a thing]. [The existence of a thing] is not [established] through [the fact] that [it has practical efficiency]. Conversely, [if a thing has no practical efficiency], it is not [therefore established] that [it] is otherwise [than existent].

17. Moreover, [that is] because [your argument, *viz.* that the Existent has no practical efficiency] is not established, since [the Existent] is the [very] cause of [your] investigation[13] and duality is emitted from It through [Its] *Māyā*.[14] [The Existent] is thus established through the *Śrutis*, the *Smṛtis*, and reasoning. But otherwise [It] is not reasonably [established].[15]

18. Furthermore, as the *Śrutis* say, the Non-dual is different in Its nature from any false assumption, and [that is also] because It is established before [there is any] false assumption. And similarly what has been falsely assumed is also negated here [in this sentence], "Not thus! Not so!", in order to establish the remainder (= *Ātman*).

19. Though [It] is thus not what is falsely assumed, [but is] unborn, non-dual, and non-perishable, people always undergo birth, old age, and death, which arise from the illusion of their own mind,[16] falsely assuming [It] to be "being" and "non-being."

20. If the birth [of a thing] were not [itself] without birth, there would be *regressus ad infinitum*; [in other words] this [brith] would have another [and that one yet another . . .]. Otherwise, there is no birth [at all], since [if the existent were to have been born,] the existent would have been non-existent, and [if the non-existent

were to be born] the non-existent would be existent. And there is neither action [of birth] nor [its] agent. Therefore [everything] is unborn.[17]

21. If the agent [of birth] is taken to be [something] devoid of action [and] no more than that, [then] there is surely no[thing] which is not an agent of [birth]. [But in fact] there is no [agent at all], because [if the agent were the existent, it would create everything] since the [merely] existent has no particularity, and [if the agent is the non-existent, then too it would create everything] since the non-existent [has no particularity] if [the non-existent is taken to be] the destruction of the existent, and because no [cause and effect relation] is determinable, as in the case of the two ends of a balance beam [moving up and down].

22. If it is unacceptable that the existent becomes the non-existent and *vice versa,* how could birth take place, when the existent and the non-existent are [firmly] fixed? These two are fixed in isolation [from each other]. Therefore, O Mind, nothing is born.

23. Even if I should, at your desire, admit your birth, I still declare that your activity is of no use to Me. There is neither loss nor gain [for Me] since what is non-existent is born neither of itself nor of something else. Even if there were both [loss and gain your activity would still be of no use to Me].

24. Things constant are not connected with things inconstant; neither things constant nor things inconstant are connected with each another. Therefore it is not reasonable that there is any effect of one upon another, and so it is to be accepted that nothing belongs to anything else. And the Truth Itself is not within the range of etymological explanation of words.

25. Therefore the wise man, examining by means of reasoning and the *Śrutis* [the *Ātman*] which is the same [in all beings], ever radiant, and free from duality which is falsely assumed to be "being" or "non-being," goes to the perfect *Nirvāṇa*[18] (extinction) as a lamp [is extinguished].

26. A man who is not possessed by the attributes [of *Brahman*], scrutinizing in the above manner the One, the Attributeless, which is not seen by those who know the identity [of *Ātman* with *Brahman*] but is easily seen by the bad logician,[19] does not undergo

delusion since he is released from the fault of being possessed [by the attributes].

27. It is not acceptable that [the fault of] being possessed [by attributes] is destroyed in no other way than this. Only [the fault of] being possessed is the cause of the notion due to delusion. Just as fire with no more fuel, so also [the fault of] being possessed, which is without cause, comes to the ultimate extinction.

28. Salutation to the teachers who churned out from the ocean of the *Veda* what they held to be supreme, this knowledge, as the gods, the great souls, [churned] out from the great ocean the elixir of immortality.[20]

Notes

[1]All the commentators consider this the view of the Sāṃkhya and interpret "*para*" as *puruṣa*. Cf. *Sāṃkhyakārikā* 31; 36; 37; 56; 57; 58; 60.

[2]See Upad I,14,12; 18,103; 18,203.

[3]The *Smṛti* and *nyāya* according to the three commentators.

[4]See BhG II,16 and Śaṅkara's commentary on it. Cf. GK III,28.

[5]"*Dvayam*" here may means "duality." Cf. GK III,29.

[6]My text reads *tathādvayā*, but it should be corrected to *tathā dvayā*.

[7]See GK IV,50; *dravyatvābhāvayogataḥ*, which Śaṅkara interprets as *vastutvābhāvāt* in his GKBh.

[8]This (*alātacakra*) is a circle which is seen when one whirls a torch in the air. In Buddhist texts (*e.g. Laṅkāvatāra* [ed. by B. Nanjio. Bibliotheca Otaniensis, vol. I, Kyoto, 1923], p. 92, etc.) this simile is used to illustrate the unreality of the phenomenal world. The fourth chapter of the GK is entitled "Quenching of the Torch" (*Ālātaśānti*) and it is an important idea in the GK. The simile is also used in the *Maitri Up.* (VI, 24) and the *Mahābhāṣya* (III,2,124; 125) but in a different sense.

[9]Cf. Bṛh. Up. I,4,7; IV,3,23–30; Upad I,17,14–17.

[10]Rāmatīrtha quotes Taitt. Ā 3,14; *Ṛg-Veda* X,114,5; Kaṭh. Up. V,9 in this context.

[11]The Buddhist.

[12]The word *anarthavattva* is interpreted as *arthakriyāśūnyatva* by Ānandajñāna, as *arthakriyākāritvābhāva* by Bodhanidhi, and as *arthakriyārahitatva* by Rāmatīrtha. The Sautrāntikas and Vijñānavādin logicians such as Dignāga and Dharmakīrti regard *arthakriyākāritva* (practical efficiency) as a criterion of existence. See, for example, *Nyāyabindu* I,12–15. According to the Advaita Vedānta *Ātman* is actionless (*akriya*), changeless, and eternal (*kūṭasthanitya*). Therefore Buddhists assert that that *Ātman* is not existent, since It has no practical efficiency. Cf. S. Dasgupta, *A History of Indian Philosophy*,, vol. I, pp. 117–118; p. 154, note 1; Th. Stcherbatsky, *Buddhist Logic*, vol. II (Reprint ed. New York: Dover Publications, Inc., 1962), p. 7, note 2; pp. 120–121, note 6.

[13]See stanzas 14 and 15.

[14]Cf. GK III,19; Mayeda Upad, p. 38.

[15]The three commentators interpret this line quite differently. Bodhanidhi takes "*vastu*" viz. *Ātman* as the subject of the sentence: *prasiddhyati* . . . *yujyate* . . . . Ānandajñāna takes "*brahmaṇo jagaddhetutvam*" as the subject of the sentence with the verb *prasiddhyati*; and "*brahmaṇo jagaddhetutvaṃ hitvā*" as *anyathā*; and "*pradhānāder jagaddhetutvam*" as the subject of the verb *yujyate*. Rāmatīrtha takes "*itthaṃ kūṭasthasyāpy arthakriyākāritvaṃ*" as the subject of the verb *prasiddhyati*; "*paramārthataḥ*" as *anyathā*; and "*arthakriyākāritvaṃ sthirasya kṣaṇikasya vā*" as the subject of the verb *yujyate*.

[16]Cf. GK IV, 61–66; Nakamura III, p. 652; Dasgupta, *A History of Indian Philosophy*, vol. I, p. 145 f.

[17]The idea that nothing is born (*ajāti*) constitutes a central theme of the third and the fourth chapters of the GK, which often depends upon arguments of the Mādhyamikas and the Vijñānavādins. Cf. Nakamura III, pp. 631–654; T. M. P. Mahadevan, *Gauḍapāda* (Madras: University of Madras, 1952), pp. 128–147. Stanzas 20–22 here seem also to prove this theory by means of arguments similar to those in the GK, but they (especially stanza 21) are so brief and obscure that my translation has had to be largely based upon the commentaries, which themselves differ in the interpretation of these stanzas.

[18]The term "'*nirvāṇa*,'' which is important in Buddhism but does not occur in the early Upaniṣads at all, is used as "*sanirvāṇa*" in GK III,47.

[19]Cf. *Kena Up*. II,3.

[20]This is a famous legend (*amṛtamanthana*) which is narrated, with some variations, in the *Rāmāyaṇa*, the *Mahābhārata* and the *Purāṇas*. Cf. Upad I,17,33 and note 27; K. Rüping, *Amṛtamanthana und Kūrma-Avatāra* (Wiesbaden, 1970).

PART II. *THE PROSE PART*

CHAPTER 1

HOW TO ENLIGHTEN THE PUPIL

1. Now we shall explain how to teach the means to final release for the benefit of seekers thereafter with faith and desire.

2. The means to final release is knowledge [of *Brahman*]. It should be repeatedly related to the pupil until it is firmly grasped, if he is dispassionate toward all things non-eternal which are attained by means [other than knowledge][1]; if he has abandoned the desire for sons, wealth, and worlds[2] and reached the state of a *paramahaṃsa* wandering ascetic[3]; if he is endowed with tranquility, self-control, compassion, and so forth[4]; if he is possessed of the qualities of a pupil[5] which are well known from the scriptures; if he is a Brahmin[6] who is [internally and externally] pure[7]; if he approaches his teacher in the prescribed manner[8]; if his caste, profession, behavior, knowledge [of the *Veda*],[9] and family have been examined.

3. The *Śruti* also says:

> "Having scrutinized [the worlds that are built up by action, a Brahmin should arrive at indifference. . . . For the sake of this knowledge let him go, with fuel in hand, to a spiritual teacher who is learned in the scriptures and established in *Brahman*. To him who has approached properly, whose thought is calm, who has reached tranquility, the man of knowledge teaches] in its very truth that knowledge of *Brahman* [by which he knows the Imperishable]" (Muṇḍ. Up. I,2,12–13);

for when knowledge [of *Brahman*] is firmly grasped, it is conducive to one's own beatitude and to the continuity [of knowledge of *Brahman*]. And the continuity of knowledge [of *Brahman*] is helpful to people, as a boat [is helpful] to one wishing to get across a river. The scripture also says:

"[Verily, a father may teach this *Brahman* to his eldest son or to a worthy pupil, but to no one else at all.] Even if one should offer him this [earth] that is encompassed by water and filled with treasure, [he should say,] 'This, truly, is more than that' " (Chānd. Up. III,11,[5-]6),

since knowledge [of *Brahman*] is not obtained in any other way [than from a teacher] according to passages from the *Śruti* and the *Smṛti* such as:

"One who has a teacher knows. . ." (Chānd. Up. VI,14,2);

"The knowledge which has been learned from a teacher [best helps to attain his end" (Chānd. Up. IV,9,3);

"A teacher is a boatman; his [right] knowledge is called a boat here."[10]

4. When [the teacher] finds from some indications that the pupil has not grasped [this] knowledge, he should remove the causes which hinder his grasping it—demerit, worldly laxity, absence of firm preliminary learning concerning the discrimination between things eternal and non-eternal,[11] care about what other people think, pride of caste and the like—by the means contrary to those causes and enjoined by the *Śruti* and the *Smṛti*, that is to say, non-anger, etc.,[12] non-injury and other abstentions,[13] and the observances[14] which are not contradictory to knowledge.

5. He should also let [him] properly achieve the virtues such as modesty[15] which are the means to attain knowledge.

6. And the teacher[16] is able to consider the pros and cons [of an argument], is endowed with understanding, memory, tranquility, self-control, compassion, favor and the like[17]; he is versed in the traditional doctrine; not attached to any enjoyments, visible or invisible[18], he has abandoned all the rituals and their requisites[19]; a knower of *Brahman*, he is established in *Brahman*; he leads a blameless life, free from faults such as deceit, pride, trickery, wickedness, fraud, jealousy, falsehood, egotism, self-interest, and so forth; with the only purpose of helping others he wishes to make use of knowledge.[20]

First of all, he should teach the *Śrutis* which are concerned primarily with the oneness of *Ātman* [with *Brahman*], for example:

"In the beginning, my dear, this universe was the Existent only, one alone, without a second" (Chānd. Up. VI,2,1);

"Where one sees nothing else, [hears nothing else, understands

nothing else—that is the Fullness]" (Chānd. Up. VII,24,1);
"*Ātman*, indeed, is this all" (Chānd. Up. VII,25,2);
"*Brahman*, indeed, is this all" (Bṛh. Up. II,5,1?)[21];
"*Ātman*, verily, was this universe, one alone, in the beginning" (Ait. Up. I,1,1);
"Verily, this all is *Brahman*" (Chānd. Up. III,14,1).

7. And after teaching [these *Śrutis*], he should help [him] by means of the *Śrutis* to grasp the marks indicative of *Brahman*, for example:
"*Ātman*, which is free from evil . . ." (Chānd. Up. VIII,7,1);
"[Explain to me] what the manifest, unconcealed *Brahman* is" (Bṛh. Up. III,4,1; 5,1);
"That which transcends hunger and thirst" (Bṛh. Up. III,5,1);
"Not Thus! Not so!" (Bṛh. Up. II,3,6);
"[It is] not coarse, not fine" (Bṛh. Up. III,8,8);
"This *Ātman* is [described as] 'not, not' " (Bṛh. Up. III,9,26; IV,2,4; 4,22; 5,15);
"[Verily, O Gārgī, that Imperishable is] the unseen Seer" (Bṛh. Up. III,8,1);
"[*Brahman* is] knowledge, bliss" (Bṛh. Up. III,9,28);
"[He who knows *Brahman* as the real,] as knowledge, as the infinite" (Taitt. Up. II,1);
"[For truly, when one finds fearlessness as a foundation] in That (= *Brahman*) which is invisible, bodiless, [. . . then he has reached fearlessness]" (Taitt. Up. II,7);
"This, verily, is [the great, unborn *Ātman*]" (Bṛh. Up. IV,4,22);
"[This *Brahman* is . . .] breathless, mindless" (Muṇḍ. Up. II, 1,2);
"[This *Brahman* is] without and within, unborn" (Muṇḍ. Up. II, 1,2,);
"[This great Being . . .] is just a mass of knowledge" (Bṛh. Up. II,4,12);
"[This *Brahman* is . . .] without an inside and without an outside" (Bṛh. Up. II,5,19);
"It is, indeed, other than the known and than the unknown" (*Kena Up.* I, 4);
"Verily, what is called 'Space' [is the accomplisher of name-and-form]"[22] (Chānd. Up. VIII,14,1)

8. [He should] also [help him grasp the marks indicative of

Brahman] by means of the *Smṛtis*, if they are not incompatible with the marks indicative [of *Brahman*] described by the *Śrutis* and concerned primarily with teaching that the highest *Ātman* is not subject to transmigration and that It is identical with all—for example:

"He is not born, nor does he ever die" (BhG II,20; Kaṭh. Up. II,18);

"He does not receive [the effect of] any one's evil" (BhG V,15);

"As [the great Wind] constantly abides in space [. . . so all beings abide in Me]" (BhG IX, 6);

"Know also that I am the Field-Knower (= *Ātman*)"[23] (BhG XIII,2);

"It is called neither existent nor non-existent" (BhG XIII,12);

"Because [He] is beginningless and attributeless" (BhG XIII, 31);

"[The supreme Lord, abiding] alike in all beings" (BhG XIII, 27);

"But there is the highest *Puruṣa* (= *Ātman*)" (BhG XV,17).

9. If the pupil who has thus grasped the marks indicative of the highest *Ātman* according to the *Śrutis* and the *Smṛtis* wishes to get out of the ocean of transmigratory existence, [the teacher] should ask him: "Who are you, my dear?"

10. If he answers: "I am a Brahmin's son belonging to such and such a family. I was a student[24]—or, I was a householder[25]—[but] now I am a *paramahaṃsa* wandering ascetic.[26] I wish to get out of the ocean of transmigratory existence infested with great sharks of birth and death";

11. [then] the teacher should say: "My dear, when you are dead your body will be eaten by birds or will turn into earth right here. How then do you wish to get out of the ocean of transmigratory existence? Because if you turn into ashes on this bank of the river you cannot get across to the other side of the river."

12. If he answers: "I am different from the body. The body is born, dies, is eaten by birds, turns into earth, is destroyed by weapons, fire and so forth, and suffers from disease and so on. I have entered this body as a bird enters a nest, by force of the merit and demerit accumulated by myself. Again and again by force of the merit and demerit, when this body perishes, I shall enter another body as a bird enters another nest when its previous one

has been destroyed. Thus I am in beginningless transmigratory existence. I have been abandoning [old] bodies which have been obtained one after another in the spheres of gods, animals, men, and hells by force of my own *karman* and I have been getting other new bodies over and over again. I am forced by my own *karman* to rotate in the incessant cycle of birth and death as in a water-wheel. I have obtained this body in the course of time. I am tired of this rotation in the wheel of transmigratory existence, so I have come to you, Your Holiness, in order to end the rotation in the wheel of transmigratory existence. Therefore I am eternal and different from the body. The bodies come and go like a person's garments"[27];

13. [then] the teacher should say: "You are right. Your view is correct. [Then] why did you say incorrectly, 'I am a Brahmin's son belonging to such and such a family. I was a student—or, I was a householder—[but] now I am a *paramahaṃsa* wandering ascetic'?"[28]

14. If he says: "Your Holiness, how have I spoken wrongly?"

15. [then] the teacher should reply to him: "Because, through such statements as 'I am a Brahmin's son belonging to such and such a family,' you have identified the *Ātman*, which is free from caste, family, and purifying ceremonies,[29] with the body, which has different caste, family, and purifying ceremonies."

16. If he asks: "How does the body have different caste, family, and purifying ceremonies?" or, "How am I (= *Ātman*) free from caste, family, and purifying ceremonies?"[30]

17. [then] the teacher should reply: "Listen, my dear, [this is] how this body, different from you (= *Ātman*), has different caste, family and purifying ceremonies and how you (= *Ātman*) are free from caste, family, and purifying ceremonies."

Thereupon [the teacher] should remind him: "You should remember, my dear, that you have been taught[31] that the highest *Ātman*, the *Ātman* of all, is endowed with the marks described above according to such *Śruti* and *Smṛti* passages as:

> '[In the beginning,] my dear, this universe was the Existent only, [one alone, without a second]' (Chānd. Up. VI,2,1)

and [that you have also been taught] the marks indicative of the highest *Ātman* according to *Śruti* and *Smṛti* passages."[32]

18. When [the pupil] has recalled to mind the marks indicative

of the highest *Ātman*, [the teacher] should tell him [in answer to his first question]: "This [highest *Ātman*] which is called 'Space'[33] is something different from name-and-form,[34] bodiless,[35] characterized as 'not coarse,'[36] etc., and as 'free from evil,'[37] etc. It is not afflicted with any attributes of transmigratory existence;

> '[Explain to me] what the manifest, unconcealed *Brahman* is, ... It is your *Ātman*, which is within everything' (Bṛh. Up. III,4,1).

It is

> 'the unseen Seer, the unheard Hearer, the unthought Thinker, the unknown Knower' (Bṛh. Up. III,7,23).

It is of the nature of eternal knowledge,

> 'without an inside and without an outside' (Bṛh. Up. II,5,19),
> 'just a mass of knowledge' (Bṛh. Up. II,4,12).

It is all-pervading like ether, possessed of infinite power, the *Ātman* of all, free from hunger, etc.,[38] and free from appearance and disappearance.[39] This [highest *Ātman*] is the Evolver of the unevolved name-and-form merely by being existent since It is possessed of inconceivable power. The unevolved name-and-form[40] is different in essence from this [*Ātman*] and it is the seed of the world, abiding in It, indescribable as this or something else,[41] and known to It.

19. "[Originally] unevolved, this name-and-form took the name-and-form[42] of 'ether' in the course of its evolution from this very *Ātman*. And in this manner this element named 'ether' arose from the highest *Ātman*[43] as dirty foam from clear water.[44] Foam is neither [identical with] water nor absolutely different from water since it is not seen without water. But water is clear and different from foam which is of the nature of dirt. Likewise, the highest *Ātman* is different from name-and-form which corresponds to foam; *Ātman* is pure, clear, and different in essence from it. This name-and-form, [originally] unevolved, took the name-and-form of 'ether,' which corresponds to foam, in the course of its evolution.

20. "Becoming grosser in the course of evolution, the name-and-form becomes air[45] from ether, fire[46] from air, water[47] from fire, earth[48] from water. In this order each preceding [element] entered each succeeding one and the five gross elements, [ether, air, fire, water, and] earth, came into existence. Consequently earth is characterized by the qualities of the five gross elements.[49] And from earth, rice, barley, and other plants consisting of the five

elements are produced; from them, when they are eaten, blood and sperm are produced, related respectively to the bodies of women and men. Both blood and sperm, produced by churning with the churning stick of sexual passion driven by nescience[50] and sanctified with sacred formulas,[51] are poured into the womb at the proper time.[52] Through the penetration of fluid from the womb, they become an embryo and it is delivered in the ninth or tenth month.[53]

21. "When it is born it obtains its name-and-form, sanctified with sacred formulas by means of a birth ceremony[54] and other [purifying ceremonies]. Again it obtains the name of a student through the performance of the purifying ceremony for initiation.[55] This same body obtains the name of a householder[56] through the performance of the purifying ceremony for union with a wife.[57] This same body obtains the name of an ascetic[58] through the purifying ceremony of becoming a forest-dweller. This same body obtains the name of a wandering ascetic[59] through the purifying ceremony which ends the ritual actions. Thus the body is different from you (= *Ātman*) and is possessed of different caste, family, and purifying ceremonies.

22. "The mind and the sense organs consist only of name-and-form according to the *Śrutis* such as:

> 'For, my dear, the mind consists of food'[60] (Chānd. Up. VI,5,4; 6,5; 7,6).

23. "[The second question you asked me earlier was,][61] 'How am I (= *Ātman*) free from caste, family, and purifying ceremonies?' Listen to what [I am going to say]. The Evolver (= the highest *Ātman*) of name-and-form, by nature different in essence from name-and-form, created this body in the course of evolving name-and-form. And [the Evolver] entered the name-and-form [of the body], Itself being free from the duties of purifying ceremonies. Itself unseen by others, [the Evolver] is seeing; unheard, It is hearing; unthought, It is thinking; unknown, It is knowing.[62]

> 'The wise one who having distinguished all forms and having created [their] names, sits calling' (Taitt. Ā. III,12,7).

There are thousands of *Śruti* passages which have this same meaning, for example:

> 'Having created it, It,indeed,entered into it'(Taitt.Up.II,6,1);
> 'The Ruler of the creatures entered into [them]' (Taitt. Ā. III, 11,1);

'It entered here, [even to the fingertips]' (Bṛh. Up. I,4,7);
'It is your *Ātman*, [which is in everything]' (Bṛh. Up. III,4,1; 5,1);
'So, cleaving asunder this very top of the skull, It entered by that door' (Ait. Up. I,3,12);
'Though It is hidden in all things, that *Ātman* [does not shine forth]' (Kaṭh. Up. III,12);
'That divinity thought, "Come! Let me [enter] these three divinities [(*i.e.*, heat, water, and food) with this living *Ātman* and evolve name-and-form]" ' (Chānd. Up. VI,3,2);
'[*Ātman* which is] the bodiless among bodies' (Kaṭh. Up. II,22).

24. "There are also *Smṛti* passages [which have this same meaning], for example:
'*Ātman* is truly all gods' (Manu XII, 119);
'The embodied *Ātman* in the city of nine gates' (BhG V, 13);
'Know also that I am the Field-Knower (= *Ātman*)'[63] (BhG XIII,2);
'[The supreme Lord abiding] alike in all beings' (BhG XIII, 27);
'The onlooker and consenter, [the highest *Ātman* . . . is also declared to be the highest *Puruṣa*, in this body]' (BhG XIII, 22);
'But there is the highest *Puruṣa*, different [from this]' (BhG XV, 17).
It is, therefore, established that you (= *Ātman*) are free from caste, family, and purifying ceremonies."

25. If he says: "I am one [and] He[64] is another[65]; I am ignorant, I experience pleasure and pain, am bound and a transmigrator [whereas] He is essentially different from me, the god not subject to transmigration. By worshipping Him with oblations, offerings, homage, and the like and through the [performance of] the actions prescribed for [my] class and stage of life,[66] I wish to get out of the ocean of transmigratory existence. How am I He?"

26. [then] the teacher should reply: "My dear, you should not hold such a view since it is prohibited to understand that [*Ātman*] is different [from *Brahman*]."

[The pupil may say:] "How is it prohibited to understand that [*Ātman*] is different [from *Brahman*]?"

Then the teacher replies:

" 'So whoever worships another divinity [than his *Ātman*], thinking that He is one and I another, he does not know' (Bṛh. Up. I,4,10);

'Brahmanhood has deserted him who knows Brahmanhood as different from *Ātman*' (Bṛh. Up. II,4,6);

'He who thinks he sees manifoldness in this world attains death after death' (Bṛh. Up. IV,4,19).

27. "These *Śruti* passages indeed reveal that transmigratory existence results from the understanding that [*Ātman*] is different [from *Brahman*].

28. "And thousands [of *Śruti* passages] reveal that final release results from the realization of the identity [of *Ātman* and *Brahman*]. [For example, through the statement,]

'That is *Ātman*, Thou art That' (Chānd. Up. VI, 8,7, etc.),

[the *Śrutis*] establish that [*Ātman*] is the highest *Ātman* (= *Brahman*). Then [they] state,

'One who has a teacher knows' (Chānd. Up. VI,14,2),

and [they] show final release with the words,

'He is delayed only until [he is freed from bondage of ignorance; then he will arrive at his final goal]' (Chānd. Up. VI,14,2).

With the simile about the [man] who was not a thief and [therefore] not burned [in the ordeal of the heated axe, the *Śrutis*] teach that he who covers himself with truth does not undergo transmigratory existence since he knows that [*Ātman*] is identical [with *Brahman*]; [on the other hand], with the simile about the[man] who was a thief and was [therefore] burned, [the *Śrutis*] teach that he who covers himself with the untruth undergoes transmigratory existence since [he holds] the view that [*Ātman*] is different [from *Brahman*].[67]

29. "And with such [similes] as,

'Whatever they are in this world, whether tiger or [lion . . . mosquito, they become That Existent]' (Chānd. Up. VI,9,3),

[the *Śrutis*] say that because of the view of the identity [of *Ātman with Brahman*]

'[he] rules himself' (Chānd. Up. VII,25,2).

And with the words,

'But they who know otherwise than this are ruled by another; theirs are perishable worlds' (Chānd. Up. VII, 25, 2),

the *Śrutis* [continue to] teach that on account of the contrary view, *viz.* the view that [*Ātman*] is different [from *Brahman*], he undergoes transmigratory existence. This is what is taught in every school of the *Veda.* So you were indeed wrong in saying, '[I (= *Ātman*) am] a Brahmin's son belonging to such and such a family[68]; [I (= *Ātman*) am] a transmigrator, essentially different from the highest *Ātman.*'[69]

30. "For the above reason it is prohibited [by the *Śrutis*] to hold the view that [*Ātman*] is different [from *Brahman*]; use of the rituals is [made] in the sphere of [the view] that [*Ātman*] is different [from *Brahman*]; and the sacred thread[70] and the like are requisites for the rituals. Therefore, it should be known that the use of rituals and their requisites is prohibited, if the identity [of *Ātman*] with the highest *Ātman* is realized, since [the use of] rituals and their requisites such as the sacred thread is contradictory to the realization of the identity [of *Ātman*] with the highest *Ātman.* [The use of] rituals and their requisites such as the sacred thread is indeed enjoined upon a transmigrator [but] not upon one who holds the view of the identity [of *Ātman*] with the highest *Ātman*; and the difference [of *Ātman*] from It is merely due to the view that [*Ātman*] is different [from *Brahman*].

31. "If rituals were to be performed and it were not desirable to abandon them, [the *Śrutis*] would not declare in such unambiguous sentence as,

'That is *Ātman*, Thou art That' (Chānd. Up. VI, 8,7, etc.),

that the highest *Ātman*, unrelated to the rituals, their requisites, and such factors of the rituals as castes and stages of life, should be realized to be identical with [the inner] *Ātman*; nor would [the *Śrutis*] condemn the realization that [*Ātman*] is different [from *Brahman*], [in passages] such as,

> 'This is the constant greatness of the knower of *Brahman*; [it does not increase nor decrease by action]' (Bṛh. Up. IV,4,23);
> '[He] is unaffected by good, unaffected by evil, [for then he has transcended all sorrows of the heart]' (Bṛh. Up. IV,3,22);
> 'In this state a thief is no thief [. . . a mendicant no mendicant, an ascetic no ascetic]' (Bṛh. Up. IV,3,22).

32. "[The *Śrutis*] would not declare that [*Ātman*] is by nature unrelated to the rituals, by nature unconnected with the class and other factors of the rituals, if it were not desirable that the rituals and such requisites of the rituals as the sacred thread be

abandoned completely. Therefore, the seeker after final release should abandon the ritual together with its requisites since [they] are contradictory to the view of the identity [of *Ātman*] with the highest *Ātman*. And [he] should realize that [his] *Ātman* is the highest [*Ātman*] since It has characteristics stated [about *Brahman*] by the *Śrutis*."

33. If [the pupil] says: "Your Holiness, when the body is burned or cut, I (= *Ātman*) evidently perceive pain and I evidently experience suffering from hunger, etc. But in all the *Srutis* and the *Smṛtis* the highest *Ātman* is said to be

> 'free from evil, ageless, deathless, sorrowless, hungerless, thirstless' (Chānd. Up. VIII,1,5),

free from all attributes of transmigratory existence. I (= *Ātman*) am different in essence from It and bound up with many attributes of transmigratory existence. How then can I realize that the highest *Ātman* is [my] *Ātman* and that I, a transmigrator, am the highest *Ātman*?—it is as if I were to hold that fire is cold! Though I am [now] a transmigrator, I am entitled to the means of [attaining] all prosperity and beatitude.[71] How then should I abandon the rituals and their requisites such as the sacred thread which lead [me] to prosperity and beatitude?"

34. [then the teacher] should answer him: "Your statement, 'When the body is burned or cut, I (= *Ātman*) evidently perceive pain,' is not correct."

"Why?"

"The body, like a tree which is burned [or] cut, is the object [which is perceived by the perceiver]. The pain of burning or cutting is perceived in the body, which is the object; so the pain has the same locus as the burning [or cutting], since people point out the pain of burning [or cutting] right there where [the body] is burned or cut and not in the perceiver of burning [or cutting]."

"How?"

"When a man is asked, 'Where do you have pain?', he points to the locus where [the body] is burned [or cut] and not to the perceiver, saying, 'I have pain in the head' or 'In the chest' or 'In the stomach.' If pain or the cause of pain such as burning and cutting were located in the perceiver, he would point to [the perceiver] as the locus of pain just as [he points to a part of the body as] the locus of burning and so forth.

35. "And [pain] itself would not be perceived as the form-and-color in the eye [are not perceived by the eye]. Therefore, pain is perceived as having the same locus as burning, cutting, and so on; so pain is merely an object like burning and the like.

As [pain] is of the nature of 'becoming,'[72] [it] has its substratum like the cooking of rice. The impression of pain [also] has exactly the same substratum as the pain, since [the impression of pain] is perceived only simultaneously with the recollection [of pain]. The aversion to pain and its causes also has precisely the same substratum as the impression.[73] So it is said,

> 'Passion and aversion have, and the latent impression of form-and-color, a common substratum [the intellect], and what is perceived as fear has the intellect as its substratum; therefore, the Knower is always pure and free from fear' (Upad I,15,13)."

36. [The student may ask:] "What locus do then the impressions of form-and-color and the like have?"

[Then the teacher] answers: "[The locus] where there are desire and so forth."

"Where are there these desire and the like?"

"Right in the intellect according to such *Śruti* passages as,

> 'Desire, volition, doubt, [faith, lack of faith, steadfastness, lack of steadfastness, shame, meditation, fear—all this is truly mind]' (Bṛh. Up. I,5,3).

Right there are also the impressions of form-and-color and the like according to the *Śruti*,

> 'And on what are the colors and forms based?—On the heart'[74] (Bṛh. Up. III,9,20).

Impurity [such as desire and aversion] is in the object and not in *Ātman* [which is the subject] according to hundreds of *Śruti* passages such as,

> 'The desires that are based on heart' (Bṛh. Up. IV,4,7; Kaṭh. Up. VI, 14);
>
> 'For [then] he has passed beyond [all sorrows of the heart]' (Bṛh. Up. IV,3,22);
>
> 'This [person] is without attachments' (Bṛh. Up. IV,3,16);
>
> 'Even this is His form that is beyond desire' (Bṛh. Up. IV,3,21),

and according to *Smṛti* passages such as,

> 'He is declared to be unchangeable' (BhG II, 25);

'Because [He] is beginningless and attributeless' (BhG XIII, 31); moreover,

'Desire, aversion' and so on are the attributes of 'the Field,'[75] *i.e.*, the object, and not those of *Ātman* (BhG XIII, 6).

37. "For this reason you (= *Ātman*) have no relation with the impressions of form-and-color and the like; so you (= *Ātman*) are not different in essence from the highest *Ātman*. As there is no contradiction to sense-perception and other [means of knowledge], it is reasonable to realize that I (= *Ātman*) am the highest *Ātman* according to such *Śruti* passages as,

'It knew only Itself, ["I am Brahman!"] (Bṛh. Up. I,4,10);
'As a unity only is It to be looked upon' (Bṛh. Up. IV, 4,20);
'I, indeed, am below. [I am above. . . .]' (Chānd. Up. VII, 25, 1);
'*Ātman*, indeed, is below. [*Ātman* is behind. . . .]' (Chānd. Up. VII, 25,2);
'One should see everything as *Ātman*' (Bṛh. Up. IV,4,23);
'Where truly everything [has become] one's own *Ātman*, [then whereby and whom does] one smell?' (Bṛh. Up. II,4,14);
'This all is what this *Ātman* is' (Bṛh. Up. II,4,6);
'That one [is without parts, immortal]' (Praś. Up. VI,5);
[This *Brahman* is . . .] without an inside and without an outside' (Bṛh. Up. II,5,19);
'[This is] without and within, unborn' (Muṇḍ. Up. II,1,2);
'*Brahman* indeed is this [whole] world' (Muṇḍ. Up. II,2,12);
'[So, cleaving asunder this very top of the skull,] He entered by that door' (Ait. Up. I,3,12);
[All these, indeed, are] names of intelligence' (Ait. Up. III, 1,2);
'[He who knows *Brahman* as the real,] as knowledge, as the infinite' (Taitt. Up. II, 1);
'[Space] arose indeed from this [*Ātman*]' (Taitt. Up. II, 1);
'Having created it, It indeed entered into it' (Taitt. Up. II,6,1);
'The one God, hidden in all things, [all-pervading]' (Śvet. Up. VI, 11);
'[*Ātman* which is] the bodiless among bodies' (Kaṭh. Up. II,22);
'[The wise one] is not born, nor dies' (Kaṭh. Up. II, 18);
'[Thinking on the great all-pervading *Ātman*, by which one

contemplates both] the dreaming state and the waking state, [the wise man is not grieved]' (Kaṭh. Up. IV,4);
'One should know that It is my *Ātman*' (Kauṣ. Up. III,8);
'Now, he who on all beings [looks as indeed in *Ātman* and on *Ātman* as in all beings—he does not shrink away from It]' (*Īśā Up.* VI);
'It moves. It does not move' (*Īśā Up.* V);
'Vena (the longing one?), seeing It, [knows all creatures, where all have the same nest]' (M.N.Up. II,3)[76];
'It is, indeed, Agni, [It is Āditya, It is Vāyu . . .]' (Taitt. Ā. X,1,2);
'I was Manu[77] and the Sun' (Bṛh. Up. I,4,10; *Ṛgveda* IV,26,1);
'The Ruler of the creatures entered into [them]' (Taitt. Ā III, 11,1);
'[In the beginning,] my dear, [this universe was] the Existent only, [one alone, without a second]' (Chānd. Up. VI,2,1);
'That is the Real, That is *Ātman*, Thou art That' (Chānd. Up. VI,8,7, etc.).

38. "From *Smṛti* passages as well it is established that, being one alone, you, *Ātman*, are the highest *Ātman* [and] free from all the attributes of transmigratory existence—for example:
'[All] beings are the bodies of Him who lives in the hearts' (*Āpastamba Dharmasūtra* I,8,22,4);
'*Ātman* is indeed [all] gods' (Manu, XII, 119);
'[The embodied *Ātman*,] in the city of nine gates' (BhG V,13);
'[The supreme Lord abiding] alike in all beings' (BhG XIII, 27);
'[The wise see the same thing] in a learned and well-behaved *Brahman*, [in a cow, in an elephant, and in a mere dog, and in an outcaste]' (BhG V,18);
'Unmanifold in the manifold' (BhG XVIII,20; cf. BhG XIII, 16);
'Vāsudeva (= Kṛṣṇa)[78] is all' (BhG VII, 19)."

39. If [the pupil] says: "If, your Holiness, *Ātman* is
'without an inside and without an outside' (Bṛh. Up. IV,5,13),
'without and within, unborn' (Muṇḍ. Up. II,1,2),
'entirely a mass of knowledge' (Bṛh. Up. IV,5,13),
like a mass of salt,[79] devoid of all the varieties of forms, and homogeneous like ether, then how is it that the object, means, and agent

of actions are [either actually] experienced or stated in the *Śrutis*? This is well-known in the *Śrutis* and *Smṛtis* and among common people, and is a matter which causes differences of opinion among hundreds of disputants";

40. [then] the teacher should reply, "It is the effect of nescience that the object, means, and agent of actions are [either actually] experienced or stated in the *Śrutis*; but from the standpoint of the highest truth[80] *Ātman* is one alone and [only] appears as many through the vision [affected] by nescience just as the moon [appears] as many to sight [affected] by *timira* eye-disease.[81] Duality is the effect of nescience, since it is reasonable [for the *Śrutis*] to condemn the view that [*Ātman*] is different [from *Brahman*] by saying,

'Verily, where there seems to be another, [there the one might see the other]' (Bṛh. Up. IV,3,31);

'For where there is a duality, as it were, there one sees another' (Bṛh. Up. II,4,14);

'Death after death attains he [who thinks he sees manifoldness in this world]' (Bṛh. Up. IV,4,19);

'But where one sees something else, hears something else, understands something else—that is the small. . . . but the small is the same as the mortal' (Chānd. Up. VII,24,1);

'[As, my dear, by one clod of clay everything made of clay may be understood;] the modification is a verbal distinction, a name' (Chānd. Up. VI,1,4), [untrue][82];

'[So whoever worships another divinity than his *Ātman*, thinking that] He is one and I another, [he does not know]' (Bṛh. Up. I,4,10).

And [the same conclusion is reached] from *Śruti* passages which establish oneness, for example:

'[In the beginning, my dear, this universe was the Existent only,] one alone, without a second' (Chānd. Up. VI,2,1);

'Where, verily, [everything has become] one's own [*Ātman*, then whereby and whom would one smell?]' (Bṛh. Up. II,4,14; cf. Bṛh. Up. IV,5,15);

'[Then] what delusion, what sorrow is there [for him who perceives the oneness!]' (*Īśā Up.* 7)."

41. [The pupil may ask:] "If this be so, Your Holiness, for what purpose is difference in object, means, etc., of actions as well as origination and dissolution [of the world] stated in the *Śrutis*?"

42. Then [the teacher] replies: "A man possessed of nescience, being differentiated by the body, etc., thinks that his *Ātman* is connected with things desirable and undesirable; [and] he does not know how to distinguish the means of attaining things desirable from that of abandoning things undesirable, although he desires to attain things desirable and to abandon things undesirable by some means. The scripture gradually removes his ignorance concerning this matter, but it does not establish the difference in object, means, etc., of actions, since the difference [constitutes] transmigratory existence which is undesirable by nature. Thus [the scripture] uproots nescience which is the view that [*Ātman*] is different [from *Brahman*], the root of transmigratory existence, by showing the reasonableness of the oneness of the origination, dissolution, etc. [of the world].

43. "When nescience has been uprooted by means of the *Śrutis*, *Smṛtis*, and reasoning, the only knowledge of one who sees the highest truth[83] is established right in this [*Ātman*] that is described as follows:

'Without an inside and without an outside' (Bṛh. Up. II, 5, 19);
'Without and within, unborn' (Muṇḍ. Up. II,1,2);
like a mass of salt[84];
'[Entirely] a mass of knowledge' (Bṛh. Up. IV,5,13);

and the homogeneous *Ātman* which is all-pervading like ether. It is not reasonable that [in *Ātman*] even a trace of impurity should arise from the difference in object and means of actions, origination and dissolution [of the world], and so forth.

44. "A man who wishes to attain this very view of the highest truth should abandon the fivefold form of desire, *viz.*, desires for a son, wealth, and worlds,[85] which result from the misconception that [his] caste, stage of life, etc., [belong to his *Ātman*]. And as this misconception is contradictory to the right conception, the reasoning for negating the view that [*Ātman*] is different [from *Brahman*] is possible; for, when the conception that the sole *Ātman* is not subject to transmigratory existence has occurred by means of the scripture and reasoning, no contradictory conception persists [any more]; for a conception that fire is cold, or that the body is not subject to old age and death, does not exist. Therefore, since all the rituals and their requisites such as the sacred thread are

the effects of nescience, they should be abandoned by him who is established in the view of the highest truth."

Notes

[1]According to the BSBh (I,1,1, pp. 36–37) the following four requirements are referred to as conditions for the study of the Vedānta: (1) discrimination between things eternal and non-eternal (*nityānityavastuviveka*), (2) dispassion toward the enjoyment of the things here and in the other world (*ihāmutrārthabhogavirāga*), (3) the attainment of the means such as tranquility and self-control (*śamadamādisādhanasampad*), and (4) being a seeker after final release (*mumukṣutva*). The condition stated in the Upad that one must be dispassionate toward all things non-eternal which are attained by means other than knowledge seems to correspond to the first requirement mentioned above (cf. note 2), which is also referred to in Upad II,1,4. Such conditions for the study of the Vedānta are again mentioned in Upad I,13,27; 16,72; 17,52; 17,85; 17,86. As for the qualifications of a teacher, see section 6, below, and also Introduction, IV,F, pp. 90–91. Cf. *Vedāntasāra* [IV] 4–27; P. Deussen, *The System of the Vedânta*, pp. 79–82.

[2]Bṛh. Up. III,5,1 reads: "Having known that *Ātman*, Brahmins overcome desire for sons (*putraiṣaṇā*), desire for wealth (*vittaiṣaṇā*) and desire for worlds (*lokaiṣaṇā*) and live the life of mendicants." Cf. Bṛh. Up. IV,4,22; Śaṅkara *ad* Bṛh. Up. III,5,1; IV,4,22. The compound *tyaktaputravittalokaiṣaṇa* is also used in GBh II,55, p. 65. Here "worlds" means three worlds, *viz.* the world of men (*manuṣyaloka*), of the fathers (*pitṛloka*), and of the gods (*devaloka*). According to Śaṅkara the world of men is obtained by means of the son alone, that of the fathers by means of actions (*karman*), and that of the gods by means of the lower knowledge, namely by means of meditation and worship of *Brahman* as a personal god. These three worlds are non-eternal and should be abandoned by the seekers after final release. Cf. Bṛh. Up. I,5,16; Upad I,18,228; II,1,44. This condition seems to correspond to the second requirement for the study of the Vedānta (see note 1).

[3]The life of a Brahmin is divided into four stages (*āśrama*), namely that of the student (*brahmacārin*), of the householder (*gṛhastha*), of the forest-dweller (*vanastha*), and of the ascetic (*saṃnyāsin*). In many works ascetics are classified into four groups, namely *kuṭīcaka*, *bahūdaka*, *haṃsa*, and *paramahaṃsa*. Each succeeding one is higher than each preceding one. The *paramahaṃsa* ascetic always stays under a tree, in an uninhabited house, or in a burial place. He begs alms from persons of all castes. He regards all as *Ātman*. For a detailed description, see P. V. Kane, *History of Dharmaśāstra*, vol. II-II, pp. 930 f. Cf. notes 6; 26.

[4]The attainment of these virtues constitutes the third condition for the study of the Vedānta (see note 1). This condition is based upon Bṛh. Up. IV,4,23, which reads: "He who knows thus becomes tranquil, self-controlled, withdrawn, patient, and collected . . ."

[5]What Śaṅkara means by "the qualities of a pupil" is not certain. Cf. Upad I,16,72; 17,52; 17,87. Ānandajñāna refers to BhG XIII,7, which mentions the following virtues: absence of pride (*amānitva*), absence of deceit (*adambhitva*), non-injury (*ahiṃsā*), patience (*kṣānti*), uprightness (*ārjava*), service to the teacher (*ācāryopāsana*), internal and external purity (*śauca*), steadfastness (*sthairya*), self-control (*ātmavinigraha*). Rāmatīrtha

quotes a stanza from an undertermined source, which enumerates nine virtues. *Smṛtis* such as the Manu (II,109; 112) and *Yājñavalkyasmṛti* (I,28) prescribe the qualifications of a student who deserves to be taught. See P. V. Kane, *History of Dharmaśāstra*, vol. II-I, pp. 330–333.

[6]The *Smṛtis* are not in agreement with regard to whether the ascetic life (*saṃnyāsa*) is open to all the upper three classes or only to the Brahmins. In Śaṅkara *ad* Bṛh. Up. (III,5,1, p. 454; IV,5,15, p. 725) Śaṅkara definitely states that only a Brahmin can be a *saṃnyāsin*. Here in the Upad he excludes all the classes except Brahmin. It is to be noted here that in his *Vārttika*(v.1651,p. 758) on his teacher's commentary of Bṛh.Up. (III,5,1) Sureśvara rejects Śaṅkara's view and that in his commentary on Sureśvara's *Vārttika* (p. 759) Ānandajñāna quotes passages from the *Mahābhārata* to support that Kṣatriya can enter the ascetic life. Cf. P. V. Kane, *History of Dharmaśāstra*, vol. II-II, pp. 942–944. According to the BS (I,3,34–39) the upper three classes of people, excluding Śūdras, are entitled to the knowledge of *Brahman*. Moreover, not only the *saṃnyāsin* but also the householder is accepted as qualified for it; and even a person who does not belong to any state of life because of lack of means, etc., is regarded as qualified for knowledge of *Brahman* (BS III,4,36–39). Cf. Nakamura II, pp. 402–404; pp. 470–475; P. Deussen, *The System of the Vedânta*, pp. 60–64. It should be kept in mind in order to understand Śaṅkara's doctrine that he accepts as qualified for his teaching a Brahmin who is in the state of *paramahaṃsa* wandering ascetic (see note 3). It may, however, be interesting to note here that in the next chapter (section 45) it is a *brahmacārin* who approaches a teacher in the prescribed manner. Cf. note 26.

[7]One of the observances (*niyama*). See note 14.

[8]What rules Śaṅkara has in mind is not known. However, there are certain rules. For example, one should not approach empty-handed one's parents, *ācārya*, sacred fires, houses, and the king, if the latter has not heard of him before. Another rule is not to pronounce the name of one's teacher without prefixing or affixing an honorific addition (such as *śrī, bhāṭṭa, ācārya*). *Smṛtis* prescribe rules about *upasaṃgrahaṇa*, which consists in repeating one's *gotra* and name, saying 'I salute,' touching one's ears, and clasping the feet of the teacher with one's hands, when one meets his teacher. See P. V. Kane, *History of Dharmaśāstra*, pp. 333–346. Cf. Muṇḍ. Up. I,2,12–13 (see the next section); Bṛh. Up. IV,2,1; Chānd. Up. VII,1,2.

[9]Śaṅkara presupposes the study of the *Veda*, which is required of a *brahmacārin*, and knowledge of it as indispensable condition. Cf. P. Deussen, *The System of the Vedânta*, pp. 77–78.

[10]The source of this quotation is probably *Mahābhārata*, *Mokṣadharma*, 12, 313, 23ab (Poona Critical ed.): "*ācāryaḥ plāvitā tasya jñānaṃ plava ihocyate*." Some manuscripts (A_4, A_5, As_6, and S_4) takes it as a quotation from a *Śruti* but it is not traced there as far as I have tried.

[11]See note 1.

[12]Ānandajñāna says that "etc." indicates "*anugraha*" and the like while Rāmtīrtha explains it as denoting "*akāma*" and so on. *Āpastamba Dharmasūtra* I,8,23,6 reads: *akrodho 'harṣo 'roṣo 'lobho'moho 'dambho 'drohaḥ . . .* ; *Śivopaniṣad* VII,101 reads: *akrodhādyā niyamā siddhivṛddhikarāḥ*; BhG XVI,2: *ahiṃsā satyam akrodhas tyāgaḥ śāntir apaiśunam*.

[13]According to *Yogasūtra* II,30, the abstentions (*yama*) are five: non-injury (*ahiṃsā*), non-lying (*satya*), non-theft (*asteya*), non-incontinence (*brahmacarya*), and non-possession (*aparigraha*). *Yama* constitutes the first of the eight-limbed practice of *Yoga* (*Yogasūtra* II,29). But *yama* in *Yājñavalkyasmṛti* III,312 has ten constituents: non-incontinence (*brahmacarya*), compassion (*dayā*), patience (*kṣānti*), giving (*dāna*), non-lying (*satya*),

honesty (*akalkatā*), non-injury (*ahiṃsā*), non-theft (*asteya*), sweetness (*mādhurya*), self-control (*dama*).

[14]According to *Yogasūtra* II,32, the observances (*niyama*) are five: purity (*śauca*), contentment (*saṃtoṣa*), self-mortification (*tapas*), study (*svādhyāya*), and devotion to the Lord (*īśvarapraṇidhāna*). According to the *Yogasūtrabhāṣya* on this *sūtra*, purity means both internal purity, which consists in washing away the blemishes of the mind, and external purity, which is produced by earth, water, or the like, and by the consumption and other requirements with regard to pure sacrificial food, *viz.* the barley mixed with cow's urine and the rest (*Tattvavaiśāradī* II, 32). *Niyama* constitutes the second limb of the eight-limbed practice of *Yoga* (*Yogasūtra* II,29). *Yājñavalkyasmṛti* III,313 gives different *niyama* consisting of ten observances: bathing (*snāna*), silence (*mauna*), fasting (*upavāsa*), rite (*ijyā*), study (*svādhyāya*), restraint of sexual desire (*upasthanigraha*), obdience to one's *guru* (*guruśuśrūṣā*), purity (*śauca*), non-anger (*akrodha*), and attentiveness (*apramādatā*).

[15]See BhG XIII, 7–11. Cf. note 5.

[16]Here Śaṅkara prescribes the qualifications of a teacher (*ācārya*), which are not so different from those of a pupil (see section 2). The essential difference between the qualified pupil and the teacher seems to be in the fact that a pupil is a seeker after final release (*mumukṣu*) whereas a teacher is released (*mukta*). Cf. Upad I,17,50–52. For the qualifications of an *ācārya* who is to perform the *upanayana* (see note 55) and to teach him the *Veda*, see P. V. Kane, *History of Dharmaśāstra*, vol. II-I, pp. 324–325.

[17]Cf. section 2.

[18]Cf. section 2.

[19]Cf. section 30.

[20]Hindu law books direct a teacher to teach learning to a pupil without hiding anything from him in all matters of duty (see *Āpastamba Dharmasūtra* I,2,8,25–28; I,4, 14,2–3). Cf. P. V. Kane, *History of Dharmaśāstra*, II-I, pp. 329–330.

[21]The sentences "*ātmaivedaṃ sarvam*" and "*brahmaivedaṃ sarvam*" are also quoted in GKBh II,32, p. 91. The former comes from Chānd. Up. VII,25,2, but the latter is problematic. As far as I have investigated, the same sentence occurs only in the *Nṛsiṃhottaratāpanīya Up.* (VII,3), from which Śaṅkara cannot be expected to quote. As I have discussed elsewhere, I would think that this is a quotation from the Bṛh. Up. This quotation must have originally been *brahmedaṃ sarvam* which occurs in Bṛh. Up. II,5,1. Furthermore, there is a possibility that *brahmedaṃ sarvam* was assimilated to *ātmaivedaṃ sarvam* which occurs just before the quotation in question (see S. Mayeda, "On the Author of the Māṇḍūkyopaniṣad- and the Gauḍapādīya-Bhāṣya," *The Adyar Library Bulletin*, vols. 31–32, 1967–68, p. 81, note 1).

[22]Cf. section 18.

[23]See note 2 of Upad I,15.

[24]*Brahmacārin, viz.* the first of the four stages of life. See note 3.

[25]*Gṛhastha, viz.* the second of the four stages of life. See note 3.

[26]There are three different opinions about the four stages of life: (1) exclusion (*bādha*), (2) orderly co-ordination (*samuccaya*), and (3) option (*vikalpa*). The first, exclusion, which is held by the *Gautama Dharmasūtra* (III,1 and 35), is that there is really one stage of life, *i.e.*, that of a householder; the other stages are regarded as inferior to it. The Manu (IV,1; VI,1; VI,33–37; VI,81–83) represents the second opinion, that a man should resort to the four stages of life one after another in order without skipping any one of them. The third opinion, as seen in the Jābālopaniṣad (4), is that there can be an option after the stage of a student. In other words, a man may become a wandering

ascetic (*parivrājaka*) immediately after he finishes the stage of a student or the stage of a householder. The BS suggests that Jaimini, founder of the Mīmāṃsā school, held the first opinion (BS III,4,18), whereas Bādarāyaṇa, founder of the Vedānta school, might have been a supporter of the second opinion (BS III, 4,19, and 20). The Upad reveals that Śaṅkara may have held the third opinion. Śaṅkara himself is said to have become a *saṃnyāsin* without resorting to the life of a householder (cf. T. M. P. Mahadevan, *Homage to Śaṅkara*, pp. 3–11).

[27]BhG II,22 reads as follows: "Just as a man leaves aside worn-out garments and takes other new ones, so the embodied *Ātman* leaves aside worn-out bodies and goes to other new ones."

[28]See section 10.

[29]The word *saṃskāra* is sometimes translated as (Hindu) "sacrament." It generally means religious purificatory rites and ceremonies for sanctifying the body, mind, and intellect of an individual so that he may become a full-fledged member of the Hindu community. There is a great divergence of opinion among the law books concerning the number of *saṃskāras*. The *Gautama Dharmasūtra* gives a list of forty *saṃskāras* with eight virtues of *Ātman*. It is, however, said that sixteen are the most popular *saṃskāras*, though the enumeration differs in different books. In the Upad Śaṅkara refers to several *saṃskāras* (see Upad II,1,20, and 21) such as birth ceremony (*jātakarman*) and initiation ceremony (*upanayana*). Cf. P. V. Kane, *History of Dharmaśāstra*, II-I, pp. 188–267; Raj Bali Pandey, *Hindu Saṁskāras* (Banaras: Vikarama Publications, 1949).

[30]See section 23.

[31]See section 6.

[32]See sections 7 and 8.

[33]The whole section is based upon Chānd. Up. VIII,14,1 (*ākāśo vai nāma nāmarūpayor nirvahitā*) and BS I,3,41 (*ākāśo 'rthāntaratvādivyapadeśāt*). See Mayeda Upad, pp. 31–32.

[34]Here, as in the BSBh, Śaṅkara uses the term name-and-form (*nāmarūpa*) in the sense of the primary material of the universe, which corresponds to *prakṛti* (or *pradhāna*) in the Sāṃkhya system. This usage of the term is peculiar to Śaṅkara. According to later Advaitins, the primary material of the universe is *avidyā* or *māyā* and not *nāmarūpa*. For a detailed discussion, see Introduction, III,A,1, pp. 18–22.

[35]Cf. Chānd. Up. VIII,12,1.

[36]Bṛh. Up. III,8,8. Cf. Upad II,1,7.

[37]Chānd. Up. VIII,7,1. Cf. Upad II,1,7.

[38]Bṛh. Up. III,5,1. Cf. Upad II,1,7.

[39]Cf. Chānd. Up. VII,26,1.

[40]See notes 33 and 34.

[41]By the expression, "indescribable as this or something else" (*tattvānyatvābhyām anirvacanīya-*), Śaṅkara indicates, as in the BSBh, the unsteadiness of the primary material *nāmarūpa* (see note 34) which will be transformed into something. The expression denotes the unstable condition of the unevolved name-and-form (*avyākṛte nāmarūpe*), of which we can neither say, "It is this" nor "It is different from this." The expression is peculiar to Śaṅkara. The term *anirvacanīya* appears as an attribute of *avidyā* first in Maṇḍanamiśra's *Brahmasiddhi* (S. Kuppuswami Sastri, *Brahmasiddhi by Ācārya Maṇḍanamiśra with Commentary by Śaṅkhapāṇi*. Madras: Government Press, 1937, p. 9, line 14. Cf. S. Dasgupta, *A History of Indian Philosophy*, vol. II, p. 89; Eigen, p. 255, note 1). The association of the term with *avidyā* occurs in the thinking of all Advaitins except Śaṅkara, Sureśvara, and Toṭaka. See Eigen, pp. 261–264; D. H. H. Ingalls, "Śaṁkara on the Question: Whose Is Avidyā?", *Philosophy East and West*, vol. 3 (1953), no. 1, p. 69;

do, "The Study of Śaṅkarācārya," *Annals of the Bhandarkar Oriental Research Institute*, vol. 33 (1952), p. 7; Mayeda Upad, pp. 32–34.

[42]The name-and-form in this case means the effect of the unevolved name-and-form. See Eigen, pp. 259–261; Mayeda Upad, p. 32.

[43]See BS II,3,1–7; Taitt. Up. II,1,1.

[44]As P. Hacker points out in his *Upadeshasāhasrī von Meister Shankara*, p. 19, note 71, this simile shows that Śaṅkara is at the transitional stage between the realistic view (*pariṇāmavāda*) of the BS and the remarkable illusionism (*vivartavāda*) of later Advaita. See Introduction, III,A,2, pp. 22–26.

[45]See BS II,3,8.

[46]See BS II,3,10; Taitt. Up. II,1.

[47]See BS II,3,11; Taitt. Up. II,1; Chānd. Up. VI,2,3.

[48]See BS II,3,12; Taitt. Up. II,1; Chānd. Up. VI,2,4.

[49]There are two different theories which explain how the subtle elements (*sūkṣmabhūta*) are combined to produce the gross elements (*sthūlabhūta*): one is the *trivṛtkaraṇa* and the other is the *pañcīkaraṇa*. Śaṅkara's description here seems to point to the *pañcīkaraṇa*. For a detailed discussion, see Introduction, III,A,3, pp. 26–27.

[50]Nescience (*avidyā*) is treated as a kind of psychic affection (*kleśa*). See Introduction, IV,D,1, p. 78.

[51]Probably these sacred formulas (*mantra*) are those which are uttered when the *garbhādhāna saṃskāra* is performed. The *garbhādhāna* is the rite through which a man places his seed in a woman. See Bṛh. Up. VI,4,1–22; P. V. Kane, *History of Dharmaśāstra*, II-I, pp. 201–213; R. B. Pandey, *Hindu Saṁskāras*, pp. 79–98.

[52]The *garbhādhāna saṃskāra* (see note 51) should be performed at the time of *ṛtu* when the wife is physically prepared to conceive. The proper time for conception is from the fourth to the sixteenth night after menstruation. See P. V. Kane, *History of Dharmaśāstra*, II-I, pp. 204–205; R. B. Pandey, *Hindu Saṁskāras*, p. 79.

[53]For Indian medical views of conception, see *Carakasaṃhitā* IV,2–3.

[54]A birth ceremony (*jātakarman*) is performed before the umbilical cord is cut (cf. Manu II,29), but there is no agreement among writers. There is also great divergence on the details which constitute the birth ceremony. According to Bṛh. Up. VI,4,24–28, which gives fairly elaborate description of the ceremony, it consists of the following parts: (1) a sacred fire (*homa*) of curds with ghee to the accompaniment of the sacred formula (Bṛh. Up. VI,4,24), (2) repeating in a child's right ear "Speech!" three times (Bṛh. Up. VI,4,25), (3) feeding him curds, honey, and ghee out of a golden spoon (Bṛh. Up. VI,4,25), (4) giving him a name, which becomes his secret name (Bṛh. Up. VI, 4,26), (5) putting him to the mother's breast to the accompaniment of a sacred formula (Bṛh. Up. VI,4,27), and (6) addressing the mother with sacred formulas (Bṛh. Up. VI, 4,28). See P. V. Kane, *History of Dharmaśāstra*, II-I, pp. 228–237; R. B. Pandey, *Hindu Saṁskāras*, pp. 116–129.

[55]The initiation (*upanayana*) is one of the purifying ceremonies, by which a boy is taken to a teacher for learning the *Veda*. Later the performance of the ritual and the commandments for observing vows (*vratādeśa*) become more important than the study of the *Veda*. If a boy is a Brahmin, this ceremony is performed at the age of eight; if he is a Kṣatriya, it is performed at the age of eleven; if he is a Vaiśya, it is performed at the age of twelve. There are many other opinions about the age of initiation. This ceremony is called a second birth, and by virtue of its performance the initiated boy becomes twice-born (*dvija*) and is distinguished from the Śūdras (*ekaja*) who have only one physical birth. In the course of the ceremony he is invested with a sacred thread

(*yajñopavīta*, see Upad II,1,30). See P. V. Kane, *History of Dharmaśāstra*, II-I, pp. 268–415; R. B. Pandey, *Hindu Saṁskāras*, pp. 187–240.

[56]See note 3.

[57]The purifying ceremony for union with a wife (*patnīyogasaṃskāra*) may mean the marriage ceremony (*vivāha*). For a detailed description of the marriage ceremony, see P. V. Kane, *History of Dharmaśāstra*, II-I, pp. 427–541; R. B. Pandey, *Hindu Saṃskāras*, pp. 261–406.

[58]See note 3. The word *tāpasa* is used as a synonym of *vānaprastha* (forest-dweller). When Śaṅkara comments on BS III,4,20, he says that *tapas* (self-mortification) is a distinctive attribute of the forest-dweller whereas *indriyasaṃyama* (restraint of the senses) and so on are the distinctive attributes of the mendicants (*bhikṣu*). The forest-dweller who may go to the forest with his wife has to keep fires and perform the daily and other rites (*yajña*), at least in the beginning.

[59]See notes 3 and 58.

[60]Cf. note 49.

[61]Section 16.

[62]Cf. Bṛh. Up. III,7,23; Upad II,1,18.

[63]Cf. Upad I,15,2.

[64]The pupil, who does not know the truth that he himself is *Brahman*, regards impersonal *Brahman* as a personal god to be worshipped.

[65]The sentence "*anya evāham . . . anyo 'sau*" is based upon Bṛh. Up. I,4,10 (see section 26).

[66]See note 3.

[67]This is based upon Chānd. Up. VI,16,1–3. See Upad I,17,65 and 73.

[68]Section 13.

[69]Section 25.

[70]The sacred thread (*yajñopavīta*), the composition of which is full of symbolism, consists of three threads of nine strands and is worn under the right arm and over the left shoulder. It is prescribed that the sacred thread of a Brahmin should be made of cotton, that of a Kṣatriya of hempen threads, and that of a Vaiśya of woolen threads (cf. Manu II,44). But the option of cotton thread is available for all. It should reach as far as the navel and is said to be spun by a virgin Brahmin girl and twisted by a Brahmin. At the time of *upanayana* (see note 55) the *ācārya* invests the student with this sacred thread. It is also prescribed that a man must wear it when waiting upon teachers, elders, guests, at the time of handling sacred fire (*homa*), in performing *japa* (murmuring prayer), in taking meals and in sipping water (*ācamana*), and at the time of daily Vedic study (cf. *Āpastamba Dharmasūtra* I,5,15,1). Cf. P. V. Kane, *History of Dharmaśāstra*, II-I, pp. 287–300; R. B. Pandey, *Hindu Saṃskāras*, pp. 224–227.

[71]Prosperity (*abhyudaya*) is the reward for worship of *Brahman* but belongs to transmigratory existence (*saṃsāra*). On the other hand beatitude (*niḥśreyasa*) is generally a synonym for final release (*mokṣa*). Cf. P. Deussen, *The System of the Vedânta*, p. 104.

[72]*Bhāvarūpa* is used as an attribute of *avidyā* or *ajñāna* by later Advaitins. Here Śaṅkara uses it as an attribute of pain (*duḥkha*). Cf. S. Dasgupta, *History of Indian Philosophy*, vol. II, p. 105 and p. 114; Eigen, pp. 254–256; Mayeda Upad, p. 29.

[73]See Introduction, III,B,4, pp. 40–43.

[74]According to Śaṅkara's commentary on the Bṛh. Up. (III,9,20, p. 508), the word "heart" (*hṛdaya*) comprises both *buddhi* and *manas* (*buddhimanasī ekīkṛtya nirdeśaḥ*). Śaṅkara probably understands it as a synonym of the internal organ (*antaḥkaraṇa*).

[75]Cf. Upad I,15,2.

[76]*venas tat paśyan viśvā bhuvanāni vidvān yatra viśvaṃ bhavati ekanīḍam*, M. N. Up. II,3.

Cf. *Vājasaneyi-Saṃhitā* XXXII, 8; Taitt. Ā. X,1,3; *Atharvaveda* II,1,1; *Śāṅkhāyana Śrautasūtra* XV,3,8. The word *ekanīḍa* is also used in Upad I,12,4; I,16,51.

[77]Manu is regarded as the first man, father of the race and the establisher of sacrifice. Cf. A. A. Macdonell, *The Vedic Mythology*, pp. 138–140; A. B. Keith, *The Religion and Philosophy of the Veda and Upanishads*, vol. I (HOS, vol. 31. Cambridge: Harvard University Press, 1925), pp. 228–230.

[78]See Upad I,15,11 and note 9.

[79]Cf. *sa yathā saindhavaghanaḥ* . . . , Bṛh. Up. IV,5,13.

[80]By accepting two standpoints, *paramārthāvasthā* (standpoint of the highest truth) and *vyavahārāvasthā* (standpoint of the daily life) or *avidyāvasthā* (standpoint of nescience), Śaṅkara tried to interpret consistently the mutually contradictory Upaniṣads, BS and so forth, and to explain contradictions between daily experiences and the truth. Cf. P. Deussen, *The System of the Vedânta*, pp. 98–115; S. Radhakrishnan, *Indian Philosophy*, vol. II, pp. 518–520. The word *paramārtha* (Pāli: *paramattha*) is not found in the ancient *Upaniṣads* but appears in old Buddhist texts (cf. *Suttanipāta* 68; 219; *Saddharmapuṇḍarīka* (ed. by U. Wogihara and Tuchida), p. 92, line 23; p. 93, line 1; p. 122, line 21; p. 257, line 3; *Saundarānanda* XV, 19); it has come to be a very important term in Mahāyāna Buddhism. Such a conception of the highest truth was first introduced into the Vedānta system by the author of the *Māṇḍūkyakārikā* (I,17; II,32; III,18; IV,73; 74), in which a Buddhistic distinction between the highest truth (*paramārthasatya*) and the conventional truth (*saṃvṛtisatya*) is recognized (IV,73 and 74). Śaṅkara adopted it for his purpose. See Nakamura III, pp. 509–510.

[81]*Timira* is a class of morbid affection of the coats of the eye.

[82]See variant readings in Mayeda Upad. D. V. Gokhale suggests in his edition of the Upad (Bombay: Gujarati Printing Press, 1917) that this is a quotation from Chānd. Up. VII,2,1, etc. It is, however, to be noted here that in his BSBh (II,1,14, p. 373) Śaṅkara quotes the same sentence (*yathā* . . . *vācārambhaṇam vikāro nāmadheyaṃ mṛttikety eva satyam*) from the Chānd. Up. and that he explains the sentence, interpreting "*nāmadheya*" as "*nāmadheyamātraṃ hy etad anṛtam.*" Therefore, "*anṛtam*" may not be a quotation but Śaṅkara's explanatory insertion.

[83]See note 80.

[84]Cf. note 79.

[85]See section 2.

CHAPTER 2
AWARENESS

45. A certain student,[1] who was tired of transmigratory existence characterized by birth and death and was seeking after final release, approached in the prescribed manner[2] a knower of *Brahman* who was established in *Brahman* and sitting at his ease, and asked him, "Your Holiness, how can I be released from transmigratory existence? I am aware of the body, the senses and [their] objects; I experience pain in the waking state, and I experience it in the dreaming state after getting relief again and again by entering into the state of deep sleep again and again. Is it indeed my own nature or [is it] due to some cause, my own nature being different? If [this is] my own nature, there is no hope for me to attain final release, since one cannot avoid one's own nature. If [it is] due to some cause, final release is possible after the cause has been removed."

46. The teacher replied to him, "Listen, my child, this is not your own nature but is due to a cause."

47. When he was told this the pupil said, "What is the cause? And what will remove it? And what is my own nature? When the cause is removed, the effect due to the cause no [longer] exists; I will attain to my own nature like a sick person [who recovers his health] when the cause of his disease has been removed."[3]

48. The teacher replied, "The cause is nescience; it is removed by knowledge. When nescience has been removed, you will be released from transmigratory existence which is characterized by birth and death, since its cause will be gone and you will no [longer] experience pain in the dreaming and waking states."

49. The pupil said, "What is that nescience? And what is its

object?[4] And what is knowledge, remover of nescience, by which I can realize my own nature?"[5]

50. The teacher replied, "Though you are the highest *Ātman* and not a transmigrator, you hold the inverted view, 'I am a transmigrator.' Though you are neither an agent nor an experiencer, and exist [eternally], [you hold the inverted view, 'I am] an agent, an experiencer, and do not exist [eternally]'[6]—this is nescience."

51. The pupil said, "Even though I exist [eternally], still I am not the highest *Ātman.* My nature is transmigratory existence which is characterized by agency and experiencership, since it is known by sense-perception and other means of knowledge. [Transmigratory existence] has not nescience as its cause, since nescience cannot have one's own *Ātman* as its object.[7]

Nescience is [defined as] the superimposition of the qualities of one [thing] upon another.[8] For example, fully known silver is superimposed upon fully known mother-of-pearl, a fully known person upon a [fully known] tree trunk, or a fully known trunk upon a [fully known] person; but not an unknown [thing] upon [one that is] fully known nor a fully known [thing] upon one that is unknown. Nor is non-*Ātman* superimposed upon *Ātman* because *Ātman* is not fully known, nor *Ātman* [superimposed] upon non-*Ātman*, [again] because *Ātman* is not fully known."

52. The teacher said to him, "That is not right, since there is an exception. My child, it is not possible to make a general rule that a fully known [thing] is superimposed only upon a fully known [thing], since it is a matter of experience that [a fully known thing] is superimposed upon *Ātman.* [For example,] if one says, 'I am white,' 'I am dark,' this is [the superimposition] of qualities of the body upon *Ātman* which is the object of the 'I'-notion.[9] And if one says, 'I am this,' this is [the superimposition of *Ātman*,] which is the object of the 'I'-notion, upon the body."

53. The pupil said, "In that case *Ātman* is indeed fully known as the object of the 'I'-notion; so is the body as 'this.' If so, [it is only a case of] the mutual superimposition of body and *Ātman*, both fully known, just like [the mutual superimposition] of tree-trunk and person, and of mother-of-pearl and silver. So, is there a particular reason why Your Holiness said that it is not possible to make a general rule that two fully known [things] are mutually superimposed?"

54. The teacher replied, "Listen. It is true that the body and *Ātman* are fully known; but they are not fully known to all people as the objects of distinct notions like a tree-trunk and a person."

"How [are they known] then?"

"[They are] always [known] as the objects of constantly non-distinct notions. Since nobody grasps the body and *Ātman* as two distinct notions, saying, 'This is the body, that is *Ātman*,' people are deluded with regard to *Ātman* and non-*Ātman*, thinking, '*Ātman* is thus' or '*Ātman* is not thus.' This is the particular reason why I said that it is impossible to make a general rule."

55. [The pupil raised another objection:] "Is it not experienced that the thing which is superimposed [upon something] else through nescience does not exist [in the latter]? For example, silver [does not exist] in a mother-of-pearl nor a person in a tree-trunk nor a snake in a rope; nor the dark color of the earth's surface in the sky. Likewise, if the body and *Ātman* are always mutually superimposed in the form of constantly non-distinct notions, then they cannot exist in each other at any time. Silver, etc., which are superimposed through nescience upon mother-of-pearl, etc., do not exist [in the latter] at any time in any way and *vice versa;* likewise the body and *Ātman* are mutually superimposed through nescience; this being the case, it would follow as the result that neither the body nor *Ātman* exists. And it is not acceptable, since it is the theory of the Nihilists.[10]

If, instead of mutual superimposition, [only] the body is superimposed upon *Ātman* through nescience, it would follow as the result that the body does not exist in *Ātman* while the latter exists. This is not acceptable either since it is contradictory to sense-perception and other [means of knowledge]. For this reason the body and *Ātman* are not superimposed upon each other through nescience."

"How then?"

"They are permanently connected with each other like bamboo and pillars [which are interlaced in the structure of a house]."

56. [The teacher said,] "No; because it would follow as the result that [*Ātman* is] non-eternal and exists for another's sake[11]; since [in your opinion *Ātman*] is composite, [*Ātman* exists for another's sake and is non-eternal] just like bamboo, pillars, and so forth. Moreover, the *Ātman* which is assumed by some others to be

connected with the body exists for another's sake since it is composite. [Therefore,] it has been first established that the highest [*Ātman*] is not connected with the body, is different [from it], and is eternal.

57. [The pupil objected:] "Although [the *Ātman*] is not composite, It is [regarded] merely as the body and superimposed upon the body; from this follow the results that [the *Ātman*] does not exist and that [It] is non-eternal and so on. Then there would arise the fault that [you will] arrive at the Nihilists' position that the body has no *Ātman*."

58. [The teacher replied,] "Not so; because it is accepted that *Ātman*, like space, is by nature not composite.[12] Although *Ātman* exists as connected with nothing, it does not follow that the body and other things are without *Ātman*, just as, although space is connected with nothing, it does not follow that nothing has space. Therefore, there would not arise the fault that [I shall] arrive at the Nihilists' position.

59. "Your further objection—namely that, if the body does not exist in *Ātman* [although *Ātman* exists], this would contradict sense-perception and the other [means of knowledge][13]: this is not right, because the existence of the body in *Ātman* is not cognized by sense-perception and the other [means of knowledge]; in *Ātman*—like a jujube-fruit in a pot, ghee in milk, oil in sesame and a picture on a wall[14]—the body is not cognized by sense-perception and the other [means of knowledge]. Therefore there is no contradiction with sense-perception and the other [means of knowledge]."

60. [The pupil objected,] "How is the body then superimposed upon *Ātman* which is not established by sense-perception and the other [means of knowledge], and how is *Ātman* superimposed upon the body?"

61. [The teacher said,] "That is not a fault, because *Ātman* is established by Its own nature. A general rule cannot be made that superimposition is made only on that which is adventitiously established and not on that which is permanently established, for the dark color and other things on the surface of the earth are seen to be superimposed upon the sky [which is permanently established]."

62. [The pupil asked,] "Your Holiness, is the mutual superimposition of the body and *Ātman* made by the composite of the body and so on or by *Ātman*?"[15]

63. The teacher said, "What would happen to you, if [the mutual superimposition] is made by the composite of the body and so on, or if [it] is made by *Ātman*?"

64. Then the pupil answered, "If I am merely the composite of the body and so on, then I am non-conscious, so I exist for another's sake; consequently, the mutual superimposition of body and *Ātman* is not effected by me. If I am the highest *Ātman* different from the composite [of the body and so on], then I am conscious, so I exist for my own sake; consequently, the superimposition [of body] which is the seed of every calamity is effected upon *Ātman* by me who am conscious."

65. To this the teacher responded, "If you know that the false superimposition is the seed of [every] calamity, then do not make it!"[16]

66. "Your Holiness, I cannot help [it]. I am driven [to do it] by another; I am not independent."

67. [The teacher said,] "Then you are non-conscious, so you do not exist for your own sake. That by which you who are not self-dependent are driven to act is conscious and exists for its own sake; you are only a composite thing [of the body, etc.]."

68. [The pupil objected,] "If I am non-conscious, how do I perceive feelings of pleasure and pain, and [the words] you have spoken?"

69. The teacher said, "Are you different from feelings of pleasure and pain and from [the words] I have spoken, or are you identical [with them]?"[17]

70. The pupil answered, "I am indeed not identical."

"Why?"

"Because I perceive both of them as objects just as [I perceive] a jar and other things [as objects]. If I were identical [with them] I could not perceive either of them; but I do perceive them, so I am different [from both of them]. If [I were] identical [with them] it would follow that the modifications of the feelings of pleasure and pain exist for their own sake and so do [the words] you have spoken; but it is not reasonable that any of them exists for their own sake, for the pleasure and pain produced by a sandal and a thorn are not for the sake of the sandal and the thorn, nor is use made of a jar for the sake of the jar. So, the sandal and other things serve my purpose, *i.e.*, the purpose of their perceiver, since I who am different from them perceive all the objects seated in the intellect."[18]

71. The teacher said to him, "So, then, you exist for your own sake since you are conscious. You are not driven [to act] by another. A conscious being is neither dependent on another nor driven [to act] by another, for it is not reasonable that a conscious being should exist for the sake of another conscious being since they are equal like two lights.[19] Nor does a conscious being exist for the sake of a non-conscious being since it is not reasonable that a non-conscious being should have any connection with its own object precisely because it is non-conscious. Nor does experience show that two non-conscious beings exist for each other, as for example a stick of wood and a wall do not fulfill each other's purposes."

72. [The pupil objected,] "Is it not experienced that a servant and his master, though they are equal in the sense of being conscious, exist for each other?"[20]

73. [The teacher said,] "It is not so, for what [I] meant was that you have consciousness just as fire has heat and light. And [in this meaning I] cited the example, 'like two lights.'[21] This being the case, you perceive everything seated in your intellect through your own nature, *i.e.*, the transcendentally changeless, eternal,[22] pure consciousness which is equivalent to the heat and light of fire. And if you admit that *Ātman* is always without distinctions, why did you say, 'After getting relief again and again in the state of deep sleep, I perceive pain in the waking and dreaming states. Is this indeed my own nature or [is it] due to some cause?'[23] Has this delusion left [you now] or not?"

74. To this the pupil replied, "Your Holiness, the delusion has gone thanks to your gracious assistance; but I am in doubt as to how I am transcendentally changeless."

"How?"

"Sound and other [external objects] are not self-established, since they are not conscious. But they [are established] through the rise of notions which take the forms of sound and other [external objects].[24] It is impossible for notions to be self-established, since they have mutually exclusive attributes and the forms [of external objects] such as blue and yellow. It is, therefore, understood that [notions] are caused by the forms of the external objects; so, [notions] are established as possessing the forms of external objects, *i.e.*, the forms of sound, etc. Likewise, notions, which are the modifications of a thing (= the intellect),[25] the substratum of the 'I'-notion, are also composite, so it is reasonable that they are non-conscious; therefore, as it is impossible that they exist for their own sake, they, like sound and other [external objects], are established as objects to be perceived by a perceiver different in nature [from them]. If I am not composite, I have pure consciousness as my nature; so I exist for my own sake. Nevertheless, I am a perceiver of notions which have the forms [of the external objects] such as blue and yellow [and] so I am indeed subject to change. [For the above reason, I am] in doubt as to how [I am] transcendentally changeless."

75. The teacher said to him, "Your doubt is not reasonable. [Your] perception of those notions is necessary and entire; for this very reason [you] are not subject to transformation. It is, therefore, established that [you] are transcendentally changeless. But you have said that precisely the reason for the above positive conclusion—namely, that [you] perceive the entire movement of the mind—is the reason for [your] doubt [concerning your transcendental changelessness]. This is why [your doubt is not reasonable].

If indeed you were subject to transformation, you would not perceive the entire movement of the mind which is your object, just as the mind [does not perceive] its [entire] object and just as the senses [do not perceive] their [entire] objects,[26] and similarly you as *Ātman* would not perceive even a part of your object. Therefore, you are transcendentally changeless."

76. Then [the pupil] said, "Perception is what is meant by the verbal root,[27] that is, nothing but change; it is contradictory [to this fact] to say that [the nature of] the perceiver is transcendentally changeless."

77. [The teacher said,] "That is not right, for [the term] 'perception' is used figuratively in the sense of a change which is meant by the verbal root; whatever the notion of the intellect may be, that is what is meant by the verbal root; [the notion of the intellect] has change as its nature and end, with the result that the

perception of *Ātman* falsely appears [as perceiver]; thus the notion of the intellect is figuratively indicated by the term, 'perception.' For example, the cutting action results [in the static state] that [the object to be cut] is separated in two parts; thus [the term, 'cutting,' in the sense of an object to be cut being separated in two parts,] is used figuratively as [the cutting action] which is meant by the verbal root."[28]

78. To this the pupil objected, "Your Holiness, the example cannot explain my transcendental changelessness."

"Why not?"

" 'Cutting' which results in a change in the object to be cut is used figuratively as [the cutting action] which is meant by the verbal root; in the same manner, if the notion of the intellect, which is figuratively indicated by the term 'perception' and is meant by the verbal root, results also in a change in the perception of *Ātman*, [the example] cannot explain *Ātman*'s transcendental changelessness."

79. The teacher said, "It would be true, if there were a distinction between perception and perceiver. The perceiver is indeed nothing but eternal perception. And it is not [right] that perception and perceiver are different as in the doctrine of the logicians."[29]

80. [The pupil said,] "How does that [action] which is meant by the verbal root result in perception?"

81. [The teacher] answered, "Listen, [I] said that [it] ends with the result that the perception [of *Ātman*] falsely appears [as perceiver].[30] Did you not hear? I did not say that [it] results in the production of any change in *Ātman*."

82. The pupil said, "Why then did you say that if I am transcendentally changeless I am the perceiver of the entire movement of the mind which is my object?"

83. The teacher said to him, "I told [you] only the truth. Precisely because [you are the perceiver of the entire movement of the mind], I said, you are transcendentally changeless."[31]

84. "If so, Your Holiness, I am of the nature of transcendentally changeless and eternal perception whereas the notions of the intellect, which have the forms of [external objects] such as sound, arise and end with the result that my own nature which is perception falsely appears [as perceiver]. Then what is my fault?"

85. [The teacher replied,] "You are right. [You] have no fault. The fault is only nescience as I have said before."[32]

86. [The pupil said,] "If, Your Holiness, as in the state of deep sleep I undergo no change, how [do I experience] the dreaming and waking states?"

87. The teacher said to him, "But do you experience [these states] continuously?"

88. [The pupil answered,] "Certainly I do experience [them], but intermittently and not continuously."

89. The teacher said [to him,] "Both of them are adventitious [and] not your nature. If [they] were your nature [they] would be self-established and continuous like your nature, which is Pure Consciousness. Moreover, the dreaming and waking states are not your nature, for [they] depart [from you] like clothes and so on.[33] It is certainly not experienced that the nature of anything, whatever it may be, departs from it. But the dreaming and waking states depart from the state of Pure Consciousness-only. If one's own nature were to depart [from oneself] in the state of deep sleep, it would be negated by saying, 'It has perished,' 'It does not exist,' since the adventitious attributes which are not one's own nature are seen to consist in both [perishableness and non-existence]; for example, wealth, clothes, and the like are seen to perish and things which have been obtained in dream or delusion are seen to be non-existent."

90. [The pupil objected,] "[If] so, Your Holiness, it follows [either] that my own nature, *i.e.*, Pure Consciousness, is also adventitious, since [I] perceive in the dreaming and waking states but not in the state of deep sleep; or that I am not of the nature of Pure Consciousness."

91. [The teacher replied,] "No, Look. Because that is not reasonable. If you [insist on] looking your own nature, *i.e.* Pure Consciousness, as adventitious, do so! We cannot establish it logically even in a hundred years, nor can any other (*i.e.* non-conscious) being do so. As [that adventitious consciousness] is composite, nobody can logically deny that [it] exists for another's sake, is manifold and perishable; for what does not exist for its own sake is not self-established, as we have said before.[34] Nobody can, however, deny that *Ātman*, which is of the nature of Pure Conscious-

ness, is self-established; so It does not depend upon anything else, since It does not depart [from anybody]."[35]

92. [The pupil objected,] "Did I not point out that [It] does depart [from me] when I said that in the state of deep sleep I do not see?"[36]

93. [The teacher replied,] "That is not right, for it is contradictory."

"How is it a contradiction?"

"Although you are [in truth] seeing, you say, 'I do not see.' This is contradictory."

"But at no time in the state of deep sleep, Your Holiness, have I ever seen Pure Consciousness or anything else."

"Then you are seeing in the state of deep sleep; for you deny only the seen object, not the seeing. I said that your seeing is Pure Consciousness. That [eternally] existing one by which you deny [the existence of the seen object] when you say that nothing has been seen, [that precisely is the seeing] that is Pure Consciousness. Thus as [It] does not ever depart [from you] [Its] transcendental changelessness and eternity are established solely by Itself without depending upon any means of knowledge. The knower, though self-established, requires means of knowledge for the discernment of an object to be known other [than itself]. And that eternal Discernment, which is required for discerning something else (= non-*Ātman*) which does not have Discernment as its nature—that is certainly eternal, transcendentally changeless, and of a self-effulgent nature. The eternal Discernment does not require any means of knowledge in order to be Itself the means of knowledge or the knower since the eternal Discernment is by nature the means of knowledge or the knower. [This is illustrated by the following] example: iron or water requires fire or sun [to obtain] light and heat since light and heat are not their nature; but fire and sun do not require [anything else] for light and heat since [these] are always their nature.

94. "If [you object,] 'There is empirical knowledge[37] in so far as it is not eternal and [there is] no [empirical knowledge], if it is eternal,'

95. "[then I reply,] 'Not so; because it is impossible to make a distinction between eternal apprehension and non-eternal ap-

prehension; when apprehension is empirical knowledge, such distinction is not apprehended that empirical knowledge is non-eternal apprehension and not eternal one.'

96. "If [you object,] 'When [empirical knowledge] is eternal [apprehension, it] does not require the knower, but when [empirical knowledge] is non-eternal [apprehension], apprehension requires [the knower], since it is mediated by [the knower's] effort. There would be the above distinction,'

97. "then, it is established that the knower itself is self-established, since [it] does not require any means of knowledge.

98. "If [you object,] 'Even when [apprehension or empirical knowledge] does not exist, [the knower] does not require [any means of knowledge], since [the knower] is eternal,' [my reply is,] 'No; because apprehension exists only in [the knower] itself. Thus your opinion is refuted.

99. "If the knower is dependent upon the means of knowledge for its establishment, where does the desire to know belong? It is admitted that that to which the desire to know belongs is indeed the knower. And the object of this desire to know is the object to be known, not the knower, since if the object [of the desire to know] were the knower, a *regressus ad infinitum* with regard to the knower and the desire to know would result: there would be a second knower for the first one, a third knower for the second, and so on. Such would be the case if the desire to know had the knower as its object. And the knower itself cannot be the object to be known, since it is never mediated [by anything]; what in this world is called the object to be known is established, when it is mediated by the rise of desire, remembrance, effort, and means of knowledge which belong to the knower. In no other way is apprehension experienced with regard to the object to be known. And it cannot be assumed that the knower itself is mediated by any of the knower's own desire and the like. And remembrance has as its object the object to be remembered and not the subject of remembrance. Likewise, desire has as its object only the object desired and not the one who desires. If remembrance and desire had as their object the subject of remembrance and the one who desires respectively, a *regressus ad infinitum* would be inevitable as before.

100. "If [you say,] 'If apprehension which has the knower as its

object is impossible, the knower would not be apprehended,'

101. "not so; because the apprehension of the apprehender has as its object the object to be apprehended. If [it] were to have the apprehender as its object, a *regressus ad infinitum* would result as before. And it has been proved before[38] that apprehension, *i.e.*, the transcendentally changeless and eternal light of *Ātman*, is established in *Ātman* without depending upon anything else as heat and light are in fire, the sun, and so on. If apprehension, *i.e.*, the light of *Ātman* which is Pure Consciousness, were not eternal in one's own *Ātman*, it would be impossible for *Ātman* to exist for Its own sake; as It would be composite like the aggregate of the body and senses, It would exist for another's sake and be possessed of faults as we have already said."

"How?"

"If the light of *Ātman* which is Pure Consciousness were not eternal in one's own *Ātman*, it would be mediated by remembrance and the like and so it would be composite. And as this light of Pure Consciousness would therefore not exist in *Ātman* before Its origination and after Its destruction, It would exist for another's sake, since It would be composite like the eye and so on. And if the light of Pure Consciousness exists in *Ātman* as something which has arisen, then *Ātman* does not exist for Its own sake, since it is established according to the existence and absence of that light of Pure Consciousness that *Ātman* exists for Its own sake and non-*Ātman* exists for another's sake. It is therefore established that *Ātman* is the eternal light of Pure Consciousness without depending upon anything else."

102. [The pupil objected,] "If so, [and] if the knower is not the subject of empirical knowledge, how is it a knower?"

103. [The teacher] answered, "Because there is no distinction in the nature of empirical knowledge, whether it is eternal or non-eternal, since empirical knowledge is apprehension. There is no distinction in the nature of this [empirical knowledge] whether it be non-eternal, preceded by remembrance, desire, and the like, or transcendentally changeless and eternal, just as there is no distinction in the nature of what is meant by verbal root[39] such as *sthā* (stand), whether it is a non-eternal result preceded by 'going' and other [forms of actions], or an eternal result not preceded [by 'going' or any other forms of actions]; so the same expression is

found [in both cases]: 'People stand,' 'The mountains stand,' and so forth.[40] Likewise, although the knower is of the nature of eternal apprehension, it is not contradictory to designate [It] as 'knower,' since the result is the same."

104. Here the pupil said, "*Ātman*, which is of the nature of eternal apprehension, is changeless, so it is impossible for *Ātman* to be an agent without being connected with the body and the senses, just as a carpenter[41] and other [agents are connected] with an axe and so on. And if that which is by nature not composite were to use the body and the senses, a *regressus ad infinitum* would result. But the carpenter and the other [agents] are constantly connected with the body and the senses; so, when [they] use an axe and the like, no *regressus ad infinitum* occurs."

105. [The teacher said,] "But in that case [*Ātman*], which is by nature not composite, cannot be an agent when It makes no use of intruments; [It] would have to use an instrument [to be an agent]. [But] the use [of an instrument] would be a change; so in becoming an agent which causes that [change], [It] should use another instrument, [and] in using this instrument, [It] should also use another one. Thus if the knower is independent, a *regressus ad infinitum* is inevitable.

And no action causes *Ātman* to act, since [the action] which has not been performed does not have its own nature. If [you object,] 'Something other [than *Ātman*] approaches *Ātman* and causes It to perform an action', [I reply,] 'No; because it is impossible for anything other [than *Ātman*] to be self-established, a non-object, and so forth; it is not experienced that anything else but *Ātman*, being non-conscious, is self-evident. Sound and all other [objects] are established when they are known by a notion which ends with the result of apprehension.[42]

If apprehension were to belong to anything else but *Ātman*, It would also be *Ātman*, not composite, existing for Its own sake, and not for another.[43] And we cannot apprehend that the body, the senses, and their objects exist for their own sake, since it is experienced that they depend for their establishment upon the notions which result in apprehension."[44]

106. [The pupil objected,] "In apprehending the body nobody depends upon any other notions due to sense-perception and other [means of knowledge]."

107. [The teacher said,] "Certainly in the waking state it would be so. But in the states of death and deep sleep the body also depends upon sense-perception and other means of knowledge for its establishment. This is true of the senses. Sound and other [external objects] are indeed transformed into the form of the body and senses; so, [the body and the senses] depend upon sense-perception and other means of knowledge for [their] establishment. And 'establishment' (*siddhi*) is Apprehension, *i.e.*, the result of the means of knowledge as we have already said, and this Apprehension is transcendentally changeless, self-established, and by nature the light of *Ātman*."

108. Here [the pupil] objected, saying, "It is contradictory to say that Apprehension is the result of the means of knowledge and that It is by nature the transcendentally changeless and eternal light of *Ātman*."

To this [the teacher] said, "It is not contradictory."

"How then [is it not contradictory]"?

"Although [Apprehension] is transcendentally changeless and eternal, [It] appears at the end of the notion [forming process] due to sense-perception and other [means of knowledge] since [the notion-forming process] aims at It.[45] If the notion due to sense-perception and other [means of knowledge] is non-eternal, [Apprehension, though eternal,] appears as if it were non-eternal. Therefore, [Apprehension] is figuratively called the result of the means of knowledge."

109. [The pupil said,] "If so, Your Holiness, Apprehension is transcendentally changeless, eternal, indeed of the nature of the light of *Ātman*, and self-established, since It does not depend upon any means of knowledge with regard to Itself; everything other than This is non-conscious and exists for another's sake, since it acts together [with others].

And because of this nature of being apprehended as notion causing pleasure, pain, and delusion, [non-*Ātman*] exists for another's sake; on account of this very nature non-*Ātman* exists and not on account of any other nature.[46] It is therefore merely non-existent from the standpoint of the highest truth. Just as it is experienced in this world that a snake [superimposed] upon a rope does not exist, nor water in a mirage, and the like, unless they are apprehended [as a notion], so it is reasonable that duality in the waking and dreaming states also does not exist unless it is apprehended [as a notion]. In this manner, Your Holiness, Apprehension, *i.e.*, the light of *Ātman*, is uninterrupted; so It is transcendentally changeless, eternal and non-dual, since It is never absent from any of the various notions. But various notions are absent from Apprehension. Just as in the dreaming state the notions in different forms such as blue and yellow, which are absent from that Apprehension, are said to be non-existent from the standpoint of the highest truth, so in the waking state also, the various notions such as blue and yellow, which are absent from this very Apprehension, must by nature be untrue. And there is no apprehender different from this Apprehension to apprehend It; therefore It can Itself neither be accepted nor rejected by Its own nature, since there is nothing else."

110. [The teacher said,] "Exactly so it is. It is nescience that is the cause of transmigratory existence which is characterized by the waking and dreaming states. The remover of this nescience is knowledge. And so you have reached fearlessness.[47] From now on you will not perceive any pain in the waking and dreaming states. You are released from the sufferings of transmigratory existence."[48]

111. [The pupil said,] "Om."

Notes

[1]*Brahmacārin*. See notes 6 and 24 of Upad II,1.

[2]See note 8 of Upad II,1.

[3]A similar simile is used in GKBh, Introduction, p. 6 (*rogārtasyeva roganivṛttau svasthatā. tathā duḥkhātmakasyātmano dvaitaprapañcopaśame svasthatā*).

[4]For a detailed discussion of *avidyā*, see Introduction, IV,D, pp. 76–84; Mayeda Upad, pp. 23–30.

[5]Commenting on BhG IV,34 which explains how to obtain knowledge, Śaṅkara gives examples of questions to be put to teachers: "How does bondage come about? How does release come about? What is knowledge? What is nescience?" (*katham bandhaḥ kathaṃ mokṣaḥ kā vidyā kā cāvidyeti*, p. 232). Here in the Upad as well the teacher and his pupil are going to discuss the same topics. It is certain that these four topics are of primary importance in Śaṅkara's doctrine.

[6]*Avidyamāna*. This is a kind of popular etymology: *avidyā* from *avidyamāna* (not existing).

[7]See Introduction, IV,D,2, pp. 79–83.

[8]In BSBh, Introduction, pp. 10–13, Śaṅkara defines superimposition (*adhyāsa*) as the appearance, in the form of remembrance, of one thing previously perceived, in an-

other (*smṛtirūpaḥ paratra pūrvadṛṣṭāvabhāsaḥ*). Then he gives his only definition of nescience: "The learned men regard this superimposition thus defined as *avidyā*." (BSBh, Introduction, p. 19). In other words, nescience is superimposition, *i.e.*, mutual superimposition of *Ātman* and non-*Ātman* such as the body, the senses, and the internal organ. See Introduction, IV,D,1, pp. 76–79.

[9]*Ahampratyaya*. See Introduction, III,B,3, pp. 38–40.

[10]"The Nihilists" (*Vaināśika*) indicates the Buddhists, especially the Śūnyavādins (or Mādhyamikas) who hold the view that everything is empty (*śūnya*) and who have Nāgārjuna (150–250) as their founder.

[11]*Sāṃkhyakārikā* 17 proves the existence of *Puruṣa* (Spirit) from several reasons, one of which is that the composite things exist for another's sake (*saṃghātaparārthatva*). The Unmanifest (*avyakta*), the great (*mahat*), "I"-consciousness (*ahaṃkāra*), and so forth are all considered to be composite of pleasure, pain, and delusion and they are compared to the bedstead, the chair, and other things (cf. Vācaspatimiśra on *Sāṃkhyakārikā* 17). And the "another" (*para*) for which they exist is the non-composite *Ātman*. Cf. P. Hacker, "Śaṅkara der Yogin und Śaṅkara der Advaitin," WZKSO, vols. XII-XIII (1968/1969), pp. 142–143.

[12]See section 56.

[13]Section 55.

[14]The simile "a picture on a wall" is not intelligible, but may mean that in a dark place like a cave.

[15]This question, which is discussed in sections 62–85, is a variation of the question, "Whose is *avidyā*?" or "What is the locus (*āśraya*) of *avidyā*?" Here Śaṅkara does not give any definite answer to it (see note 16). See Introduction, IV,D,2, pp. 79–83.

[16]This answer is very characteristic of Śaṅkara's attitude toward the problem of the locus of *avidyā*. See Introduction, IV,D,2, pp. 79–80.

[17]See Upad II,1,33–38.

[18]See Upad I,7,1 and note 1; 18,155–157; Introduction, III,B,2, p. 36.

[19]A similar discussion takes place in BSBh II,1,4, p. 356.

[20]In reply to the same question Śaṅkara gives elsewhere the following answer: "This analogy does not hold good because in the case of servant and master also only the non-conscious part of the former is subservient to the conscious part of the latter, for a conscious being subserves another conscious being only with the non-conscious part belonging to it, such as the intellect, etc., but a conscious being itself acts neither for nor against any other conscious being" (BSBh II,1,4, p. 356).

[21]Cf. Section 71.

[22]In the Sāṃkhya system both *Puruṣa* and *Prakṛti* are eternal, without either beginning or end. But the eternity of the *Puruṣa* is different from that of the *Prakṛti*; the former is described as "*kūṭasthanitya*" (eternal without change) and the latter as "*pariṇāminitya*" (eternal with change). Cf. Vijñānabhikṣu on *Sūtra* I,75; R. Garbe, *Die Sâṃkhya-Philosophie* (Leipzig: Verlag von H. Haessel, 1894), p. 289. According to Śaṅkara's non-dualism eternity with change is not acceptable, since everything subject to change is non-eternal; everything, with the only exception of *Brahman-Ātman*, which is changeless (*kūṭastha*), is non-eternal. The word *kūṭastha* is used as an antonym of *pariṇāmin* (Upad II,2,75) and *vikriyāvat* (Upad II,2,74). See note 3 of Upad I,13 and the discussion starting in section 74, below.

[23]Section 45.

[24]Introduction, III,B,2, pp. 35–37.

[25]Rāmatīrtha interprets "a thing" (*vastu*) as the internal organ (*antaḥkaraṇa*).

[26]See Upad I,18,156–157.

[27]Among Indian grammarians there are various opinions about the meaning of the verbal root (*dhātvartha*). Cf. R. C. Pandeya, *The Problem of Meaning in Indian Philosophy* (Delhi: Motilal Banarsidass, 1963), pp. 117–123. As in *Mahābhāṣya* III,2,84, the meaning of the verbal root is here conceived to be "action" (*kriyā*). Cf. L. Renou, *Terminologie Grammatical du Sanskrit*, pp. 168–169. In the Nyāya and the Vaiśeṣika "*upalabdhi*" and "*jñāna*," which are considered to be (the nature of) *Ātman* by Śaṅkara, are treated as synonyms of "*buddhi*" and "*pratyaya*" (see *Nyāyasūtra* I,1,15; *Vaiśeṣikopaskāra* VIII,1,1; *Nyāyakośa*, pp. 604–608).

[28]For a detailed discussion, see Introduction, III,B,3, pp. 38–40.

[29]In the Nyāya and the Vaiśeṣika perception is a quality (*guṇa*) of *Ātman, i.e.*, perceiver. The Sāṃkhya and the Yoga regard it as a modification (*vṛtti*) of the intellect (*buddhi* or *citta*). The Buddhist and the Mīmāṃsā systems commonly describe it as an activity. Cf. S. Chatterjee, *The Nyāya Theory of Knowledge*, pp. 9–20.

[30]See section 77.

[31]See section 75.

[32]See sections 48–50.

[33]Cf. BhG II,22; Upad II,1,12.

[34]Cf. sections 56; 74; etc.

[35]Cf. sections 89; 93.

[36]Section 90.

[37]*Pramā*, which is here translated as "empirical knowledge," generally indicates the valid knowledge which results from the means of knowledge (*pramāṇa*). The pupil wants to say here that *pramā* requires *pramāṇa* for its establishment; so *pramā* is non-eternal.

[38]Cf. sections 93–98.

[39]See note 27.

[40]Cf. Unters p. 1944; Naiṣ III,19.

[41]See BS II,3,40 and Śaṅkara's commentary on it.

[42]According to Rāmatīrtha this is a refutation of the Mīmāṃsākas.

[43]Rāmatīrtha suggests that this is a refutation of the Naiyāyikas.

[44]Rāmatīrtha suggests that this is a refutation of the Lokāyatikas.

[45]Cf. section 77.

[46]Rāmatīrtha suggests that this is a refutation of the Sāṃkhya.

[47]Cf. Bṛh. Up. IV,2,4.

[48]This is the conclusion of the discussion which started in sections 48 and 49.

CHAPTER 3

PARISAṂKHYĀNA MEDITATION

112. This *parisaṃkhyāna* meditation[1] is described for seekers after final release, who are devoting themselves to destroying their acquired merit and demerit and do not wish to accumulate new ones. Nescience causes faults (= passion and aversion); they cause the activities of speech, mind, and body; and from these activities are accumulated *karmans* of which [in turn] the results are desirable, undesirable, and mixed.[2] For the sake of final release from those *karmans* [this *parisaṃkhyāna* meditation is described].

113. Now, sound, touch, form-and-color, taste, and odor are the objects of the senses; they are to be perceived by the ear and other [senses]. Therefore, they do not have any knowledge of themselves nor of others, since they are merely things evolved[3] [from the unevolved name-and-form] like clay and the like. And they are perceived through the ear and other [senses].

And that by which they are perceived is of a different nature since it is a perceiver. Because they are connected with one another, sound and other [objects of the senses] are possessed of many attributes such as birth, growth, change of state, decay, and destruction[4]; connection and separation; appearance and disappearance; effect of change and cause of change; field (= female?) and seed (= male?). They are also commonly possessed of many [other] attributes such as pleasure and pain. Their perceiver is different in its nature from all the attributes of sound and the other [objects of the senses], precisely because it is their perceiver.

114. So the wise man who is tormented by sound and the other [objects of the senses] which are being perceived should perform *parisaṃkhyāna* meditation as follows:

115. I (= *Ātman*) am of the nature of Seeing, non-object (= subject) unconnected [with anything], changeless, motionless, endless, fearless, and absolutely subtle. So sound cannot make me its object and touch me, whether as mere noise in general or as [sound] of particular qualities—pleasant [sounds] such as the first note of music or the desirable words of praise and the like, or the undesirable words of untruth, disgust, humiliation, abuse, and the like—since I am unconnected [with sound]. For this very reason neither loss nor gain is caused [in me] by sound. Therefore, what can the pleasant sound of praise, the unpleasant sound of blame, and so on do to me? Indeed a pleasant sound may produce gain, and an unpleasant one destruction, for a man lacking in discriminating knowledge, who regards sound as [connected with his] *Ātman* since he has no discriminating knowledge. But for me who am endowed with discriminating knowledge, [sound] cannot produce even a hair's breadth [of gain or loss].

In the very same manner [touch] does not produce for me any change of gain and loss, whether as touch in general or as touch in particular forms—the unpleasant [touch] of cold, heat, softness, hardness, etc., and of fever, stomachache, etc., and any pleasant [touch] either inherent in the body or caused by external and adventitious [objects]—since I am devoid of touch, just as a blow with the fist and the like [does not produce any change] in the sky.

Likewise [form-and-color] produces neither loss nor gain for me, whether as form-and-color in general or as form-and-color in particular, pleasant or unpleasant, such as the female characteristics of a woman and the like, since I am devoid of form-and-color.

Similarly, [taste] produces neither loss nor gain for me who am by nature devoid of taste, whether as taste in general or as taste in particular forms [, pleasant or unpleasant,] such as sweetness, sourness, saltiness, pungency, bitterness, astringency which are perceived by the dull-witted.

In like manner [odor] produces neither loss nor gain for me who am by nature devoid of odor, whether as odor in general or as odor in particular forms, pleasant or unpleasant, such as [the odor] of flowers, etc., and ointment, etc. That is because the *Śruti* says:

> "That which is soundless, touchless, formless, imperishable, also tasteless, constant, odorless, . . . [— having perceived that, one is freed from the jaws of death]" (Kaṭh. Up. III,15).

116. Moreover, whatever sound and the other external [objects of the senses] may be, they are changed into the form of the body, and into the form of the ear and the other [senses] which perceive them, and into the form of the two internal organs[5] and their objects [such as pleasure and pain],[6] since they are mutually connected and composite in all cases of actions. This being the case, to me, a man of knowledge, nobody is foe, friend or neutral.

In this context, if [anybody,] through a misconception [about *Ātman*] due to false knowledge,[7] were to wish to connect [me] with [anything], pleasant or unpleasant, which is characteristic of the result of action, he wishes in vain to connect [me] with it, since I am not its object according to the *Smṛti* passage:

"Unmanifest he, unthinkable he, [unchangeable he is declared to be]" (BhG II,25).

Likewise, I am not to be changed by [any of] the five elements, since I am not their object according to the *Smṛti* passage:

"Not to be cut is he, not to be burnt is he, [not to be wet nor yet dried]" (BhG II,24).

Furthermore, paying attention only to the aggregate of the body and the senses, [people, both] devoted and adverse to me, have the desire to connect [me] with things, pleasant, unpleasant, etc., and therefrom results the acquisition of merit, demerit, and the like. It belongs only to them and does not occur in me who am free from old age, death, and fear, since the *Śrutis* and the *Smṛtis* say:

"Neither what has been done nor what has been left undone affects It" (Bṛh. Up. IV,4,22);

"[This is the constant greatness of the knower of *Brahman*]; he does not increase nor become less by action" (Bṛh. Up. IV,4,23);

"[This is] without and within, unborn" (Muṇḍ. Up. II,1,2);

"[So the one inner *Ātman* of all beings] is not afflicted with the suffering of the world, being outside of it" (Kaṭh. Up. V,11); etc.

That is because anything other than *Ātman* does not exist,—this is the highest reason.

As duality does not exist, all the sentences of the *Upaniṣads* concerning non-duality of *Ātman* should be fully contemplated, should be contemplated.[8]

Notes

[1]As far as I have investigated, this is the only place where Śaṅkara describes the *parisaṃkhyāna* meditation. P. Hacker translates it as "Rekapitulierende Betrachtung." Judging from its description here given, it seems to be a kind of meditation which consists in recapitulating the conclusion which has been arrived at through one's previous study and discussion with a teacher. It is interesting to note that Śaṅkara rejects the *prasaṃkhyāna* meditation (or *prasaṃcakṣā*, see Upad I,18,9 ff. and note 13 of Upad I,18) but recommends the *parisaṃkhyāna* meditation (cf. PBh I,5,29, p. 24). But the difference between them is not clear.

[2]See Upad I,1,3–5.

[3]See Upad II,1,18–20.

[4]According to *Nirukta* I,2, there are six modifications of becoming (*ṣaḍbhāvavikāra*): (1) birth (*jāyate*), (2) existence (*asti*), (3) alteration (*vipariṇamate*), (4) growth (*vardhate*), (5) decay (*apakṣīyate*), and (6) destruction (*vinaśyati*).

[5]Śaṅkara points out a self-contradiction in the Sāṃkhya system, saying that it describes the internal organ as three in one place and as one in another place (BSBh II, 2,10, p. 425), but he himself does not make his position clear with regard to the number and concept of the internal organ. See Introduction, III,B,1, pp. 30–31.

[6]Rāmatīrtha interprets their objects as pleasure and pain. Cf. Upad I,15,13; 18,201; II,1,34–35.

[7]False knowledge (*mithyājñāna*) is a synonym for nescience (*avidyā*) in Śaṅkara's usage. See Mayeda Upad, pp. 24–25; Introduction, IV,D,1, p. 78.

[8]As in *Upaniṣads* such as Chānd. Up., Ait. Up., Kauṣ. Up., *Kena Up.*, and Śvet. Up., the Prose Part ends with a repetition of the last word. See Mayeda Upad, p. 66.

INDEX TO INTRODUCTION

Note: An index of Sanskrit words in the *Upadeśasāhasrī* is attached to *Śaṅkara's Upadeśasāhasrī, Critically Edited with Introduction and Indices* by Sengaku Mayeda (Tokyo: Hokuseido Press, 1973).

ābhāsa (false appearance), 37–39, 63n-64n; (reflection), 37–39, 75
abhāva (disappearance), 37
abheda (identity), 34
abhihitānvaya theory, 50–51
abhinnavṛtta (leading a blameless life), 93
Ācāryavijayacampū. *See* Parameśvara
action (*karman*), 40, 57, 69, 71–72, 78, 84–88, 91–92, 94; result of, 85
ādhāra, 83–84
adharma (demerit), 71
adhiṣṭhāna, 83–84
adhyāsa (superimposition), 24, 77–78, 80, 83–84
Adhyātmapaṭala, 6, 97
adhyavasāya, 31
Advaita Vedānta School, 7, 14, 19, 25, 31, 33, 37, 43, 46, 62n, 63n, 81, 82, 89, 93; illusionistic, 14
advaitavāda (non-dualism), 14, 17n, 49; of Saṅkara, 16n
Advaitins, 4, 5, 8n, 16n, 17n, 35, 38, 40, 50, 51, 54, 55, 64n, 78, 89
advaya (non-dual), 45
Āgamaśāstra, 8n
Agniṣṭoma, 87
aham. *See* "I"-consciousness
"*aham brahmāsmi*" ("I am *Brahman*"), 50, 57, 58
ahaṃdhī. *See* "I"-consciousness
ahamkāra. *See* "I"-consciousness
ahaṃkārādisaṃtāna (individual continuity of the "I"-notion), 75
ahaṃkartṛ (bearer of *ahaṃkāra*), 40, 57–58, 75, 78
ahaṃkriyā. *See* "I"-consciousness
ahaṃpratyaya. *See* "I"-consciousness
ahaṃpratyayaviṣaya (object of *ahaṃpratyaya*), 40, 57
ahiṃsā (injury), 88, 92
Aitareya, 6
aja (unborn), 45
ajaḍa, 67n
ajahallakṣaṇā (*ajahatsvārthā lakṣaṇā*), 53
ajñāna (ignorance), 45, 64n, 72, 74, 79, 81, 84, 86
akāma (free from desire), 45
akriya (actionless), 39
akrodha (non-anger), 92
Amalānanda, 26
amānitva (modesty), 92
aṃśa (portion), 12, 15n
anādi (beginningless), 83
ānanda (bliss), 20, 27, 58n, 60n, 67n
Ānandagiri (author of *Śaṅkaravijaya*), 7n
Ānandānubhava, 17n
Anantānandagiri (author of *Guruvijaya*), 7n
ananyadṛś, 44
anatiśaṅkyatva (not to be doubted), 47
anekavṛttika (having various modifications of *manas*), 30
anṛta (falsehood), 93
antaḥkaraṇa (internal organ), 28, 30–31, 35–43, 57, 74, 77
antaḥkaraṇadvaya (twofold *antaḥkaraṇa*), 30
antaḥkaraṇavṛtti (modification of the *antaḥkaraṇa*), 41
antaḥkaraṇopahitam caitanyam (consciousness having the *antaḥkaraṇa* as its limiting adjunct), 34
āntarapratyakṣa (internal perception), 34